Television Dramas and the Global Village

Television Dramas and the Global Village

Storytelling through Race and Gender

Edited by
Diana I. Ríos
Carolyn A. Lin

LEXINGTON BOOKS
Lanham • Boulder • New York • London

Published by Lexington Books
An imprint of The Rowman & Littlefield Publishing Group, Inc.
4501 Forbes Boulevard, Suite 200, Lanham, Maryland 20706
www.rowman.com

86-90 Paul Street, London EC2A 4NE, United Kingdom

Copyright © 2021 by The Rowman & Littlefield Publishing Group, Inc.

All rights reserved. No part of this book may be reproduced in any form or by any electronic or mechanical means, including information storage and retrieval systems, without written permission from the publisher, except by a reviewer who may quote passages in a review.

British Library Cataloguing in Publication Information Available

Library of Congress Cataloging-in-Publication Data

Names: Ríos, Diana Isabel Arredondo, 1962– editor. | Lin, Carolyn A., editor.
Title: Television dramas and the global village : storytelling through race and gender / edited by Diana I. Ríos, Carolyn A. Lin.
Description: Lanham : Lexington Books, [2021] | Includes bibliographical references and index. | Summary: "This book analyzes the ways in which television dramas allow audiences to vicariously experience fantasy-indulging, escapism-satisfying, and reality-reckoning stories. Contributors discuss how our innate desire to tell human stories both binds us together and motivates us to persevere as a community on a global scale"—Provided by publisher.
Identifiers: LCCN 2021033552 (print) | LCCN 2021033553 (ebook) | ISBN 9781793613523 (cloth) | ISBN 9781793613530 (epub)
Subjects: LCSH: Television programs. | Television viewers.
Classification: LCC PN1992.5 T3653 2021 (print) | LCC PN1992.5 (ebook) | DDC 791.45—dc23
LC record available at https://lccn.loc.gov/2021033552
LC ebook record available at https://lccn.loc.gov/2021033553

Diana I. Ríos

To my family located in different parts of the globe. Especially those who like espectáculos de televisión dramática, including procedurals, crime scene investigations, "Plus Belle La Vie," and "Amour Gloire et Beauté."

Carolyn A. Lin

This book is dedicated to my parents, who taught me how to always empathize with others and respect all living things.

Contents

Introduction: Television Dramas as Storytellers of Race and Gender for the Global Village   1
Diana I. Ríos and Carolyn A. Lin

SECTION I: FANTASY SCIENCE FICTION, HORROR, AND MYSTERY   7

1. *Luke Cage* Is Harlem's Captain America: Black Masculinity and Vulnerability in the Marvel Cinematic Universe   9
   Graeme John Wilson

2. *Doctor Who*'s 13th Doctor: Redefining the Female Lead in Science Fiction Television   25
   Gwendelyn S. Nisbett and Newly Paul

3. A Woman in Trouble in *Twin Peaks: The Return:* Gothic Texts, Magical Technology, and Dreams Within Dreams   39
   Joseph Boisvere

4. Arya and Sansa Stark of HBO's *The Game of Thrones*: Abuse, Agency, Trauma Survival, and Redefined Destinies   51
   Diana I. Ríos, Mary Helen Millham, Karin A. Haberlin, and Graciela Quiñones-Rodriguez

5. The Protagonists of the Fantasy Drama *Lost*: From Stereotypes to Flexible Identities   65
   Jérôme David

SECTION II: SOAP OPERAS AND TELENOVELAS   79

6   Pakistan Television Drama Serials and Telenovelas from 1964 to 2019: Gendering in Different Political Regimes   81
Saleem Abbas

7   Primetime Brazilian Telenovelas and Gender Violence Representation   95
Lorena Caminhas

8   French Television and the Audience: Examining Serial Dramas *Un Si Grand Soleil* and *Plus Belle La Vie*   111
Patricia Jullia and Frédéric Marty

9   Brazilian Telenovelas and Multi-platform Audiences: Overviews and Industry Insights   127
Rosane Svartman

SECTION III: HISTORICAL AND PERIOD DRAMA   141

10   Korean Historical Television Dramas: Cultural Meanings, Confucian Values, and Transcultural Identities   143
Suji Park and Carolyn A. Lin

11   Thoroughly (Un)Modern *Downton Abbey*: Interrogating Gender/Sexual Dynamics and Whiteness Boundaries   159
Gordon Alley-Young

12   From *The Crown* to *Madmen*: Historical Television as Commentary on Twenty-first-Century Ideologies   175
Nettie Brock

13   *The Story of Zheng Yang Gate:* Chinese Television Representation of Female Entrepreneurs   189
Mei Zhang

14   Exploring Gendering in Iranian Television Drama Serials   203
Ali Zohoori

SECTION IV: COMEDY DRAMA   217

15   Being a Black Man on *Being Mary Jane*: Considering Complexities of Black Masculinity in a Female-centric Drama   219
George L. Daniels

16 HBO's *Insecure* and Issa Dee: Black Women's
Interpretations on Facebook 233
Morgan W. Smalls

17 Pregnancy and the Back-to-Work Narrative: How
Television Comedy Dramas Navigate the Social
Norms of Motherhood 249
Elizabeth Fish Hatfield

SECTION V: CRIME AND MEDICAL DRAMA 261

18 Historical Drama *Peaky Blinders*: Pitching Racial Allegiances
and Ethnocentric Populism 263
Inna Arzumanova

19 *Zero Tolerance*: Genre and the Politics of Reconciliation in
a South African Crime Show 277
Ian-Malcolm Rijsdijk

20 Doctor(ed) Representations: Physician Portrayals on
Medical Television Shows 291
*David Lynn Painter, Sarah Parsloe,
and Hannah Jureller*

Index 307

Contributors 317

Introduction

Television Dramas as Storytellers of Race and Gender for the Global Village

Diana I. Ríos and Carolyn A. Lin

Dramatic serials have thrived through generations and have deep roots in the sociocultural imaginations of many different societies around the globe. This long life is intimately connected with the growth and economic viability of media technologies, and how, when, and why audiences use media. In particular, the year 2021 saw tremendous increase in television viewing and online streaming in many parts of the world (BBC, 2020; Spangler, 2021; Stoll, 2021). People had no choice but to increase internet use for work and maintaining family connections, as well as finding much-needed escape from news about COVID-19 and political turmoil through video streaming entertainment programs.

In this edited volume, we offer a collection of analyses on different kinds of dramatic television series. This excellent collection will examine several genres as well as consider the larger dramatic serial world in which particular genres reside. Integral to the analysis of program content will include consideration of character gender roles, sexualities, race, violence, and a series' economic value as a cultural product. This collection is valuable, because academics and critical publics alike will continue to be concerned about popular media imparting messages and their possible impact on different sectors of society. After all, television series are made extensively available through multiple modalities such as legacy television, cable television, tablets, and laptops and streaming services such as Netflix, HBO, Hulu, and Amazon Prime.

Programs take stands through representation of captivating, beautiful or twisted people and about severe social, racialized, gender hierarchies in real places and fantastical spheres. Furthermore, the life of a television series is extended beyond its permeable time or national boundaries in our hyper-digital era. Popular social media platforms such as Facebook, YouTube, Twitter, and Tumblr provide spaces for global viewers to vent their feelings and claim their voice in the virtual world. They rapidly compose and post reactions, create character art, pay homage, direct frustration at producers, writers, showrunners, and other fans for breaking unspoken trust, and personalize stories about admired characters beyond the original television program.

This book will examine many facets of the dramatic television series. The volume is organized into five sections. These sections include (1) fantasy, science fiction, horror, and mystery dramas; (2) soap operas and telenovelas; (3) historical and period dramas; (4) comedy dramas; and (5) crime and medical dramas. Grouping together television series by major genres allows us to recognize the commonalities between subgenres and each of their uniqueness within a major genre category. Television series do not always fall neatly into one genre. In particular, writers, producers, and other media professionals apply styles they find to be effective for the ideas, topics, issues, and emotions they wish to impart. Likewise, as the reader has experienced in their mediated lives, there are particular textures, atmospheres, or tragic structures of feeling encouraged by one or more television programs.

Section one addresses the often overlapping genres of fantasy, science fiction, horror, and mystery. Recent revivals of this kind of programming have revealed how this major genre and its subgenres are relatively ubiquitous. Concomitant with wide availability, there are connections to other media such as graphic novels and comics (legacy print and web), fan art, games, industry and fan fiction literature, and Comic-cons (fan conventions). Cross-platform spillage and energetic fans create tensions between industry and public, but this only lends more mystery and dynamism to inherently fantastical characters and themes. These subgenres point to a strong existence in the future as viewers manage anxieties and needs, including imagining past and future time travel in order to fix circumstances in the present world; wishing to communicate with the dead to gain important information; longing for superheroes and heroines to help combat personal and social problems.

Section two presents the dramatic or melodramatic genres called soap operas and telenovelas. These classic genres have transformed themselves separately and in parallel over many decades and across many countries. These are more than "weepies" depicting filiality, forbidden love, kidnapped child-heirs, and family feuds. Some telenovelas and soaps integrate political and religious attitudes aiming to support a society of particular cultural values. Some of these melodramas disseminate public policy information in attempts to inform and protect women against partner and family violence. Other dramas impart views on ethnic diversity and cultural tolerance as societies struggle with colonial legacies and/or new migration trends. It is also true that too many series present content that denigrates women and lean on violence as a technique for creative interest and narrative spark. As soap operas and telenovelas present relatable aspects of daily and multigenerational life, they will thus continue to be enduring genres.

Section three is composed of historical and period drama serials. These are set in geographic settings of the past such as in Britain, China, Korea, Iran, the United States, and Pakistan. Of particular viewer interests are historical period sets and elaborate indoor and outdoor settings that envelope fans in fictional and based-on-some-truth stories. This genre has been embraced by viewers in different parts of the world and by fans who wish to maintain ethnic, folkloric connections while residing elsewhere. This genre has the unique opportunity to recast real historical events and reinvent old figures. Creative license allows an accentuation of beauty, heroism, human rights, and courageous outcomes. Story arcs and long narratives can make statements about policies, social values, the status of women and stigmatized gendered others, and intersections of ethnicity/race/religion. Overall, the genre encourages fictional or make-believe nostalgia among viewers who see idealized people and societies of the past.

Section four contains comedy dramas, an unexpected vehicle for analysis on issues of race and gender. Chapters look at facets of Black masculinity in close relationships, African American female identity development, and women's perpetual balancing act to fulfill work and family role demands. The programs under analysis shed light on difficult cultural and societal pressures that people face. Characters often awkwardly manage their worries through better decision-making and a sense of humour. In particular, young people in these dramadies are maturing and trying to find and define themselves at the intersections of race and gender. Viewers can become engaged in the career, marriage, partner, and family disappointments faced by these characters because these characters' stories echo the challenges faced by the viewers themselves at different stages of their own lives.

Section five brings together crime and medical dramas. As genres are permeable, one chapter examines criminals in a historical period drama set in Britain. Issues of ethnic group and cultural stigmatization are carefully discussed using a fictional narrative based on a nonfiction character and community. Views and debates on race and racial tolerance come forth in two of the chapters. In a chapter focusing on a South African cop show, criminal investigation cases are more than looking for law-breakers. Racial policies, spiritual practices, ethnicity, race, and collective cultural memories come into play. Another chapter conducts an empirical examination on several well-known medical dramas in order to shed light on the demographic characteristics of medical doctors in these shows. This study on representation draws attention to the missed opportunities that are common in medical series, because they can showcase ethnic and racial diversity and inspire future generations to enter the health professions.

The COVID-19 pandemic has inevitably revealed the social inequities and health disparities in society across the world. Predictably, an individual's gender and race became the reason or even target for the exhibition of social injustice. In the United States, women bore the heaviest burden to home school their children and maintain employment by remote work. Many women experienced increased levels of domestic violence abuse, in addition to disproportional loss of employment and hence inability to feed their families (Croda & Grossbard, 2021). Racial, ethnic, and indigenous communities (i.e., Blacks, Latinos, and Native Americans) paid the ultimate price via the highest pandemic infection rates and fatalities, resulting from lack of access and inadequate access to healthcare (CDC, 2020; Ford et al., 2020).

Amidst Donald Trump's vitriolic "Kung Flu" reference about the pandemic, a majority of 6,000 Britons and Americans surveyed also considered East Asians the "undesirables" in society (Geldsetzer, 2020; Lin, 2020). East Asian-looking individuals in the United States were socially ostracized, shunned, verbally abused and/or physically assaulted (BBC, 2021); severe injuries and deaths have occurred among elderly individuals and women, including six women who were targeted and gunned down (Hauser, 2021). This racial hatred has sparked a social movement to stop Asian hate, in addition to the Black Lives Matter (BLM) movement. BLM reawakened much of society to care about racism because viewers saw videos of extreme police brutality and the agonizing, public death of an African American man (Shanga, 2020).

Against the backdrop of this social turmoil, the chapters in this book were reworked, edited, and finalized during the COVID period when we were in "lockdown" and during the debut of an effective vaccine. It is of peculiar irony that we were writing about dramatic media, and tales of tragedy and courage, while it seemed as if the world was caught inside a kaleidoscopic dream with giant hopes of happier days, in another time dimension. Nonetheless, even after people have recovered from the special COVID epoch and walked out into the real world again, the public will still feel pulled to watch their favorite dramatic series.

With the "new" world of vaccinated freedom and renewing our hope for working toward a more socially just world, we will try to get lost on a special island, have viewing parties over "tea time" or local beer or even visit parts of the world we only saw through streaming the most interesting foreign dramas. Television drama allows us to vicariously experience fantasy-indulging, escapism-satisfying and reality-reckoning stories that bring us tears, solace, comfort, and delight. Our human stories are at the heart of these dramatic series, including triumphs and failures in fighting for social justice as well as racial and gender equality. Our innate desire to tell these human stories both binds us and motivates us to share our humanity and to persevere as a human community.

We are grateful to colleagues, family, and friends for encouragement and helping with this project. Our authors were eager to contribute to what is known about television drama, and found a meaningful home for their original research in this book. Special thanks for the institutional support made possible by El Instituto: Institute of Latinx/Latin American and Caribbean Studies at the University of Connecticut. Finally, *mil gracias, moltes gràcies, merci infiniment* to our network of fellow researchers, professionals, and family around the globe.

REFERENCES

BBC (2020). TV watching and online streaming surge during lockdown. https://www.bbc.com/news/entertainment-arts-53637305.

BBC (2021, April 2). Covid 'hate crimes' against Asian Americans on rise. British Broadcasting Corporation. https://www.bbc.com/news/world-us-canada-56218684.

CDC (2020, December 10). COVID-19 Racial and Ethnic Health Disparities. Centers for Disease Control and Prevention. https://www.cdc.gov/coronavirus/2019-ncov/community/health-equity/racial-ethnic-disparities/disparities-deaths.html.

Croda, E. & Grossbard, S. (2021, February 15). Women pay the price of COVID-19 more than men. *Review of Economics of the Household, 19*, 1–9. https://link.springer.com/article/10.1007/s11150-021-09549-8.

Ford, T. N., Reber, S., & Reeves, R. V. (2020, June 16). Race gaps in COVID-19 deaths are even bigger than they appear. https://www.brookings.edu/blog/up-front/2020/06/16/race-gaps-in-covid-19-deaths-are-even-bigger-than-they-appear/.

Geldsetzer, P. (2020, July 21). Knowledge and perceptions of COVID-19 among the general public in the US and the UK: A cross-sectional online survey. *American Internal Medicine*. https://doi.org/10.7326/M20-0912.

Hauser, C. (2021, March 17). Asian-Americans were targeted in nearly 3,800 hate incidents in the past year. *The New York Times*. https://www.nytimes.com/2021/03/17/us/hate-crimes-against-asian-americans-community.html.

Lin, C. A. (2021). A year like no other: A call to curb the infodemic and depoliticize a pandemic crisis. *Journal of Broadcasting & Electronic Media, 64*(5), 661–671.

Shanga, G. (2020, July 9). How Black Lives Matter became a multicultural awakening An increasing number of white activists are taking part. *ABC News*. https://abcnews.go.com/US/black-lives-matter-multicultural-awakening/story?id=71635471.

Spangler, T. (2021). US consumers now pay $47 monthly for streaming services up 24% since COVID hit, survey finds. https://variety.com/2021/digital/news/us-consumers-pay-average-47-dollars-monthly-svod-streaming-1234890534/.

Stoll, J. (2021). Latin America: Increase in pay TV use due to COVID-19, by country. https://www.statista.com/statistics/1115907/latin-america-pay-tv/.

Section I

FANTASY SCIENCE FICTION, HORROR, AND MYSTERY

Chapter 1

Luke Cage Is Harlem's Captain America

Black Masculinity and Vulnerability in the Marvel Cinematic Universe

Graeme John Wilson

The superhero is arguably the most prominent archetype in US fiction. Today, the most recognizable modern superhero franchise is the Marvel Cinematic Universe, a multimedia franchise encompassing various interconnected superhero films and television series based on Marvel Comics characters (Beaty, 2016). Writers often utilize superhero narratives to address societal concerns and provide social commentary on a variety of subjects. However, superhero fiction has historically been criticized for reinforcing white hegemony, particularly through lack of minority representation. For decades, black characters were relegated to supporting roles, often as stereotyped caricatures (Nama, 2011). The term "black" is used to "signif[y] all non-White minority populations," including the African American and African Caribbean populations. Although "the term Black has a long service in social, political, and everyday life and in its use to denote African ancestry," African American specifically describes "descendants of [African] persons brought to the Americas as slaves between the 17th and 19th century" (Agyemang et al., 2005, p. 1016).

Marvel Comics began introducing black superheroes in the late 1960s, including African (i.e., Black Panther) and African American characters (i.e., Falcon and Luke Cage). Cage, who was introduced in 1972, followed Marvel's trend of greater diversification. Originally informed by contemporary Black Power politics (Nama, 2011), Cage, born Carl Lucas, is a former convict framed for a crime he never committed. While incarcerated, Cage is forcibly subjected to an experimental procedure that grants him "steel-hard skin that can repel bullets and superhuman strength" (Ledrum, 2005, p. 367).

Although he was not the genre's first black superhero, Cage was notably the first to be featured as a title character, beginning in 1972 with *Luke Cage, Hero for Hire*. Throughout his comic history, Cage has been utilized by Marvel to explore sociocultural issues relevant to African Americans and has been described as "the most inherently political and socially profound black superhero to ever emerge" (Nama, 2011, p. 55). Forty-four years after his debut, Cage breaks further ground by becoming the first black superhero in the Marvel Cinematic Universe to headline his own project. This self-titled television series airs on Netflix between 2016 and 2018, totaling two seasons and 26 episodes.

The debut season of *Luke Cage* premiered in its entirety in September 2016, in the midst of considerable social unrest in the United States. The controversial shooting deaths of Trayvon Martin, Michael Brown, Eric Garner, and other unarmed African Americans by law enforcement officials inspired the creation of Black Lives Matter, a social activist movement that campaigns against racial profiling and police brutality. The movement was a focal point of discussion during the 2016 presidential election, although Republican candidates were largely dismissive of Black Lives Matter, suggesting the movement was actually at fault for promoting racial division and anti-police bias (Altman, Frizell & Rhodan, 2015). Cheo Hodari Coker and Mike Colter, the showrunner and star, respectively, of *Luke Cage*, indicated in promotional interviews that the series would address the country's current racial climate and epidemic of police brutality, alluding to Black Lives Matter (Dockterman, 2016). Coker famously compared *Luke Cage* to *The Wire*, an eminent HBO series renowned for its sociopolitical themes and realistic portrayal of urban life in Baltimore (Nolfi, 2016).

Many series starring black characters or ensembles have been criticized for embodying a certain pejorative post-racial ideology, which asserts that "black people's problem is not disenfranchisement through racist institutions and histories, but . . . the disrespectable cultural standards that black people [maintain]" (Joseph, 2016, p. 304). However, *Luke Cage* is different because it actively disrupts the perpetuation of respectability politics, which refers to the efforts of marginalized communities in a society to conform to majority community values, rather than challenge the societal status quo and advocate for the acceptance of their own values (Di Leonardo, 2016; Harris, 2014; Newman & Obasogie, 2016; Patton, 2014). *Luke Cage* provides a voice for progressive racial politics by directly commenting on prominent stereotypes of African American males, contemporary concerns of police brutality, and the complexity of black identity and language. To provide context, this chapter cites interviews conducted with both Coker and Colter and draws from critical sources. Marketed and positioned as a breakthrough text before its premiere, *Luke Cage* ultimately continues the character's legacy of challenging systemic oppression and rebuking cultural stereotypes.

FRAMEWORK AND METHODOLOGY

This chapter employs critical race theory, an interpretive model designed to examine the relationship between race and hegemonic power in society, particularly in terms of racial inequality and domination (Crenshaw, 1995; Wing, 2016). This theoretical framework is appropriate when considering the tense race relations of contemporary America and *Luke Cage*'s advertised commentary on them. For its method, this chapter applies rhetorical criticism, a form of textual analysis, to particular scenes and dialogue from *Luke Cage*'s debut season.

Textual analysis is one of the most popular methods within television studies (Gray & Lotz, 2012) and is harnessed by scholars to distinguish "between the primary, linguistic meaning of a text's component parts and the secondary, or textual meaning" (Altman, 1984, p. 15). Textual analysis encompasses various submethods, including rhetorical criticism. Cultural scholars specifically employ rhetorical criticism to explicate the messages and themes of a media text. Rhetorical criticism is an appropriate method through which to engage in social criticism by identifying how media texts comment on contemporary sociocultural trends, thus influencing their audiences' perceptions of a subject or topic (Botan, Frey & Kreps, 1999). Rhetorical criticism is an effective form of textual analysis through which to analyze the racial commentary of *Luke Cage* and its targeted deconstruction of respectability politics.

Respectability Politics

As a concept, respectability politics was first articulated by scholar Evelyn Brooks Higginbotham in her book *Righteous Discontent: The Women's Movement in the Black Baptist Church: 1880 – 1920*. Higginbotham's book focused on the efforts of African American women to promote "self-esteem, a sense of agency, and the courage to . . . challenge and resist the racism and dehumanization that they faced" (Patton, 2014, p. 730). Other scholars have since contributed to the development of respectability politics as a distinct field of research, with greater emphasis on the African American community as a whole. Advocates of respectability politics argue "that Blacks can minimize or evade the injustices associated with discriminatory attitudes by behaving in a so-called respectable manner, i.e., dressing, acting, speaking, and even protesting in certain acceptable ways" (Newman & Obasogie, 2016,

p. 541). Respectability politics has witnessed a significant increase in interest over the past decade, largely attributed to the 2008 election of Barack Obama, the country's first black president (Harris, 2014). Today, some African Americans engage in respectability politics to combat prominent racial stereotypes and stigmas, such as "intellectual inferiority, perceived laziness, and presumed moral bankruptcy" (Patton, 2014, p. 730). However, conforming to such norms "limits the construction of African Americans, [and] also caters to and reinforces dominant, hegemonic ideologies" (p. 731). In contrast, the Black Lives Matter movement aims to expand notions of black respectability:

> As a social movement, Black Lives Matter can be understood as growing out of a specific opposition to respectability politics by insisting that regardless of any ostensibly non-respectable behavior . . . their lives matter and should not be treated with deadly force (Newman & Obasogie, 2016, p. 541).

Recently, discussions of respectability politics have extended to media representation. There are very few black showrunners and producers in US entertainment, and thus their projects are subject to greater scrutiny and analysis (Gray, 2000; Joseph, 2016). Tyler Perry has been criticized for promoting respectability politics in his various sitcoms, as well as inauthentic models of black masculinity that are more readily accepted by white audiences (Di Leonardo, 2016; Jones, 2018). Although Shonda Rhimes has been praised for developing strong black protagonists in her dramas *Scandal* and *How to Get Away with Murder*, she has also been criticized by some for "avoid[ing] discussing issues of racial difference or racial inequality" in these series (Joseph, 2016, p. 315). However, *Luke Cage* breaks this established trend. *Luke Cage* strives to expand notions of respectability toward African Americans, emphasizing how systemic racism and institutional practices such as police brutality and racial profiling are more detrimental to the community's well-being.

THE SOCIOPOLITICAL COMMENTARY OF *LUKE CAGE*

Black Masculinity

As a whole, *Luke Cage* serves as a faithful adaptation of the comics' source material. After gaining his powers, Carl Lucas escapes from prison and settles in Harlem, a neighborhood in New York City, where he adopts Luke Cage as his nom de guerre and begins fighting crime. The character's personality in the television series is largely unchanged from his modern depiction in the comics, thus breaking several prominent stereotypes. As observed by Gray (2013), portrayals of African Americans in scripted television are "often characterized by the persistence of stereotypes" (p. 258). Such stereotypes include propensity for violence, heterosexual hypersexuality, materialism, and other behaviors commonly associated with social deviancy (Jackson, 2006; Ward, 2004). While several factors have contributed to this particular model of black masculinity entering the cultural mainstream, it "has developed largely as a result of the commodification of hip-hop culture" (Henry, 2004, p. 119), which emphasizes aggressive posturing and urban aesthetics. In contrast, Cage represents a conscious deviation from such norms. As explained by Adrian Younge, the music composer for the series, Cage is "a different type of black alpha male. He's not bombastic. You rarely see a modern black male character who is soulful and intelligent" (Dockterman, 2016, p. 49). Coker further elaborates:

> Anytime you see a big black guy depicted [in live-action superhero entertainment], they're always either angry or docile to the point that they're funny.... I wanted to show the complexities that actors of Mike Colter's size never get to portray because they're always cast as a thug. [. . .] It was about showing that an African American male character can be all the things you think he is, but also show other elements that you weren't expecting (Flood, 2018, paras. 18–19).

The sensitive treatment afforded to Cage's character also carries over to the neighborhood of Harlem, a community recognized as a major cultural and residential hub for African Americans (Gill, 2011). *Luke Cage* is heavily invested in Harlem's history and culture, and throughout the series characters namedrop black musicians, literary figures, and civil rights leaders. Cage himself declares in the first season finale called "You Know My Steez" that "Harlem is supposed to represent [black] hopes and dreams. It's the pinnacle of black art, politics, innovation. It's supposed to be a shining light to the world." In *Luke Cage*, this light is threatened by Cornell "Cottonmouth" Stokes and Willis "Diamondback" Stryker, crime lords that maintain gun-running operations in Harlem.

As in the comics, Stryker is Cage's childhood friend. However, after a falling out with Cage, Stryker frames him for a crime that results in Cage's incarceration. The criminal charges and prison sentence result in Cage being disowned by his father. Much of superhero fiction ruminates on the protagonists' relationships with their parents. However, in many of these narratives, the superheroes are orphans, which motivates their crusade for justice. These narratives commonly "evoke father-son drama, thereby emphasizing heroics as masculine and homosocial stories about men as most essential" (Kvaran, 2017, p. 219). Additionally, the majority of these narratives feature white protagonists. Cage is not an orphan, yet struggles with his father's absence, thus addressing a different racial trope in television: the absentee black father.

Due to higher statistics of African Americans being raised by single mothers, "it is frequently assumed that black men father children but seldom *are* fathers" (Coles & Green, 2010, p. 1). According to Patricia Hill Collins, this assumption builds from another prominent stereotype that African Americans are sexually promiscuous and unwilling to dedicate themselves to committed relationships (Collins, 2004). Collins argues that such misguided views have promoted African American culture as socially degenerate, as "the absence of black patriarchy is used as evidence for black cultural inferiority" (Collins, 2002, p. 77). This stereotype has historically been exaggerated in popular television, with many series depicting African Americans "as being in single parent homes or unmarried, thus providing no model of a stable nuclear family for the viewing audience" (Jones & Staples, 1985, p. 18).

The truth is that African American family structures historically reflect greater demographic and economic trends. It is observed that black males face greater socioeconomic disadvantages than white males when fulfilling their roles as providers to their partners and children, including "institutionalized factors [such as] poverty, persistent racial inequality and discrimination" (Mills, 2010, p. 345). Refusing to acknowledge societal trends such as these safeguards white hegemonic privilege in the United States, and instead portrays African Americans at fault for their lower social standings (Roberts, 1998).

Black fatherhood is a key theme of *Luke Cage*'s debut season, with the series specifically addressing the trope of the absentee black father. After settling in Harlem, Cage finds a substitute father in his new mentor, Henry "Pop" Hunter. Pop is a reformed gangster who earned his nickname for fist fighting. After prison, Pop opened a barbershop in Harlem and became a respected public figure, serving as a father figure to many neighborhood youths and providing them with direction. As observed by Moss (2016), *Luke Cage* "delves into the subject of legacies and fatherhood as a way to address the incarceration of young black men, and the impact that American criminal-justice policies have had on black families" (para.10). This theme is reinforced throughout *Luke Cage*, even as early as its first episode, "Moment of Truth," in which Cage laments to Pop that "Everyone [in Harlem] has a gun. No one has a father." After Pop is killed during a shootout at the climax of the subsequent episode "Code of the Streets," his death reverberates throughout the season. Not only has Cage lost a father, but so has the entire Harlem neighborhood. It is Pop's murder that motivates Cage to combat Cottonmouth and Diamondback, as Pop had encouraged a reluctant Cage to use his powers to protect and heal the community prior to his death.

In US popular media, black masculinity has historically been associated with stereotypes of criminality, violence, and hypersexuality (Jackson, 2006; Ward, 2004). As observed by Park (2015):

The relationship between race and masculinity has always been one vested with popularized stereotypes that . . . involve representational practices that classify and categorize members of another group, reducing those members to simplified and exaggerated characteristics, which are then communicated as fixed by nature. (p. 370)

Cage rebukes many stereotypes associated with African American masculinity and the series highlights systemic factors that break apart black families and remove black fathers. As explained by Coker, "Fatherhood is something that is personal to me because I didn't grow up around my father" (Moss, 2016, para. 11). One such factor is police brutality, a phenomenon that *Luke Cage* also ruminates on at length.

Police Brutality

Prior to *Luke Cage*'s premiere, Coker affirmed that race and its relationship to "the issue of police-community relations" would be addressed in the series (Dockterman, 2016, p. 50). In an interview with *The Frame* (Kim & Shifflett, 2016), Coker explains that the death of Trayvon Martin had particularly influenced his writing. Martin was an African American teenager who was fatally shot in 2012 by George Zimmerman, a volunteer for a local neighborhood watch. Zimmerman argued that Martin, who had been wearing a hoodie, appeared suspicious and confronted him, prompting an altercation that resulted in Martin's death (Boyle, 2012). Zimmerman was acquitted of murder in 2013, despite continued allegations that his targeting of Martin was motivated by racial bias, particularly "racial stereotypes of black criminality" (Perry, 2014, p. 59). Following Zimmerman's acquittal, hoodies became "a key part of widespread public conversations on whether certain attributes or cues signal danger in a manner that might reasonably elicit fear or concern of a kind that could lead police or a concerned citizen to engage someone with deadly force" (Newman & Obasogie, 2016, p. 542). Coker explains that in the series, Cage eschews his classic costume from the comics and instead wears hoodies in deliberate evocation of Martin:

> Of course I wanted there to be a . . . not so subtle nod to what one faces as a black man in society wearing a hood. Unfortunately, what happens is that people will make assumptions about who you are based on that hoodie and that's the whole thing. I wanted to show that heroes could wear hoodies, too (Kim & Shifflett, 2016, para. 6).

Cage's first major encounter with law enforcement occurs in the episode "DWYCK," after he has been framed by Diamondback's organization for the murder of Cottonmouth. Now wanted by the NYPD, Cage is stopped by two police officers in Harlem. Complying with instructions, Cage raises his hands, evoking arguably the most famous slogan of Black Lives Matter, "hands up, don't shoot." This slogan was adopted after the purported final gesture of Michael Brown, another African American man fatally shot during an altercation with a white police officer (Apel, 2014). The officers ultimately open fire upon Cage, who subdues them both and escapes. The incident is recorded by the police car's dashcam.

In "Take It Personal," Priscilla Ridley, a black police captain, warns her subordinates against provoking a racial incident during their search for Cage. Jacob Smith, a white police officer, protests the lecture, exclaiming, "I'm from the South Bronx, I'm 28 years on the job. I'm not some idiot who's afraid of blacks and Hispanics," affirming a lack of racial bias. Smith later states to Ridley that "the *good* people in Harlem have no problem with me. Just the assholes." The subtext of this statement is that if they are innocent of crime, no black individual would be in danger of police brutality. This is a gross oversimplification of contemporary race relations in the United States, where police misconduct against African Americans remains a major societal concern.

Such misconduct is replicated in *Luke Cage*. After the dashcam footage goes viral, the police experience increased pressure to locate Cage. In the penultimate episode of the season, "Soliloquy of Chaos," the police begin widespread racial profiling, which "refers to the use of race as a key factor in police decisions to stop and interrogate citizens" (Tuch & Weitzer, 2002, p. 435). Racial profiling is largely rooted in stereotypes of black criminality. Because "a prevalent representation of crime is that it is overwhelmingly committed by young Black men . . . the familiarity many Americans have with the image of a young Black male [is] a violent and menacing street thug" (Welch, 2007, p. 276). In the United States, racial profiling of African Americans is a sadly common occurrence and contributes to the community's mistrust of police (Tuch & Weitzer, 2002). Therefore, its portrayal in *Luke Cage* is both authentic and socially relevant.

In "Soliloquy of Chaos," a reporter following police activity informs her audience that "There have been numerous false sightings" of Cage in Harlem, with many black residents "wearing hoodies with holes as a sign of solidarity with an outlaw some people still perceive to be a hero." This choice of clothing is significant. Since Martin's death, the hoodie has emerged as a prominent symbol of Black Lives Matter (Boyle, 2012). When a bulletproof black man wears a hoodie in *Luke Cage*, it generates a powerful symbol for civil rights, suggesting that in order to survive, black men must be impervious to pain. In addition to black masculinity and police brutality, another topic *Luke Cage* engages throughout its debut season is the use of "n---a" within the black community.

Language

Luke Cage is notably the first property within the Marvel Cinematic Universe to use the term "n---a," which many, although not all, black characters use casually in the series. In an interview with *The Washington Post* (Betancourt, 2016), Coker explains that this enhances the authenticity of the show, due to the term's prominence in African American vernacular (para. 12). The term itself has a long and complicated history in its meaning and usage. "N---a" is derived from "n---er," a racial slur directed against the black community. Etymologists believe the slur "was derived from a Northern English word–'neger'—that was itself derived from 'Negro,' the Spanish word for black" (Kennedy, 2000, p. 86). Its specific connotation of "a black figure [possessing] animalistic tendencies and lacking intelligence emerged at a time when racial inferiority was established through legal, scientific, and philosophical discourses" (Nguyen, 2013, p. 296) in colonial America, where slavery of imported Africans operated as a legal institution. Therefore, "There is little dispute over the fact that [n---er] has been a staple of white supremacist discourse often employed to shorthand commonly held societal beliefs about black folk as being less than human" (Neal, 2013, p. 557). Cultural critics such as Asim (2007) suggest that African Americans should "adhere to post-civil rights notions of public decorum" (p. 230) and refrain from using the term in public.

One primary motivation for African Americans to adhere to white hegemonic standards of respectability is potential access to privilege or career ascension (Patton, 2014). In *Luke Cage*, this is Mariah Dillard's motivation for conforming to respectability politics. Dillard, Cottonmouth's cousin, is originally introduced as an aspiring but corrupt politician who, over the course of *Luke Cage*'s first season, evolves into an antagonist and arguably succeeds Diamondback as Cage's archenemy. At the beginning of the series, Cottonmouth helps finance Dillard's political campaigns with his gun-running profits. Dillard views their cooperation as a necessary evil and intends to abandon the partnership later. In "Moment of Truth," Dillard states to her cousin that "politics is where the power is," rather than crime. The subtext in this scene is that politics is where white hegemonic power is; power that Dillard can access by projecting a respectable and acceptable black identity for her white political peers. Because word choice and appropriate language are recognized elements of respectability politics (Newman & Obasogie, 2016, p. 541), Dillard attempts to project a respectable identity partly through her refusal to say "n---a," frequently admonishing Cottonmouth for casually doing so.

Pop and Cage, the series' most prominent black male role models, similarly refuse to employ the term, as well as any profanity. This is established as early as the pilot's opening scene, set at Pop's barbershop, where Luke and Pop reprimand Chico, Lonnie, and other youth for profane language. Although "Moment of Truth" establishes that Cage habitually refuses to employ profanity in his dialect, his particular opposition to "n---a" is influenced by series star Colter. Colter explains (2016), "I remember talking to [Coker] about it and I was adamant that Luke was not a person that used that language" (para. 9). This viewpoint is not uncommon within the African American community. However, this was construed by a segment of the audience as the series endorsing the politics of respectability. Addressing these critiques, Coker explained:

> Because Luke Cage doesn't love the N-word, it doesn't make him a conservative. It makes him an old head from the '90s. Because back in the '90s, there was a period of time when if you were going to use the N-word, you were going to talk about why you're using it. [. . .] What about the fights that I had to have with Marvel to even use that word? So people want to talk to me about respectability politics without even realizing all the different levels of fights that I had to have to even use the word within a Marvel property (Harris, 2018, para. 119).

Coker argues that due to Cage being an "old head," a term referring to informal mentors of young men in African American communities (Carter & Duneier, 1999), his use of the term would be inauthentic to his character. Marcano (2016) observes that while Cage himself does not use the term, many other African American characters in *Luke Cage* do so freely. Marcano praises the series for showcasing a diversity of attitudes toward the term from within the community, "*Luke Cage* avoids depicting Black people as a monolith, and that's the best possible scenario for a show seeking to represent, and reach, the Black community" (para. 5).

This discussion is correctly framed as a debate. The past century has witnessed efforts by some African Americans to reclaim "n---er" and reappropriate it as "n---a." As explained by Kennedy (2000), "What many gays and lesbians have done with 'queer' and 'dyke' is what many African Americans have done with n---er—transformed it from a sign of shame to be avoided if possible into a sign of pride to be worn assertively" (p. 90). In the 1980s and 1990s, black hip-hop artists such as Dr. Dre, Ice Cube, and Tupac Shakur began to freely include the term "n---a" in their songs in an effort "to locate an authentic self in the midst of increasing commodification" of black culture (Neal, 2013, p. 558). This influenced young African American consumers of hip-hop music, who began to employ "n---a" in their own vernacular (Kennedy, 2000). This generation viewed their usage of the term as distinct from its historically pejorative meanings, with the term instead affirming unity. However, many African Americans, including celebrities as Oprah

Winfrey, refute any usage of the term, arguing that it continues to reinforce stereotypes of the community as unintelligent and inferior (Nguyen, 2013). This argument has in turn been criticized by promoting respectability politics by "ignor[ing] context in a move that both refuses to recognize cultural difference and accommodate hegemonic whiteness" (Nguyen, 2013, p. 296). From a critical perspective, *Luke Cage* is noteworthy because the series does not portray its usage as ubiquitous within the community, nor does the series endorse respectability politics by portraying its use as regressive or indicative of criminality.

CONCLUSION

Luke Cage debuted at a critical time in US civil rights history. Debates regarding police brutality and other forms of systemic oppression have reached a zenith. When considering this sociocultural context, *Luke Cage* received considerable interest leading up to its premiere. Not only was it the first property in the Marvel Cinematic Universe to feature a black protagonist, itself notable in terms of representation, but the series centered on a bulletproof black male: an undeniably relevant concept, thereby making *Luke Cage* "inherently political" (Dockterman, 2016, p. 48). Aware of this, Coker announced that *Luke Cage* would continue the tradition of previous Marvel television series produced for Netflix by commenting on contemporary social concerns. Specifically, *Daredevil* and *Jessica Jones*, both of which premiered in 2015, mediated respectively on the criminal justice system and rape culture. In contrast, Cage had historically been utilized by Marvel to explore issues specific to African Americans. Coker also drew comparisons to *The Wire* in terms of *Luke Cage*'s sociocultural insight, generating high expectations for the series. As explained by Coker, "I just always feel that any black art should address our perpetual struggle for progress and freedom, period" (Harris, 2018, para. 3).

In the episode "Manifest," Cottonmouth sarcastically refers to Cage as "Harlem's Captain America," alluding to one of Marvel's flagship characters, a superpowered World War II veteran. While Cottonmouth is mocking Cage's aspirations of heroism, it is not an unfair characterization. Historically, even television series heavily rooted in black culture and representation generally "operate under the creative control and direction of white studio and network executives" (Gray, 2000, p. 283), thus privileging majority white viewing audiences and conforming to respectability politics. This is indicative of political economy, which encompasses the production, distribution, and ownership of media texts (Kellner, 1995). Because the system of production informs both what and how media texts shall be produced, political economy has heavy social implications (Armstrong, 2006). Therefore, *Luke Cage* deserves recognition for directly rebuking politics of respectability. It challenges prominent media stereotypes of black masculinity, addresses systemic oppression against African Americans, and discusses the usage of the word "n---a" within the community. *Luke Cage* and its eponymous protagonist are not concerned with respectability politics but rather with the dominant frame of racism.

As the first property in the Marvel Cinematic Universe to feature a black protagonist, adapted from the first black character to star in his own comic series, *Luke Cage* possesses a high degree of influence that few other superhero projects can boast. It, therefore, enjoys a unique position within contemporary popular culture. In comics, television, and other entertainment media, the African American community has historically been denied authentic heroes and strong role models, thus making Cage and his expression of community values especially praiseworthy. The rapper Method Man, who contributed music to the series, plays himself in "Soliloquy of Chaos." A fan of Cage, he relates that "there's somethin' powerful about seeing a black man that's bulletproof and unafraid." During a period characterized by African American mortality at the hands of police, *Luke Cage* asserts its sociopolitical relevance and offers a true hero for this moment.

REFERENCES

Agyemang, C., Bhopal, R., & Bruijnzeels, M. (2005). Negro, Black, Black African, African Caribbean, African American or what? Labelling African origin populations in the health arena in the 21st century. *Journal of Epidemiology & Community Health, 59*(12), 1014–1018. http://dx.doi.org/10.1136/jech.2005.035964.

Altman, A., Frizell, S., & Rhodan, M. (2015). Black Lives Matter. *Time, 186*(25–26), 116–120.

Altman, R. (1984). A semantic/syntactic approach to film genre. *Cinema Journal, 23*(2), 6–18. http://dx.doi.org/10.2307/1225093.

Apel, D. (2014). "Hands up, don't shoot": Surrendering to liberal illusions. *Theory & Event,* 17(3), 1.

Armstrong, J. (2006). Applying critical theory to electronic media history. In D.G. Godfrey (Ed.), *Methods of historical analysis in electronic media* (pp. 145–166). Lawrence Erlbaum Associates.

Asim, J. (2007). *The N word: Who can say it, who shouldn't, and why.* Houghton Mifflin.

Beaty, B. (2016). Superhero fan service: Audience strategies in the contemporary interlinked Hollywood blockbuster. *The Information Society, 32*(5), 318–325. http://dx.doi.org/10.1080/01972243.2016.1212616.

Betancourt, D. (2016). Inside the making of 'Luke Cage,' Marvel's first black superhero show. *The Washington Post.* https://www.washingtonpost.com/news/comic-riffs/wp/2016/09/27/inside-the-making-of-luke-cage-marvels-first-black-superhero-show/?utm_term=.1e5a533505a3.

Botan, C., Frey, L., & Kreps, G. (1999). *Investigating communication: An introduction to research methods* (2nd ed). Allyn & Bacon.

Boyle, K. (2012). Trayvon Martin's death has put spotlight on perceptions about hoodies. *The Washington Post.* https://www.washingtonpost.com/lifestyle/style/trayvon-martins-death-has-put-spotlight-on-perceptions-about-hoodies/2012/03/24/gIQAwQ6gaS_story.html?utm_term=.c634ffbe9972.

Carter, O., & Duneier, M. (1999). *Sidewalk.* Douglas & McIntyre Ltd.

Coles, R. L., & Green, C. (2010). Introduction. In R. L. Coles & C. Green (Eds.), *The myth of the missing black father* (pp. 1–16). Columbia University Press.

Collins, P. H. (2002). *Black feminist thought: Knowledge, consciousness, and the politics empowerment* (2nd ed.). Routledge.

Collins, P. H. (2004). *Black sexual politics: African-Americans, gender, and the new racism.* Routledge. http://dx.doi.org/10.4324/9780203309506.

Crenshaw, K. W. (1995). Introduction. In K.W. Crenshaw, N. Gotanda, G. Peller, & K. Thomas (Eds.), *Critical race theory: The key writings that formed the movement* (pp. xi–xxxii). The New Press.

Di Leonardo, M. (2016). Partyin' with a purpose: Black respectability politics and the Tom Joyner Morning Show. *Souls: A Critical Journal of Black Politics, Culture, and Society, 18*(2–4), 358–378. http://dx.doi.org/10.1080/10999949.2016.1230816.

Dockterman, E. (2016). The making of Luke Cage: A hero for this moment. *Time, 188*(12), 48–50.

Flood, A. (2018). What should we expect from Luke Cage Season 2? The brains behind Marvel's superhero series spill some secrets. *NME.* https://www.nme.com/blogs/luke-cage-season-2-marvel-netflix-cheo-hodari-coker-lucy-liu-2330457.

Gill, J. (2011). *Harlem: The four hundred year history from Dutch village to capital of Black America.* Grove Press.

Gray, H. (2000). The politics of representation in network television. In H. Newcomb (Ed.), *Television: The critical view* (6th ed.) (pp. 282–305). Oxford University Press.

Gray, J., & Lotz, A.D. (2012). *Television studies.* Polity Press.

Harris, A. (2018). 'Luke Cage' season 2: A new villain and respectability politics. *The New York Times.* https://www.nytimes.com/2018/06/21/arts/television/luke-cage-season-2-netflix.html.

Harris, F. C. (2014). The rise of respectability politics. *Dissent, 61*(1), 33–37. http://dx.doi.org/10.1353/dss.2014.0010.

Henry, M. (2004). He is a "bad mother*$%@!#": "Shaft' and contemporary black masculinity. *African American Review, 38*(1), 119–126.

Jackson II, R. L. (2006). *Scripting the masculine body: Identity, discourse and racial politics in popular media.* State University of New York Press.

Jones, J. (2018). It still matters: The Cosby Show and sociopolitical representation on television. In A. Barlow & L. Westengard (Eds.), *The 25 Sitcoms that changed television: Turning points in American culture* (pp. 180–195). Praeger.

Jones, T., & Staples, R. (1985). Culture, ideology and black television images. *The Black Scholar, 16*(3), 10–20.

Joseph, R. L. (2016). Strategically ambiguous Shonda Rhimes: Respectability politics of a black woman showrunner. *Souls: A Critical Journal of Black Politics, Culture and Society, 18*(2–4), 302–320. http://dx.doi.org/10.1080/10999949.2016.1230825.

Kellner, D. (1995). Cultural studies, multiculturalism and media culture. In G. Dines & J. M. Humez (Eds.), *Gender, race, and class in media* (1st ed.) (pp. 5–17). Sage.

Kennedy, R. L. (2000). Who can say "nigger"? … And other considerations. *The Journal of Blacks in Higher Education, 26*, 86–96.

Kim, J., & Shifflett, J. (2016). Why Luke Cage creator made his superhero costume a hoodie. *The Frame.* http://www.scpr.org/programs/the-frame/2016/09/15/52135/why-luke-cage-creator-made-his-superhero-costume-a/.

Kvaran, K. M. (2017). Super daddy issues: Parental figures, masculinity, and superhero films. *The Journal of Popular Culture, 50*(2), 218–328.

Ledrum, R. (2005). The super black macho, One baaad mutha: Black superhero masculinity in 1970s mainstream comic books. *Extrapolation, 46*(3), 360–372. https://doi.org/10.3828/extr.2005.46.3.8.

Marcano, A. (2016). 'Luke Cage' doesn't like the n-word, but you don't have to agree. *Inverse.* Retrieved from https://www.inverse.com/article/21814-luke-cage-nigga-n-word.

Mills, C. E. (2010). Fostering fatherhood: Understanding the effects of child-support policy on low-income, noncustodial African American fathers. In R.L. Coles & C. Green (Eds.), *The Myth of the Missing Black Father* (pp. 327–350). Columbia University Press.

Moss, C. (2016). Luke Cage is truly a hero for his time. *The Atlantic.* https://www.theatlantic.com/entertainment/archive/2016/09/luke-cage-gets-a-new-story/502229/.

Nama, A. (2011). *Super Black: American pop culture and black superheroes.* University of Texas Press.

Neal, M. A. (2013). Nigga: The 21st-century theoretical superhero. *Cultural Anthropology, 28*(3), 556–563.

Newman, Z., & Obasogie, O.K. (2016). Black Lives Matter and respectability politics in local news accounts of officer-involved civilian deaths: An early empirical assessment. *Wisconsin Law Review, 2016*(3), 541–574.

Nguyen, K. H. (2013). Hearing what we see: Censoring "nigga," vernaculars, and African American agentic subjects. *Howard Journal of Communications, 24*(3), 293–308. http://dx.doi.org/10.1080/10646175.2013.805988.

Nolfi, J. (2016). Luke Cage producer compares Netflix's Marvel series to The Wire. *Entertainment Weekly.* http://ew.com/article/2016/04/13/cheo-hodari-coker-compares-luke-cage-wire/.

Park, M. K. (2015). Race, hegemonic masculinity, and the "Linpossible!": An analysis of media representations of Jeremy Lin. *Communication & Sport, 3*(4), 367–389.

Patton, L. D. (2014). Preserving respectability or blatant disrespect? A critical discourse analysis of the Morehouse appropriate attire policy and implications for intersectional approaches to examining campus policies. *International Journal of Qualitative Studies in Education, 27*(6), 724–746. http://dx.doi.org/10.1080/09518398.2014.901576.

Perry, S. P. (2014). The deaths of Trayvon Martin: Photographs and representation in protest. *Argumentation & Advocacy, 51*(1), 58–71. http://dx.doi.org/10.1080/00028533.2014.11821839.

Riesman, A. (2016). How Luke Cage got Marvel to say the N-word. *Vulture.* http://www.vulture.com/2016/09/luke-cage-n-word.html.

Roberts, D. (1998). The absent black father. In C.R. Daniels (Ed.), *Lost fathers: The politics of fatherlessness in America* (pp. 145–162). St. Martin's Griffin.

Tuch, S., & Weitzer, R. (2002). Perceptions of racial profiling: Race, class, and personal experience. *Criminology, 40*(2), 435–456.

Ward, L. M. (2004). Wading through the stereotypes: Positive and negative associations between media use and black adolescents' conceptions of self. *Developmental Psychology, 40*(2), 284–294. http://dx.doi.org/10.1037/0012-1649.40.2.284.

Welch, K. (2007). Black criminal stereotypes and racial profiling. *Journal of Contemporary Criminal Justice, 23*(3), 276–288.

Wing, A. K. (2016). Is there a future for critical race theory? *Journal of Legal Education, 66*(1), 44–54.

Chapter 2

Doctor Who's 13th Doctor

Redefining the Female Lead in Science Fiction Television

Gwendelyn S. Nisbett and Newly Paul

In 2017, the traditionally male role of *Doctor Who* (*DW*) went to Jodie Whittaker who was cast as the 13th Doctor. This chapter examines portrayals of gender and race in one of the biggest and most influential science fiction (sci-fi) shows, which now stars its first female lead. It is important to study a television series like this, particularly at this time, because sci-fi has long been regarded as a genre dominated by men. But critics and fans have praised the 2000's reboot of *DW* for its increasing use of social commentary, the evolving role of the Doctor's companion, and attempts at cast diversity. Perhaps, most importantly, *DW* has a massive global fandom. The fans, known as Whovians, are some of the most active and critical components of the *DW* transmedia space. When the show addresses gender and racial issues, the content enters the fandom discursive space where the issues have an even greater impact. In short, sci-fi and *DW* hold immense cultural clout, and this chapter adds to sci-fi scholarship by analyzing a beloved character from the perspective of gender and race.

UNDERSTANDING GENDER AND RACE IN SCIENCE FICTION

Despite the masculine appeal of the field, sci-fi shows' portrayal of gender has improved through the decades (Merrick, 2003). In the 1930s and 1940s, women characters and people of color were marginalized and stereotyped (Merrick, 2003), but this changed in the 1950s, when a number of women sci-fi writers introduced feminist ideas into the field. Their texts featured strong women as central characters, interrogated traditional gender roles and celebrated the power of the feminine hero. The 1960s further challenged gendered assumptions and portrayed "women as fully 'human,' rather than 'female men'" (p. 246). This era also featured futuristic narratives that included women of color. The 1970s further promoted the concept of gender as a social construct and presented alternatives to traditional social mores such as the idea of parenting being a woman's job. Following the 1980s which were marked by dystopian works of sci-fi, in the 1990s and 2000s, sci-fi began to portray "increasingly nuanced explorations of gender" (p. 250) and disrupted "the conventionally 'masculinist' narratives of 'hard' sf (characterized by scientific accuracy and logic) and military sf (involving weapons and military activity)" (p. 250).

With reference to scientists in sci-fi, scholars have found that there is a dearth of women depicted as scientist characters (Long et al., 2010; Flicker, 2003). Women tend to be portrayed as less competent than male scientists (Flicker, 2003). They are valued for their social skills rather than their expertise and are depicted as young and beautiful characters (Steinke, 2005).

Scholarship on race and sci-fi has documented the exclusion of people of color from sci-fi, especially during the field's formative years (Bould, 2007; Nama, 2010). From the 1950s through the 1990s, black characters in sci-fi shows were either tokenized (Nama, 2010), or portrayed as silent mystical characters, witch doctors, and destructive people. Plotlines in sci-fi shows often wrote off black characters by killing them off early in the show. Some shows challenged the status quo by featuring "black-viewpoint characters" (Bould, 2007, p. 178) and incorporating narratives from important historical events such as the US Civil Rights movement (Guerrero, 1993).

The racial stereotyping extended to Hispanics as well. They were portrayed as outer space aliens—threatening creatures who were culturally dissimilar to Western civilization (Ramirez, 2008). According to Berg (2002), sci-fi shows incorporated political rhetoric on immigrant rights and undocumented immigration to create a racialized alien trope that demonized the image of Hispanics. Aliens were portrayed in two ways—as sympathetic aliens or destructive monsters. Sympathetic aliens allowed viewers to see the positive qualities of the characters, but at the same time, they were portrayed as very distinct from humans, who were mostly characterized as citizens of the Western world. It was in the aliens' best interests to return home, and if they refused, they assumed the characteristics of destructive monsters who needed to be killed by humans.

The attitude toward Asian characters in sci-fi is also characterized by xenophobia, stemming largely from US immigration rules through the mid-1960s, which strictly controlled Asian immigration (Cheng, 2019). During this time, Asians were portrayed as aliens and represented Americans' fear of

Communism (Berg, 2002). They were also depicted using Orientalist tropes such as the "Yellow Peril" which portrayed them as cunning, violent, and a danger to Western ideals. Sci-fi shows also adopted tropes of "Techno-Orientalism" (Morley and Robins, 2002) where they portrayed Asians as consumed by capitalism, and "as unfeeling aliens . . . cyborgs and replicants" (p. 170).

In the late 1990s, these patterns started to change with movies such as *The Matrix* (1999), and *Avatar* (2009), featuring multiethnic characters and depicting a future world inhabited by black people. They ushered in an era of "Afrofuturism" (Dery, 1994). This new crop of sci-fi shows fundamentally altered the sci-fi field to portray black characters occupying spaces that were unconditionally white. Presenting a more complex black identity, these characters were no longer constrained by racial stereotypes. Despite the positive changes in plotlines and characterizations with reference to race, sci-fi on the whole remains an overwhelmingly white and male-centric field. The next section discusses how racial and gender tropes affected the characterization of *DW*.

CASE STUDY: *DOCTOR WHO'S* 13TH DOCTOR

The British Broadcast Corporation's (BBC) *DW* first aired on November 23, 1963, in the United Kingdom. From the outset, the show was different and bolder than anything that had been broadcast on children's television. More than 50 years later, *DW* is still going strong with global success (Schaefer, 2018). Early *DW* distinguished itself from other sci-fi shows by functioning as an educational program that addressed history, ethics, and morality (Edwards, 2015). While the show has changed in terms of audience and production value, it is still regarded as a show that seeks to explore ethical and moral issues.

The show can be thought of in two iterations—early *DW* that ran from 1963 to 1987 featuring the first Doctor through the seventh Doctor, and new *DW*, currently airing, featuring the ninth through 13th Doctors. Aside from a made-for-television movie version of the show featuring the only time fans would see the 8th Doctor, the show was put on an 18-year hiatus. In 2005, under showrunners Russell T. Davies and Julie Gardner, the show made a return and renewed its popularity.

This new version of *DW* featured the same premise as the original: a madman in a box who travels through space and time. New Who did get a reboot, however, that distinguished it from early *DW*. The Doctor was still white, male, and British, but the role of the "companion" was reconceptualized. The companion was reimagined to be a deeper, fuller character that matched the Doctor in wit and bravery.

In 2017, as 12th Doctor Peter Capaldi was finishing his term as the character, it was announced that the 13th Doctor would, for the first time, be a woman. Actress Jodie Whittaker took over as the Doctor in season 11 which began airing in fall 2018. During Whittaker's tenure, the role of the companion was reconceptualized, the story flow was altered to focus on singular stories, and guest stars and story lines included increased diversity.

The 13th Doctor travels with three companions named Yasmin "Yaz" Kahn, Ryan Sinclair, and Graham O'Brien. Ryan is the step-grandson of Graham, who is married to Ryan's grandmother Grace (she is killed in episode 1). Yaz is a police officer who is also an old school friend of Ryan. Like many companion origin stories in *DW*, the companions collide with the Doctor when aliens invade their community.

The role of women and people of color in *DW* is complicated. The original version was very white and the women were often subjugated to supporting characters. Even the term "companion" has a pejorative gloss. New Who introduced more diversity, including LGBTQ companions (Captain Jack Harkness and later Bill Potts) and companions of color (Mickey Smith, Martha Jones, and Bill Potts), but the Doctor was still the same. Much of the diversity, especially in season 11, comes from the guest stars and extra cast. As Gupta (2013) notes, the casting in *DW* has increasingly reflected the diversity of Britain. Behind the scenes, however, progress was slow as the writers and directors of the program were still mostly men (Lorna, 2014).

While *DW* steers away from overt gender stereotypes, it has a mixed record in terms of a nuanced representation of women characters. The show has been praised for engaging with various gender-related issues (Orthia & Morgain, 2016), increasing the prominence of the female companions (Wallace, 2010), and portraying both male and female scientists as competent. It has also been criticized for reinforcing gender stereotypes (Franke & Nicol, 2018). Similarly, the show has an inconsistent record in portraying race. Seasons before the 2000s were criticized for various issues such as the subtle confirmation of imperialism (Gregg, 2004; Charles, 2007; Orthia, 2010), and the portrayal of minorities as one-dimensional characters whose lives strictly revolved around the Doctor (Welch, 2013). Against this chequered history of *DW*, we seek to explore the following research questions:

> RQ1: What are the major themes in Season 11 of *DW* in terms of gender and race?
>
> RQ2: How does the 13th Doctor compare to previous incarnations?

METHOD

In order to answer our research questions, we performed a thematic analysis on all ten episodes of *DW* season 11. Following the method described in

Nowell et al. (2017, p. 4), we followed six steps to arrive at the results. First, both researchers spent time familiarizing themselves with the data. One of the researchers is a fan of the show, while the other is new to the show. The researchers watched every episode of the season independently via a streaming service and documented their thoughts on the plot, settings, characters, and dialogues. Next, they met for a peer-to-peer debriefing session and discussed their thoughts about the show. This helped fill gaps in understanding and drew attention to aspects that one or the other researcher might have overlooked in the initial viewing.

In the third phase, the researchers used a deductive approach to search for themes in the episodes (Nowell et al., 2017, p. 8). They paid special attention to the following aspects of the show: (1) the Doctor and companions' characterizations (appearance, personality, manner of interaction with other characters); (2) insights into the Doctor's philosophy toward life as depicted through her actions and dialogues; (3) the group's reaction to various crises; (4) the issues explored in the show; (5) the connection to current politics; and (6) the extent to which the female Doctor differed from the previous male Doctors. During this phase, they made extensive notes and rewatched some episodes. The fourth and fifth phases involved reviewing the notes and defining and naming the themes. In these phases, they finalized the themes and ensured that they were coherent and sufficiently supported by the data gathered from the episodes. The last phase involved producing the report, that is, describing the themes, incorporating quotes to support them, and providing context and interpretation.

ANALYSIS

Disrupting Gender Roles

The show does not portray the Doctor as a sexualized being, which is in contrast to many female characters in sci-fi. She is shown wearing the 12th Doctor's battered Crombie coat, instead of overly feminine clothes. Viewers do see a flare of the (stereotypical) feminine when the episode concludes with a shopping trip to find new clothes, but every Doctor is a bit of a clothes horse. For example, after the 10th Doctor finishes his regeneration, we see him picking through a massive wardrobe in the TARDIS. The 13th Doctor's costume, in keeping with past Doctors, has a tinge of feminine lines but is overall quite masculine. She wears boots, baggy pants with suspenders, and an oversized trench coat.

The second thing a viewer would notice is the Doctor's disposition. She is quirky and friendly, but she is not warm, empathetic, or nurturing. The Doctor is "the Doctor" and thus is not the mother hen of the crew (even though she keeps trying to call them "fam"). Also, the Doctor is in charge. Even when her brain is a bit foggy or she is making quirky side remarks, she is the leader. As the 12th Doctor says as he is regenerating into the 13th, "Always try to be nice, but never fail to be kind." The Doctor is driven by an internal moral compass to try to help when she is needed, but we do not see the Doctor being particularly nurturing. If anything, she is socially awkward and a bit rude. For instance, in the episode "It Takes You Away," the Doctor balks at the unwise sentimentality of Graham and Eric (a father they are trying to save from an alien). She even calls Eric an idiot, which is very much keeping with past Doctors.

Indeed, the nurturing center of the show is Graham. He is unfailingly kind, good humored, and persistently concerned with the emotional well-being of his fellow travelers. He often references his late wife Grace, whom we see from time to time as a memory or specter. With the growth of the relationship between grandson Ryan and Graham, we see Ryan also becoming a nurturer. In the episode "It Takes You Away," Ryan takes on the role of carer for a young girl called Hanne.

Another example where gender stereotypes are questioned is the episode "The Tsuranga Conundrum." While the main male characters are shown helping with the birth of a baby, the women characters are performing the role of protectors, fighting the alien, and trying to save the ship from damage. Further, a male character's pregnancy brings out the fatherly, nurturing side in Ryan and Graham—a concept that is severely underrepresented in the media. The scenes depicting them cheering on the pregnant man while he is in labor serve to overturn stereotypes about women's primary roles as caregivers, and about women being naturally maternal and empathetic. The scenes depict a new dimension of male bonding, one that is not associated with typical male stereotypic interests such as sports or beer, but the birth of a baby.

Feminism

One issue that is sparingly addressed is respect for women and women's rights. Generally, the Doctor's authority is not questioned, but her identity as a woman is not fully explored either. She is shown stumbling at times, forgetting that she is not a man. In "The Ghost Monument" episode, she tells the TARDIS to "Come to daddy, I mean mummy."

She occasionally runs into male characters that belittle her. For example, recurring villain Tzim-Sha calls her "little one," to insult her intelligence, and in the episode "Arachnids in the UK," a billionaire real estate tycoon questions her authority as leader of the group. The Doctor handles these misogynists in stride, deliberately mispronouncing the alien's name as Tim Shaw and by asking the tycoon if he is Ed Sheeran.

The episode that tackles gender and women's rights head-on is "The Witchfinders," which is set in early seventeenth-century England and addresses the dark era of the Witch Hunts that targeted women. The plot revolves around a wealthy landowner, Becka Savage, who killed 36 women by a ducking stool (drowning them), because she suspected them of being witches. The Doctor and her companions introduce themselves to Savage as witchfinders sent to assist her. When King James arrives to help the villagers, he refuses to acknowledge the Doctor's expertise and assumes that Graham—an older white man—must be the leader of the group. He addresses the Doctor as "lassie," and determines that on account of her gender, she has an "innate aptitude for nosiness and gossip."

Reflecting on the general condition of women during this period, the Doctor says, "These are hard times for women. If we're not being drowned, we're being patronized to death." Later, Savage and King James accuse the Doctor of being a witch at which she says, "Honestly, if I was still a bloke, I could get on with the job and not have to waste time defending myself." Her experiences help the audience reflect on the double standards applied to women.

Eventually, the episode shows that the Doctor had a positive impact on Willa, a teenager whose grandmother was killed for being a witch. Initially, she told the king that the Doctor might be a witch because she had introduced herself as the Doctor, but at the conclusion of the episode, Willa decides to carry on her grandmother's medicine practice and become a doctor herself. In showing a change in Willa, the episode highlights the resilience of women and the power of positive women role models in affecting change.

Focus on Family

A major theme and the primary story arc from season 11 explored family. We see the back stories and families of each companion, though we never explore the Doctor's past. The three companions struggle with what family means to them, how they fit into their real families, and how they create a new family with the Doctor. The primary relationship at the center of the season is that of companions Ryan and Graham. Ryan chafes at the notion that Grace is married to Graham, and scoffs at Graham's request to call him grandad. For instance, Graham asks "So we're sticking with Graham then, and not Grandad?" to which Ryan retorts, "Yes, Graham." When Ryan and Graham lose Grace as their connection point, they must seek solace in each other. Their story arc is at the center of season 11 as they wrestle with becoming a family for each other. In the final episode, in trying to convince Graham not to seek revenge for Grace's death, Ryan finally tells Graham, "You're my family, and I love ya."

Yaz also explores the notion of family (though does not have the primacy of the Ryan/Graham story arc). We are introduced to her family in "Arachnids in the UK" and explore her Pakistani heritage further in "Demons of the Punjab." Though we catch a glimpse of her stereotypically overbearing family, it is not fully explored.

Moreover, as they travel in their adventures, the Doctor and her companions encounter characters who also reference family. The characters in the "Ghost Monument" are competing for their families. The "Demons of the Punjab" episode explores tension and conflict within families, while "The Tsuranga Conundrum" episode explores the notion of fatherhood.

Bearing Witness

In the episode "Demons of the Punjab," the alien presence explains to the Doctor that they are bearing witness to an atrocity and death lost to history. In many ways, a theme of the season finds the Doctor bearing witness to racism, colonialism, and sexism. This is a marked change from seasons past. The episode features Yaz's grandmother as a young Muslim girl who is getting married to her Hindu neighbor on the eve of Partition (when India and Pakistan were carved as separate nations on the basis of religion). The Doctor solemnizes the marriage, but the groom is killed shortly after by his own brother. Despite the hopelessness of the situation, the Doctor and her companions simply observe, rather than intervene to change the events.

Another example is the third episode of the season, "Rosa," occurs in 1955 Montgomery, Alabama, and the plot revolves around the Doctor and her companions preventing time-travelling criminal Krasko from stopping Rosa Parks from carrying out her act of defiance—giving up her seat for a white passenger in a segregated bus. This act is a culturally important moment because it started the bus boycott movement, which is widely considered the first large-scale demonstration against segregation in the United States. The episode weaves in details about Parks' life and the Civil Rights Movement, thereby simultaneously entertaining and educating audiences.

Ryan, a black man, is shown getting physically assaulted by a white man, and being asked to leave an establishment that was for whites only, while Yaz, who is of South Asian origin, is labeled a Mexican woman because of her brown skin, and treated with contempt. These enactments of overt racism are jarring and emotional, and the show makes the point that though overt racism might be a thing of the past, covert racism or subconscious racial bias is still prevalent today.

In his conversation with Yaz, Ryan admits that he is having to work very hard to keep his temper. He says, "I could have slapped that guy back there as soon as we arrived," referring to the white man who assaulted him.

"Thank God, my nan taught me how to keep my temper. Never give them the excuse," he says, highlighting a common reality in the lives of black men in the United States who contend with negative stereotypes of criminality and the need to present a nonthreatening image. Later, upset with the racism he witnesses, Ryan says that Rosa Parks's act was not able to wipe out racism from the world forever, and he points out that back home, he gets stopped by the police more frequently than his white friends. Yaz, who is a police officer, agrees and recounts that she is called a "Paki" (derogatory term for a person of Pakistani origin) when she's sorting out domestic violence incidents, or a terrorist when she walks home from the mosque. The show also features a moment with Graham, the Doctor's white, male companion, who is devastated to know that he needs to be the white passenger for whom Parks has to give up her seat. His feelings of despair and reluctance embody the complexity of racism, showing that whites are not homogenous in their attitudes.

Though the episode highlights the absurdity of racial classifications and comments on the persistence of negative stereotypes, it leaves audiences with a broader message of hope. In response to Ryan's pessimism about the endurance of racism, Yaz says, "But they don't win, those [racist] people. Because I can be a police officer now because people like Rosa Parks fought those battles for me. For us. And in 53 years they will have a black president as leader. Who knows where they'll be 50 years after that. That's proper change."

This uplifting message is combined with a powerful message about the power of small acts of defiance. The scene where police handcuff Parks and lead her away from the bus plays out in slow motion, focuses on close-ups of Parks, and features the song "Rise Up" by black singer Andra Day, all of which puts the focus squarely on the true hero of the episode—Rosa Parks—and her small act of defiance. This sensitive treatment of a landmark cultural moment saves the episode from falling into the trap of using the "white savior" trope where white characters are shown as being solely responsible for protecting and guiding characters of color.

FAN RESPONSES TO A REIMAGINED *DOCTOR WHO*

The Whovian fandom is regarded as one of the most engaged groups in the pop culture transmedia space, and the casting of Whittaker was seen as an important step in terms of positive female representation in sci-fi. The fandom's response has been largely accepting of the first female Doctor and have adopted her as a role model. As a character, Whittaker's casting inspired a large number of young girls to tune in to the show ("Jodie Whittaker's Doctor Who draws more young, female viewers," 2018). Given that sci-fi shows are known to boost an interest in science-related careers (Simis et al., 2015), the show could be a catalyst to correcting the gender bias in science and correcting misperceptions about women's abilities.

In exploring how the 13th Doctor compares to past incarnations, the obvious question among fans was whether Whittaker is simply a woman cast in a man's role and whether she is playing a man. In many ways, the 13th Doctor is still the Doctor, displaying traits that have been consistent for 50 years. In keeping with past incarnations, the 13th Doctor is a pacifist. At one point, in the "Ghost Monument" episode, the Doctor disarms an armed character using Venusian Aikido and calls herself a "Grandmaster Pacifist" (harkening back to the third Doctor). Throughout the season, she rails against using guns specifically, but generally abhors violence as a solution. The 13th Doctor also displays the quintessential wackiness that is a hallmark of the character. As with past incarnations, she lacks the usual filters that mark her as human. For instance, she is awful at making small talk without sounding completely bizarre. The show and the characterization were widely regarded among fans as keeping with the spirit and canon of the show.

There were some fans that argued the show missed the mark in not making the first female Doctor more feminine and for not taking the opportunity to explore the Doctor's inherent male privilege (Harris & Ridley, 2018). We argue, however, that keeping the Doctor consistent with past incarnations was beneficial for a number of reasons. First, by allowing the 13th Doctor to be like other Doctors, it emphasizes that the character (at least in new *DW*) was already disrupting gender roles. At the 2015 San Diego Comic Con *DW* panel, then 12th Doctor Peter Capaldi was asked about whether the Doctor was a nice guy. Capaldi balked at this a bit, and explained, "The Doctor is mysterious; he's a Time Lord; he's not a guy. You know, he's a special creature. I don't even know really if he even has a corporeal being. He may project this to everyone, but he may exist on a totally different plane. So, he's not a guy." This statement captures the essence of who the Doctor should be—a mysterious alien unrestricted by normative gender traits.

With the 13th Doctor maintaining the characteristics of past Doctors, other characters are more free to explore and upend traditional gender roles. Yaz is brave and bold, Ryan is vulnerable and goofy, and Graham is nurturing and sentimental—all playing against traditional tropes. Moreover, in disrupting the Doctor, the show is more political and open to interrogating racial and gender stereotypes. Episodes comment on issues such as gun violence, racism, colonialism, the impact of automation on workers' rights, climate change, and separation of families (though they stop short of making strong ideological statements on any issue). The production also emphasized diverse casting of guest stars, including people of color, LGBTQ, and visually impaired actors. Such depictions filled a void in representation and very well may have expanded the Whovian fandom even further.

Despite the season's plotlines integrating important historical events, the episodes tend to discuss issues such as gender and race in isolation rather than incorporating these topics in a cohesive manner throughout the season. For example, when gender issues are at the forefront in "The Witchfinders" episode, the Doctor is shown challenging gender-stereotypical assumptions about her credibility. However, gender issues are not directly addressed in other episodes. Similarly, in the episode on Rosa Parks, the Doctor's companions suffer the effects of racism, but she refrains from making statements about racial discrimination and white privilege. This siloed treatment of race and gender could create the impression among audiences that while the season tapped into important debates of the day, it did not explore them in their full complexity. It ignored the intersection of race and gender with other issues such as economic inequality, thus failing to reflect the fan's own experiences.

Moreover, though the show depicts the atrocities during the Jim Crow era and the racism that persists today, it still falls prey to the racial trope of minimizing African heritage characters. For instance, the influential black woman character, Grace, is killed off in the very first episode. Moreover, the origin story for Ryan falls into racist tropes—he has a wayward absentee father that gives his son over to grandmother Grace to be raised. Ryan finds solace in his growing relationship with Graham (an older white man), who is portrayed as kind and persistently caring toward Ryan, which comes close to a white savior trope.

CONCLUSION

Diverse casts are underrepresented in sci-fi, often relying on characters that are stereotypically portrayed. A woman taking over the lead of a top sci-fi transmedia empire was a useful opportunity to better understand gender and race in the genre. This chapter brought forth valuable insights. It was found that the show does not portray the Doctor as a sexualized being, thereby overturning the trope of sexualized female sci-fi characters. In addition, the show questions gender and racial stereotypes through the supporting characters. The theme of family runs through most episodes this season, and the family ties between companions Ryan and Graham are highlighted. We see male characters displaying their nurturing side, and women taking on the role of protector and leader. Though the show incorporates issues such as women's rights and racism, it stays away from making these issues an ongoing part of the show or exploring in detail the implications of a woman in the Doctor's role. Part of the reason for this could be the creators' uncertainty about fan reactions.

We see the Doctor and her companions bearing witness to racism, colonialism, and sexism, and though they help save some characters from persecution and death, for the most part, they let history run its course uninterrupted. There are two reasons for this: First, the show refrains from implying that the Doctor and her companions are the architects of history and leaves the spotlight on real-life heroes such as Rosa Parks. Second, this allows the show to give a broader message about the importance of hope, positivity, and the power of small acts of defiance.

The 13th Doctor is only getting started and the fandom is excited to see how the characters grow. There is a tremendous opportunity in the show and within the *DW* transmedia space to further explore the intersection of gender and race. Despite flaws in the show, *DW* has tremendous potential for both further research enquiry and as a vehicle for audience discussions about gender and race. Further research should examine how the Doctor progresses as a disruptive sci-fi character. Researchers could also use surveys and experiments to gauge fan reactions to the show and explore antecedents and effects of viewers' attitudes. For example, do people who support a female Doctor also tend to support a woman candidate as president? Sci-fi reflects aspects of contemporary reality and also offers an alternate vision of the world (Seed, 2011) by critiquing social and political issues and proposing solutions to these issues (Orthia, 2011). These "fantastical approaches to solutions" (p. 77) often act as "a mental health necessity for viewers" (p. 77), and future research can examine the extent to which this is true.

REFERENCES

Attebery, B. (2014). *Decoding gender in science fiction*. Routledge.

Avery-Natale, E. (2013). An analysis of embodiment among six superheroes in DC Comics. *Social Thought & Research: A Continuation of the Mid-American Review of Sociology*, 71–106.

Berg, C. R. (1989). Immigrants, aliens, and extraterrestrials: Science fiction's alien "other" as (among other things) new Hispanic imagery. *CineAction, Fall*, 3–17.

Bould, M. (2007). The ships landed long ago: Afrofuturism and Black SF. *Science Fiction Studies*, 177–186.

Charles, A. (2007). The ideology of anachronism: Television, history and the nature of time. In D. Butler (Ed.), *Time and relative dissertations in space: critical perspectives on Doctor Who* (pp. 108–122). Manchester University Press.

Cheng, J. (2019). Asians and Asian Americans in Early Science Fiction. In *Oxford Research Encyclopedia of Literature*.

Cocca, C. (2014). The 'Broke Back Test': a quantitative and qualitative analysis of portrayals of women in mainstream superhero comics, 1993–2013. *Journal of Graphic Novels and Comics*, *5*, 411–428.

Dery, M. (1994). Black to the Future: Interviews with Samuel R. Delany, Greg Tate, and Tricia Rose. *Flame Wars: The Discourse of Cyberculture*, 179–222.

Dodson, L. (2013). Conscious color-blindness, unconscious racism in *Doctor Who* companions. In L. Orthia (Ed.), *Doctor Who and race* (pp. 29–34). Intellect.

Edwards, O. D. (2015). "As We See, So We Learn": Doctor who as religious education. *Implicit Religion*, *18*(4), 527–540.

Elasmar, M., Hasegawa, K., & Brain, M. (1999). The portrayal of women in U.S. prime time television. *Journal of Broadcasting & Electronic Media*, *43*(1), 20–34.

Franke, A., & Nicol, D. (2018). 'Don't make me go back': Post-feminist retreatism in Doctor Who. *The Journal of Popular Television*, *6*(2), 197–211.

Gierzynski, A. (2018). *The Political Effects of Entertainment Media: How Fictional Worlds Affect Real World Political Perspectives*. Rowman & Littlefield.

Guerrero, E. (2012). *Framing Blackness: The African American image in film*. Temple University Press.

Gupta, A. (2013). Doctor Who and race: Reflections on the change of Britain's status in the international system. *Round Table*, *102*(1), 41–50.

Gregg, P. B. (2004). England Looks to the Future: The Cultural Form Model and" Doctor Who". *Journal of Popular Culture*, *37*(4), 648–661.

Harris, K., & Ridley, P. (2019). "I never did this when I was a man." *Soundings*, (71), 107–115.

Harwood, J., & Anderson, K. (2002). The presence and portrayal of social groups on primetime television. *Communication Reports*, *15*(2), 81–97.

Jodie Whittaker's Doctor Who draws more young, female viewers than ever. (2018, October 9). https://www.telegraph.co.uk/tv/2018/10/09/jodie-whittakers-doctor-draws-young-female-.

Jowett, L. (2014). The girls who waited? Female companions and gender in Doctor Who. *Critical Studies in Television*, *9*(1), 77–94.

Leiserowitz, A. A. (2004). Before and after the day after tomorrow: A US study of climate change risk perceptions. *Environment*, *46*(9), 23–37.

Merrick, H. (2003). Gender in science fiction. In E. James & S. Mendlesohn (Ed.), *The Cambridge companion to science fiction* (pp. 241–252). Cambridge University Press.

Morley, D., & Robins, K. (2002). *Spaces of identity: Global media, electronic landscapes and cultural boundaries*. Routledge.

Nama, A. (2010). *Black space: Imagining race in science fiction film*. University of Texas Press.

Nowell, L. S., Norris, J. M., White, D. E., & Moules, N. J. (2017). Thematic analysis: Striving to meet the trustworthiness criteria. *International Journal of Qualitative Methods*, *16*(1), 1–13.

Orthia, L. (2010). "Sociopathetic abscess" or "yawning chasm"? The absent postcolonial transition in Doctor Who. *The Journal of Commonwealth Literature*, *45*(2), 207–225.

Orthia, L. (2011), Paradise is a little too green for me: Discourses of environmental disaster in Doctor Who 1963-2010. *Colloquy: Text Theory Critique, 21*, 56–80.

Orthia, L. (2019). How does science fiction television shape fans' relationships to science? Results from a survey of 575 Doctor Who viewers. *Journal of Science Communication, 18*(4), 1–18.

Orthia, L. & Morgain, R. (2016). The gendered culture of scientific competence: A study of scientist characters in Doctor Who 1963–2013. *Sex Roles, 75*(3–4), 79–94.

Parrott, S., & Parrott, C. T. (2015). US television's "mean world" for white women: The portrayal of gender and race on fictional crime dramas. *Sex Roles, 73*(1–2), 70–82.

Prior, M. (2007). *Post-broadcast democracy: How media choice increases inequality in political involvement and polarizes elections.* Cambridge University Press.

Schaefer, S. (2018, October 8). Jodie Whittaker's Doctor Who scores record-breaking ratings & reviews. https://screenrant.com/doctor-who-season-11-ratings-reviews-jodie-whittaker/.

Seed, D. (2011). *Science Fiction: A very short introduction* (Vol. 271). Oxford University Press.

Simis, M., Yeo, S.., Rose, K., Brossard, D., Scheufele, D., Xenos, M. and Pope, B. (2015). New media audiences' perceptions of male and female scientists in two sci-fi movies. *Bulletin of Science, Technology & Society, 35*, 93–103.

Streeby, S. (2018). *Imagining the future of climate change: World-making through science fiction and activism* (Vol. 5). University of California Press.

Vandenbosch, L., Vervloessem, D., & Eggermont, S. (2013). I might get your heart racing in my skin-tight jeans: Sexualization on music entertainment television. *Communication Studies, 64*, 178–194.

Welch, R. (2013). When white boys write black: Race and class in the Davies and Moffat eras. In L. Orthia (Ed.), *Doctor Who and race* (pp. 67–72). Intellect.

Womack, Y. (2013). *Afrofuturism: The world of Black Sci-Fi and fantasy culture.* Chicago Review Press.

Chapter 3

A Woman in Trouble in *Twin Peaks: The Return*

Gothic Texts, Magical Technology, and Dreams Within Dreams

Joseph Boisvere

With its initial 30 episode run during 1990–1991, creators Mark Frost and David Lynch made television history in more ways than one with their iconic ABC prime time drama series *Twin Peaks* (*TP*). The show's hip stylization, chilling ambience, and challenging subject matter combined with innovative televisual storytelling techniques engendered a cult following that endures today. Canceled suddenly and leaving devotees on a quarter-century cliff-hanger, Frost and Lynch were able to resurrect the show for an 18-episode run on Showtime with nearly unlimited creative freedom, capping off the show's original run with *Twin Peaks: The Return* (*TP:R*) in 2017. In the interim and around the debut of *TP:R*, there was a flurry of supplemental texts, that is, media that engages with or informs how viewers perceive the series itself. These were David Lynch's critically reviled film *Fire Walk with Me* (1992), a book called *The Secret Diary of Laura Palmer* (1990), written by Lynch's daughter, Jennifer, and *Diane: The Twin Peaks Tapes of Agent Dale Cooper* (1990), written by Frost's son, Scott, and available as an audiobook read by none other than leading *TP* actor Kyle Maclachlan. These texts served to simultaneously enrich, enliven, complicate, and often refute what dedicated viewers had learned (or thought they understood) from the show. This treatment was particularly appropriate for *TP* because it is a show of texts within text, framed by still more texts. For example, the television soap opera parody, *Invitation to Love*, plays at opportune times in the background of the show's interior scenes. The plot is influenced, and character motives are disclosed, by letters that are misplaced or misinterpreted. Sentence fragments are repeated nonsensically by a mynah bird named Waldo, and the readout from a sensitive high-tech listening array enigmatically contains Agent Cooper's name several times in sequence. All of these texts-within-texts have led Lewdon (1994) to designate *TP* a Gothic television show. She explains how *TP* follows in the centuries-old Gothic tradition of creating an atmosphere of uncanniness and uncertainty through use of mysterious intradiegetic texts to convey information between characters and influence the plot.

Another critical feature of both *TP* and *TP:R* is its peculiar designation as an auteur series. As the work of renowned filmmaker David Lynch, viewers come into *TP* with certain expectations of quality and complexity. Therefore, although the original show was directed by many people over the course of its 30 episodes, and although scripts were written in collaboration with many writers besides Frost and Lynch, the project is considered a distinct David Lynch and Mark Frost product. It can also be argued, then, that David Lynch's other works are particularly relevant to the two shows. As Lynch's feature film, *Inland Empire* (2006) provides viewers of *TP* and *TP:R* with stylistic and thematic link between the two series. Although all of the intervening films in Lynch's repertoire have a bearing on his development as a storyteller, *Inland Empire* represents two important links to *TP:R*. First, the narrative tagline for *Inland Empire*, "A Woman in Trouble," appeared on movie posters and the DVD case. This paratext, a text that is outside of the imaginary world of the film but which primes viewers with certain expectations, resonates through both Nikki Grace's existential crisis and Laura Palmer's entire life(s) as told by all *TP*-related writings, television, and film. The second link has to do with how the film tells its story. That is to say, it is narratological. It has to do with the breakdown between diegeses, or the multiple story-worlds within the film, and how the narrative moves from one diegetical reality to another via sex, technology, and dreams.

All of the above texts use sexual acts, gender-based iconography, and an engagement with processes of sexual identification to contextualize and motivate both conventional plot and character development as well as to represent a gateway between different realities, perspectives, or timelines. In *TP:R*, Diane and Cooper engage in a prolonged and bizarre sex scene which results in their identity change to Linda and Richard. These fresh identities are new to the viewers; Richard and Linda do not correspond to any characters in either *TP:R* or the original series. This is a cue that they have slipped into a different level of reality within the *TP* universe. In *Inland Empire*, when Nikki and Devon consummate their affair, Nikki becomes Susan Blue (or thinks she has, or is unsure). The plots of both cinematic worlds hinge upon the feminine identity of Nikki Grace and Laura Palmer, the gendered violence they face, and how that violence is systemically inscribed.

Technology plays a critical triple role in this story arc, subplot, from *TP* to *TP:R*. It serves as a site through which metatexts and intradiegetic messages may be passed around the economy of the show. These shows also portray technology as an unsettling element, engendering a sense of existential uncanniness best described in Avital Ronell's innovative *The Telephone Book: Technology, Schizophrenia, Electric Speech* (1989). Ronell analyzes communications technology through her reading of controversial German philosopher Martin Heidegger's fundamental texts, or perhaps it elucidates Heidegger's life and work through a technological mode. As the following analysis will demonstrate, it is the blurry line between communications technology in the story reality of *TP* technology, its potential, and the world of dreams that finally complicates the diegesis in *TP:R*.

Through these elements, Frost and Lynch create a text whose narrative conclusions are undecidable and even contradictory. Frost, for his part, added the "novels," *The Secret History of Twin Peaks* and *Twin Peaks: The Final Dossier*, to the oeuvre, texts which often report "facts" in the form of declassified FBI files that are at odds with what audiences experienced in the televisual world of northeastern Washington State. This dense and mysterious text then draws its story world closer to our "real" world. *TP:R* engages with our reality in novel ways. For example, the actress Monica Bellucci appears as herself in *TP:R*, as do several musical acts. Also, the world that Cooper/Richard traverses in the final episode of *TP:R* is our own, a reading which is legitimized by the appearance of a Valero station and a run down, abandoned RR Diner. These artifacts are foreign to the television reality of *TP:R*, but television viewers would be able to readily identify them. The series is then best understood in audio/visual modes of meaning related to the resonating images surrounding sex and gender, existentialist philosophy, and the symbolic logic of myth. Laura Palmer's trouble is not simply diegetic, but one of unstable diegesis. *TP:R* finds itself straddling the line between television miniseries and long form auteur cinema by the same characteristics, two birds with one stone.

TWIN PEAKS AS POSTMODERN GOTHIC

Genre studies on *TP* abound, tying the show with many literary traditions. Most important for accessing *TP:R* are the insights of two scholars on the original series. Lewdon (1993) frames the show as a contemporary version of Gothic literature that relies not on the familiar tropes of time and setting, but rather on the use of many internal texts to create an atmosphere of mystery. She considers the Gothic a process of storytelling and states, "the result of this process is a series in which the domestic is the Gothic and television becomes the ghost in the home" (Lewdon, 1993, p. 260). This observation is salient across all 30 hours of the original series as well as throughout the film *Fire Walk with Me,* which serves as a prequel to *TP.* From Cooper's iconic tape recorder, which records his messages for the mysterious Diane, to Audrey's waylaid letter to Cooper, *TP* is a tapestry of recorded messages spun from ink and radio waves and woven onto television screens. At other times, as in the example of Audrey's letter, the communication is delayed or misplaced, leading to increased suspense. The audience helplessly watches Cooper walk past the note under his bed as danger draws nearer at the brothel to the north. In the background, episodes of the soap opera parody *Invitation to Love* plays on household television sets, a show within a show, that delves into melodrama hardly more extreme than the goings-on of Twin Peaks, Washington, in the wake of Laura Palmer's untimely demise.

Related to this confluence of information threading within and without the diegesis of the show, *TP* is a show that is notorious for its intertextuality, or engagement with its precursors. That is to say, it engages with other shows, films, and literature. As Lafky (1999) points out, the show assumes that viewers have an awareness of Western cultural production of the last half century, and the show "seizes on the idiosyncrasies and eccentricities of murder mysteries, soap operas, cop shows, musicals, '50s teenage culture, and numerous films, simultaneously paying homage to and ridiculing these genres" (p. 9). *Invitation to Love* lampoons the daytime soap while enhancing the grasp of the same, on the audience's reading of *TP.* The character James Hurley appears to be straight from a 1950s teenage rebellion B-movie, which reaches its hysterical height when he, Donna, and Maddie perform their ballad "Just You."

INLAND EMPIRE: A WOMAN IN TROUBLE

In preparing to discuss *TP:R* in terms of its relationship with *TP,* it is useful to think of David Lynch's feature film, *Inland Empire* as an interlocutor text. The point of departure here is the tagline for the film, which marketers pulled from Lynch's own terse explanation of the enigmatic film, "A woman in trouble." Not only does this phrase give the audience a mantra while trying to piece together the onscreen images of *Inland Empire,* it clearly resonates throughout *TP* and *TP:R.* Nikki Grace and Laura Palmer are both in trouble, and this trouble takes many forms throughout the twists and turns of both narratives.

In the simplest of psychoanalytical terms, *TP* is an Oedipal narrative, concerned with intergenerational incest and the male possession of the woman. This reading maps onto several main relationships among the characters, most notably those between Laura and Leland Palmer, Laura Palmer and Dale Cooper, some of the Audrey Horne plots, and the Shelley/Leo/Laura relationship. These relationships are rooted in sexuality. They are often realized on screen through violence. This has led some feminist scholars to conclude that *TP* betrays David Lynch's latent misogyny, since the filmmaker and his audiences seem to enjoy a show so steeped in images of women in pain (George, 1994; Lafky, 1999). This criticism is grounded on solid observations, namely that (mostly male) critics and audiences thought favorably of the show and that the show is preoccupied with themes of violence against women. However, the notion of enjoyment or pleasure itself is not given enough nuance in such criticisms, leading to an indictment of patriarchal creative culture that is incomplete.

In her essay, Mulvey (1988) sets out to articulate the relationship between the gaze of the viewer of a film, which she posits as generally male or male inflected, and the eroticized image of women onscreen through "a political use of psychoanalysis" (p. 57). While scholars such as Lafky (1999) use terms such as "celebrate" when discussing reception of *TP*, Mulvey uses the term "fascination" when articulating her argument regarding sexualized onscreen images and their inscription in patriarchal modes of cinematic production and consumption. The difference is stark and leads from the argument that the male viewer (or filmmaker) derives a prurient pleasure from the very image of the woman who suffers to the concept that processes of developing a sexual identity. The male gaze itself is locked in a heteronormative system of ego-driven identification and voyeuristic observation, according to these theorists. This normative system engenders an obsession, on the part of this masculine perspective, with narratives that engage with the eroticization of gender-based violence. Mulvey goes on to identify her objective, "it is said that analyzing pleasure, or beauty, destroys it. That is the intention of this article . . . leaving the past behind without rejecting it, transcending outworn or oppressive forms, or daring to break with normal pleasurable expectations" (1988, p. 59). The pleasure is not merely in what is looked at but in looking itself, and in psychoanalytical terms the image of the woman is the embodiment of that which, paradoxically, is pleasant in form and threatening in content for the male gaze.

More than a decade after *TP* and *Fire Walk with Me*, *Inland Empire* represents a reversal of this preoccupation that anticipates and contextualizes the recalibration of both content and form of *TP:R*. Ellis and Tyler (2019) write of "the general move made in the new series away from the Freudian oedipal grid structured around crimes of the obscene father to the pre-Oedipal, distinctly Kleinian world of the mother," including, "the possession of Sarah Palmer" (p. 23). Ellis and Tyler describe the takeover as seemingly "the result of her swallowing an evil insect—in Kleinian terms, the 'bad object' put into the mother that results in her 'splitting' into two figures: the 'good,' loving mother, and the 'bad,' persecuting mother" (p. 23). This move, however, is already at work in *Inland Empire*. Nikki Grace is in trouble, but not simply because of her parallel existence with the Lost Girl or because her affair is in danger of being found out. These are marginal dramatic elements that merely structure the more pressing trouble that Nikki finds herself in, that of her constantly shifting identity and how this identity corresponds with the reality she is inhabiting. Ellis and Theus go on to posit that traditional interpretive readings represent a mere "re-encoding" of the text into a new set of equally unclear terms, but that for these creative works, these frameworks become an effective tool for "its potential to illuminate some of its formal narrative features" (2019, p. 24). *Inland Empire* is then to be read not as a chaotic but plot-driven metonym for the process of sexual identification, but rather through the crises of identity that Mulvey's "sexually mature non-mother" undergoes through the signs of sexual difference as they are manifested in the form of the film (1988, p. 58).

Galow (2019) articulates this affinity between *TP:R* and *Inland Empire* as one that "explores the relationship between trauma and fantasy through a multi-layered approach with more fluid boundaries [compared to earlier films]. The narrative opens up layers of stories within stories within stories that blend and fragment in unexpected ways" (p. 212). Whereas *TP* is focused on binary splitting of identity (Leland/BOB, Black Lodge/White Lodge), *Inland Empire* represents a shift to fragmented narratives, places, and characters that overlap, turn inside out, and contradict one another in ways that prefigure what is to come in *TP:R*. Galow's observation is in line with Ellis and Theus's Kleinian interpretation of *TP:R*. It displaces a causal or linear interpretation of plot onto interpretation of audio/visual elements in terms of their relation to the various crises that arise throughout female sexuation against phallocentrism in general. As the narrative arcs overlap and the film's causal flow is increasingly disrupted, the viewer can and should be sensitive to cinematic cues indicating narrative slippage and its bearing on Nikki's crisis, or "trouble."

POSTMODERN GOTHIC

Aside from plot elements of *Inland Empire* which quickly become marginal as the text fragments, recombines, and its very consistency comes into doubt, the film is also framed technologically. It is, after all, a film about the making of a film from the perspective of the lead actress. Nikki Grace finds herself unable to separate her life from the script of *On High in Blue Tomorrows* at various times throughout *Inland Empire*. This reality is often framed with shots that put Panaflex 35mm cameras on the margins of the mise-en-scene, cuing the audience that what is transpiring is on a set in the context of a film.

This device leads the audience all the way to the climactic scene at the end when Lynch's camera pans out, revealing that Nikki's death on the streets of Hollywood is the climactic scene not just of *Inland Empire* but also of *On High in Blue Tomorrows*. The text of the film is then that of a film about the making of a film, from a lost script, which was derived from a Polish folktale. The text telescopes and consumes itself, with such uncanny moments as when, after delivering a monologue to Devon/Billy on set, Nikki/Sue exclaims with a laugh that what she just said was so dramatic that it might have come right out of the script of the film they are working on. Of course, the monologue is assumed to have come out of the script, but a moment of uncertainty such as this one does more nuanced work in articulating the crisis of identity and reality than a concrete shift in space or time. These spaces and times overlap in disturbing ways and lead to some very satisfying, if disorienting, cinematic twists as in the two moments recalled above.

This discomfort and difference between digital filmmaking and the 35mm production being depicted in the plot of *Inland Empire* is borrowed and transposed into the much broader universe of *TP:R*. Published just before the release of *TP*, Ronell (1989) offers a meditation on Heideggarian ontology in *The Telephone Book: Technology, Schizophrenia, Electric Speech* which is useful to understand the uncanniness inherent to communications technology and revealed through the televisual moments of the above texts. In her prolonged meditation on Heidegger and how his existential thinking can be applied to late twentieth-century technology (or on how the logic of such technologies can explain Heidegger's life and work), Ronell implicates telecommunication in the rise of fascism, among other things, as a medium that "offers a certain untried access code to terrorism that, in the first place, is technologically constellated" (p. 8). This technological gateway to terrorism creates a false sense of immediacy, and therefore unity—a founding dogma of totalitarianism. Further on, she argues in a full Heideggerian mode that information technology as tool disappears into its function when transmitting such information correctly, and in the event of a break or a failure "the transmission puts itself in-the-world" (p. 44). As the site of a problem, formerly transparent technologies become visible in their resistance against their purported uses.

Regarding the telephone, Ronell asserts, "the question of *Unheimlichkeit* [uncanniness or weirdness] awaits restlessly—does the telephone, despite mere appearances, not fundamentally belong to the structure of not-being-at-home, of a being expropriated from a *chez-soi*?" (p. 51). This brings us back to *TP:R*. While there were certainly sinister technological signs in *TP*—Cooper's tape recorder, the phone at the sheriff's department, the televisions playing *Invitation to Love*—*TP:R* employs these technologies as the most dominant sites of the aforementioned Gothic internal texts. Ronell reminds that from the outset there must be at least two phones, and where the other line connects is important (p. 3). This props up multiple narrative threads throughout *TP:R*, as Diane's sinister doppelganger exchanges mysterious text messages with an unknown phone number, Lucy is horrified by cellular technology which she cannot understand, and Gordon Cole spends time on the phone with numerous agencies and characters trying to wrangle the loose ends of his multiple cases. These mysterious calls, texts, and their off-screen origins and destinations function just like a found letter, a hidden diary, or an ancient folktale. They engender a feeling of the uncanny and simultaneously provide information to motivate the plot of the show while often creating accompanying mysteries.

Furthermore, as the show progresses these technologies become signs themselves that link their cinematic representation with their role as narrative tool in intradiegetic communications as well as foreboding link to the disembodied other. In episode 17 of *TP:R*, the opening credits end and the first thing onscreen is the face of Gordon Cole, played by none other than David Lynch. He is wearing his trademark hearing aid and is surrounded by telephones. These are not cellular phones, although we know that Cole has at least one of those as well. He has three land-line connected phones with him on his desk and a fourth is in the extreme foreground. He explains to Albert and Tammy, ensconced in communications technology, how the top-secret Blue Rose Task Force figures into their investigations. It is a moment of confession for Cole, who finally brings into the diegesis what the viewer has known or suspected all along—that the supernatural and the technological are two sides of the same coin in the world of *TP:R*.

A PLACE BOTH WONDERFUL AND STRANGE

Not only do these texts serve the narrative in the above roles, or even as signs of the uncanniness of technology as such; various audio and visual technologies take on mythic significance in the diegeses of both *TP:R* and *Inland Empire*. The latter puts the viewer in a mise-en-abyme of a film about a film. There is already an overlap of Laura Dern playing Nikki Grace playing Susan Blue. This relationship is mediated by a screen that shows what Lynch captured on his DV camcorder. Recordings are images of a crew filming a movie on 35mm cameras. Then, the viewer is told that the script for the film *On High in Blue Tomorrows* is actually the script of a film called *4-7* which was never finished because the lead actors were murdered during filming. Finally, this script is based on a Polish folktale, which Grace Zibriskie's character foreshadows from the beginning when she drops in on her new neighbor, Nikki Grace.

Before this arrangement of texts, however, the film begins with a scene shot in black and white and spoken in Polish, seemingly between a prostitute and a john, their faces blacked out. The scene ends with another woman, known only in the credits as the Lost Girl, crying and watching a television. On television is an episode of *Rabbits*, a series of short films that Lynch made in 2002 and which he has integrated into the feature film *Inland Empire*. The show depicts a room shot from a very high angle wherein a trio of anthropomorphic rabbits enact an absurd "sitcom," punctuated by random bursts of canned laughter. At a certain point, one of the rabbits leaves the room through a door and enters the diegesis of another narrative with what appear to be two mafiosi in negotiation. Here, the television is a gateway between different realities or levels of reality (Galow, 2019). The most bizarre element of this arrangement is that *Rabbits* is a show which we can watch in our reality, implying that the mysterious character of the Lost Girl inhabits a fictional space that is in some way closer to our own than that of the other characters. From the perspective of one character or another, all of these narrative worlds are texts being read by someone else and transmitted through a notion of time and space through information technology, even if at some degrees of removal.

These narrative slippages as cued by the communications apparatuses that mediate them are an example of how these technologies signify "returning in general, disappearance/ reappearance—what was earlier cited as relation to absence—and transferring oneself into an object or placing a call to the not-there, and identifying with it" (Ronell, 1989, p. 85). In *TP:R*, one can begin with "the television in the haunted home of Sarah Palmer . . . [which] plays the same black and white loop of an ancient boxing match again and again" (Fallis & King, 2019, p. 55). This is a text that signals/is a sign of that haunting itself, indicates Sarah Palmer's trauma, and foreshadows her fate. This culminates in the scene in which Sarah Palmer hysterically smashes her daughter's iconic photograph as the image speeds up, slows down, and skips in episode 18. Fallis and King also refer to the digital cameras that surround the mysterious glass box in the first episode, poised to catch footage of whatever dark thing might appear within its transparent walls. Here, the link between camera and the reality of the Black Lodge/Red Room is plain, the camera is the medium for the conveyance of material between realities.

These technologies are also linked by electricity, a common trope in *TP:R*. The series begins with a scene in the dwelling of the Fireman, a supernatural being who gives Cooper several pieces of advice and shows him the sound of electricity which plays through the (not-electrical) phonograph. At this point, the Fireman's dwelling is completely mysterious in terms of where it is and what the nature of its reality is. The Fireman himself speaks in the trademark backward-forward manner of denizens of the Red Room, but Cooper speaks normally. Also, the Fireman refers to him as "Agent" Cooper, foregrounding his occupation as FBI agent and narrative role as hero and problem-solver, which reduces him to his own instrumentality. Other supernatural beings repeatedly call out (in reverse) "e-lec-trici-ty!" An electrical shock finally frees Cooper from his stupor, and the series ends with Cooper and Diane driving alongside humming high-tension wires. Even the shape of these high-tension wires recalls the shape of the insignia on the jade ring found at the scene of Laura's murder. Power lines are like veritable highways between the supernatural realm and various locations in the United States of *TP:R*. The moment that unifies the technological uncanny, with the origination of technology as a gateway between worlds, is the bizarre sequence depicting the first ever nuclear explosion in White Sands, New Mexico, in 1945. This explosion, evoking both the scientific and the supernatural, serves as an origin story for the entire *TP* universe, ironically an event of unprecedented destruction.

"WE LIVE INSIDE A DREAM"

There is now a narrative that partially explains the supernatural existence of alternate worlds or realities in quite a literal way. This representation of the reality of *TP* in general maps onto the interpretation that *TP:R* and takes place along multiple timelines or simultaneously existing possible worlds. These worlds could also be interpreted as multiple layers of dream reality. This is especially salient after Gordon Cole's dream of Monica Bellucci, who tells him that "we live inside a dream," but, "who is the dreamer?" This assertion is spoken again, just after Mr. C and BOB are dispatched in episode 17, by the superimposed spectral face of Cooper that hangs over the action. Certainly, this clue is an invitation to interpret the nature of fiction itself in its relation to television.

This dream or dreams within dreams, as it pertains to *TP:R*, has a peculiar ontological consequence. A fan theory published as *TP:R* was mid-run takes on the enigmatic Audrey storyline. A fan favorite from the original series, *TP* season two ends with Audrey, Pete Martell, and Andrew Packard in a bank vault when a bomb goes off. It is a cliffhanger. When *TP:R* began airing, Sherilynn Fenn (Audrey Horne) was among the names on the leaked list of cast members, so she must have survived. *TP:R* finds Audrey arguing with her husband/accountant Charlie, a new character about whom the audience knows nothing. She is desperately trying to find "Billy," still another mysterious character. Just after one such scene, a young boy runs through the RR Diner shouting, "where's Billy?" As he exits the diner, there is a sudden cut to the same shot of the dining room, but all the people are different.

Eventually, Charlie gives in and takes Audrey to the Bang Bang Bar to look for Billy. When she arrives, the emcee announces that the next song is "Audrey's Dance." As the unforgettable Angelo Badalamenti jazz track begins, Audrey loses herself in dancing, closes her eyes, and when she opens them, she is shocked to find herself in a white room wearing white hospital garb looking into a mirror (Theone3's blog 8/31/2017).

The key for the author of this blog post is where Monica Bellucci, "Audrey's Dance," and even the musical acts that play at the *Bang Bang Bar* exist—in real life. Monica Bellucci is in Gordon Cole's dream, but she is the only actress, indeed the only real person (besides historical figures) who is mentioned on the show. It is also telling that the emcee announces "Audrey's Dance," which is a piece of music on the *TP* soundtrack, an item that could never exist in the *TP* universe. This means that the scenes in the Bang Bang Bar that contain live music by such in-our-reality bands as the Chromatics and Nine Inch Nails are happening in or overlapping with *real* reality. This leads back to "Billy," who Theone3's blog assumes is none other than Billy Zane, the actor who played John Justice Wheeler in season two of *TP*. Audrey and John Justice Wheeler become lovers before he is called away on business, and she is involved in the bank explosion. When Audrey finds herself in a white room, she has just awoken in *TP* reality where she has suffered mental health problems, as Mark Frosts supplemental texts tell us, since her near-death in the bank explosion and giving birth to a son who may have been fathered by the evil Mr. C. Until she has awakened, her crisis involves living on the threshold of a dream. She is dreaming herself into our world and looking for her lost lover whose existence she cannot fully comprehend. Is he Billy or is he the long-lost John Justice Wheeler? The RR Diner changes suddenly in the aforementioned scene because it has just snapped between the RR Diner in *TP:R* and the real diner that fans of the show visit on pilgrimages to the Pacific Northwest. The day's actual customers are replaced with extras on a television set (Theone3's blog 8/31/2017).

CONCLUDING WITH COMPLEX TELEVISION: A WOMAN IN WHAT KIND OF TROUBLE?

The ways in which *TP*, especially in its second season, progressed its many plots and subplots strongly influenced the hallmark conventions of numerous primetime and streaming series. The creators of *TP* embarked on more than two decades of intervening works before writing and producing *TP:R*, including Mark Frost's supplemental *TP* novels and the evolution of David Lynch's perspective on storytelling within art house cinema. Lynch's latest feature, *Inland Empire*, is identified with this art house. It treats similar themes using conventions much like those found in *TP:R*. *TP:R* is also an auteur series with a finite beginning and ending, eschewing the open-ended seriality of most television formats even in this golden age of prestige television. Is it still appropriate, then, to think of *TP:R* as television, or more importantly, to think of other contemporaneous television shows in terms of *TP:R?* This comparison raises important and novel questions about seriality in general, signaling perhaps not entering a period of more cohesive episodic television, but open-ended cinema parsed into hour-long installments. Deciding on a dividing line between television and cinema, then, is no longer the important question; rather, this uncertain reality, and even less certain way of reading these media, mirrors the nature of the "trouble" in which Nikki and Laura find themselves.

REFERENCES

Fallis, J. & King, T. K. (2019). Lucy finally understands how cellphones work: Ambiguous digital technologies in Twin Peaks: The Return and its fan communities. In A. Sanna (Ed.), *Critical essays on Twin Peaks: The Return* (pp. 53–68). Palgrave Macmillan.

Galow, T. W. (2019). From Lost Highway to Twin Peaks: Representations of trauma and transformation in David Lynch's late works. In A. Sanna (Ed.), *Critical essays on Twin Peaks: The return* (pp. 211–218). Palgrave Macmillan.

George, D. H. (1994). Lynching women: A feminist reading of Twin Peaks. In D. Lavery (Ed.), *Full of secrets: Critical approaches to Twin Peaks* (pp. 109–119). Wayne State.

Lafky, S. (1999/2000). Gender, power, and culture in the televisual world of Twin Peaks: A feminist critique. *Journal of Film and Video, 51*(3/4), 5–19.

Lewdon, L. (1993). Twin Peaks and television gothic. *Literature/Film Quarterly, 21*(4), 260–270.

MacLachlan, K. (1990). *Diane: The Twin Peaks tapes of Agent Cooper.* Simon and Schuster.

Ellis, M. and Theus, T. (2019). Is it happening again? Twin Peaks and "The Return" of history. In A. Sanna (Ed.), *Critical essays on Twin Peaks* (pp. 23–36). Palgrave Macmillan.

Mulvey, L. (1988). Visual pleasure and narrative cinema. In C. Penley (Ed.), *Feminism and Film Theory* (pp. 57–69). Routledge, Chapman and Hall.

Ronell, A. (1989). *The telephone book: Technology, schizophrenia, electric speech.* University of Nebraska Press.

Theone3's Blog. (2017). Twin Peaks: Audrey, Billy, and living inside a dream. https://ozba.wordpress.com/2017/08/31/twin-peaks-audrey-billy-and-living-inside-a-dream/.

Chapter 4

Arya and Sansa Stark of HBO's *The Game of Thrones*

Abuse, Agency, Trauma Survival, and Redefined Destinies

Diana I. Ríos, Mary Helen Millham,
Karin A. Haberlin, and
Graciela Quiñones-Rodriguez

The Home Box Office (HBO) blockbuster television series *The Game of Thrones* (2011–2019) is celebrated and vilified for stylistic presentation and selections of dramatic spectacle. This show features, what have become, two popular culture icons Arya and Sansa Stark, sisters with disparate values and behaviors. These characters have different perceptions of agency and how to deploy it; are traumatized and abused by power brokers; and, in surviving and thriving, must redefine their respective destinies. This chapter will examine the problematic nature of these important female characters as heroines, role models, and for some viewers—vicarious friends. Our analytical framework draws from established literature on tough girls and action women in popular culture (Deuber-Mankowsky, 2005; Frankel, 2014; Inness, 1999, 2006; McCaughey & King, 2001; Neroni, 2005; Schubart, 2007). Research on women's representation in television, film and other media, discusses how strong girls and women tend to be developed with intrinsic and commonplace limitations and restrictions that must be overcome. To amplify our framework, and elaborate our character analysis of imperfect heroines, we draw upon select clinical literature on abuse, trauma, agency, and survival (Ben-Ari et al., 2003; Dufour et al., 2000; Staller & Nelson-Gardell, 2005). This approach is uncommon in analysis of females in media.

The #MeToo and #TimesUp movements have assisted with placing abuse issues higher on the social agenda in recent years (Backus & De Pinto,

2020). This energy inspires scholars to reexamine storylines of "survivor" female characters and to question and challenge representations consumed by millions around the world. Key female characters have the potential to inspire and inform audiences about systemic social problems such as violence against women. Taking this a step further beyond raising general awareness, we will argue that a close reading of Sansa and Arya's lives could assist viewers in critical, yet compassionate perspective-taking about survivors of violence in popular culture, as well as in real life.

GAME OF THRONES OVERVIEW AND VIEWING TRENDS

Showrunners and executive producers David Benioff and D. B. Weiss adapted George R. R. Martin's incomplete medieval fantasy book series to the drama of several royal families competing for hegemony in the seven kingdoms of Westeros. The "game" refers to the constant machinations amongst noble and not-so-noble characters to obtain the Iron Throne, the seat of power.

Debuting on the premium pay cable channel HBO in April 2011, the show ran for eight seasons with a total of 73 episodes and saw its ratings rise even as viewers and critics complained of gratuitous and sensationalized violence, especially against female characters. The series finale aired on May 19, 2019, and the US viewership of 19.3 million for the final episode set records for both the show and for single episode viewership for HBO (Otterson, 2019; Porter, 2019). The average viewership for each season grew from 2.32 million viewers in the United States for season one in 2011 (TV by the Numbers, 2011 as cited by Clarissa, 2011) to 19.3 million viewers for season eight in 2019 (Mitovich, 2019).

GENDER REPRESENTATION: HEROINES, TOUGH GIRLS, VIOLENT WOMEN

There has been a noticeable upswing of females in dramatic leading roles over the years. Many types of media present characters who break gender roles, display emotional grit and uncharacteristic physical agency while facing serious barriers. Feminist media scholars discuss several facets of tough females who defy traditional gender roles. A requisite commonality among these, and similar heroines, is their tapping into personal power reserves and demonstrating great skill to protect and avenge. Inness (1999) describes adult and very young femme fatales who kill to survive. Sarah Connor, the svelte woman lead in the *Terminator* media franchise (1984–2019) initially appears unassuming but quickly becomes "pretty tough," and a "post apocalyptic tough girl" (p. 74) in order to save humans from annihilation. Viewers note her latest armed companion is the teen/adult woman Dani Ramos, who is thrust into the defense killing life soon after colliding with senior citizen, super kick-ass, Sarah. In *The Professional* (1984), Mathilda is a pre-adolescent orphan, with moments of sexualization, who yearns to kill and avenge her family. Similarly, the nine-year-old Cataleya of *Colombiana* (2011) leaps from innocent school girl to cunning, avenging young woman. In later renditions of Lisbeth Salander of the *Millennium* media franchise, fans see a more fighting-ready and mentally acute character who avenges abused women.

Inness (2004) and others suggest that sexualizing serves to undermine female power as this satisfies a masculinized gaze when it falls into gratuitous territory. A blogger coined the term "sexposition" to describe this phenomenon (McNutt, 2011); applied to GOT's portrayals of women, this refers to an exposition of excessive sex and unnecessary scenes. The camera's voyeurism does not strengthen female character roles or advance the narrative. An example of this working against narratives of strategy and endurance can be seen in the *Nikita* media franchise, which is overwhelmingly defined by Nikita's sexualized body.

SISTERS AND AGENCY: DIFFERENT PATHS

The Stark sisters display different levels of agency through the multiyear narrative, which are contingent on external forces, internal instincts, and reactions. Over time, they are forced to learn the rules of the game; their changing roles within the larger game; and the kaleidoscope of changing alliances. It might seem natural for the Stark sisters to band together as a sisterhood bloc to fend off transgressors; however, they have distinct perspectives about what power is and where their aspirations fit in the Westeros patriarchal power structure.

Sansa the High-Born

Sansa, as a girl with high-born blood, believes that she should at least maintain her social position, if not improve it. In her eyes, she must marry into a prominent family or royal house to achieve future agency for her well-sired descendants. This line of thinking is standard in Westeros, where men constitute the nucleus of power and enforce societal rules. Sansa is less a person than a well-bred, virginal commodity to be appraised, bargained for, and purchased. However, she does not see herself as a victim in a game of sociopolitical hierarchies, but as an admired beauty with princess-quality manners. At the outset of the series, she accepts her agency as contingent to her father's political influence, wealth, and the strategic battle location of her family's castle.

It may seem apparent early in the series for viewers to consider Sansa as someone easily influenced by those with power despite their dangerous personality flaws. For example, on a sunny day strolling with her potential future husband, Prince Joffrey, she witnesses him bullying and tormenting a humble baker's boy. When Arya, who is also present at the scene, tries to help the boy, Joffrey swings his sword several times in attempts to hurt Arya (season one). Instead of reacting to threats to her sister Arya's safety, Sansa's reactions are to reprimand her sister, dismiss the incidents, and continue her docile and pliant interactions with the prince. In her early life, Sansa adheres to her ideals of femininity and young womanhood, and does this to the detriment of her family members. At one point, her father Eddard Stark opposes matching her with the turbulent Prince Joffrey, and she wishes to persuade him otherwise. Her words tumble out: "I can't go. I'm supposed to marry Prince Joffrey. I love him and I'm meant to be his Queen and have his babies" (season one, episode six). She knows he is not "gentle and strong" but desperately attempts to shape a narrative for herself and her future life; she is an adolescent dreaming of queenhood and royal progeny.

When Sansa is informed by the royal council in season one that her father killed King Baratheon and is a traitor, she tearfully defends her father while simultaneously attempting to leverage her potential connection with the evil-minded Lannisters. It appears that Sansa sees herself only possessing the agency that others allow her to have; she still wishes to marry into a royal house that has labeled her own father a traitor and murderer. Sansa is swiftly betrayed; her father is soon executed in a degrading public display; and Joffrey brutally forces her to view her father's execution and his head displayed on a stick (season one).

Sansa's privileged upbringing would not have easily anticipated her life worsening; however, she descends into a period of tragic victimhood, enduring repeated emotional and physical abuses. Her high-bred class position does not protect her from partner violence, and her ideals of becoming a royal betrothed, princess, and royal wife are transformed into nightmares. Under Joffrey's command, she is badly beaten, humiliated, and traumatized in public (season two). As kind Tyrion, Joffrey's uncle, escorts her away from the court where she was battered, she quietly insists, "I'm loyal to King Joffrey, my one true love." Despite her knowledge of Joffrey's mental instabilities and firsthand experience of his violence, she continues to maintain she will marry this abuser.

Discussion regarding why Sansa's agency is stifled should include consideration of her age, education, skills, and options. As a girl, Sansa is dependent on her parents and authority figures, and has had little need to develop self-efficacy. As an adolescent virgin and budding woman, she accepts her role as a daughter to be married off. Her training and education are limited to that which is suitable for females to serve husbands, and she follows cultural rules of female comportment, learning to sew and embroider—acceptable, womanly skills that are nonthreatening to males. Additionally, Sansa dresses and arranges her hair according to traditional norms, and often uses a deferential speaking style. Her reading is largely limited to fairy tales and royal romances, which serve to create a glorified mirage of the world beyond the family estate of Winterfell; a world inevitably including a royal happy ending. Some viewers may wonder whether she truly favors the norms or if she is swept into the powerful currents of a prescribed destiny or fate. By her action or inaction at key moments, Sansa stays inside a system that beats her down, and does not exit this system early on when she has chances to leave.

Social media fans appear to be of two general minds about Sansa. Some viewers dislike her intensely, as in the following statement: "She's a smug, annoying, terrible character, who falls ass backwards into survival—maybe that's why people don't like her" (morgadc1887, 2018). In contrast, other viewers such as "khaleesikirk" admire her:

> I think she makes the most realistic decisions in the show (and the book). While other characters are pushed forward by honor, or some far off goal, or because they are "different," Sansa just wants to survive. When she finds out what Joffrey is like, she is scared, but knows that in order to keep her head, she has to please him, or at least not displease him. . . . She becomes stronger as the show progresses because she learns. She figures out who she needs to be to survive (khaleesikirk, 2020).

From a perspective looking at survivors of domestic violence, women who stay in violent relationships picture no other options or support systems waiting for them beyond their immediate circumstances, explains a senior psychotherapist and coauthor of this chapter. Research on battered women who stay shares this view (Ben-Ari et al., 2003). As a noblewoman, Sansa was trained to behave within the phallocentric marriage system. This female was socialized, as many females in the real world are, to be nice despite facing aggressive male behavior (Murnen et al., 2002). This system barters, exchanges and sells her, deceiving and victimizing her several times over. With her options running out, she reluctantly accepts to marry into the family that sacked her home of Winterfell and killed her brother. Once inside the encampment, she is a prisoner. She appears to be interminably lodged inside a misogynist system where women are pawns. She and many women in Westeros cannot develop full personal agency within their restricted boundaries. In order to fully rein in and dominate his new wife Sansa, Ramsay Bolton repeatedly and sadistically beats, rapes, and tortures her. Ramsay gains gleeful satisfaction and titillation from hurting Sansa. Fans and critics alike were divided about the need for the gratuitous sexual violence Sansa was made to suffer during her marriage to Ramsay. It is under these extreme circumstances that Sansa finally escapes, marking a key turn in her world views and self-agency. After the defeat of the undead at Winterfell, Sansa confides to Sandor Clegane that the difficulties she endured made her wiser and ready to act.

However, many viewers feel emotionally manipulated by what they perceive to be the showrunners' ham-handed attempt at female character development. A viewer posting on Reddit comments:

> Sansa has internalised the psychological abuse she's suffered to the extent that she tells herself she is stupid—because she's repeatedly been told so by her abusers. And then fandom . . . takes this at face value to mean that she really is stupid (themurphysue, 2017).

The commenter takes this observation further by critiquing what "they" the showrunners thought they had to do in order to develop the character and draw viewers:

> So Sansa got "tough and got sharp and shrewd" with the not-so-subtle implication here being that it was the rape+revenge, the "painful experience" . . . that made her strong, and hardened, and by extension worthy of our attention as a leader. All the shoulder pads in the world can't make up for the fact that this is what they thought had to be done to make her "interesting" (themurphysue, 2017).

True fans of Sansa see through these machinations, tagging posts with "#sansa stark defense squad." One fan posted statements describing Sansa's change from demure to bold:

> Sansa Stark S1: A gentle, trusting and naive little girl with dreams of marrying her prince charming. Sansa Stark S7: Lady of Winterfell, current regent of the North, a strong intelligent young woman who has to overcome and deal with her PTSD, and is currently trying to work out how to feed and shelter refugees from the upcoming war, while trying to ensure her people are safe. [N]one of that "Sansa Stark S1-S7—annoying girl but slightly older" bullshit (sxpiosexualx, 2018).

Toward the end of the series, when Arya bitterly confronts Sansa about her role in their father's execution at Joffrey's hands. Sansa retorts, "You should be on your knees thanking me. We're standing in Winterfell again because of me. ... You didn't win it back. ... While you were training, I suffered things you can never imagine" (season seven, episode six). Unlike her sister Arya, Sansa never imagines herself living on the fringes of society. She sees herself as an emotionally tough champion of the Stark family, withstanding the system in order to protect the family legacy.

Arya the Future Sword Master

Arya's self perception and ideas for her future contrast with the rules and demands of Westeros society. Unlike her sister, who yearns to be a lady of a prestigious house through the vehicle of marriage, Arya is an anticonformist (Frankel, 2014) and dreams of being a knight and sword master. She chooses a masculine path, desiring to fight with a "pointy" utensil comparatively larger than her sister's sewing needle. When she demonstrates keen interest in weaponry, her father assigns her an expert dueling instructor from the city of Braavos. She exhibits self-agency early on when she takes it upon herself to rescue a boy being harassed by cowardly Prince Joffrey, while her sister looks on. Furthermore, she knocks Joffrey to the ground, takes his sword and tosses it in the river. This symbolic castration of the prince leads to punishments. The punishment-as-training relegates Arya to a subordinated gender role and reinforces male domination. The lesson she is to learn is that she is not to be physically strong and athletically superior to males and should not dispossess males or their phallus-as-sword.

It is not surprising that Arya has a conversation with her father where she rejects marriage and domesticity. She tells him clearly, "that's not me." It is through Arya's defiance of systemic expectations that she builds her agency. Choosing a traditionally masculine path of armed defense allows her to express a gender identity that is outside a predefined femininity. As a "butch-girl" or "tomboy," she resists being like her sister, who focuses on domestic arts, and thereby resists being defined by Westeros society. As a novice swordsman, not a swordswoman, she sees a larger world in which to live and a larger terrain of future possibilities. As she progresses in her life and improves attack skills, she dons masculine clothing cut to better hold and manage weapons. She can pull a sword swiftly in a moment of defense or easily unsheath a knife while prowling the perimeter of an enemy camp.

Arya's self-agency allows her to escape the wrath of Joffrey and the dangers of Casterly Rock after her father's execution. While escaping, she takes the advice to cut her hair short and masculinize her name in order to transform into a boy. By cross-dressing using authentic boy's clothing, she will save her life; the royals are not hunting for a boy named Ary. At this crisis, she has an opportunity to submerge girlness, a normative quality she did not like, and form a new male-like identity. As a female, the Westeros system sees her as weak and fragile. As a male, she gains new levels of agency and freedom of movement. She travels more safely; sits with mercenaries in pubs; rides in the open with boys and men; and gains food and shelter. Women cross-dressing for safety and freedom is not an uncommon strategy, as this affords security, higher gender status, and avoids poverty and harassment in the outside world. Aspects of this type of cover, or performativity, have been depicted in popular culture such as in *Queen Christina* (1933), *The Lieutenant Nun* (1944), *Albert Nobbs* (2012), *Enola Holmes* (2020), and *Mulan* (2020).

Arya exhibits self-agency and survival intuition in choosing to live outside the margins of the traditional power structure. Her parents are killed as a result of political machinations and her sister is caught in a system of deception and brutality. By living in the margins and actively recreating her identity, she is not bartered or sold off to other high-born families. Her assumption of a masculinized gender identity removes her from focus as a pretty accessory and mother of heirs. Arya's agency and comfort level with nontraditional paths places her out of reach of royals that want her dead; as a commoner lad, Ary is no threat to royal or landowner systems.

Significant events in Arya's life include distant travel, entering a secret society, and expanding agency. Participation in the cult of the god of death and in its subsequent training elevates her physical abilities and senses for fighting and anticipating modes of attack. As a young assassin (Schubart, 2007), a "faceless man," she identifies with a male power, or god, and becomes highly skilled and deadly. Both sisters are beaten in this series; but in contrast to her sister, Arya is never raped. To a mercenary who thought to violate her, she talks back in a steady voice, "You said you would put a stick in my c--- and kill me." He is soon dead by her hands. In the last series episodes, wanting to know "what it feels like," she exhibits sexual agency by selecting the specific young man she wants to have sex with.

At first blush, Arya is a kick-ass, Amazon girl, a young woman who can demonstrate self-agency and independent decision-making for female viewers. The problematic nature of Arya's life is that she continually denigrates females ("girls are stupid"), and turns into a brutal assassin. As a faceless "man," she is a murderer for hire and is sent on jobs to poison men and women. During her travel quests alone or with others, she repeats a list of names every night, including royals, rapists, and abusers she condemns to death. The apex of her vengeance-kill, presented in the narrative as justified, is her visit to Lord Walder Frey's family. She deftly enters a well-guarded home, and disguises herself as a lowly kitchen maid. She serves a meat pie to the cranky, hungry Walder and he proceeds to voraciously tuck into it. Arya slowly reveals her deed, as the man discovers pieces of his sons are cooked into the pie. While he howls in disgust and fury, she slits his throat. Blood gushes and viewers see her with blood splattered on her smiling face as she holds her weapon and observes her victim. The brutality of this revenge-kill erases any remaining cute, butch-girl attributes. Arya's tough girl, "fille fatale" world has no beauty or light. Her living and training in the shadows has shaped her as an instrument of dark arts, prowling among games of domination and oppression.

Abuse and Trauma Survival: Coping with Emotional and Physical Harm

Given the tremendous amount of violence in GOT, viewers may ask how Sansa and Arya could cope. The experiences of these sisters, and much of the content of the series, normalizes violence against women and suggests that women must suffer in order to achieve their goals. The longer narrative and smaller story arcs reinforce that the system of patriarchy of Westeros is not easily challenged; challenging it leads to death or marginalization. The lessons to be learned in Westeros are to gain agency, hold power, use power to oppress and dominate others. Furthermore, to avenge a wrong, one must kill.

Sansa and Arya do not have traditional happy endings, but perhaps acceptable ones given their escapes from death. Survivors of abuse and trauma suffer emotionally and physically for the remainder of their lives. They hold the experiences "in their hearts" (Staller & Nelson-Gardell, 2005) as a heavy burden, and survivors work to live productive lives and to resist envelopment by dark clouds of violent memories. Girls and women tend to keep their secrets from others because they are too easily judged and condemned within a real-world social system that blames women for being weak, stupid, and willing victims.

Scars "follow" women when they are asked to explain themselves. The process of "telling" is different or impossible for survivors who cannot easily trust, or know who will spread gossip and turn community opinions against them (Staller & Nelson-Gardell, 2005). Disclosing to others about abuse is one way for a person to receive social support, because this can alleviate feelings of isolation, loneliness, and self-doubt regarding how the incident(s) came about (Staller & Nelson-Gardell, 2005) and could help a victim's resilience when people are supportive (Dufour et al., 2000). Support outside oneself also makes the incidents "real," even when there are no physical scars, and family members pretend the violence never happened (Staller & Nelson-Gardell, 2005). Sansa tells Littlefinger portions of what she suffered as a consequence of his exchanging her for soldiers. Arya tells no one, not even her chosen lover who asks her about scars on her back.

The real-world contemporary movements of #MeToo and #TimesUp encouraged women to tell of their violations, and ignited a process where high-level celebrities and people in the public eye revealed emotional and sexual abuse at work and other parts of their lives. The intent of those revelations was to offer recognition and support to others who had suffered similarly, and to put a stop to serial abusers. Many of these revelations came from women in the media industry who had suffered at the hands of powerful male decision-makers. The movements pulled the curtain back from the power monopoly of patriarchy in the industry.

Statements from some actors, who were famous in television series known for violence were controversial. The GOT actor Sophie Turner explains that her character Sansa "always had that strength" and resilience (Ordoña, 2019) and that the experiences Sansa had made her the strong woman she became by the end of the series (Ordoña, 2019). A counterpoint to this view is that not all people survive torture and sexual violence. Those that do survive may decide to tell the painful tale. Evan Rachel Wood of HBO's *Westworld* testified before US Congress about being a rape survivor, explained the emotional tolls of rape and how she was able to direct the rage of being violated into emotionally demanding scenes and episodes (Ryzik, 2018). Additionally, Wood used her interview platform to explain how "gaslighting" is used by perpetrators against their victims in order to create denial of the incidents and the criminal acts (Ryzik, 2018). Her experiences were voiced to help other survivors and prevent sexual assault victimization. It is unclear if the #MeToo and #TimesUp movements, which were going strong while GOT was running—along with public criticism—pressured HBO's producers and writers to reduce the amount of gratuitous sex, girl-on-girl sexual action, and violence against women in GOT. However, after a production hiatus, the show proceeded to showcase females in power during the last episodes of the series.

During closing episodes of the series, Sansa has transformed into a composed, tough young woman who avenges her family. Sansa is able to turn the tables on Ramsay Bolton by having him tied-up in a cell and consumed by starving hunting dogs. Sansa slowly walks away, grinning in quiet satisfaction; she learned savage lessons and agency through her long, painful, and violent journey. When she becomes Queen of the North, she carefully traps Littlefinger at a meeting of family leaders. With little emotion, she sentences him to death and watches Arya slit his throat. This and other episodes that completed the GOT run, show a more mature Sansa who knows how to play the man's game in Westeros. She learned from a system that emotionally and physically abused her. It may appear that Sansa emerges victorious at the end of her story because she gains a high position, saves Winterfell, and conducts revenge-kills on evil men. However, it is important to remember that Sansa's emergence as a queen comes at a high price of emotional and physical damage. She did not ascend the steps to her dream life by gracefully working inside a system. By killing two male leaders, she used the same violent tools of their toolbox, and this is displayed to viewers as the way a survivor navigates societal problems. Thus, in the end, it turns out that Sansa and Arya are not so different after all; the sisters deploy similar strategies to achieve their goals.

CONCLUSION

This chapter examined the lives of Sansa and Arya from House Stark in the global hit television series GOT. While much has been written about action females, tough women, kick-ass girls, and contemporary heroines, this chapter sought to add to the literature by providing a closer look at agency, emotional and physical abuse and trauma experienced by two lead female characters. Female agency deserves attention, because too often stories undermine and subvert female abilities. Agency is compromised for the Stark sisters, who must navigate through systems and structures of power. They are never superheroines and survive by surpassing great barriers. Emotional and physical abuses suffered by females in television fiction need our attention, because these stories continually inform viewers that girls and women should follow male-defined rules in male-defined systems of power. These are risky and dangerous messages to present to audiences, especially to female viewers. Such ideologies serve to support and not contradict current societal problems.

Some may say the portrayals and stories of the two lead women could be interpreted simply as examples of females charging through adversity, skirting death, and achieving hard-won goals. Perhaps Sansa and Arya just worked hard and "leaned-in" toward favorable destinies (Sandberg, 2013). However, that is a partial reading of the GOT narrative. Much of the GOT story, as seen through the lives of Sansa and Arya, is dark, twisty, and nasty with "aurum crusta" or golden veneer. As the real world must wrestle with problems of gender inequities, gender oppression, trafficking of girls, and violence against females, giving attention to certain issues may promote a more media literate viewer regarding female leads in popular culture. We ask viewers not to dismiss the extreme maltreatment of these characters but to recognize how ideas are conveyed through vividly beautiful and elaborate fiction. In the world of Westeros, the violent system of oppression becomes normalized across all seasons. Abuse, trauma, and near-death survival should not be requisite tickets to female character success. The blockbuster GOT will continue to make its mark as a uniquely dramatic television series beyond its full run. It behooves media researchers and intellectually curious scholars to continue to piece out the intricacies of this series.

REFERENCES

Backus, F., & DePinto, J. (2020, January 7). #MeToo and Time's Up: Most think the movements are making progress-CBS News poll. *CBS News.* https://www.cbsnews.com/news/metoo-and-times-up-most-think-the-movements-are-making-progress-cbs-news-poll/.

Ben-Ari, A., Winstok, Z., & Eisikovits, Z. (2003). Choice within entrapment and entrapment within choice: The challenge facing battered women who stay. *Families in Society: The Journal of Contemporary Social Services, 84*(4), 539–546. https://doi.org/10.1606/1044-3894.132.

Clarissa. (2011). Game of thrones: How did season 1 do for ratings overall? *TV Over Mind.* https://www.tvovermind.com/game-thrones-season-1-ratings/.

Deuber-Mankowsky, A. (2005). *Lara Croft: Cyber heroine.* University of Minnesota Press.

Dufour, M. H., Nadeau, L., & Bertrand, K. (2000). Les facteurs de résilience chez les victimes d'abus sexuel: État de la question. *Child Abuse & Neglect, 24*(6), 781–797. https://doi.org/10.1016/s0145-2134(00)00141-1.

Frankel, V. E. (2014). *Women in Game of thrones: Power, conformity and resistance.* McFarland.

Funnell, L. (2010). Assimilating Hong Kong style for the Hollywood action woman. *Quarterly Review of Film and Video, 28*(1), 66–79. https://doi.org/10.1080/10509200802530148.

Inness, S. A. (1999). *Tough girls: Women warriors and wonder women in popular culture.* University of Pennsylvania Press.

Inness, S. A. (2006). *Action chicks: New images of tough women in popular culture.* Macmillan.

khaleesikirk. (2020). I want to talk about Game of thrones for a moment...Queen of my heart, 29 October 2020. Tumblr.com. https://khaleesikirk.tumblr.com/post/633355569251696640/i-want-to-talk-about-game-of-thrones-for-a-moment.

McCaughey, M., & King, N. (2001). *Reel knockouts: Violent women in the movies.* University of Texas Press.

McNutt, M. (2011, May 29). Game of Thrones "You Win or You Die". *Cultural Learnings.* https://cultural-learnings.com/2011/05/29/game-of-thrones-you-win-or-you-die/.

Mitovich, M. W. (2019, May 20). Ratings: Game of Thrones Series Finale Breaks Records, Tops 19 Million Viewers. *TVLine.* https://tvline.com/2019/05/20/game-of-thrones-finale-ratings-season-8-iron-throne/.

morgadc1887. (2018, December 01). [Comment on the online forum post Spoilers Why do people on reddit hate Sansa Stark so much?]. Reddit. https://www.reddit.com/r/gameofthrones/comments/a20qt0/spoilers_why_do_people_on_reddit_hate_sansa_stark/.

Murnen, S.K., Wright, C. & Kaluzny, G. (2002). If "Boys Will Be Boys," Then Girls Will Be Victims? A Meta-Analytic Review of the Research That Relates Masculine Ideology to Sexual Aggression. *Sex Roles 46*, 359–375. https://doi.org/10.1023/A:1020488928736.

Neroni, H. (2005). *The violent woman: femininity, narrative, and violence in contemporary American cinema*. State University of New York Press.

Ordoña, M. (2019, August 12). Sophie Turner sees 'Game of Thrones' heroine Sansa Stark's future and it's looking bright. *Los Angeles Times*. https://www.latimes.com/entertainment-arts/awards/story/2019-08-09/sophie-turner-game-of-thrones-sansa-stark-emmy-nominee.

Otterson, J. (2019, May 20). 'Game of Thrones' Finale Sets New Series High With Staggering 19.3 Million Viewers. *Variety*. https://variety.com/2019/tv/ratings/game-of-thrones-series-finale-draws-19-3-million-viewers-sets-new-series-high-1203220928/.

Porter, R. (2019, May 21). Game of Thrones Series Finale Sets All-Time HBO Ratings Record. *The Hollywood Reporter*. https://www.hollywoodreporter.com/live-feed/game-thrones-series-finale-sets-all-time-hbo-ratings-record-1212269.

Ryzik, M. (2018, April 4). Evan Rachel Wood Turns Her Trauma Into Good. On 'Westworld' and in Life. *The New York Times*. https://www.nytimes.com/2018/04/04/arts/television/evan-rachel-wood-westworld-interview.html.

Sandberg, S., & Scovell, N. (2013). *Lean in: Women, work, and the will to lead*. Knopf.

Schubart, R. (2007). *Super bitches and action babes: The female hero in popular cinema, 1970-2006*. McFarland.

Staller, K. M., & Nelson-Gardell, D. (2005). A burden in your heart: Lessons of disclosure from female preadolescent and adolescent survivors of sexual abuse. *Child Abuse & Neglect, 29*(12), 1415–1432. https://doi.org/10.1016/j.chiabu.2005.06.007.

sxpiosexualx. (2018). Sansa Stark S1: a gentle, trusting, and naive.... Tumblr.com. https://sxpiosexualx.tumblr.com/post/169915986702/sansa-stark-s1-a-gentle-trusting-and-naive.

themurphysue. (2017, August 29). [Online forum post Spoilers Extended Sansa's Bolton plotline, two years later: what did it bring and what did it rob us of?] Reddit. https://www.reddit.com/r/asoiaf/comments/6wrad3/spoilers_extended_sansas_bolton_plotline_two/.

TV Listings- Find Local TV Listings and Watch Full Episodes - Zap2it.com. *Zap2It*. (2011, June 19). http://tvlistings.zap2it.com/.

Chapter 5

The Protagonists of the Fantasy Drama *Lost*

From Stereotypes to Flexible Identities

Jérôme David

The early 2000s marked the beginning of a so-called post-network era (Lotz, 2010) in the US television industry. Audiences for traditional national channels collapsed, before platforms established themselves as major audiovisual content providers, on a global level. The last creative and commercial peak of free-to-view US television was the 2004–2005 season. The new series *Lost*, *Desperate Housewives*, *Grey's Anatomy*, and *House, M.D.* attracted 10–20 million US viewers each week (David, 2019, p. 122). The year 2005 also saw a shift in the competitive landscape. NBC, the network that brought out "quality drama" in 1982 was not responsible for these successes. For the first time in thirty years, its competitor ABC dominated the scene; it went from fourth to first place among the networks. It was ABC's first breakthrough since its acquisition in 1996 by the Walt Disney Company. Its first hit show was the fantasy show *Lost*, scheduled at 8:00 p.m. It was a massive success for ABC, and also an online phenomenon, thanks to its ambitious transmedia storytelling (Scolari, 2013). During its three last seasons (2007–2010), the show continued popularity online and was the most illegally downloaded television show on BitTorrent (Strangelove, 2015). Studying *Lost*, therefore, means scrutinizing the way a particular national media group adjusted its supply to a global and connected audience.

Through a socioeconomic and semiological analysis of the content of the six seasons broadcast between 2004 and 2012, this chapter examines why the protagonists of *Lost* responded to an internationalization of the audience, characteristic of the post-network era. First, the series was produced by the Walt Disney Company for its channel, ABC. Its high-concept format (Wyatt, 1996) meant that it could set itself against the social realism that had prevailed under the creative industrial leadership of NBC and favorite heroes, albeit stereotyped, of various nationalities. Second, the final seasons were marked by synchronization with a cosmopolitan audience. While it became the most pirated "content series" in the world (Combes, 2013, p. 29), *Lost* made the identities of these characters "flexible" (Balle, 2020).

A WALT DISNEY COMPANY PROGRAM

Lost was, above all, a revolution for US primetime. First of all, it was a fantasy drama scheduled for 8:00 p.m. Second, unlike popular US fiction programming of the 1990s, the main action was not set in a US city but on a lost island in the Pacific. Third, this high-concept approach allowed it to fit into the Disney editorial line because it offered entertainment that broke with US social reality. Yet, its characters were racially and culturally stereotyped by European standards (Marie, 2009).

A FAMILY TELEVISION FANTASY DRAMA

NBC experienced a historic fall from first to fourth place in 2005, behind Fox and CBS. NBC reigned over the period 1980–1990, the period of the "multi-channel transition" (Lotz, 2010), marked by an increase in the supply of free and pay channels. Under NBC's commercial leadership, primetime began at 8:00 p.m. with a comedy program to capture a family audience, and ended at 10:00 p.m. with a drama series targeting a more adult audience. Thus, on Thursdays, the most competitive evening of the week, the sitcom *Friends* started the evening's viewing, and the medical drama *ER* ended it. On Fox on Sundays, comedies preceded *The X-Files*, the most popular fantasy series of the 1990s (Lavery, 1996). NBC also laid down the creative standards for the entire US industry. Following the example of *Hill Street Blues* in 1982, *ER* (NBC), *NYPD Blue* (ABC), *Chicago Hope* (CBS), and *The X-Files* (Fox) were considered quality dramas. Night programming aimed at delivering dark, realistic, and critical visions of US society. The fantasy series *The X-Files* explored the mysteries of US political history and folklore in a combination of political thriller and horror. ABC's breakthrough seemed to launch a new cycle. Its first successful drama, *Lost*, was scheduled for Thursdays at 8:00 p.m., just before the reality show *The Bachelor*. Consequently, the industrial mission of a dramatic series would change. It could now appear at the beginning of primetime. Some changes were more ideological in scope because *Lost* was the custodian of ABC's editorial line in terms of the symbolic capital of its owner, the Disney conglomerate. Thus, in the 2000s, a fantasy series would not be dark and disturbing like *The X-Files*, but more attuned to the spectacular and the exotic. In an era marked by online piracy of audiovisual content, *Lost* elevated television genre fiction into an international blockbuster (Abbott, 2009). If *The X-Files* had been the fantasy series of the multi-channel transition, *Lost* would play the same role for the beginning of the post-network era.

THE ISLAND, AN ENCHANTED KINGDOM

The first three seasons of *Lost* tell how castaways stranded on a strange desert island after a plane crash, turn out to have mysterious pasts. This initial premise allows ABC to offer content that matches the symbolic capital of the Walt Disney Company. According to co-showrunner Damon Lindelof, *Lost* recounts how individuals with unhappy lives find that the island gives them an opportunity to rethink those lives (Vandwerff, 2010). It constitutes an escape. Thus, *Lost* depicts an "imaginary kingdom," as carefully separated from reality as an amusement park. In each of the areas on the island, there is a control station bearing symbols and names that suggest something marvellous, such as Hydra, Arrow, Swan, Flame, Pearl, and Orchid. There are many areas of the park for the characters and viewers to explore. Proceeding from the initial California theme park Disneyland, a Disney theme park was created in Florida in 1971, followed by other versions in Japan, China, and France.

As in Disneyworld theme parks, the heroes of *Lost* discover buildings reminiscent of the imaginary world of adventure films. This includes a nineteenth-century ship stranded in the jungle (the *Black Rock*), a twin-engine plane from Nigeria, an abandoned temple and even a haunted house. It is soon suggested that the island has mysterious faculties. As in a theme park, the magic of the island is fabricated behind the scenes. The indigenous population of the island is like the staff of Disneyworld. The latter appear in disguise to visitors but circulate backstage, through underground passages. Everything that is part of the preparation of the spectacle is hidden from public view. The way the island mimics Disneyworld confirms the editorial coherence of its high-concept approach, thereby making the series a new avatar of the Disney empire. There is a similar ideology in both. In *Lost*, the fantasy does not allow the US audience to confront its historical reality (Lavery, 1996, p. 79), but rather to distract it from that reality.

Disneyworld's escape from reality is a flight from the present, in favor of nostalgia and utopia. It is a form of "hyperreality" (Baudrillard, 1993). Baudrillard sees Disneyworld as an allegory of the United States, a "utopia becom(ing) reality" (p. 246). From his European point of view, he concludes that since America has not accumulated enough history, "unlike our referential cities, which have a territory, a memory and a history, these are exponential cities" (id.), it "lives in perpetual simulation" (p. 245).

Bryman (1995) finds that a reconstructed reality "exaggerates positive elements and plays down or altogether omits negative ones" (id.), such as "racism, conflict, poverty and unemployment" (p. 108). In his overview of the art devoted to hyperreality, Bryman identifies three main rules at work in Disneyworld. He says, "The problems created by industry and corporations are given little if any attention. Second, issues of class and race (and gender too, which is less apparent from these lists) are side-stepped. Third, conflict is all but eliminated from the depiction of the past" (p. 101).

In 1975, Mattelart and Dorfman, specialists in American cultural imperialism, had already observed that, in the comic books produced by Disney, "the proletariat are expelled from the society they created, thus ending all antagonisms, conflicts, class struggle" (Dorfman & Mattelart, 2009, p. 65). In *Lost* there is, for example, a certain denunciation of capitalism in the way the role of antagonist is ascribed to ruthless businessmen, thus presenting the corporate world as corrupt. However, flashbacks revealing the heroes' pasts often give them privileged social backgrounds.

Above all, *Lost* avoids the staging of racial tensions, for the basic reason that its action takes place on a remote island. Bryman (1995) notes that Disneyworld stays away from big cities for a specific reason, "cultural diversity and productive labor disappear from view: exchange, interdependence, the struggle for power—all the everyday functions of the city have been hidden, or banished" (p. 101).

RACIAL AND CULTURAL STEREOTYPES

The scholar Marie states, "To the extent that a stereotype is part of a process of categorization and generalization, it simplifies and prunes the real; it can thus favor a schematic and distorted vision of the other which leads to prejudice" (Marie, 2009, para. 1). Each episode in the first three seasons contains flashbacks retracing the past of one of the castaways. These flashbacks reinforce stereotypes. The poor white Americans Kate and Sawyer are solitary people living in illegal circumstances, the rich white male US doctor has a savior complex; the English rock star is a drug addict with an unbridled sex life; the obese Latino male works in a fast-food restaurant and thinks only of food; African heritage people live in a state of misery and war. In season four, a new character, an Asian, talks with spirits. Other protagonists also revealed stereotypical and melodramatic modes of writing.

Of Iraqi origin, the character Sayid was a delicate role to write for, three years after the September 11 attacks in the United States. However, the production decided to make him an ex-soldier who tortures the American character Sawyer. In addition, Sayid is in love with a female Iraqi insurgent, for whom he searches across the world. The authors and the actor (of Anglo-Indian origin) declared that they wanted to defend a heroic vision of an Iraqi (Gray, 2009), the polar opposite of the paranoid and conservative discourse of action series *24*, produced by the Fox channel, where Muslims are often terrorists (Nurullah, 2010). However, the result is ideologically ambiguous. If Sayid is a courageous protagonist whose expertise is of great value, he is also presented as a violent man. While his past tells his story as an ex-torturer, his future stages him as an assassin.

The South Korean couple Jin and Sun is also very stereotypical, revealing a common past worthy of a telenovela. Sun is a wealthy young woman in a setting that would suit a melodrama, while Jin has two life prospects, both archetypical of Asian people in the Hollywood imagination (Park, Gabbadon, Chernin, 2006), ruthless mafioso or impoverished fisherman. Season three introduces the story of a pregnancy and a mystery surrounding the biological father. Sun has had a lover, but the latter is murdered at the request of her father, who wishes to avoid scandal. With this fictionalized representation, the series distances itself from the reality effect that preoccupied the scriptwriters of *ER* and *NYPD Blue* where men and women of Asian origin were sometimes depicted. On the other hand, it confirms the way the series is rooted in ABC's editorial line, well before its acquisition by Disney. The editorial approach was both progressive and stereotypical.

In 1972, thirty-two years before *Lost*, ABC broadcast *Kung-Fu*, the story of a mixed-race Shaolin monk who is a fugitive on both sides of the Pacific. The "eastern western" show was hailed for marking a turning point in the representation of Asians on television, but was also the subject of heavy scholarly and Asian community critique since the lead actor David Carradine was not Asian at all, but white.

Said (1978) discusses "orientalism" to refer to representations of the Eastern world by Western arts and literature. In 2011, the US scholar Iwamura examined the "eastern monk" promoted by the *Kung-Fu (1972–1975)*. She initially approved of Said's reading, noting that "rather than offering perspicuous insight into its Oriental object, this system of representation reveals much about the Occidental subjectivity from which it emerges" (p. 7). She went further, by proposing the concept of "virtual orientalism" to designate the cultural stereotypes conveyed by the visual media (id.). By "virtual," she refers to broadcasting techniques (image, sound) supported by digital media, and individuals favoring the circulation of cultural stereotypes. Thus, an individual does not imagine an "oriental monk" outside the image that has been relayed to him or her by the media. Stereotypes are constructed on a global scale, notably by US representations, which benefit from media infrastructures and from "products ready for immediate consumption." These representations go beyond the postcolonial dimension of the British orientalism. In her view they contribute to "romanticizing traditions and cultural traits" (id.). Thus, Iwamura regrets the way Asian culture is reduced to being a "spiritual other" for the American gaze, while reinforcing the image of an affable and docile culture. She also recognizes that *Kung-Fu* also sends a peaceful message in a tense sociopolitical context due to the Vietnam War.

In the chapter author's view, this ambiguity can be seen in *Lost*. Unlike *Kung-Fu*, the series does not resort to "whitewashing" (Gabriel, 1998). The production recruited actors of Korean origin who speak in their mother tongue, an innovation for a US series. However, the possibility of *Lost* being consumed worldwide, in less than 24 hours, also confirms Iwamura's fear of seeing "virtual" stereotypes circulating more easily. When Asians are depicted, their cultures are illogically consolidated. Asian men tend to be portrayed as either wicked martial arts masters or as non-sexualized men. Women are submissive or highly sexualized exotic beauties (Towbin et al., 2004). *Lost* manages to bypass some of these clichés.

This points to economic explanations. ABC was targeting a predominantly female and family audience (David, 2019, p. 219). For this, the channel opted for an editorial line turned toward soap operas and entertainment (series such as *Desperate Housewives*, *Grey's Anatomy*, and *Scandal*, but also the reality show *The Bachelor*), distancing itself from the documentary realism of NBC, which historically targeted an audience that was male, urban and had high purchasing power. It was this difference between the products of the two national media that led ABC to present stereotypical and romanticized characters, but also to avoid taking a critical look at US multiculturalism.

A GLOBAL "CONTENT SERIES"

During its last three seasons, *Lost* was the most illegally downloaded series in the world, while its live-time audiences decreased. It became a "content series" (Combes, 2013, p. 29), a show better suited to be watched and discussed online. The series could then openly slip toward the fantasy genre because its characters bore witness to flexible identities, while the island took on the appearance of a global village. By so doing, the show advocated a discourse of reconciliation.

FLEXIBLE IDENTITIES

The French political scientist Constant identifies three major phases in the history of multiculturalism: (1) a phase marked by the failure of the Civil Rights Movement in the United States in the 1960s, which established an inequality of opportunity between Blacks and Whites; (2) a phase which consolidated a divided and isolationist American society until the end of the 1990s; (3) a third period, that of a "celebration of cultural and identity diversity as well as the cultural shaping of social conflicts" (pp. 25–26).

The police series *NYPD Blue* and the legal drama *The Practice*, ABC's two successes in the 1990s, echoed the second phase of multiculturalism, in line with NBC's "quality dramas." The first season of *Lost*, focused on the group as it settled on the island and also confronted this issue briefly. Three characters are employed: the American Sawyer, a swindler from the south; the African American from New York, Michael, an engineer by profession and father of a boy named Walt; and Jin, a Korean businessman. Upon their arrival on the island, Sawyer is best known for giving his companions sometimes racist nicknames. For his part, Jin lives in isolation with his wife, with whom he speaks exclusively in Korean, the only language he knows. Showrunner Damon Lindelof says that a survey conducted by ABC showed that Sawyer and Jin were the characters least liked by the public (Vandwerff, 2010). It is interesting to note that they are the only ones to display isolationist behavior.

At the end of the season, Sawyer, who has redeemed himself, joins Jin and Michael on a raft to leave the island and seek help. The group fraternizes in the face of adversity, as if the absence of "residential segregation" (id.) allowed by the island had allowed these individuals from different cultures and religions to coexist peacefully.

In a manner that masks cultural markers, the heroes are confronted with indigenous people of the island, whom they call "the Others." Thus, while this term is usually a metonym for foreigners, the series attributes it to individuals who reside on the island. The latter adopt offensive behavior toward the castaways, kidnapping and killing some of them. They also send out spies, who are individuals who pass themselves off as castaways under false identities. Part of the suspense of the first three seasons is thus based on the mystery of the identity of the Others.

These Others are mostly white and first appear in rags, reinforcing the stereotype of savages who attack "settlers." The audience discovers in season two that they were actually wearing disguises and false beards. In season three, the series reveals that they live in a village similar to a Western holiday camp. Finally, season four reveals that some are returning to the continent, where they can enjoy the benefits of civilization. Thus, these antagonists turn out to be all endowed with fluid identities. It is impossible for the viewer (as for the heroes) to know who they really are.

The castaways are not to be outdone. In flashbacks, the principle of change of identity is recurrent. Many seem to have experienced several lives and to be hiding their true identity from their companions in misfortune. The flashbacks of the first seasons of *Lost* resort to different dramatic mechanisms characteristic of a soap opera of the 2000s.

On the island, the series maintains the same discourse. On several occasions, the survivors can choose a group or a side. However, in episode 4x01 that a really decisive choice poses itself: either to follow the hero Jack, who announces that he has found a way to leave the island, or the solitary Locke, who prefers to stay. *Lost* thus confirms that its heroes all the choice of belonging to a group or taking a completely different direction. In this, they have "flexible identities," in the sense of the French sociologist Balle (2004): "The inhabitants of global society are both here and elsewhere. . . . We are constantly cobbling together a new identity to become what we think we want to be" (p. 11).

In *Lost*, the heroes are no longer confined to "closed social environments" and many of them hope for an "elsewhere." In doing so, the fiction distances itself from the recurrent discourse of the fantasy dramas produced under the leadership of NBC. Fox Mulder, the federal agent of *The X-Files* is hidden in the basements of the FBI, obsessed by his desire to understand what happened to his sister. Buffy the vampire slayer is trapped in her destiny. Angel, the vampire with a soul, is doomed to seek his redemption. Buffy and Angel thus share, with the heroes of the dramas *NYPD Blue* and *The Practice*, the weight of a professional and personal priesthood. They have only one identity. However, *Lost* does not advocate any individualism. Each of the heroes must choose a side. From the very first episodes, the hero Jack insists on the collective as a source of hope in his phrase about living together or dying alone.

THE ISLAND, A GLOBAL VILLAGE

One of *Lost*'s gimmicks is to bring up, in the flashbacks of a given character, another protagonist, often stealthily and in the background. This is to encourage viewers to pay attention to the details that they can comment on via the Internet, but also to establish a geographical proximity between all the heroes. In the same spirit, the last season replaces flashbacks and flashforwards with "flashsideways," imagining what life would have been like for the heroes if they had never met on the island. It turns out that they would have ended up encountering each other (again), despite the millions of kilometers that separate them.

In the late 1960s, philosopher Marshall McLuhan developed the idea that technological advances would lead to the emergence of a global village, a unique, shared, worldwide culture shaped by the media. The immediacy of the means of communication would lead to the elimination of distances between individuals, entailing a shrinking of the world and a weakening of national borders. It was the Internet that would be identified as the concrete realization of what was fundamentally a utopia. Forty years later, *Lost* seems to question the fantasized dimension of a global village. The island constitutes a space of reinvention for characters whose lives before the crash were a source of misfortune and despair. If it embodies every possibility, this is in particular because it offers a historical and cultural link between all the castaways.

Lost initially distinguishes itself by a fascination for "religions from elsewhere" (Constant, 2000, pp. 27–28). As the seasons go by, the island starts to appear as a patchwork of symbols and myths from different continents. A polar bear attacks the castaways in the middle of the tropical jungle, mysterious hieroglyphs appear on the chronometer of a secret station on the island, the foot of a statue that the heroes spot at the bend of a cove turns out to be that of the Egyptian goddess Taweret; the Others all find refuge in a temple. Finally, in one of the final episodes, the showrunners reveal how the island's genesis drew on a mixture of biblical influences and Roman mythology. The island's guards appear to be two men, one dressed in white and the other in black, demiurgic entities, at once complementary and contradictory. Both guards were raised by a woman who killed their real mother and hid the origins of their birth from them. Thus, it is by assembling several artefacts from Asian and African cultures, like the Adventureland of Disneyworld, that the island manages to build a global village. It superimposes internationally familiar myths and religions.

The series therefore echoes the third phase of multiculturalism according to Constant (2000), by participating in "a superficial way of experiencing multiculturalism on a daily basis, which mixes desire for escape and desire for authenticity" (pp. 27–28).

This spatio-temporal compression crosses a decisive frontier at the end of season 4, which definitively projects the story into science fiction. A central wheel located at the heart of the island allows the latter to be projected in time and space; in particular, anyone who operates the wheel can travel from the Indian Ocean to the Tunisian desert in a few seconds. The season will thus relate to a complex story of time travel. The heroes find themselves separated into two groups, one having escaped the island, and living in the present, and the other stuck on the island, but this time in the 1970s. Here again, fantasy, and even science fiction, put themselves at the service of a common history. The island becomes less and less like some lost place on the planet, but on the contrary like the hidden center of the entire world.

This creative choice seems to echo the synchronization of the series with its connected audience (Pearson, 2011). Indeed, the Internet has made it possible to compress time and space in the consumption of television series, giving everyone the possibility of seeing the series almost at the same time, and of discussing it online together. *Lost* metatextually embraces its status as a world series, by providing a plot capable of satisfying its status as a "content series."

Mattelart (2009) reminds us that a "compression of the world" into a single village would create "an exacerbation of 'collisions' between cultures or societies, putting under pressure the categories used to perceive these" (p. 54). *Lost* answers any such concern by reducing peculiarities to artefacts from the past, but also by endowing each of the characters with similar plot lines, inspired by soap operas.

Lost did indeed play a key role in asserting ABC's editorial line in the post-network era. On Thursday evenings, at the end of the 2000s, it was the fictions produced by the African American showrunner Shonda Rhimes that would for a long time proceed after *Lost*. *Grey's Anatomy* and then *Scandal* would go on to promote an openly post-racial discourse, imagining teams of US professionals whose racial and cultural singularities are obscured (Joseph, 2016). *Lost* thus paved the way for an equally progressivist discourse, devoid of any critical gaze directed at US society.

A description of "human collectivities, perceived as plural groups made up of diverse communities" in "conflicts over state resources" (Constant, 2000, pp. 33–34) does indeed belong to the cycle of symbolic production previously created by NBC, when US television was still addressing an US audience. At that time, when *X-Files* related the North American Indigenous genocide, for example, it presented, as did its contemporaries *ER* and *NYPD Blue*, the multiculturalist model as "a zero-sum game, where the gains of one community are always obtained at the expense of another" (ibid.). Faced with an international, connected audience, *Lost* preferred to advocate a discourse of reconciliation between people of various nationalities, based on common values.

A DISCOURSE OF RECONCILIATION

The majority of French academic work dedicated to *Lost* highlights the universal dimension of the series. Whether in terms of research in the field of classic literature (Hatchuel, 2013), or of philosophy (Thiellement, 2014), all emphasize that *Lost* is addressed to "humanity." Hatchuel (2013) sees the romances in the series as one of the bonds of a community "formed by common sufferings and joys, grief, solidarity, friendship and love" (p. 93). Above all, the chapter author perceives in it a distinctive feature of the editorial line of the ABC channel, which allows *Lost* to have a universal language of emotion and love.

The final season ended with a revelation. All of the survivors died when a bomb exploded at the end of the previous season. The sequences identified by the audience as flashsideways turned out to be "flashaheads." These are realities imagined by the heroes after their death. Cornillon (2016) describes "an outside of time so that the characters may come together again after death" (para. 21). During the very last moments of the series, the survivors find themselves in a purgatory resembling a church, but whose stained glass windows symbolize different religions: Islam, Hinduism, Judaism, Buddhism. The survivors embrace and the separated couples meet when Jack's father, Christian Shephard, opens the main door, letting a warm stream of light flood the room. Hatchuel (2016) notes that this final resolution resembled "syrupy transcendence" and proclaimed "a religiosity without cynicism." It disappointed "an audience of postmodern skeptics" (para. 72), who were accustomed to irony and the construction of multiple universes and realities.

It is possible to qualify this view. First of all, the ironic dimension of the first seasons can be put into perspective, with regard to their strong soap opera tone (David, 2019, p. 388), part of a stereotypical Hollywood-style representation of the countries from which the protagonists come. The way the series follows the ABC editorial line continues on another level. When Hatchuel mentions "romances (which) could provide contemporary viewers with precious clues on how to respond to the challenges of the historic period that is now beginning," it is difficult not to think of the "votive" mission that Laborde and Jullier (2015, p. 13) identify in *Grey's Anatomy*.

Likewise, if the series puts the fates of its heroes before the solving of its mysteries, this is in line with the values promoted by the channel. That is why the love lives of the doctors in *Grey's Anatomy* swallow up the end of each season, while, on NBC, *ER* was primarily concerned with criticizing the US hospital system. It is also why the main secret of the heroine of *Scandal* is an affair with the president of the United States, while on NBC, *The West Wing* modestly allowed viewers to follow the men and women who work in his shadow. For all these reasons, *Lost* was therefore, editorially speaking, a fiction doomed to disappoint at the level of its overall plot, preferring as it did to focus on interpersonal relationships and emotions.

The sociopolitical context also strongly justifies this conclusion, one turned toward the idea of a better world. Hatchuel sees the fiction as a "post-September 11 iconography" (Hatchuel, Laist, 2016, para. 36). Indeed, when *Lost* was launched in September 2004, George W. Bush was waging a highly publicized "war on terror." However, when the show ended on ABC in early

2010, it was precisely a year after Barack Obama unexpectedly entered the White House.

In the space of six years of broadcasting, *Lost* provided an accompaniment to a difficult period in the history of the country and world. The series, based on a cast of various nationalities, enabled a country and a world population traumatized by the September 11 events, to escape together from the geopolitical reality that ensued. Chan (2012) speaks of "critical cosmopolitanism" (p. 145) to refer to such a discourse, in his study of the fantasy series *Heroes*, launched by NBC in 2005 as a response to *Lost*.

CONCLUSION

In the 1970s, during its first commercial golden age, ABC already offered "jiggle television" (Mittell, 2013, p. 161) based on colorful, exotic, and spectacular worlds to divert the United States and the rest of the world from gray sociopolitical realities. Thirty years later, its editorial line, now consolidated by the Walt Disney Company, regained all its social, political, cultural and above all commercial relevance. This chapter discussed how *Lost* embodied the tendency of the conglomerate to deliver utopias relying heavily on stereotypes, then trying to develop characters easy to identify with for a broad audience. Ultimately, *Lost* did not try to tell a story about the United States but about the world. That, incidentally, is why most French academics who studied the show focused on its humanism and underlined its potential of identification. It was indeed a form of "escape television" (David, 2019, p. 70) that prevailed in a post-network era, characterized by the internationalization of audiences for serial content on the Internet. From this point of view, the way *The Game of Thrones* (2011–2019) took over from *Lost* to head the list of the most pirated television series in the world (Strangelove, 2015) makes perfect sense. Fantasy soap opera has never unified so many audiences as in the digital age.

REFERENCES

Abbott, S. (2009). How *Lost* found its audience: The making of a cult blockbuster. In R. Pearson (Ed.), *Reading Lost* (pp. 9–26). I.B. Tauris.

Balle, F. (2020). *Les medias*. Presses Universitaires de France.

Baudrillard, J. (1993). Hyperreal America. *Economy and society*, 22(2), 243–252.

Bryman, A. (1995). *Disney & His Worlds*. Routledge.

Chan, K. (2012). Heroes' internationalism. In S. David (Ed.), *Investigating heroes: Essays on truth, justice and quality TV* (pp. 144–155). McFarland.

Combes C. (2013). *La pratique des séries télévisées: une sociologie de l'activité spectatorielle*, PhD dissertation, École Nationale Supérieure des Mines de Paris.

Constant, F. (2000). *Le multiculturalisme*. Flammarion.

Cornillon, C. (2016). Lost, fiction kaléidoscopique. *TV/Series*, (Hors séries 1) https://journals.openedition.org/tvseries/1632.

David, J. (2019). "Les séries télévisées des chaînes historiques américaines de 2004 à 2014: lignes éditoriales et stratégies de programmation à l'ère post-network," PhD dissertation, Université Paris 2, Panthéon-Assas.

Dorfman, A., & Mattelart, A. (1975). *How to Read Donald Duck*. International General.

Gabriel, J. (1998). *Whitewash: Racialized politics and the media*. Psychology Press.

Gray, J. (2009). We're not in Portland anymore. In R.E. Pearson (Ed.), *Reading lost* (pp. 221–239). I.B. Tauris.

Hatchuel, S (2013). *Lost, fiction vitale*. Presses Universitaires de France.

Hatchuel, S., & Laist, R. (2016). Lost: une «romance» shakespearienne?. *TV/Series* (Hors séries 1) https://journals.openedition.org/tvseries/1656.

Iwamura, J. N. (2011). *Virtual orientalism*. Oxford University Press.

Joseph, R. L. (2016). Strategically ambiguous Shonda Rhimes: Respectability politics of a black woman showrunner. *Souls*, *18*(2–4), 302–320.

Laborde, B., & Jullier, L. (2015). *Grey's Anatomy. Du coeur au care*. Presses Universitaires de France.

Lavery, D., Hague, A., & Cartwright, M. (Eds.). (1996). *Deny all knowledge: Reading the X-Files*. Syracuse University Press.

Lotz, A. (Ed.). (2010). *Beyond prime time*. Routledge.

Marie, V. (2009). La Sémantique des Possibles Argumentatifs: un modèle de description-construction-représentation des significations lexicales. *Cahiers de Narratologie. Analyse et théorie narratives*, (17). http://journals.openedition.org/narratologie/1337.

Mattelart, T. (2009). Globalization theories and media internationalization: In D.K. Thussu (Ed.), A critical appraisal. In *Internationalizing media studies* (pp. 62–74). Routledge.

McLuhan, M., & Powers, B. R. (1989). *The global village: Transformations in world life and media in the 21st century*. Communication and Society.

Mittell, J. (2013). *Genre and television: From cop shows to cartoons in American culture*. Routledge.

Nurullah, A. S. (2010). Portrayal of Muslims in the media: "24" and the 'Othering' process. *International Journal of Human Sciences*, *7*(1), 1020–1046.

Park, J. H., Gabbadon, N. G., & Chernin, A. R. (2006). Naturalizing racial differences through comedy: Asian, Black, and White views on racial stereotypes in Rush Hour 2. *Journal of Communication*, *56*(1), 157–177.

Pearson, R. (2011). Cult television as digital television's cutting edge. *Television as Digital Media*, 105–131.

Rojek, C. (1995). Disney culture. *Leisure Studies*, *12*(2), 121–135.

Said, E. W. (1979). *Orientalism*. Vintage.

Scolari, C. A. (2013). Lostology: Transmedia storytelling and expansion/compression strategies. *Semiotica*, *2013*(195), 45–68.

Strangelove, M. (2015). *Post-TV: Piracy, cord-cutting, and the future of television.* University of Toronto Press.

Thiellement, P. (2014). *Les mêmes yeux que Lost.* Editions Léo Scheer.

Towbin, M. A., Haddock, S. A., Zimmerman, T. S., Lund, L. K., & Tanner, L. R. (2004). Images of gender, race, age, and sexual orientation in Disney feature-length animated films. *Journal of Feminist Family Therapy, 15*(4), 19–44.

Vandwerff, T. (2010). The Lost Interviews: https://www.vox.com/a/lost-damon-lindelofinterviews.

Wyatt, J. (1994). *High concept: Movies and marketing in Hollywood.* University of Texas Press.

Section II

SOAP OPERAS AND TELENOVELAS

Chapter 6

Pakistan Television Drama Serials and Telenovelas from 1964 to 2019

Gendering in Different Political Regimes

Saleem Abbas

The tradition of Pakistani Urdu television drama is more than 50 years old. Among other types of television entertainment programs—stage shows, morning shows, docudramas, and music programs—drama serials are the most popular and well-received genre by Urdu drama lovers within and outside Pakistan (Bhattacharya & Nag, 2016). This chapter discusses a brief history of Pakistani Urdu television drama serials/telenovelas in four phases—from 1964 to 2019—and explores gender representation in the content of television shows during different political regimes of the country. Generally, these drama stories present one to three female protagonists in every serial. The majority of the drama narratives revolve around Pakistani patriarchal society and women's lives (Kothari, 2005). They allow female writers to raise their voices for women's rights. In these dramas, resistance and transgression against patriarchy and social oppression can also be observed. Despite the popularity of drama serials in Pakistan, academic research on the content of these television shows remains very limited.

Pakistan Television (PTV) is the first television channel of Pakistan that began its transmission in 1964 during an early martial law regime of Gen. Ayyub Khan (1958–1969). It is a state-owned channel and displays fluid media policies. These policies vary with the change of Pakistani governments. Before the proliferation of private television channels in 2002, PTV was viewed across the country and was believed to be the major source of information and entertainment for the Pakistani audience. Currently, there are 92 satellite private Pakistani television channels (PEMRA, 2020) that broadcast news and entertainment shows including soap operas, telenovelas, and drama serials. All these shows were regulated by the Pakistan Electronic

Media Regulatory Authority (PEMRA), which oversees Pakistan's electronic media policies and policy implementation.

For this chapter, an analysis of the top five Urdu television shows of every year during the period of 1970–2008 were discussed and the history of Pakistani television drama during this period was divided into four phases. The first phase consists of eight years (1970–1977), which included dramas of initial years of PTV. Although PTV was started in 1964, the country did not adopt recording facilities until 1970. For this reason, this study examination began examination from 1970 and proceeded onward. This phase represents a major shift from acoustic to visual medium. Here, despite the perplexing and challenging production environment of initial Urdu television drama, government media policies were moderate and progressive.

Phase two discusses twelve years of dramas—from 1978 to 1988—during the regime of military dictator General Zia-ul-Haq. This phase is also called the period of "Islamization." In this section, it is argued that a gender-discriminated media policy of the government can be observed in Urdu television drama serials. During this phase, the archetypal and traditional roles assigned to women are common. Generally, females were portrayed in domestic confines, while male characters are showcased in powerful, aggressive, independent, and professional roles.

The third phase describes Pakistan's television dramas of another eleven years (1989–1999). In this post-Islamization period, civil governments of two political parties came up with more moderate media policies. During this phase, the Pakistani audience experienced a plethora of international television shows through cable television networks. Private drama production houses also received licenses from the government. Hence, for the first time, Pakistani drama was included in national and international comparisons. During this phase, the popularity trend of Pakistani dramas was low, but the visibility of diverse female portrayals in Pakistani Urdu dramas remained very high. PTV's overall shows exemplified the government's vision of women empowerment. The majority of female leading characters in this era were comparatively less conservative and dependent.

Phase four begins with new discussions of dramas from the new millennium until 2019. It included proliferation of private television channels in Pakistan and a vast production network of Urdu drama serials and telenovelas. During this phase, PTV shows not only gained back their popularity, but female dramatists also outnumbered male writers. Although the majority of drama stories revolved around family issues and love affairs, female protagonists represented a variety of strong and independent roles. A progression in female empowerment throughout this phase is noticeable. The female protagonists mainly belonged to urban, middle-class traditional families. While these drama heroines were educated, progressive, and independent, they had a strong bond with their culture. Their progress and approach can be seen as considerate and collective, rather than being egotistical and self-centered. In this section, a phenomenon of "new womanhood" (Dotoya, 2018) in Pakistani dramas was explored.

To present a holistic view of all four phases of the Pakistani television drama industry, one drama per year out of the top five popular Urdu dramas was selected for the study for each criterion year. The popularity of these dramas was gauged by using the following resources: (1) available archives at the Pakistan Television Corporation, (2) a rigorous cherry-picking from the columns of leading Pakistani newspapers from the relevant time period, (3) focus groups of Urdu television drama lovers, (4) interviews with people involved in the productions of these drama serials (i.e., directors, writers, cast, and other associates), and (5) online information provided by relevant drama companies and television channels.

For phase one (1970–1977) and two (1978–1988), published drama reviews in leading national dailies were considered. For phase three (1989–1999), focus group discussions and interviews of the relevant people were conducted. As for phase four (2000–2019), the study relied on the Internet Movie Database (IMDb) rating for Pakistani Urdu television dramas. For the first three phases, data from an unpublished PhD thesis (Abbas, 2010) was used. In the next sections, a detailed discussion was provided for each phase of gender representation in television dramas.

PHASE I: PAKISTANI DRAMA AND PROGRESSIVE MOVEMENT

After an armed conflict between Pakistan and India in 1971, a civil government of the Pakistan People's Party (PPP) replaced the 12-year-long military dictatorship. Displaying a Marxist inclination, the PPP government provided a congenial and encouraging atmosphere to the progressive Urdu writers (Sadeed, 1985). Most of these Urdu writers (Shaukat Siddiqi, Ibraheem Jalees, Kamal Ahmad Rizvi, Munnu Bhai, and Ahmad Nadeen Qasmi) had written serials and assorted plays for PTV during the early years of PTV. In their serials, these playwrights highlighted issues of underprivileged and neglected communities. In their stories, they suggested multiple ways for social development. Generally, dramatists of the first phase (1970–1977) believe in liberty, gender equality, enlightenment, and a nonconservative approach toward religion.

That was the time when television was newly introduced in Pakistan as a powerful visual medium where people could see live human images on their home screens. In particular, the portrayal of female characters had to undergo severe criticism because of the cultural heterogeneity among viewers (Désoulières, 1999). Although the civil government of Zulfiqar Ali Bhutto (the PPP leader) adopted progressive media policies for his regime (Shah & Panhwar, 2014), the gendering in television content was still an issue. Instead of equal gender representation, the diverse provincial cultural depiction was the priority for the PTV administration. That is why representing a patriarchal society, rife with examples of female subjugation, the drama serials from the provinces of Balochistan and Khaiber Pakhtoonkha (KP) feature diminutive female representation during the first phase. On the contrary, the drama serials of other provinces (Punjab and Sindh) seem open for diversity and liberty. In terms of behind-the-camera female participation, the situation was not much different. The visibility of educated and creative females in the drama industry was limited. The writer and director of PTV's first telenovela, entitled *White Shadow* (*Safaid Saya*, 1970), were females: Jamila Shaheen, and Raana Sheikh, respectively. During this period, prolific female writers like Hasina Moin and Fatima S. Bajia also started writing for the television drama. Moin and Bajia were among a few female writers who set the tone and trend of drama in Pakistan. They mostly wrote on family issues and showcased a typical picture of a Pakistani woman, who is the custodian of Eastern family values. Hasina Moin tried to bridge the gap of tradition and modernity. Her female protagonists are traditional but strong, educated, and confident. For the first time, Moin introduced a character of hyperactive and independent heroine in her stories on the Pakistani screen. Her dramas—*Shehzori* (1973), *Kiran Kahani* (1973), and *Uncle Urfi* (1974)—received fame and acceptance from both traditional and progressive circles.

PHASE II: ISLAMIZATION AND GENDERING IN TELEDRAMAS

After an initial perplexing and challenging phase, the Pakistani Urdu television drama serial established its identity by the late 1970s (Ahmed, 1990). Throughout the history of Pakistani drama serials, eleven years (1978–1988) of General Zia-ul-Haq's military dictatorship stand out because of the general's ultraconservative media policies. The regime of Gen. Zia-ul-Haq, also known as a period of Islamization, was infamous for its media censorship (Hasan, 2000a). The "veil and four walls," traditional clothing, and gender segregation were the salient features of this era. The majority of female drama characters were showcased in confines of domestic space. All kinds of performing arts were considered "un-Islamic" (Kothari, 2005). Concurrently, many human rights and women's movements started as a response to Zia's coercing and debilitating women's policies (Mumtaz & Shaheed, 1987).

Many researchers consider this military dictatorship indelible and damaging to women's rights (Kothari, 2005). The intensification of control over women's lives was visible on the television screen. During this period, female visibility at public spheres was discouraged in dramas. The slogan of "veil and four walls for women" was publicized in a way that their visibility was likened to indecency and obscenity.

Naqvi (2017) describes that during his regime, General Zia-ul-Haq exercised absolute power and altogether transformed the country's political and social structure. Many scholars (Haqqani, 2005; Hasan, 2000a; Rashid, 2013; Shah & Panhwar, 2014) argue that Zia-ul-Haq's entire regime laid a foundation for many issues, including religious bigotry, gender inequality and male chauvinism. A strict "dupatta" (headscarf) policy was enforced for all female actresses and news anchors who appeared on screen (Hasan, 2000b). The television shows of that era depicted stereotypical images of women, including caring housewives, sacrificing sisters, loving mothers, and obedient daughters. The definition of "a good woman" was linked with a woman's piety, docility, and subservience.

Archetypal and traditional roles assigned to female characters were highly visible in the Pakistani telenovelas and dramas serials from 1977 to 1988 (Abbas, 2018; Hasan, 2000b; Kothari, 2005; Mumtaz & Shaheed, 1987). Drama serials *Waris* (1979), *Dehleez* (1981), *Aakhri Chatan* (1980), *Dewarain* (1983), *Shaheen* (1983), *Jangal* (1984), *Khwaja and Son* (1988) portrayed male characters in dominating and strong/aggressive roles. The men in these dramas were presented as family heads, managers, professionals, and other leading positions. On the other hand, average women in the same dramas were showcased in acquiescent roles. Essentially, women in these dramas were depicted with major responsibilities of housekeeping, child care, and providing assistance to male members of the family or other social spheres (Vandello & Cohen, 2003). In a thematic analysis of 12 drama serials, the majority of female characters are depicted in domestic and passive roles.

Throughout the Zia regime (1978–1988), the images of male supremacy can be found in abundance. The reinforcement of patriarchal values in Pakistan was justified by mentioning omnipresent male dominance in all Islamic courtiers (Christ, 2013). Telenovelas based on Islamic history were telecast more frequently than other regimes. *Aakhri Chatan* and *Shaheen* are the two sample telenovelas in which mainly male protagonists were showcased as ideal human beings to embody virtuous and noble qualities. They were brave, genuine, honest, committed, and saviors of mankind, particularly the protector of women's honor.

In Pakistani society, the honor of a family is mainly associated with the family's females. Women are considered to be the guardians of the honor.

Men are supposed to provide food and shelter to their families and safeguard them from any potential danger. Furthermore, men are expected not to tolerate any disrespectful comportment toward females of their families. In the drama serials *Waris*, *Dehleez*, *Waqat*, and *Daria*, all male characters are breadwinners and protectors of their families. *Jangal* (1984) is the first drama serial in which a female writer raises a voice against honor killing. In Pakistani traditional society, the narrative of "honor" and "shame" is stapled with a woman's body (Atakav, 2020). This concept drives honor-based violence against women (Zia, 2019) and "immoral behavior" can be punished by killing the person.

The "immoral behavior" is defined differently in different Pakistani provincial cultures. The most common reasons for honor killings are alleged marital infidelity, refusal to submit to an arranged marriage, or being raped (Raza, 2006). In the majority cases, women become the target of this honor-based violence. Pakistani television dramas also depict honor-based violence against women in many television shows [see drama serials *Waris* (1979), *Jangal* (1984), *Zard Dopehar* (1993), *Marvi* (1993), *Baghi* (2017), *Yaqeen Ka Safar* (2019)]. Honor is a gendered social construct, which appears as a male trait, while shame appears as a female trait (Vandello & Cohen, 2003). In patriarchal and religious societies, saving honor is more important at the cost of a woman's life. It is a phenomenon embedded in the system of power relations. Honor killing is one of the older tribal customs that has existed since pre-Islamic times (Raza, 2006). Most of the Muslim countries, including Pakistan are labeled for their patriarchal culture (Abu Lughud, 2011). In patriarchal cultures, a family's respect and honor is knotted with a woman's chastity. The concept of "veil and four walls" in which adoption of "hijab" (veil) and women's segregation to "zannan khana" (living quarters reserved for wives and female relatives) is a measure of safeguard and protection.

Having said that, these dramas generate many debates, including gender occupational power and prestige (Sang et al., 2016; Signorielli, 2004, 2009). As male characters are depicted in managerial and controlling prestigious positions (see dramas: *Waris, Seriyan, Dewarian*), and women are either presented as housewives or in some stereotypical professions like teachers or medical staff, researchers argue that media is perpetuating patriarchy by showcasing gendered stereotypically assigned roles (Kothari, 2005; Signorielli & Bacue, 1999).

Many research studies found a high degree of consistency in the male and female characters' attributes (Christ, 2013; Signorielli, 2004; Signorielli et al., 2018; Vandello & Cohen, 2003). They found that female characters are generally depicted in stereotypical roles such as week, submissive, and less important characters. The female characters are rarely shown in Western-style clothing (e.g., jeans, pants, and tee-shirts). In many cases, Western-style clothing is only used in the negative portrayal of female characters (Hasan, 2000b). In the dramas of this period, female antagonists are shown inciting their men to use unfair means and shortcuts to become rich and powerful (Mumtaz & Shaheed, 1987). This indirectly reinforces the biblical notion that Adam was innocent, and it was Eve who provoked him to eat from the knowledge tree thereby committing sin. The ideology also provides context to another stereotype related to females in which, besides money and land, women are considered major causes of conflict between men. Overall, the content of numerous PTV dramas of phase two depict a typical conventional and conservative representation of females.

PHASE III: DRAMA IN POST-ISLAMIZATION PERIOD AND WOMEN'S EMPOWERMENT

The post-Islamization era witnessed three aspects, (1) a milieu of political change, (2) the inception of cable television, and (3) the beginning of private drama production houses. The general elections of 1989, after an 11 year's long military dictatorship, marked a historical change in the political scenario of the country. Benazir Bhutto was elected as the first female prime minister of Islamic Republic of Pakistan (Bhutto, 2008). The impact of this political change can be observed on every field of life. We see female-friendly media policies in which female artists, writers, and television producers worked in a congenial environment without unnecessary restrictions (like wearing a dupatta or veil) on their physical appearances. A female-headed government had an aura of encouragement and empowerment among women at a grass-roots level. Moreover, a content analysis of television dramas (from 1989 to 1999) depicts a trend of drama stories based on issues of oppressed women. The Urdu drama serials—*Nile Hath* (1989), *Hawa Ki Beti* (1990), *Aahat* (1992), *Marvi* (1993), and *Zard Dopehar* (1993)—thus represent a whole spectrum of Pakistani women.

Hassina Moin, in a serial named *Aahat*, expounds important and delicate complications of family structures in our society. Giving birth to girls is not seen with pride in Pakistani society, whereas the birth of a baby boy is always wished. There is an expectation that a son will help parents in their old age and advance the lineage of his forefathers. One of many reasons for the population explosion in the country is the wish to have a baby boy. The desire persists, despite births of girls, one after the other. This phenomenon impinges on the health of the mother and increases social problems. The practice of bemoaning the birth of a baby girl still persists in the society. This very fact is shown in the play *Aahat*, when the grandmother expressed fretfulness over the birth of the fourth daughter of Rabeea. The drama shows that children were also much affected by extensive discussion over the wish for a baby boy, making the girls feel inferior to boys. This point is well depicted in the girls' talk to their Aunt Nahid:

1st girl: Auntie! Papa didn't have sufficient money; that is why he could not buy a brother.
2nd girl: Auntie! Why is a girl so inexpensive?
   (*Aahat Episode 2* | *Sania Saeed* | *Salman Ahmad* | *Sameena Ahmad* | *Talat Naseer* | *Ahmad Kapadia*, n.d.)

Another social issue that was connected to a debate of a sister's inheritance is represented in the drama serial *Zard Dopehar* (1993). An oppressed female Saira Begum is presented as the victim of patriarchal society in this drama. She is a sister of Malik Mehrban Ali, a powerful and unkind politician of a Punjabi village. He does not allow his sister to marry her university fellow, just to avoid division of his land and eschew her due share in the family property. *Zard Dopehar* is one of those dramas in which forceful women's activism can be seen.

Although the family dramas named *Mandi* and *Uroosa* do not propagate much activism on women's rights, their female protagonists are bold, independent, brave, and self-committed. In the drama serial *Uroosa*, Anjum (Uroosa's mom) is a brave and confident lady. She is an embodiment of self-commitment and high spirits. After her divorce, Anjum becomes a lawyer. Being an intelligent and hardworking woman, Anjum earns prominence in the profession. She makes her profession not only a source of income but also a support to helpless and poor women. Similarly, in the drama serial *Mandi* (1991), Fauzia (a female protagonist) works in her father's office and does not lose self-esteem or social status after her first husband divorces her. Instead, Fauzia recollects her spirit and becomes a lawyer. She leads a successful life as a successful barrister. Besides her regular caseload, she accepts cases from helpless women free of cost and becomes a support resource for them. Also, she successfully manages her son's pursuit of an engineering degree.

In Pakistani male-oriented society, where there are fewer examples of protection of women's rights and fair treatment to them, women are exploited in every arena of life. Even within the bounds of the household, men reign as superior. Women are held responsible for every ill, a practice that brings satisfaction to men's ego. Sometimes women are actually portrayed as responsible for harassing other women. Fatima S. Bajia (writer) depicted the same situation in her telenovela (*Uroosa*), where two unmarried, overaged sisters shatter their brother's smooth married life. In the same telenovela, Bajia also presents a typical Eastern-style drama heroine named *Uroosa*. *Uroosa* is a pretty, middle-class girl with a strong character. She admires traditional garments and cultural decorum. Moreover, *Uroosa* is altogether angelic in nature. She does not want others to be angry or woeful and tries to cheer them up, regardless of her own discomfort.

During phase three dramas, a variety of female occupations is visible. Female characters were cast in the professions like lawyer, journalist, and small entrepreneur, along with doctors, professors, and school teachers. Overall, women were depicted inside as well as outside of domestic confines. Another important aspect of this phase is the easy access to and popularity of international television channels. This was the first time when Pakistani Urdu drama faced international competition. The international television channels brought a huge diversity in television shows that was full of extravaganza, glamour, and special technological effects in the shows. Consequently, Urdu drama series started losing its viewership. To offset this flow of entertainment and information, the Pakistani government allowed private productions of television dramas.

On the political horizon, people observed instability in political governments. Two political parties—the PPP and the Pakistan Muslim League (PML)—were elected, one after the other, but could not complete their five-year term each time. The PPP is considered a left-wing political party, while the PML advocates right-wing ideology. Due to the rapid change of governments, no standard media policy lasted. Thus, this period witnessed confusion between traditionality and enlightenment. During this period, the PTV dramas fluctuated between two ideologies. However, PTV increased the ratio of social communication, and PTV drama accelerated this process by portraying gendered characters according to popular ideology (Parvez, 1998). On the other hand, the primary focus of private drama production houses was attracting more viewers by showing popular stuff. Thus, from the end of 1990s onwards, different aspects of popular culture could be seen in Pakistani television shows.

PHASE IV: PAKISTANI DRAMA SERIALS AND NEW WOMANHOOD

After an eleven-year break, Pakistan witnessed another coup in 1999. General Pervez Musharraf turned over Prime Minister Nawaz Sharif's civil government and ruled over Pakistan for almost nine years (1999–2008). He created the slogan "enlightened moderation," that is reflected in government media policies (Afzal-Khan, 2008). Another difference in his government was the proliferation of Pakistani private television channels in 2002. The majority of them only focused on entertainment programs. Hum TV, Geo Entertainment, ARY Digital, Urdu 1, and Geo Kahani were the main channels that telecast

Urdu dramas. During phase four, a vast production of Urdu drama serials and telenovelas presented a wide range of family dramas focusing on gender issues. The majority of these dramatists were females and prominent digest writers in their early careers. Although stories revolved around family issues and love affairs, drama heroines represented a normative model of "new womanhood" (Dutoya, 2018). A progression in female empowerment occurred throughout this phase. Here, women in dramas mainly belonged to urban, middle-class, traditional families. These heroines were educated, progressive, and independent. At the same time, these women had a strong bond with their culture. Their approach to life is to be considerate and collectivistic, rather than being egotistical.

It could be argued that Dutoya's socially permissible model of the "new woman" is noticeable in the majority of contemporary Urdu dramas. The heterogeneous portrayals of "new womanhood" in Pakistani Urdu television dramas emphasize moral character and women's self-empowerment. In the dramas of this period, women's consistency toward self-empowerment through education, and a respectful attitude toward their own culture's values differentiate them from what they consider to be Western-style radical feminism. These new women appear to balance values of traditional piety and contemporary modernity. An assertion can be made that the Pakistani version of the new woman is a response to Western waves of feminism, religious orthodoxy at home, and cultural conservatism prevalent in Pakistan.

Traces of the new womanhood can be found in the traditional Muslim writings of Urdu literature. Writers like Sir Syed Ahmad Khan and Deputy Nazeer Ahmad (1869) were from the colonial era, after the 1957 war of independence. The Victorian "superwoman" (Hussein, 2018) and colonial Indian idea of a "super wife" (Dutoya, 2018; Walsh & Chatterjee, 2001) can also be considered antecedent, crude forms of the concept of new womanhood. In the post-Islamization period (1988 to date), especially during the last two decades in Pakistan, this normative model of the new woman is apparent in Urdu dramas. This model seems to continue Hassina Moin's progressive, energetic, independent, and loving heroines. The seemingly singularity of this normative model of the new woman is an embodiment of diverse qualities.

For the phase four of this study, 10 leading female characters of contemporary popular drama serials from 2010 to 2019 were examined. These characters are all educated, self-made, and progressive ladies. Out of ten, four characters (Zara, Faarah, Dua, and Zubia) completed their education in medicine, and the rest of six characters (Khirad, Shandana, Kashaf, Farida, Gul, and Sanam) have bachelor's and master's degrees in different fields. These characters are shown to be incredibly committed to achieve their goals. Their efforts to improve their economic status through education provides testament to their progressive attitudes.

The dramas of phase four appear to break the mold of past archetypal, meek, and passive women and present a comparatively liberal, progressive, and independent model. These powerful women have the courage to raise their voices for their rights. These female protagonists appear on screen quietly, but gradually, with their courteous attitude and constant struggle, earn dominating positions in the drama narratives. For example, in the drama serial *Yaqeen Ka Safar* (2017), in spite of a controlling and egoistic father, the female protagonist Zubia empowers herself with professional education and begins her own successful life. All heroines of the corpus reflect respect toward religious ethics and family values. These women establish their individuality through persistent learning and rigorous hard work. Moreover, their bonding to the local culture and religion protects them from alienation in Pakistani society.

CONCLUSION

The popularity of Pakistani dramas within and outside the borders has been a major attraction for political governments to use this genre for social change (Pervez, 1999). Drama producers used social constructs for continuation and representation of male and female gender roles (Hall et al., 1997). The four different phases of Pakistani drama history depict specific gendered images and patterns. During the first phase, besides multiple technical challenges, dramas portray progressive images of women, whereas the phase of "Islamization" (also the second phase) marks gender segregation and oppressed media policies. In this phase, archetypal and traditional assigned roles for women are common, though male characters are showcased in powerful, aggressive, independent, and professional roles.

The post-Islamization period—phase three—brings a wave of women empowerment that is reflected on television with the visibility of diverse women portrayals. In these shows, most of the female protagonists are less conservative and a little less docile. Of note, in the new millennium, the proliferation of Pakistani private television channels and a vast production of Urdu drama serials and telenovelas develop a normative model of the new woman. The new woman does not represent a perceived radical feminism. Rather, she maintains a strong bond to her native culture and religion. In real sense, she maintains respect and love for her culture. The belief that Islam has given more security and rights of women empowerment, as compared to other ideologies, provides the foundation to the new womanhood. Overall, there is a progression in both on- and off-screen female participation in Pakistan's Urdu drama industry.

REFERENCES

Aahat Episode 2 | *Sania Saeed* | *Salman Ahmad* | *Sameena Ahmad* | *Talat Naseer* | *Ahmad Kapadia*. (n.d.). Retrieved March 10, 2020, from https://www.youtube.com/watch?v=vgYfre4JiAE.

Abbas, S. (2010). *A Critical and analytical study of PTV Urdu drama serials (1970-2000)* [Ph.D. Dissertation].

Abbas, S. (2018). Conventional female images, Islamization and its outcomes: A study of Pakistani TV dramas. *Online Journal of Communication and Media Technologies*, 8(2).

Afzal-Khan, F. (2008). What lies beneath: Dispatch from the front lines of the Burqa Brigade. *Social Identities*, 14(1), 3–11. https://doi.org/10.1080/13504630701848408.

Ahmed, M. (1990). *Pakistan Television Kay 25 Saal*. Media Home, P.O.Box 2198.

Atakav, E. (2020). Growing up married [2016]: Representing forced marriage on screen. *Critical Discourse Studies*, 17(2), 229–241. https://doi.org/10.1080/17405904.2019.1665078.

Bhattacharya, S., & Nag, A. (2016). Watching Zindagi: Pakistani social lives on Indian TV. *South Asian Popular Culture*, 14(1–2), 61–72. https://doi.org/10.1080/14746689.2016.1260865.

Bhutto, B. (2008). *Reconciliation: Islam, democracy, and the West* (1st ed). Harper.

Christ, C. P. (2013, February 18). *Patriarchy as a system of male dominance created at the intersection of the control of women, private property, and war, Part 1 by Carol P. Christ*. https://feminismandreligion.com/2013/02/18/patriarchy-as-an-integral-system-of-male-dominance-created-at-the-intersection-of-the-control-of-women-private-property-and-war-part-1-by-carol-p-christ/.

Désoulières, A. (1999). A study of Kamal Ahmad Rizvi's Urdu TV drama Alif Nun. *Annual of Urdu Studies*, 14, 55.

Dutoya, V. (2018). The new heroine? Gender representations in contemporary Pakistani dramas. In N. Hussein (Ed.), *Rethinking new womanhood* (pp. 71–93). Springer International Publishing. https://doi.org/10.1007/978-3-319-67900-6_4.

Hall, S. (ed), Laclau, E., & University, O. (1997). *Representation: Cultural representations and signifying practices*. Sage.

Haqqani, H. (2005). *Pakistan: Between mosque and military*. Carnegie Endowment for Int'l Peace.

Hasan, B. (2000a). *Uncensored: An eyewitness account of abuse of power and media in Pakistan*. Royal Book Company.

Hasan, B. (2000b). *Uncensored: An eyewitness account of abuse of power and media in Pakistan*. Royal Book Company.

Hussein, N. (2018). *Rethinking new womanhood: Practices of gender, class, culture and religion in South Asia*. Springer.

Kothari, S. (2005). From genre to zanaana: Urdu television drama serials and women's culture in Pakistan. *Contemporary South Asia*, 14(3), 289–305. https://doi.org/10.1080/09584930500463719.

Mumtaz, K., & Shaheed, F. (1987). *Women of Pakistan: Two steps forward, one step back?* Zed Books.

Naqvi, S. (2017, August 18). *This is very much Zia's Pakistan, the most influential man after Jinnah.* DAWN.COM. https://www.dawn.com/news/1352139.
Parvez, N. (1998). *Pakistan television drama and social change: A research paradigm.* Department of Mass Communication, University of Karachi.
PEMRA. (2020). *List of satellite TV licences issued by PEMRA.* Pakistan Electronic Media Regulatory Authority (PEMRA). http://www.pemra.gov.pk/.
Rashid, A. (2013). *Pakistan on the brink: The future of America, Pakistan, and Afghanistan.* Penguin.
Raza, A. (2006). Mask of honor—Causes behind honor killings in Pakistan. *Asian Journal of Women's Studies, 12*(2), 88–104. https://doi.org/10.1080/12259276.2006.11666010.
Sadeed, A. (1985). *Urdu Adab Ki Tehreekain (Ibtadae Urdu Se 1957 Tak).* Anjuman Taraqi-e-Urdu Pakistan.
Sang, K. J. C., Richards, J., & Marks, A. (2016). Gender and disability in male-dominated occupations: A social relational model. *Gender, Work & Organization, 23*(6), 566–581. https://doi.org/10.1111/gwao.12143.
Shah, S. M. H., & Panhwar, S. H. (2014). *Bhutto, Zia and Islam.* Shaheed Bhutto Publications, Larkhana.
Signorielli, N. (2004, June). Aging on television: Messages relating to gender, race, and occupation in prime time. *Journal of Broadcasting & Electronic Media, 48*(2), 279–301. Academic OneFile.
Signorielli, N. (2009). Race and sex in prime time: A look at occupations and occupational prestige. *Mass Communication and Society, 12*(3), 332–352. https://doi.org/10.1080/15205430802478693.
Signorielli, N., & Bacue, A. (1999). Recognition and respect: A content analysis of prime-time television characters across three decades. *Sex Roles, 40*(7), 527–544.
Signorielli, N., Morgan, M., & Shanahan, J. (2018). The violence profile: Five decades of Cultural Indicators Research. *Mass Communication and Society, 0*(0), 1–28. https://doi.org/10.1080/15205436.2018.1475011.
The Global Competitiveness Report 2018. (n.d.). World Economic Forum. Retrieved March 27, 2020, from https://www.weforum.org/reports/the-global-competitveness-report-2018/.
Vandello, J., & Cohen, D. (2003). Male honor and female fidelity: Implicit cultural scripts that perpetuate domestic violence. *Journal of Personality and Social Psychology, 84*, 997–1010. https://doi.org/10.1037/0022-3514.84.5.997.
Walsh, J., & Chatterjee, I. (2001). Gender, slavery and law in colonial India. *The American Historical Review, 106*(1), 152. https://doi.org/10.2307/2652254.
Zia, A. S. (2019). Can rescue narratives save lives? Honor killing in Pakistan. *Signs: Journal of Women in Culture and Society, 44*(2), 355–378. https://doi.org/10.1086/699342.

Chapter 7

Primetime Brazilian Telenovelas and Gender Violence Representation

Lorena Caminhas

This chapter investigates the portrayal of gender violence in Brazilian primetime telenovelas, identifying the mechanisms through which these narratives frame aggression against women perpetrated by their lovers, husbands, or relatives. The analysis addresses the representation regime that governs gender violence scenes, seeking to understand how assaults are qualified and characterized within telenovela plots. Key questions guide this study. Are telenovelas trying to expose the brutality of these scenes in a framework of reflection and criticism? Or, are they exposing aggression as everyday events free from questioning? Or, in another sense, are they discerning problematic and unproblematic circumstances of gender violence? May it be asserted that there is a normalization process of gender violence in Brazilian primetime telenovelas? This inquiry starts from the first telenovela that debated domestic violence, *Mulheres Apaixonadas* (*Women in Love*) of 2003, and follows subsequent stories that displayed aggression against women, whether through the lens of spousal abuse or in the storylines of female villains. As a result, five telenovelas aired between 2003 and 2019 were selected, all of which present both forms of gender violence in their plots. From a critical diagnosis of their scenes of violence, this study reveals a dissidence in gender violence representation concerning telenovelas' narrative structuring and story building.

The argument is developed throughout four sections. The first one provides a brief overview of the role of telenovelas in Brazil and reveals their significance in debating and representing urgent national problems. Gender violence discussions are settled in this context, showing how telenovelas have expanded representations of this issue since the 2000s. The second section presents research methods and analytical tools and introduces the five telenovelas under examination. The third section describes and analyzes the scenes of aggression against women, distinguishing violent events that involve protagonists of spousal abuse and female villains. This examination reveals the narrative mechanisms that support unequal representation regimes, distinguishing women who need "care" from women who "deserve" to be beaten. The fourth section systematizes three principal mechanisms through which gender violence is deployed in telenovelas and questions the consequences of a representation regime that normalizes aggression against women.

TELENOVELAS AND GENDER VIOLENCE IN BRAZIL

This research addresses the Brazilian sociocultural context and the role that television and telenovelas play in it. In Brazil, television companies have assumed the function of debating urgent national issues (Hamburger, 2011), presenting themselves as fundamental political actors. According to Boreli (2005), television in general and telenovelas in particular have assumed the role of depicting the nation, and framing and guiding some important social and moral debates. Telenovelas started to approach the country's everyday problems in the 1970s when these fictional narratives became a legitimate space for interpreting Brazilian reality (Hamburger, 2011). Lopes (2009) explains that between 1970 and 1980, telenovelas abandoned "sentimental" narratives prevalent at the beginning of Brazilian television and assumed a "realistic" tone. At that time, "telenovelas became one of the most important spaces for problematizing Brazilian reality, ranging from private intimacy to social problems" (Lopes, 2009, p. 26). In the 1990s, a new narrative format was introduced, known as "naturalist," aiming to amplify plot verisimilitude by adopting "social merchandising" (Lopes, 2010). Social merchandising is a narrative strategy where public debates and political problems are written into a specific plot section or story arc, promoting educational and pedagogical messages.

Considering the socio-legal debate on gender violence in Brazil, television and its fictional narratives have actively provided images and discourse about the issue, accompanying changes in moral perspectives and institutional transformations (Blay, 2003). From the national feminist protests in the 1970s to the institution of the Women's Police Station in 1985 (first public policy to combat violations against women), Brazilian society witnessed the advent and expansion of stories that portrayed and discussed aggression against women (Santos, 2005). The inaugural productions were two miniseries from Rede Globo, the major Brazilian broadcast company. These were *Quem Ama não Mata* (*One Whom Love Doesn't Kill*) in 1982 and *Delegacia de Mulheres* (*Women's Police Station*) in 1990.

During the years 2000 to 2019, there was significant expansion of fictional stories depicting aggression against women, especially in primetime telenovelas. These productions dedicated their plots to portray domestic violence, following the two principal public policies to combat and restrain aggression against females. The National Policies of Prevention, Punishment, and Eradication of Violence Against Women, became Special Secretariat of Policies for Women in 2003. The second policy, known as Maria da Penha Law, Law 11.340/06, was enacted in 2006 (Bandeira, 2014). During a period of 19 years, a total of 13 primetime telenovelas discussing domestic violence were broadcast in Brazil. Two programs came from Rede Record and 11 from Rede Globo. All of them addressed the societal problem of cycles of violence in the stories using social merchandising strategies (Caminhas, 2019).

Despite the optimistic public educational efforts described above, socio-legal developments and telenovelas are part of a context in which gender violence is endemic (Saffioti, 1994). Brazil ranks fifth place in the world regarding violations against women, according to the Human Rights Watch's World Report (2019). As the 2018 Dossier Violence Against Women in Data from the Agência Patrícia Galvão (Patrícia Galvão Agency) shows, there are 13 femicides and 135 rapes every day, and 536 cases of bodily injury per hour in the country. Additionally, a 2014 report about the tolerance of violence against women by the Instituto de Pesquisa Econômica Aplicada (Brazilian Institute for Applied Economic Research) revealed a constant relativization and normalization of this kind of assault. More than half of respondents (58%) agree that "if women knew how to behave there would be fewer rapes" (p. 3) and 89% believe that marital problems should be solved at home (*a roupa suja deve ser lavada em casa*, p. 3).

In this context, it is not surprising that telenovelas have replicated these contradictions regarding the treatment of gender violence in Brazil, constructing narratives that show, at the same time, images of domestic violations and corrective flogging scenes (principally when women are the villains). Abandoning the social merchandising veil, from 2000 to 2019 there were seven primetime telenovelas displaying villainous women being beaten and threatened by their lovers, husbands, and fathers, presenting these violations as necessary and pedagogic punishment (Caminhas, 2018, 2019). Furthermore, in seven out of 11 telenovelas that addressed domestic violence in an educational tone, there are scenes of gender violence against villains.

RESEARCH METHODOLOGY AND ANALYTICAL CORPUS

This research follows a socio-anthropological approach (Rothenbuhler & Coman, 2005), considering the representation process that builds social imagery and imaginaries. To Rothenbuhler and Coman, this approach demands a reflexive approach to media, which is possible through accurate and careful observations that allow apprehending the components of media frameworks and representations. Considering specifically television melodramas, Abu-Lughod (2006) proposes applying ethnographic "thick description" to the analysis of fictional narratives of television. In this sense, it is necessary to develop thick description of melodramatic narratives and discourses, considering the sociocultural context in which they circulate. This methodological strategy produces a meticulous and detailed analysis of the narrative mechanisms that represent gender violence in primetime telenovelas.

To operationalize the analysis, this chapter works with the idea of narrative as discussed by Ricoeur (1980), considering intrigues as the story reference point, responsible for governing the succession of events. The development of the plot depends on intrigue guidelines and temporal organization that coordinate acts, thoughts, and feelings of characters. Intrigue is, therefore, a means to recognize the world proposed in the plot (Ricoeur, 1979). This chapter analyzes telenovela plots, considering its events and relations, and also its characters and their roles. Additionally, the chapter apprehends the moralities within the telenovelas that allow or deny the recognition of gender violence.

This study observed the specific storylines that deploy gender violence, examining two main elements of their narrative structures—these are content and form. Based on the content, the author identified a profile of characters, the context of violent relationships, and the consequences of violations against women. Based on the form, the author detected the organization and structuring of gender violence scenes, arranging in specific moments of the plot.

The analytical *corpus* sums five Brazilian primetime telenovelas aired between 2003 and 2019, which deployed gender violence in their plots. This compilation considers most important stories that employed social merchandising (public education appeals), reserving a particular storyline to present domestic violence, and also displayed the female villain constantly being assaulted by men in a context of discipline and punishment.

All telenovelas are from Rede Globo, the largest and most known broadcast company in Brazil: *Mulheres Apaixonadas* (*Women in Love*, 2003), *Fina Estampa* (*Looks & Essence*, 2011), *Amor à Vida* (*Trail of Lies*, 2013), *A Regra do Jogo* (*Rules of The Game*, 2015), and *O Outro Lado do Paraíso* (*The Other Side of Paradise*, 2017). Of note, the Rede Record television network aired two telenovelas discussing domestic violence: *Vidas Opostas* (*Opposite Lives*, 2006) and *Vidas em Jogo* (*Lives at Stake*, 2011), which also displayed villains being assaulted by men. However, these stories centralized the violence between women, unlike the other plots that compose the *corpus*.

PARADIGMS OF GENDER VIOLENCE REPRESENTATION

Brazilian telenovelas build their stories based on melodrama, a narrative genre that centralizes personal and familial relationships and intrigues (Lopes, 2010). Despite deep transformations in telenovela melodramatic structures since the 1970s, which assumed a "naturalistic" tone and adopted social merchandising to discuss societal problems, melodrama is still the core framework of those stories (Boreli, 2005).

Livingstone (1995) and Ang (1985) define melodrama as a combination of sociopolitical issues and interpersonal relations, in which contemporary debates are presented through intimate relations. Accordingly, melodramatic stories must combine emotions and events, building a narrated social world that dialogues with the viewers. Three main elements compose melodrama structure: a central story that moves forward the narrative; simultaneous storylines with a particular set of characters and dramas; and the arrangement of characters by roles and positions that define their moral reputation and behavior (Almeida, 2007).

Gender violence is represented and interpreted through the melodramatic narrative structure. Therefore, this phenomenon is presented within intimate and affective relationships, in which every person has a function and specific behavior. Its stories are located inside a cause-and-effect plot that determines in advance the faith of characters. Moreover, aggression against women is displayed in a particular story arc that has precise functions in the plot. All these elements cooperate with the unequal treatment of certain forms of gender violence, which appear in the story as an educational effort and a necessary moral lesson.

In 2003, Rede Globo aired *Mulheres Apaixonadas*, the first primetime *telenovela* to discuss domestic violence. This narrative tells the story of Raquel (Helena Ranaldi), a physical education teacher that moves to São Paulo to escape her violent husband, Marcos (Dan Stulbach). In episode 55, the viewer knows Marcos, a violent and controlling man who does not admit losing his wife. At this moment, the relationship between Marcos and Raquel becomes clear. This is an abusive marriage that Marcos wants to maintain and Raquel desires to abandon. Their personalities matter in this context. Raquel is a dedicated teacher and sweet woman who has good relationships with people. Marcos is impulsive, aggressive, and reveals traces of madness.

As the plot progresses, the viewer can notice a hostile and tense atmosphere that permeates the couple's home. The narrative shows Marcos pulling, pushing, slapping, and flogging Raquel several times. In episode 57, Marcos rapes his wife. Domestic violence reaches its apex when Marcos's abuses against Raquel are explicitly depicted, showing the complete chain of actions. Episode 135 presents this moment, revealing how Marcos uses a tennis racquet to spank his wife. At the end of the scene, badly injured Raquel is lying in bed in shock. In the next episode, Raquel decides to report her husband to the Women's Police Station, going through a process that begins with a formal complaint and ends with a forensic examination. The scenes that display violence apex expose the injustice and unfairness of Marcos's offenses. They establish the framework to interpret Raquel's story as a routine of abuses that demands legal mechanisms to end violence.

In 2012, *Fina Estampa* tells the story of Celeste (Dira Paes), a woman who gave up a teaching career to marry Baltazar (Alexandre Nero). While Celeste is at home taking care of their teenage daughter Solange (Carol Macedo), Baltazar works as a driver for Tereza Cristina (Cristiane Torloni). During several episodes, Baltazar beats and strangles his wife near death, revealing daily violence. Celeste, similar to Raquel, is always passive and accepts her husband's aggressive behavior in order to maintain the marriage. In episode 56, Baltazar continues to abuse Celeste by spanking, slapping, punching, and throwing her on the floor. At the end of the scene, the woman is full of bruises, lying in Solange's arms. In episode 57, Celeste decides to report her husband to the police, and he is arrested. Once again, legal mechanisms appear as a way out of domestic violence, a crime that demands the offender prison. However, Baltazar leaves prison the same day and returns home. Only in episode 179 is he definitively expelled from home, ending the violence cycle. In this telenovela, divorce is another solution to the violence, responsible for distancing the aggressor from his victim.

In both narratives, there is a pattern in the portrayal of domestic violence. The aggressive scenes are recurrent, revealing a routine of assaults and reinforcing its daily presence. While modalities of violence seen as less serious appear more frequently in the plot, such as pushing, pulling, and minor threats, extreme abuses emerge only in particular episodes, exposing severe beatings, rapes, flogging, and public humiliation. In the episodes of extreme violence, the viewer follows the climax of violent relationships, seeing the result of attacks on women's bodies. Women are physically harmed and experience mental depression. The men are represented as bad tempered, addicted to alcohol, or emotionally psychotic. They beat women because of jealousy or to control the relationship, even if such actions do not further the plot. In the stories, men's behaviors do not change, and the solution to violence is the divorce or police report. The female characters, in turn, are respectable members of the community, virtuous professionals and wives, and are unable to betray their husbands. They do not react early on to repeated violence and take a long time to file police reports. They withstand violence throughout the narrative and only react when assaults become more severe, demonstrating the domestic violence cycle that ends in a formal complaint.

Following the same plot structure discussed above, *A Regra do Jogo* tells the story of Domingas (Maeve Jinkings), an honest and generous woman, married to the perverse Juca (Osvaldo Mil). The couple lives in Morro da Macaca, a periphery location where everyone knows and helps each other. Domingas is responsible for the management of their home and financial sustenance, constantly working to support her husband's whims. Since the beginning of the narrative, we see Juca trying to take advantage of Domingas, asking for money or ordering meals, persistently humiliating her. The woman never reacts to the violence, not even to the daily menaces. She continues being a good wife, attending to her husband's desires. Like Raquel and Celeste, Domingas avoids discussing her experience with domestic violence to other people, trying to conceal the harsh relationship.

Domingas is always frighted and anxiety-ridden as a result of the daily aggressions. In episode 54, Juca has fits of jealousy, spanks his wife and slaps her in the face, calling her a bitch. He was suspicious about a lover who did not exist. In episode 76, Domingas faces severe violence. She is ill and resting at home when Juca arrives with his mistress. Trying to escape her husband, Domingas hides in the bathroom. However, this does not contain Juca, who breaks furniture and threatens to kill Domingas. The situation is pacified by neighbors who take Juca from the home. Domingas threatens to report him, citing the Maria da Penha Law. In this narrative, unlike the others, the female character does not seek institutional or police help, and the aggressor is not arrested. The violence ends after the divorce when Domingas expels Juca from home.

Amor à Vida is subtly different from the other narratives. This telenovela tells the story of Marilda (Renata Barbosa), a nutritionist in San Magno Hospital who constantly appears with face and neck bruises. When her coworkers ask about the injuries, she says that they were caused by a domestic accident. No one in the telenovela knows Marilda's partner, but everyone suspects she suffers domestic violence. In the middle of the narrative, the viewer discovers that Marilda is assaulted by Ivan (Adriano Toloza), a nurse at San Magno Hospital. Afraid of losing the relationship with Ivan, Marilda avoids reporting the aggressive behavior. This plot presents the ritualized violence only once, in episode 214. In the scene, Ivan argues with Marilda, blaming her for the end of their relationship. He interrogates her about the door lock change, demanding his house and belongings back. The nutritionist, in a fury, affirms that she is not a "punching bag" and does not support his presence in her life anymore. In a fit of anger, Ivan pushes Marilda against the wall, slaps her face, and throws her against the floor. Immediately, he is arrested under the Maria da Penha Law.

Although the telenovela does not present the routine of violence as the other narratives do, the bruises and injuries function as signals of repeated beatings.

Unlike the other plots, *Amor à Vida* does not reveal who the aggressor is at the beginning. Instead, viewers must wait for Ivan to be exposed in a scene of severe aggression. This is also a story about a man who beats a woman with whom he has an intimate relationship. The association of violence with men's behavior is another common point. In all cases of aggression, a mental, behavioral, or moral factor is emphasized. Similarly, as in other telenovelas, the assaults function as controlling the marriage or wife, preventing her from ending the relationship and finding another partner.

In *O Outro Lado do Paraíso*, Gael (Sérgio Guizé) beats his wife Clara (Bianca Bin) starting from the initial episodes. Employing a similar narrative structure of other telenovelas, this story displays various occasions in which Gael beats and humiliates Clara, revealing the physical and emotional results of the violence. On the couple's wedding night (episode two), Gael rapes Clara. He rips her dress, strangles and suffocates her near death. After this experience, Clara remains terrified, constantly suffering from Gael's hostilities and threats. Episode 6 shows Gael slapping Clara, dragging her by her hair and pushing her against the stairs. This time Clara needed medical care of her serious injuries. In episode 16, Gael spanks Clara and breaks a chair on her legs. In the sequence, Clara discovers she is pregnant, increasing the seriousness of the situation. Similarly to the other women of domestic violence storylines, Clara does not report her aggressor to the authorities. Only in episode 27, when Clara and Gael are divorced, is he arrested and forced to rethink his nefarious behavior.

In the five domestic violence storylines, aggression against women is constant and routinized, and the male's motivations are ignominious and unjustified. This dynamic points to violent relationships, in which assaults are daily based. The cycle of violence, repeated and ritualized in the scenes, reaffirms the abuse and injustice of these events. In this sense, the telenovela narratives present extreme and unjustifiable cases of violent behavior, those that are clearly interpreted as crimes in Brazil (Segato, 2003). In all the plots, the aggressor is jealous, disturbed, an alcoholic, or psychotic, beating his wife for pleasure or perversion. The victim is invariably gentle, respectful, and truthful, withstanding humiliation. This dichotomy between a victim and oppressor implies an unequal and unbalanced relationship, in which a man expresses his aggressiveness against a vulnerable other. Consequently, the narrative construction is based on the dissidence between the causes and effects of men's actions, revealing that their behavior is incorrect, reprehensible, and illegal. The content and format of the plot support an ideal type of domestic violence, which fits in the narrative morality.

The construction of violent scenes in telenovelas replicates two elements of the contextual organization of gender violence in Brazil. First, it alludes to the ritualization of aggression, which is a typical frame to explain domestic violence (Gregori, 1989). The continuous and pervasive aspects of the assaults typify them as very abusive and harmful. As Segato (2003) shows, the differences between the defense of honor and committing a crime are enacted in the situations of continuous violent aggression. Second, these scenes reinforce a paradigmatic model of violence, which is the conjugal relationship where a virtuous woman is mistreated and subjugated by an evil man (Gregori, 2016). By concatenating these two interpretative frames, the telenovelas build an imaginary of domestic violence that resembles the daily narratives in Brazil about abused women, thus confirming the brutalities and atrocities depicted in the program.

Domestic violence storylines emphasize regularities of aggressive behavior, injustices of recurrent assault, the adequacy of women to the moral standards of the telenovela, and the corrupted morality of husbands who beat without reasons. Female villain intrigues depict the opposite situation. In those plots, the viewer sees bad women being beaten whenever "needed," especially when it is "necessary" against their vile tendencies. Accordingly, violent aggressions are presented as episodic and justified. In this sense, it is possible to understand villain narratives as an example of what Moore (1994) calls the non-fulfillment of gender fantasies of identity and power. The violent acts within gender relations are attached to the frustration in performing a social role consonant with the hegemonic norms of gender. The assorted forms of physical, moral, and psychological injuries are grounded in and justified by specific male and female positions (Merry, 2009) that are reestablished in episodes of aggression or punishment against villains.

In *Mulheres Apaixonadas*, Dóris (Regiane Alves) is often beaten by her father. In the narrative, she is portrayed as an ungrateful daughter who humiliates her parents and grandparents, and is a gold digger in constant search for luxury. She is willing to do anything for money, even dating rich men in exchange for expensive gifts. Her father is tired of seeing her immoral attitudes and decides to apply educational punishments, like public humiliation and beatings. In episode 41, the father locks the girl in her bedroom and beats her with a belt. After that, he throws Dóris against the floor and humiliates her. These kinds of scenes are repeated through the plot, showing the father's efforts to change his daughter's behavior. At the end of the telenovela, he is exhausted by Dóris's antics and decides to "repair" her with brutal violence. He goes to a hotel room where Dóris is with a lover. While there, he slaps her face violently and spanks her until her dress tears. He goes to the lobby choke holding his daughter and humiliates her in front of all the guests. After this, the villain redeems herself by changing her life.

The villain of *Fina Estampa* is Zuleika (Juliana Knust), an unscrupulous and ambitious woman who falls in love with the corrupt Rafael (Marco

Pigossi). Both work at *Fashion Motos*, a motorcycle dealership. At the beginning of the narrative, Rafael forges robberies in the dealership to earn extra money by selling stolen motorbike parts. Zuleika discovers Rafael's plans and imposes a date in exchange for silence. Tired of being blackmailed by Zuleika, Rafael decides to change his life and stops stealing from the dealership. He abandons Zuleika and starts a relationship with Amália (Sophie Charlotte). In the meantime, Zuleika becomes resentful and dangerous. In episode 103, Rafael fights with Zuleika, slapping and throwing her on the floor. That was only one situation in which Rafael was violent with Zuleika. However, that was the first time Rafael is presented as applying justifiable physical violence. The plot shows Rafael beating her in a moment of impatience and anger because she "provoked" him. Rafael accuses Zuleika of provoking him and creating lies to harm him. In this telenovela, Zuleika's guilt is reinforced, showing that "provoking" violence is part of her plan to ruin Rafael's life. Like Dóris, Zuleika is held responsible for the violence, insofar as she "provoked" and "incited" men's violent behavior.

In *Amor à Vida*, two villains are attacked. The first one is Aline (Vanessa Giácomo), who wants to get revenge on the physician César (Antônio Fagundes). She plans to get a position as César's secretary at San Magno Hospital and become his mistress. Immediately César falls in love with her and abandons his family. After they get married, Aline starts poisoning César. While César falls ill, Aline maintains a secret relationship with Ninho (Juliano Cazarré), who helps her with a revenge scheme against César. In episode 216, in the final moments of the telenovela, César discovers Aline's plans and decides to kill her. He takes a knife and tries to cut her neck, but he does not succeed because of the blindness. Nevertheless, César tears off Aline's clothes, beats, and spanks her.

The second villain is Leila (Fernanda Machado), an ambitious and selfish woman. She humiliates her parents and siblings and plans financial scams. Leila dates Thales (Ricardo Tozzi), an unscrupulous and corrupt man who helps her in planning fraud. In episode 32, Thales beats her for the first time. Leila was planning to steal the fortune of a sick girl with Thales's help. Leila wanted Thales to marry the ill girl and inherit her fortune after her death. In a fit of anger, Thales accuses Leila of fraud and slaps her face aggressively. He humiliates and threatens to abandon her. After this episode, Thales beats and pushes Leila, threatening her every time he believes she might "cross the line." In episode 71, Leila's brother Daniel (Rodrigo Andrade) discovers the villain's plans and decides to educate her. Furious and annoyed with the situation, Daniel argues with his sister and demands some explanation. In a moment of anger and impatience, Daniel slaps Leila's face and throws her against the floor. While he beats her, he affirms that Leila "needs" this kind of warning and reprimand from him.

The villain from *A Regra Do Jogo* is Atena (Giovanna Antonelli), a woman who is always seeking rich friends and lovers to live a luxurious life. She is a swindler, expending her time deluding and deceiving the other characters of the telenovela. Atena starts to date Romero (Alexandre Nero), the commandant of a criminal group. Together they plan a financial coup in the criminal group, but Atena changes her mind and decides to blackmail Romero for money. Seeing himself in a trap, Romero plans an ambush to Atena, locking her in an industrial shed where he can humiliate and beat her (episode 128). He threatens to punch and kill her but realizes this is not the best idea. In episode 132, Romero abandons Atena in her ex-husband's house. Vander (Roney Villela) ties her with ropes and chains her around the neck, preventing her from obtaining food. He tortures her for days, recalling the time they were married. Atena attempts an unsuccessful escape. All these situations were inserted into the plot as justifiable punishments for Atena's evil actions.

In *O Outro Lado do Paraiso*, the villain is Sophia (Marieta Severo), a rich and ambitious woman. She is the mother of Gael, the man who beats his wife in a domestic violence storyline. The central objective of Sophia is to command an emerald deposit in Clara's farm. Because of this, she encourages the marriage of Gael and Clara and, later, prompts their divorce. In episode 63, Gael argues with his mother, blaming her for his terrible upbringing. In the scene, he is tired and irritated, threatening to beat or kill his mother Sophia. According to him, she is responsible for his bad temper and aggressiveness and also for his divorce with Clara. To Gael, Sophia benefited from his conflicts with Clara. Tired of being accused, Sophia confesses that she manipulated Gael and instigated him to beat Clara. At this moment, Gael grabs his mother, strangles and suffocates her, and throws her off the stairs. After this, intimidations and coercions from Gael are common, until the moment Sophia is found out and arrested.

Contrary to the women in domestic violence storylines, villains suffer aggressions at specific moments, especially when their plans and scams are revealed. Violence is a means of retaliating against and correcting women's behavior, working contrary to the ritualization logic present in the plots about domestic violence. The violent scenes are, at the same time, scarce and more severe. Also, these scenes have a well-demarcated space in the narrative; in a moment between the gains and losses of villains. In sum, violence appears in moments of punishment and education of "bad" women. The aggressor is, generally, a man with an intimate relationship with a villainous husband, lover, or relative. However, the man does not assume the role of persecutor or oppressor; instead, he is seen as a moral actor that reasserts the morality of the narrative. The beatings are an instrument to correct promiscuity, transgression, and misconduct. Moreover, it is worth noting that in these stories only women need domestication and education, never men.

Considering the regimes of representation analyzed above, violence against women in telenovelas is based on a "mystification of the feminine" (Moore, 1994), which supports ideals of docility, resignation, and submission. These ideals are parameters to classify good and bad women and define the fairness and unfairness of the aggressions, discerning true crimes from justified occurrences. Additionally, another critical factor reinforces the circumstantial explanation of aggression against women. In specific situations, the plot suggests the woman herself causes the situation of violence, urging men to retaliate. This happens in moments when she behaves immorally or beats her partner first. Nevertheless, this is only in the villains' storylines.

In the villain's case, in which there is a relativization of suffering, violence is interpreted as a disciplinary and educational act, justified as a way of domesticating insubordinate women (Moore, 1994). It should be noted that aggressions have a normative function in the plots, namely, to establish gender norms and hierarchies. Therefore, the villain narratives can be seen as representations of violence as a necessary means to maintain the balance between male and female roles (Gregori, 2016). Contrary to the domestic violence storylines, in which women are docile and submissive, the villains disrupt the division of power in gender relations, causing the fury of male characters around them. When "bad" women challenge the asymmetries between gender roles, violence assumes two main functions, according to Segato (2003). First, it acts as punishment and reprehension on the individual level. Second, it is a means for maintaining the social order established by the telenovelas.

CONCLUSION

Three main narrative elements support the disparity in the representation of gender violence in the Brazilian telenovelas under analysis. First, the telenovelas establish a difference between occasional and regular violence. Within the domestic violence storylines, aggressions are the result of violent relationships, in which women are constantly suffering. On the other hand, in the villain stories, violence is occasional and only occurs when "necessary" to contain women's vile behavior. In the first case, the scenes of violence are continuous, while in the second case, they are scarce and situational. Second, there is a fundamental difference between the women of the two storylines. On one side, some women fit gender norms and moral standards of the telenovela. They are good mothers and wives, respectable and submissive. On the other side, women are promiscuous and unscrupulous. They establish dubious relationships, deceiving and betraying everyone around them. The distinctions of conduct and character discern unjustified violence (when conduct and personality do not presume adjustment) and "necessary" punishment (when behavior and character need discipline). Third, the narrative typifies different situations of aggression against women, divided into needless and extreme cases and occasional and necessary events. In fact, this division depends on the moral order of the telenovela, which regulates the compass or mismatch between the cause and effect of the violence. These three elements together engender discordant images of gender violence in Brazilian telenovelas.

The unequal representation of aggression against women must be considered in conjunction with the importance of telenovelas in Brazilian society. Telenovelas assume the symbolic and moral role of discussing the country's public problems, presenting images and meaning that become part of the Brazilians' repertoire (Hamburger, 2011). In this sense, telenovelas build up "proposed worlds" (Ricoeur, 1979), being essential elements in constructing social reality. They also act as "technologies of gender" (De Lauretis, 1987), responsible for building hegemonic discourses on gender identity, establishing normative possibilities to inhabit a gender. The visibility and invisibility regimes of telenovelas have moral and ethical consequences (Silverstone, 2007). In the case of gender violence, these regimes are perverse, supporting discordant images of suffering. The first problem to be considered is the flexibility of the representation of gender violence in primetime telenovelas, which deploys these violations as contingent and circumstantial occurrences. The second problem is the categorization of women by their temperament and attitudes, defining victims as only those fitted to the moral standards of the narrative. Immoral women, instead of being victims, are seen as the principal causes of aggression. The narrative content and structure build a world in which it is possible, and even necessary, to distinguish violence from "necessary punishment." On the one hand, telenovelas educate about domestic violence, representing it as a public problem. Given the prevalence of violence against women globally and in Brazil, it is necessary to create and enforce policies that protect females. On the other hand, telenovelas also hold the potential to reinforce an array of violence against and shaming of women. Representations of gender violence send a message that authorizes aggression against women, when women are depicted as ignoring or violating gender moralities, such as being a provocateur, overly ambitious, greedy, and villainous.

REFERENCES

Abu-Lughod, L. (2006). *Local contexts of Islam in popular media*. Chicago University Press.

Agência Patrícia Galvão. (2018). *Violência contra as mulheres em dados.* https://dossies.agenciapatriciagalvao.org.br/violencia-em-dados/.

Almeida, H. (2007). Consumidoras e heroínas: Gênero na telenovela. *Estudos Feministas, 15*(1), 177–192. http://dx.doi.org/10.1590/S0104-026X2007000100011.

Ang, I. (1985). *Watching Dallas: Soap opera and melodramatic imagination.* Methuen.

Bandeira, L. (2014). Violência de gênero: A construção de um campo teórico e de investigação. *Revista Sociedade e Estado, 2*(29), 449–469.

Blay, E. (2003). Violência contra a mulher e políticas públicas. *Estudos Avançados, 49*(17), 87–98.

Boreli, S. (2005). Telenovelas brasileñas: Producción, flexibilidad narrativa, recepción. *Revista Latinoamericana de Ciencias de la Comunicación, 3*(1), 106–117.

Caminhas, L. (2018). Face e contraface da violência de gênero: Diálogos entre telenovela e contexto nacional. *Revista Mana, 24*(3), 33–62. http://dx.doi.org/10.1590/1678-49442018v24n3p033.

Caminhas, L. (2019). Imagens da violencia de gênero em telenovelas brasileiras. *Estudos Feministas, 27*(1), 1–11. http://dx.doi.org/10.1590/1806-9584-2019v27n152253.

De Lauretis, T. (1987). *Technologies of Gender: Essays on Theory, Film, and Fiction.* Indiana University Press.

Gregori, M. (1989). Cenas e queixas: Mulheres e relações violentas. *Novos Estudos CEBRAP,* (23), 163–175.

Gregori, M. (2016). Violence and gender: Political paradoxes, conceptual shifts. *Vibrant, 7*(2), 216–235.

Hamburger, E. (2007). A expansão do "feminino" no espaço público brasileiro: Novelas de televisão nas décadas de 1970 e 80. *Estudos Feministas, 15*(1), 153–175. https://doi.org/10.1590/S0104-026X2007000100010.

Hamburger, E. (2011). Telenovelas e interpretação do Brasil. *Lua Nova, 82*(1), 61–86.

Human Rights Watch. (2019, September 17). *World Report 2019.* https://www.hrw.org/sites/default/files/world_report_download/hrw_world_report_2019.pdf.

Instituto de Pesquisa Econômica Aplicada. (2014, Abril 4). *Tolerância social da violência contra as mulheres.* http://ipea.gov.br/portal/images/stories/PDFs/SIPS/140327_sips_violencia_mulheres.pdf.

Livingstone, S. (1995). Where have all the mothers gone? Soap opera's replaying of the oedipal story. *Critical Studies in Media Communication, 12*(2), 155–175. https://doi.org/10.1080/15295039509366929.

Lopes, M. (2009). Telenovela como recurso comunicativo. *Matrizes, 1*(3), 21–47.

Lopes, M. (2010). Ficção televisiva e identidade cultural da nação. *Alceu, 10*(20), 5–15.

Merry, S. E. (2009). *Gender violence: A cultural perspective.* John Wiley and Sons.

Moore, H. (1994). *A passion for difference: Essays in Anthropology and Gender.* Indianapolis University Press.

Rothenbuhler, E & Coman, M. (2005). The promise of media anthropology. In E. Rothenbuhler & M. Coman (Eds.), *Media anthropology* (pp. 1–12). Sage.

Ricoeur, P. (1979). The function of fiction in shaping reality. *Man and World*, (12), 123–141. https://doi.org/10.1007/BF01252461.
Ricoeur, P. (1980). Narrative time. *Critical Inquiry*, 7(1), 169–190.
Saffioti, H. (1994). A violência de gênero no Brasil atual. *Estudos Feministas*, (2), 443–461. https://doi.org/10.1590/%25x.
Santos, C. M. (2005). *Women's police station: Gender, violence and justice in São Paulo, Brazil*. Palgrave McMillian.
Segato, R. (2003). *Las estructuras elementales de la violencia*. Prensa de la Universidad Nacional de Quilmes.
Silverstone, R. (2007). *Media and morality: On the rise of mediapolis*. Polity Press.

Chapter 8

French Television and the Audience

Examining Serial Dramas Un Si Grand Soleil *and* Plus Belle La Vie

Patricia Jullia and Frédéric Marty

In France, it was not until 2004 that the public service media *France Télévisions* launched *Plus Belle La Vie* (PBLV; France 3), followed by *Un Si Grand Soleil* (USGS; France 2) in 2018 (translating to English as *A Very Beautiful Life* and *A Great Sun Ahead*, respectively). These daily shows are very popular among viewers. Compared to its European neighbors, France's production of daily television drama series began relatively late. The Independent Television network (ITV) introduced *Coronation Street* in 1960, and the British Broadcasting Corporation (BBC) debuted *East Enders* in 1985. Of note, the French programs were part of a strategy promoting the social good, an uncommon approach for global soap operas, telenovelas, and drama serials. For example, marking the 15th anniversary of PBLV, France Télévisions declared a plan of ideals for the organization and its productions, "its humanist and civic vision, a reflection of an open and multiple society, [which] combines proximity and modernity around the values of tolerance, solidarity and sharing, valuable for public service" (FTV, 2019a).

Programs are also shaped by production constraints and audience reception, especially in distinct cultural contexts. While daily television programs have been examined in media literature relative to national cultural regions, and based on their international circulation, the French case has received sparse attention. This research focuses on the French cultural space, where television shows strive to shift away from common Anglo-Saxon formats (e.g., British, US) to establish a unique style. Favard discusses aspects of French television programming development, "Shaped by the American cultural industry, they have shifted from an exportation approach to appropriation, and now offer a rich and diverse international panorama" (Favard, 2018, p. 15).

Before presenting our analysis, this chapter will discuss audience reception, understood as how viewers perceive the series. Of note, the authors of this chapter are seasoned media professionals as well as academics, thereby affording informed viewpoints and analysis. Before presenting field insights, interview material, and audience observations, it is necessary to highlight the different dimensions of the series. Indeed, this will provide a much broader meaning, with the objective to link content (characters, places, and stories) and strategies (audience's engagement with social issues) which are involved in the formation of what Maigret and Macé (2005) refer to as "mediacultures."

Our objective is to decipher how the French public service media addresses social issues through these two series. We will pay particular attention to gender, diversity, and discrimination issues. First, we will present the two series analyzed, and then we will analyze them as belonging to the cultural industry and "social world". (Cefaï, 2015). We will then assess the "reality effects" (Glévarec, 2010) that PBLV and USGS convey.

FROM MARSEILLE TO MONTPELLIER: FRANCE REPRESENTED IN TWO DRAMAS

PBLV and USGS are ensemble shows with a penchant for continuous drama. While they are inspired by soap opera codes (Allen, 1985), they propose some variations (Boudon, 2017). The broadcasts take on a narrative temporality, in "real-time imitation." For example, the Monday episode takes place on a Monday. Political or cultural news may be mentioned, allowing the series to be more in tune with viewership reality. Both series are broadcast during prime time, at 8:20 p.m. for PBLV (26 minutes) and 8:45 p.m. for USGS (22 minutes). The broadcasting of PBLV was advanced to avoid pitting the two series against each other and to allow viewers to watch them both, one after the other. These two series bring together more than three million spectators daily and capture approximately 15% audience share each. Moreover, the audience is extended because of nonlinear programming and the availability of content across media platforms. Audiences can get more out of their favorite shows through digital social networks such as Twitter, Facebook, YouTube, Instagram, and special online or primetime programs, podcasts, dedicated magazines, and the sale of "tie-in" products.

With regard to PBLV, this translated into approximately 430,000 replays on average per episode (+ 11% live views) in 2017 and 240,000 for USGS in 2018. Based on cumulative audience figures, these are the two programs produced by *France Télévisions* which are watched most often in replay. In addition, in 2018 PBLV was also the program most often purchased via the transactional video on demand media distribution system (CNC, 2018a). It is the most-watched program, both live and in replay, and catch-up fans spend half their viewing time on replays (Médiamat, 2019).

While these two series initially targeted an intergenerational audience, the average age of the viewers of both programs is relatively high, that is, 55 years for PBLV and 62 years for USGS (Le Plateau Télé, 2019). Nevertheless, PBLV's audience is almost 10 years younger than audiences of other programs on the channel. The objective of these two series is to rejuvenate the audience by using intrigues that concern them and increasing transmedia narratives (see Jenkins, 2006, for transmedia and convergence) in particular. Similarly, nonlinear program broadcasting attests to a younger, more active, and familial audience. Lastly, its weekly coverage varies. For instance, from October 14 to 18, 2019, 5.8 million people saw at least one episode of USGS and 1.4 million saw them all (FTV Production, 2019). This may be explained by the nature of these series, that is, ensemble shows, where multiple and varied narrative arcs are used. The broadcast is extended by recurring primetime broadcasts, more than 20 for PBLV. Moreover, the world of these series is displayed across social networks through content promoting episodes (summaries, "best-of," voluntary spoilers, etc.) or additional content (dedicated web series, augmented reality game, vlog or video log, quarterly magazines, and bimonthly podcasts).

These two series have similar narrative styles. The narrative presents the lives of social groups, often families, who face contemporary dilemmas and world challenges. In particular, these programs seek to embody the diversity of French society, which is better represented in the series than in television news stories (CSA, 2019). To this end, they avoid classic stereotypes linked to towns and cultures in the south of France. The programs do this by avoiding localized accents and customs and making few references to local news. *France Télévisions* describes overall narratives and characters from PBLV and USGS on their website:

> Summary of PBLV: "Since its emergence, fifteen years ago, the soap opera has kept its promise of entertainment and emotions, combining suspense, romance and comedy. It is an authentic story, which can be baffling from time to time, and one that is insightful and without taboos. A space that brings us together in the face of everyday life, in a daily and multicultural social reality which is open and diversified, and which helps shape the identity of the soap opera, thus ensuring its uniqueness" (FTV, 2019a).

> Summary of USGS: "Multiple characters with new destinies in a contemporary Montpellier pass through Un Si Grand Soleil. The Bastide, Estrela, Berville, Alami, Levy and Real families, and many others, are intensely involved in the present. Between romance and thriller, comedy and social issues, emotions lie at the heart of this daily encounter" (FTV, 2019b).

Both series relate to social facts, and in order to analyze them, we will use the notion of the social world and the work at this regional level of the production.

THE SERIES AS PART OF THE CULTURAL INDUSTRY, REFLECTING SOCIAL WORLDS

These series are part of cultural industries which allow us to reflect collectively on the economic, political, and social dimensions of audiovisual cultural productions (Bryon-Portet, 2011). Each episode of USGS costs €100,000 (or about 110,000 US dollars). This is approximately €41 million per season, and involves major economic stakes (approximately €140,000 per episode for PBLV). We believe, however, that special attention must be paid to the popular culture and the social worlds these series convey, and to how they relate to the construction of public opinion on social issues. These series construct representations of society and society's issues while maintaining an industrialized production.

UN SI GRAND SOLEIL: AN INDUSTRIAL, DELOCALIZED AND MASS-PRODUCED SERIES

USGS is produced in a quasi-industrial manner. Anglo-Saxon models of mass-produced series are clearly present in this planned organization of filming (FTV, 2019b)—referring to a collective writing, an industrialized production and a worldwide or massive audience. Approximately 200 people produce a 22-minute episode in 3 days. Three film crews, one in the studio and two outdoors, operate throughout the year. The filming studios are located in a metroplex area called *Montpellier Méditerranée Métropole* (Montpellier 3M). They are in the city of Vendargues. Two studios with a square footage of 1,250 m^2 each make it possible to produce an average of 40% of the episodes. Most of the filming takes place outdoors. Indeed, it is for this "sunny" reason that this site was chosen. There are 300 days of sunshine a year on average for a soap opera that has "soleil," meaning "sun," in its title.

French television production overall is very Parisian despite efforts to appear more general. The construction of studios outside Paris to produce these series reflects the desire to streamline production. It is worth noting that Montpellier and Marseille have strong cultural ecosystems. They serve as recruiting grounds for local professionals such as actors, decorators, and technicians. Local recruitment helps reduce costs and simplify. The cast is thus from Paris and Montpellier for USGS. The series brings together 50 recurring actors and many local extras.

However, the writing of the series and the postproduction still take place in Paris. For USGS, approximately 20 script writers write 260 episodes a year, creating approximately 100 hours of viewing time. Two teams work together with one writing scenes and the other focusing on dialogue structures of the narrative arcs. Five months are required between the initial writing phase and the broadcast of the episode. Rather than imagining the arcs as closed worlds, each of them line up a new story. Each episode ends with a cliffhanger that intrigues viewers and motivates them to keep returning. The narrative arcs include matters of the heart, police, or social issues. Between romantic and social issues, the series thus seeks to be perceived more as a "saga" than as a repertory of stories. PBLV operates quite similarly.

French towns and regions are currently in fierce competition to attract producers of film or fiction series to their area. The economic stakes are high since productions mean long-term jobs for technicians and several local actors. Productions also require renting filming equipment, creating sets, and even installing studios. Thus, there is a strong boost to the local cultural ecosystem.

The Occitanie region, where two—USGS (France2) and DNA (TF1)—of the three primetime series are filmed, has since been increasingly solicited for filming by all types of productions (Film France, 2017). This region went from 466 days of filming in 2015 to 1,497 in 2018. USGS and DNA filming explains this increase in part. Conversely, the neighboring and just as sunny region, that is, the Alpes-Provence-Côtes d'Azur region, experienced a certain loss of interest in 2018. This is despite the fact that the region hosts the pioneering series, PBLV. The Île-de-France Region and its capital Paris have also been faced by strong competition from the regions. Although it is still the region most filmed in France, 300 days of filming were lost between 2015 and 2018.

The National Cinema Center has assessed the economic spinoffs, or secondary economic effects, of filming (CNC, 2018b). For each euro a local authority invests in an audiovisual project, it generates close to eight euros in terms of economic activity on its territory. Furthermore, one euro investment generates seven euros through salaries paid to extras, actors, local technicians, as well as to the monetary "spinoffs" related to the hotel industry, transport, the renting of facilities and the installation of a film studio. Moreover, the series boosts tourism. Tourist offices organize guided tours of key sites. The economic benefits associated with this growth in tourism alone generate one euro, reimbursing the local authorities' initial investment.

In addition to these direct economic stakes, there are also more communicative and more diffuse strategies such as the territory's quest for notoriety at both the national and international levels (CNC, 2018a). This is obtained via series press coverage, meaning the territory is better ranked by online search engines. A win-win partnership links the production to the territory. This explains why, 10 years ago, Montpellier city set up a film reception office.

This office provided support to 98 audiovisual projects and enabled 413 days of filming in 2018 (Montpellier 3M, 2019). Films shot in this region are exempted from paying the fee for the occupation of publicly owned property. The office helps producers identify the locations best suited to specific stories. To achieve this, it makes proposals and acts as a "location scout" in order to facilitate the choice of location sets for the series in this complex territory.

This urban complex comprises 31 municipalities, as described in an official description, "The city offers a mosaic of remarkable atmospheres and sites: from a coastline bordered by preserved ponds to a hinterland filled with vineyards and scrubland, the charm of old villages and the incomparable architecture of its new neighborhoods" (Montpellier 3M, 2019). The production teams do not know the territory as well as the film reception office. To facilitate access to these different places, the city has identified correspondents in each of its 31 municipalities. The municipality, therefore, has a dual role in the series that allows it to be a key player. It participates in series production and highlights its region. The materiality of the city goes beyond simple decoration and beautiful landscapes; it is also a social matter involving people and living spaces. As Boudon (2017) points out regarding the Mistral neighborhood in PBLV, "The neighborhood becomes an actor-subject" (p. 261). This dimension is embodied by people who live in places constructed through fiction.

WORK AT THE REGIONAL LEVEL AND SOCIAL WORLDS: PLACES AND PEOPLE

Paraphrasing De Certeau (1990), we question what the series produces for the territory and what the territory produces for the series. On the one hand, the production seeks ways to industrialize filming, and the city has prepared itself to be the ideal partner. On the other, the territory receives obvious economic benefits and an enhanced city image. What, then, is the "work at the regional level" with regard to the city's image and, more specifically, to its identity? What identifiable criteria are proposed to residents, tourists, and manufacturers wishing to come and settle here? Similarly, the region validates the universe of the series and lies at its very core. What, then, does the region do for the series? This question leads us to examine the symbolic and interactive work between living spaces and the series. Noyer and Raoul (2011) define "territorial media work" as a question of:

considering an entanglement, and in particular of understanding how and why media discourse is a "territorializing discourse," knowing that a region can only gain recognition, and thus exist, through discursive authority (in which the media participates) which designates it, delimits it and accounts for it in its spatial form and materiality, and in its social history (digital section 6).

Based on this approach to work at the regional level, which considers local media, we postulate that the USGS series involves discourse on the region or "an act of language." This discourse is nestled here, within a serial fictional narrative that Beylot could describe as a "vector of identification" (Beylot, 2005).

To enable regional level work to lead to these identification processes, we must find a way to "decode the series." Both the characters and the places provide clues and meanings. According to Glaudes and Reuter, "The character plays a central role in the production of the narrative and its reception" (as cited in Sepulchre et al., 2015). Audience members are as much "typological markers" who specify the narrative language as an organizer who takes charge of the narrative. Both locations and characters are involved in the story. This leads the audience or spectator to a "psychic and social investment" which is the source of identification.

According to Shibutani and Strauss, the social world is a "universe of regularized mutual responses" (quoted in Cefaï, 2015). Within this social universe are shared norms, ways of doing and being built around a "generalized other" (in Cefaï, 2015). Each world has its own social identity which concerns its social level and its living environment. These social worlds may be structured around family groups which are all bearers of social diversity such as the Bastides, the Estrela, the Berville, of USGS. For example, the Bastide family is composed of a grandmother, her son, her daughter-in-law, and her two grandchildren. They have typical family events and rituals for Christmas, birthdays, and all other social rites. However, each of its members participate in other social worlds. Élisabeth Bastide, the grandmother, manages an investment fund and her son, Julien, a cosmetics firm. They are therefore both entrepreneurs. Alice, the mother, is a veterinarian at a zoo and part of her social life is played out in a world dedicated to protecting nature. The children escape the family world and are fully immersed in their adolescent experiences with their peers. Each family has its villa or apartment which marks its social status. The Bastide family has two architect's villas with swimming pools, and the Estrela and Berville families live in apartments. Other types of worlds connect the different members of these families. These spaces are the police station, the courthouse, the hospital, the high school, the lawyer's office, the zoo, the *L Cosmétic* firm, and so on.

In the context of USGS, the socioeconomic analysis of the characters in the series allows us to draw a fictional portrait of the city. However, this portrait oscillates between reality and imagination. After a strategic analysis of the 50 recurring characters in the series, there appears to be an absence of different types of sociocultural actors. Students, who represent 20% of the real city's population, are absent from the series. Pensioners, who currently comprise 21% of the real inhabitants, are represented by only two characters. Laborers and the unemployed are just as invisible. Put differently, the characters in the series represent only 50% of the city's population. The representation of social classes is not statistically realistic. The other types of social actors are either under or overrepresented. Employees and senior managers each represent 6% of the characters while in reality they represent 23% of the population. In contrast, traders, artisans, and entrepreneurs are overrepresented in the series. The "police-justice" world concerns 14% of the characters and education (teachers, high school students and university students), 24% of the characters.

The social portrait of Montpellier is thus presented as a young (high school students), active and entrepreneurial (executives, business leaders) city. While this representation of the social actors of the territory is fictitious, it is in line with some aspects of the city's communication strategies. To some extent, the series has the characteristics that the city seems to want to invest in. However, this desired image remains rather approximate because certain fields (cultural and creative industries, scientific research and start-ups with the French Tech label) are not represented despite being flagship sectors of the city's development. Similar to Bryon-Portet's analysis of PBLV, the series gives a "(necessarily) simplistic vision of the region" in which "the local sphere is merely a pretext to develop a global dimension" (Bryon-Portet, 2011). The question, then, is how is diversity and associated discrimination represented?

CONTEMPORARY NARRATIVE ARCS AS POSSIBLE MIRRORS OF DIVERSITY

In the French context, it is difficult to take diversity indicators into account. Indeed, the legal framework in place means that the collection of ethnic statistics is highly monitored. However, as Malonga (2008) points out, putting the issue of ethnic or visible minorities on the agenda "also shows that since the beginning of the 21st century, a new debate has emerged in French society" (p. 162). The French audiovisual regulatory body has had a diversity office since 2008 in order to ensure "that the diversity of French society is represented in the programs of audiovisual communication services and that this representation is without prejudice" (CSA, 2019, p. 5). While the daily series produced by France Télévisions appear to pay special attention to these questions, we will see that they are not free from normative discourses. Moreover, the studies undertaken on these series, PBLV in particular, show how investing in reception as an experience reexamines the audience relationship to the content of mass-produced programs.

France Télévisions and Diversity

According to Delphine Ernotte, the current president of France Télévisions:

> Public television can help make society. First because it is a common good. Public television is, by both definition and history, everyone's television. A familiar and shared place. In this sense, it cannot belong to a caste or an elite. (. . .) Lastly, because it is a place for the expression of plurality and diversity, of differences but also of what we all have in common. It is both a vector of the republican ideal and a pillar of our democracy (as cited in Jouanneau, 2019).

Armed with this assertive discourse on the role of public service media, the daily series that it broadcasts seeks to hold up a mirror between television and the audience.

Beyond the themes addressed and their representation, it is also a question of linking the narrative arcs to the experience of the public. Several "anniversary" or exclusive programs, broadcast during prime time or on social networks, also seek the deconstruction of the series through this experience: the actors are asked to chat with fans who have experienced similar ups and downs. Those programs are in a somewhat talk show setting, a paragon of "relational television" (Mehl, 2002). These "appeals for witnesses" are notably displayed across the digital social networks managed by the production. Like the "rabbit holes" in transmedia storytelling (Jenkins, 2006), they illustrate the multiple attempts to blur the boundaries between fiction and reality. The broadcast schedule of PBLV, in competition with the evening news broadcast on France 2 (which is one of the flagship programs), is also revealing of these relative boundaries. These series thus end up playing a non-negligible role in understanding reality:

> Thriving on the unspoken in the discourse of information, fiction eventually appears more real and more credible than this discourse, a paradoxical inversion of polarities reinforced by the storytelling and scriptwriting processes of the political life which have helped mask what citizens continue to perceive as the reality of power, and have blurred in parallel the boundaries between genders (Coulomb-Gully & Esquenazi, 2012).

Moreover, while these series are familiar with product placement, they have also developed the "placement of ideas" (Le Naour, 2013) and partnerships with public sector actors, in particular. This includes prevention in public health, promotion of the actions of local authorities, advertising of cultural events, and so on. As Glevarec points out with regard to contemporary US television series, the quest for likelihood through these fictions "requires a model of reception based on an inquiry about the nature of the program by the viewer more than a decoding process" (Glevarec, 2010, p. 232). From this perspective, the manner in which USGS and PBLV address diversity and discrimination is quite interesting as a public sphere of debate.

It should be noted that PBLV was the first to cast diverse characters, thereby promoting diversity in a series. According to Macé, PBLV is

> known for having introduced many non-white characters and making them appear commonplace, the series notably features non-white families such as the oldest family in the series, i.e., the Nassri family, which is of Algerian origin. Also new is the fact that non-white characters are no longer isolated but are now increasingly presented within a family setting (Macé, 2013, p. 191).

Similarly, USGS is structured around families whose role is to enhance the visibility of minorities. While the Alami family talks about North African immigration, Mo Réal and his daughter, Ines, reflect the diversity of households. In PBLV, Samia and Valère are among the characters who reflect diversity. Each of these minorities initiate narrative arcs associated with social issues of stigmatization. According to Bryon-Portet (2012), this reveals a certain cultural mix, a "representation of socio-cultural diversity, and of what Pierre-André Taguieff (1990) refers to as 'mixophilia' (. . .) a neologism which may be translated as 'a love of mixing' in the sense of pleasure in mixing" (Bryon-Portet, 2012, p. 98). It thus appears that the frequent use of narratives to highlight arguments, in a quest for recognition or even practices associated with domination, tend to provoke debate on social issues. We therefore posit that their objective is to spark debate around the issues associated with diversity within the public space.

These series are also inspired by the current issues that have a significant impact on the French scene. For example, the Lévy family, a Jewish family in USGS, replays a news item featuring anti-Semitism. In 2017, a Jewish family was kidnapped and mistreated on the grounds that, being Jews, they were undoubtedly rich. The narrative arc of the series draws on current issues in a rather similar manner and adapts them to the series. Some social issues are more common than others. Violence against women and disability trigger several narrative arcs by varying the social worlds in which they occur. It may deal with the rape of high school girls but also of adult women, workplace or street harassment, the environmental crisis, disability, and so on. In PBLV, the French version of #Metoo ("balance ton porc"or denounce your pig) gave rise to a narrative arc involving a masked avenger who branded the men found guilty of harassment. Female and male homosexuality is represented in each series through recurring characters such as Thomas (2004) and Léa (2016) in PBLV, and Sophia and Bilal in USGS (2018). These characters rarely hide their love lives and frequently assert their demands (surrogate motherhood, same-sex marriage, coming out, etc.).

This desire to express social change has an impact on audiences and this is occasionally reflected in the local press. When a USGS narrative arc presented a love story between two women, their negative comments on the "Manif pour tous" (the movement against the same-sex marriage law) against medically assisted conception, gave rise to rather virulent controversies in the local press. The series goes beyond the relationship with its spectator,

> using its own procedures, the fiction takes on an active role in the constitution of public problems and does not—in line with the common beliefs—simply reflect the terms of the controversy or the initial framework. Rather, it develops complementary and sometimes alternative meanings which are integrated into the mechanisms of the public sphere (Boudon, 2017).

The producers accept the use of some form of stereotyping of their characters, and sometimes use counter-stereotypes, which become "emblems" reflecting themes in the public sphere: "It is therefore not only a question of increasing the visibility of minorities but also of reversing the representational paradigm by varying and tempering the occurrences" (Boudon, 2017, p. 242). However, forms of "stigma" persist, and Boudon argues that they "therefore appear as a narrative reservoir from which to draw in order to focus on social issues but also outline a normative background, resulting from the tension between deviance and integration." From this perspective, PBLV and USGS are quite similar and this has an impact on audience engagement.

AUDIENCE ENGAGEMENT

As mentioned earlier, PBLV and USGS depict daily life and the ups and downs of social spaces. According to Toma de Matteis, the producer of USGS, "In [its] mission of a daily series produced by the public service, there must be a form of decoding of the social and the real in which we evolve even if this occurs through completely unreal and fictional things" (as cited in Gazzano, 2019). Audience engagement is not a simple process. It helps to extend the civic ambitions of the two series. The conversational practices of the public forge what may be referred to as "citizen-viewers" (Livingstone, 2004), particularly in the context of soap operas (Boullier, 2004; Boudon, 2017). These are obvious when they are advertised on social networks and during social interactions, or they are limited to private synchronous or asynchronous exchanges. The studies undertaken by Corroy have clearly shown how the young audiences of PBLV succeeded in turning official and unofficial forums into a "sentimental and civic education" (Corroy, 2010, p. 104). Since this study, "conversations" have shifted to social networks.

This shift has also arisen from the fact that various actors of the public space have taken ownership of the contents of the series and either denounce or support the messages the series conveys, particularly when they relate to diversity or discrimination. Media coverage of these controversies, especially local media, confirms how these series are both actors and representations of the social world in the era of social viewing.

Given that PBLV has been available longer, the impact of these conversational practices can be observed with greater hindsight compared to USGS. For example, the 30 nonofficial and most active PBLV groups at the end of 2019 represent more than 4,000 members per group on average and 134 posts per month, for a total of more than 100,000 accounts and approximately 3,000 monthly publications. In the most active group, publications can generate more than 4,500 interactions (such as likes) and 600 responses in a week. In these groups, members can exchange their opinions and their predictions on the intrigues, exclusive photos of the actors, links to view the episodes in advance or in replay, the appearances of the actors in other productions, and so on. One of the rules laid down is that members should avoid political debates, but comments on the social issues addressed by the series are allowed insofar as they are aligned with the "moral" of the series. Failure to adhere to this rule leads to the deletion of comments and/or exclusion from the group. Beyond these fan communities, the productions of the two series rely heavily on social networks to give greater weight to their programs. Certain narrative arcs or characters will mobilize these networks directly, in particular in PBLV where certain characters have dedicated accounts on a recurring or occasional basis. This has been the case for the character of Sabrina since 2016, for example. Immediately after joining the series, she began to embody the role of an "influencer" after that of a "poor worker." In 2019, this was how she was described on Facebook (81k subscribers), Twitter (53k subscribers), and Instagram (37.5k subscribers). On a more occasional basis, the characters of Emma and Baptiste staged the arrival of their child on Instagram in the form of a vlog, and Valentin highlighted his ecological and alternative globalization activism via the same channel.

An even more successful achievement is PBLV's Alternate Reality Game (ARG), which invites audiences to get involved in transmedia narratives. A narrative around video surveillance called on spectators to resolve an intrigue while getting informed about individual freedoms. This intrigue brought together "more than 70,000 players and 10,000 simultaneous connections, 100,000 YouTube video views" during the summer of 2012 and made it possible to "highlight the low mimetic mode on which the characters are based" (Boudon, 2014, p. 53). As Boudon further points out:

> by encouraging the viewers' identification with and attachment, [it] raises the public's awareness, using a comical mode, of a problem in the public arena (. . .). [This allows] to build fan networks that are genuine interpretative communities of the debate around a social problem rather than just of the fiction itself (p. 54).

Ultimately, beyond the "emotional realism" (Ang, 1996) on which these series are based and their desire to restore "the awesome everyday" (Mille, 2011), the importance they attach to social issues and their attachment to a territory shapes the experiences of the audience. In other words, creating scenes close to reality nourishes as much as it builds the frameworks for these experiences. For the public service media, these programs are an attempt to position itself. For the public, they renew the terms and conventions of their experiences.

CONCLUSION

Our research used a broad framework that includes the examining production, reception, and engagement of the public via different channels. These aspects are intricately linked to the territory in which a program series is produced. We argue that a series is an intentional object, and these analyses may later be validated through interviews and in situ observations to provide a more comprehensive analysis of audience reception and identify the regional activities implemented. The approach used in this critical examination of PBLV and USGS is necessarily complex. Both the shifting of material and its profusion is a major challenge. These drama series will continue to be successful among audiences as long as they will be able to depict and feed social and societal debates. Each day, a new episode adds more material to this social mirror.

REFERENCES

Allen, R. C. (1985). *Speaking of soap operas*. The University of North Carolina Press.

Ang, I. (2013). *Watching Dallas: Soap opera and the melodramatic imagination*. Routledge.
Beylot, P. (2005). *Le récit audiovisuel*. Armand Colin.
Boudon, H. (2014). Les enjeux des supports transmédia dérivés des séries télévisées. *Télévision*, *5*, 47–60.
Boudon, H. (2017). *Vies privées, problèmes publics: La nouvelle dramaturgie des séries télévisées françaises* [Doctoral dissertation, Université Paris 2].
Boullier, D. (2004). La fabrique de l'opinion publique dans les conversations télé. *Réseaux*, *126*(4), 57–87.
Bryon-Portet, C. (2011). Les productions télévisées, genre oublié dans la construction de l'image d'un territoire ? *Études de communication*, *37*, 79–96.
Bryon-Portet, C. (2012). La dimension politique de la série Plus belle la vie. *Mots*, *99*, 97–112.
Cefaï, D. (2015). Mondes sociaux. Enquête sur un héritage de l'écologie humaine à Chicago. *SociologieS*. http://journals.openedition.org/sociologies/4921.
Certeau, M. de. (1990). *L'invention du quotidien. I, Arts de faire*. Gallimard.
Corroy, L. (2010). Plus belle la vie, une éducation sentimentale « à la française » des jeunes–et des seniors ? *Le Télémaque*, *n° 37*(1), 99–110.
Coulomb-Gully, M., & Esquenazi, J.P. (2012). Fiction et politique: Doubles jeux. *Mots*, *99*, 5–11.
CNC. (2018a). *L'impact des tournages sur le tourisme*. https://www.cnc.fr/c/document_library/get_file?uuid=9ffc6542-6bb5-4baf-b553-33480226ec3b&groupId=18.
CNC. (2018b). *Bilan 2018*. https://www.cnc.fr/documents/36995/153434/CNC_Bilan_2018.pdf/f97eb201-5bce-38b0-3b1d-190377f4bef8.
CSA. (2019). *La représentation de la diversité de la société française à la télévision et à la radio: Bilan 2013–2018*. http://bit.ly/2JUiEHj.
Esquenazi, J.P. (2017). *Éléments pour l'analyse des séries*. L'Harmattan.
Favard, F. (2018). *Les séries télévisées*. Presses Universitaires Blaise Pascal.
Film France. (2017). *Géographie des tournages de longs métrages en France, étude 2017*.
FTV. (2019a). *Dossier de Presse–15 ans*. https://www.francetvpro.fr/index.php/france-3/dossier-de-presse/Plus-Belle-La-Vie-15ans.
FTV. (2019b). *Un si grand soleil*. Le Tigre Bleu.
FTV Production. (2019). Un si grand soleil. https://francetvstudio.fr/production/un-si-grand-soleil/.
Gazzano, C. (2019, June 7). Toma de Matteis ("Un si grand soleil"): Nous sommes la série quotidienne la plus aboutie des trois. *Ozap*. https://www.ozap.com/actu/toma-de-matteis-un-si-grand-soleil-nous-sommes-la-serie-quotidienne-la-plus-aboutie-des-trois/579404.
Glevarec, H. (2010). Trouble dans la fiction. Effets de réel dans les séries télévisées contemporaines et post-télévision. *Questions de Communication*, *18*, 214–238.
Jenkins, H. (2006). *Convergence culture: Where old and new media collide*. NYU Press.

Jouanneau, I. (2019, December, 19). Notre télévision publique est-elle entre les mains d'une caste? *Entreprendre*. https://www.entreprendre.fr/notre-television-publique-est-elle-entre-les-mains-dune-caste/.

Le Naour, J.Y. (2013). *Plus belle la vie. La boîte à histoires.* Presses Universitaires de France-PUF.

Le Plateau Télé. (2019). DNA, PBLV, USGS: Un soap, un public. https://leplateautele.com/2019/02/22/dna-pblv-usgs-un-soap-un-public/.

Livingstone, S. (2004). Du rapport entre audiences et publics. *Réseaux, 126*(4), 17–55.

Macé, É. (2013). La fiction télévisuelle française au miroir de The Wire. Monstration des minorités, évitement des ethnicités. *Réseaux*, n° 181, 179–204.

Maigret, E., & Macé, E. (2005). *Penser les médiacultures: Nouvelles pratiques et nouvelles approches de la représentation du monde.* Armand Colin/INA.

Malonga, M. F. (2008). La télévision comme lieu de reconnaissance: Le cas des minorités noires en France. *Hermès*, n° *51*(2), 161–166.

Médiamat. (2019). *Base 2017–2019*. https://www.mediametrie.fr/fr/mediamat.

Miège, B. (2004). *La pensée communicationnelle*. Presses Universitaires de Grenoble.

Mille, M. (2011). Rendre l'incroyable quotidien. *Réseaux, 165*, 53–81.

Montpellier 3M. (2019). Montpellier, studio à ciel ouvert. https://www.montpellier3m.fr/sites/default/files/plaquette-bat.pdf.

Mehl, D. (2002). La télévision relationnelle. *Cahiers Internationaux de Sociologie, 112*(1), 63–95.

Noyer, J., & Raoul, B. (2011). Le « travail territorial » des médias. *Études de Communication, 37*, 15–46.

Sepulchre, S. (Ed.). (2015). *Décoder les séries télévisées*. De Boeck.

Chapter 9

Brazilian Telenovelas and Multi-platform Audiences

Overviews and Industry Insights

Rosane Svartman

In Brazil and throughout the world, television viewing modes and ways of examining media productions have undergone rapid transformations. The arrival of broadband has fueled the expansion and migration of audiovisual content to various screens and media, regardless of the will and intent of their copyright holders. Mobile phones and tablets allow the exhibition of content where and when a viewer wishes, ignoring the linear programming of a channel or time slots. The way viewers exert influence and interact with content has changed relationships between content producers, distributors, creators, and who they perceive as their audiences. In this chapter, the author will share her experiences as head writer of four telenovelas, transmedia producer, and film and television director, in order to examine the main elements of a telenovela from a rare professional insider's view. This work aims to explore the following questions: How do telenovelas resist, negotiate, and adhere to new media and transformations in spectatorship? How can telenovelas lead the future of Brazilian television?

BACKGROUND ON BRAZILIAN TELEVISION

Four broadcasters dominate the greater part of the massive audience: Globo Television, Record Television, SBT Television, and Bandeirantes Television. Globo Television, a public concession commercially exploited by a private group, is part of the largest media conglomerate in Latin America and also the most popular open television broadcaster in Brazil. In 2017, the broadcaster celebrated a daily viewership of over 100 million people in a nationwide campaign. Telenovelas are the most sought-after content in Brazilian television today. *Bom Sucesso (A Life Worth Living)*, a 2019 telenovela written by the author of this chapter with Paulo Halm (Granada, 2020), had a daily audience of 36 million, for example. However, that does not mean the Brazilian viewers do not have other options.

Brazilian spectators may choose from among several productions of the current audiovisual ecosystem. According to the Brazilian Institute of Geography and Statistics (2010), the federal provider of national data, 29.5% of the residences, a little under 20 million people, have cable television that offers over 100 different channels. The country has 78 VOD (video on demand) platforms, and 34.5 million people subscribe to least one service. Lopes and Lemos (2019) observe that the country is considered the eighth largest VOD market in the world. They state, "However, this is the main form of watching fiction for only 8% of the population" (p. 97). Brazilian viewers prefer to watch content, mainly telenovelas, through linear programming on a television set, and 97.3% of Brazilian residences have at least one television.

Telenovelas are the most-watched genre in broadcast television and require a significant financial investment. In 2017, Globo Television's 7 p.m. telenovela, *Totalmente Demais (Total Dreamer)*, which the author of this chapter also cowrote with Paulo Halm, an International Emmy Nominee, cost an equivalent of 300,000 US dollars per episode. This data was made available by Globo Television during the International Emmy Awards show of 2017. *Totalmente Demais* is 176 episodes long, which means a total cost of approximately 52.8 million US dollars. This cost includes implementation, that is, building the studio and exterior settings, and preproduction. According to telenovela writer Alcides Nogueira, "When you write a page, you know it means work for three or four hundred technicians, production staff, directors, make-up artists, costume designers, and scenographers" (Fiuza, p. 130). Writing and producing a telenovela requires pacing, professional commitment, and industrial-level resources.

THE TELENOVELA NARRATIVE FORMAT

Telenovelas inherited much of its format and initial writers from radio fiction programs in the 1950s and 1960s, Brazilian cinema, and the Latin American melodramatic tradition in literature and theatre. In the beginning many narratives were historical pieces, but during the 1970s local everyday stories replaced these. Unlike US soap operas, *telenovelas* are daily and long serial narratives with a planned conclusion. There is a limited number of episodes that are typically broadcast for four months and can last up to one year.

Telenovelas have gone through many transformations. Episodes became longer, whereas the length of the whole telenovela became shorter—between 150 and 200 episodes. Also, secondary narratives were added to facilitate production—so now many scenes can be shot simultaneously with different scenery, crews, and actors. However, one central element has not changed over the last decades. A telenovela will be written while still being exhibited. This strategy provides a dialogue with the audience and the possibility of tuning, or adjusting, the story based on timely research. Furthermore, telenovela viewers know that if they miss an episode, because of its pleonastic (repetition or redundancy) narrative format, they will not fail to understand what happens in the plot.

Like classic narrative films and series with wide-ranging story arcs, a good synopsis for a telenovela should have strong turning points and narrative plot twists. This term is widely used by theorists and researchers to designate the moment in which the plot is completely modified by the characters' actions, through an external event or a conflict that will reach its peak. As a telenovela needs duration, at least three major turning points or plot twists must be produced along the way. A significant turning point will bring lesser (or secondary) turning points and revelations each week, and these will turn into cliffhangers at the end of each episode. To the viewer, these plot twists, revelations, turning points, and cliffhangers translate into short, medium, and long-term expectations. Mittel (2015) observes that contemporary series, also influenced by melodrama, tend to similarly invest in long narrative arcs and narrative tools like cliffhangers to interest the audience.

In film, power lies with the director; in the theatre, with the actor; in television, with the author. US television has produced the figure of the *showrunner*, a series creator and head writer who also functions as a producer of sorts and has general approval of casting and the artistic team. Such a position is uncommon in the Brazilian telenovela. Nevertheless, the entire chain of production depends on its author, who thus possesses a natural ascendancy. Comparato (1995) observes that a telenovela may have as many as four or five directors, who may change without influencing the show. On the other hand, if the scriptwriter is replaced, the same telenovela may suffer significant changes.

Filho (2001) ponders that the telenovela's narrative may be easily simplified. He states "Two people fall in love and live happily for a few episodes. Inevitably, they will be separated by the villain, who may want one of them for him [or her] self" (p. 68). For Filho, "This is the foundation, in a raw and critical manner" (p. 68). An experienced film and television director who directed and supervised telenovelas acclaimed by audiences and critics alike, his telenovela description minimizes the complexity of a format that rivets millions of viewers daily. Viewers' reactions are unpredictable and formulas do not always work. Every telenovela author tackles and leaves their mark in uniquely different subjects.

Frequently, the love story is not the starting point for their creation. The 2019 telenovela *Bom Sucesso* (*A Life Worth Living*) tells the story of Paloma, a seamstress and mother of three. Here life turns upside down when she is diagnosed with a terminal disease. She begins to think about all the things she dreamed one day of doing but could not, because of her hard life. After emotionally breaking down as a result of her bad health news, dancing in the streets, getting drunk, phoning her long-lost love, and losing her job after dissing her boss, Paloma discovers the blood exam belongs to somebody else. Alberto is a wealthy terminally ill book publisher on the verge of death, and is decades older than Paloma. Between them, a friendship blossoms inspired by a shared love of literature and an awareness of how finite life is. They do not have a love affair, though Paloma falls in love with Alberto's playboy son.

Glória Perez's *O Clone* (*The Clone*) from 2001 is remembered for the love story of the Moroccan Muslim named Jade and the Brazilian businessman Lucas. Nevertheless, the telenovela was not built around their love story. Its entire structure hung on the subject of human cloning as a metaphor for a man confronting choices that transformed his life 20 years earlier. At 40 years old, tense and depressed Lucas meets his 20-year-old carefree clone, who also falls in love with his girlfriend from his youth, Jade. In addition to cloning, Glória Perez addressed topics such as surrogate mothers, the transgender universe, and human trafficking in her telenovelas. The author's usual strategy is to seek out current subjects that will generate debate and juxtapose issues with more traditional outlooks. Additionally, Glória Perez's mark is social merchandising in her telenovelas.

Although it may not be a starting point, one of the telenovela's key elements has always been romance. Writing specifically about the telenovela, Almeida (2001) analyzed the consumption of the 1997 *O Rei do Gado* (*King of Cattle*). Almeida finds that, because it is about affective relationships, the telenovela interacts with spectators and provokes reflections on intimate and family relationships. Thus, the telenovela constitutes a cultural text capable of promoting a singular sentimental education through a reflexive process of viewers with the narrative. Almeida uses an example of mothers who use the narrative to talk about delicate topics such as sexuality and love.

Romantic novels are associated with female audiences, and women are also the major part of the telenovela's public. Lopes and Lemos (2019) discuss the 2018 viewership demographics of *O Outro Lado do Paraíso* (*The Other Side of Paradise*): 62.3% were women, 37.7% were men; 31.5% were from the AB socioeconomic level (the highest class); 49.4% were from C (middle class); and 19.1% were from DE (the lowest class). The age groups varied, indicating family viewing, but also tilted toward older age groups:

5.3% from 4 to 11 years of age; 5.6% were 12 to 17; 7.6% were 18 to 24; 13.2% were 25 to 34; 25.4% were 35 to 49; and 42.9% were over 50 years old. When writing for daily television, drama authors envision nuclei and plots that portray different social realities with characters of different ages, and scenes with different tones such as humor, drama, and action. Even with these considerations, there is no certain formula for stirring audience identification with content.

THE RELATIONSHIP BETWEEN THE TELENOVELA NARRATIVE AND THE AUDIENCE

Viewers have always created new meanings for narratives. The act of changing channels or simply turning off the television also puts the audience in a place of power over content. Feuer (1992), on criticism and contemporary television, argues that the meaning of a text and pleasure of the reader derives from relating the text to other texts. The viewer interprets the narrative according to their individuality and experience. With transformations in spectatorship, there is a resilient production of meanings and subjectivities that permeates the spectator's experience. The telenovela stands out in programming flow due to these characteristics, the relationship, and the dialogue with the audience. To Fiske (1987), the ultimate power of a work's message lies in the viewer's reading of it, rather than in the producers' ambition or proposal. According to Fiske, the relations between the texts take place in two dimensions, the horizontal and vertical. The horizontal dimension exists between primary texts such as, for example, two different telenovelas. The vertical intertextual relationship consists in the relationship of a primary text to secondary texts that use the former as reference: advertising, criticism, promotional content. The vertical intertextual relationship may also extend to tertiary texts. These occur at the level of the spectator and their social relations. A spectator relates the television text to their own lived experiences, to their own intertexts within their historical and social contexts. Consequently, each reading is unique, and every viewer actively elaborates these connections.

With millions of Brazilians watching the same content, there is a feeling of belonging. Eneida Nogueira was director of Globo Television's Research Department from 1998 to 2017. In a personal interview for this research, on July 17, 2018, she explains that some main dimensions guide the public's taste, and permeate all telenovelas. These are themes that generate discussion at home and in the social environment: expansion of repertoire, learning and reflection; new values to personal narratives; fun; hope and fantasy; and subjects for social exchange (online or offline). Muanis (2018) observes that consuming content on linear television provides a sense of up-to-date-ness, nurturing conversations and debates in one's social group. He states "In other words, the search for being part of a social community, mediated by television, continues to be possible through content, but also through all the effort of marketing and word of mouth" (p. 25). These communities exist offline and online. Nogueira especially remembers the following kinds of viewer testimonies concerning people's intimate relationship with television and content: "I come home and turn on the TV, and it stays on all day"; "If you don't have the sound of the TV it looks like the house is empty"; "With TV, I don't feel alone"; "Without the sound of the TV, it seems that something is missing"; and "On Sunday lunch, TV participates in the family circle." For Nogueira, these are strong statements that continue to be relevant.

Pursuing what the audience desires on television is fundamental for the business, and quantitative and qualitative research are the network's main strategies. Minute-by-minute audience ratings are available throughout the exhibition of a telenovela, and there is at least one focus group after the first month on the air. Research includes discussions about the plot, characters, and main couples, with assiduous and sporadic viewers that mirror the audience at home during the time slot of the telenovela. The audience of linear television programming sustains the telenovela's primary revenue, advertising. Because the focus group happens in the first month, it is the opportunity for the author to make plot or character trait changes in order to increase viewership. The intention of the author and the perceptions of the audience may not be the same.

Generally, in qualitative research, there is a moment when the moderator asks what character of the plot the participant would like to be if they could. The chosen characters are an aspirational source for these viewers. When a viewer chooses a character, this is a sign of the viewer's affection for him or her. If a character finds no audience empathy, for example, a solution may be to make the character suffer. With the director's partnership, the author of this chapter has taken steps to change a character's hair and costume after the character was criticized by the discussion groups. She was also made to suffer all sorts of setbacks in a tide of bad luck. Obstacles help in the viewer's empathy for a character, even for a villain. The character transformed herself going through the obstacles and became more generous and supportive, but did not lose her willpower. The ratings rose significantly. The author of this chapter has made other changes to telenovelas she worked in, based on focus group feedback. In an interview, author Aguinaldo Silva posits, "Why are you doing a telenovela? To get an audience and please the viewer. It is for success, not for any other reason. So it is absurd to stand against what the viewer wants" (Fiuza, p. 36).

There is no company policy forcing an author to change the plot according to focus group feedback. Oguri, Chauvel, and Suarez (2009) discuss how audience information signals problems and opportunities for the broadcaster and to the authors but does not dictate decisions. They explain, "They function as indicators that need interpretation, and only in some cases result in changes in the product, which rarely involve key elements of the plot. Also, it is clear that the initial project, the synopsis, in its great lines, is what guides the telenovela" (p. 45). However, the author knows that if audience ratings are low, he or she may have to shorten the telenovela or a supervisor may be hired by the station to intervene.

The audience has always influenced the telenovela, which in turn, changes and adapts to attract viewers that enable its business model, based on the advertising. However, this audience is changing. Jenkins (2006), Jenkins, Ford, and Green (2013), Jenkins, Ito, and Boyd (2016) discuss the growing power of the participatory television audience. According to Jenkins, Ford and Green (2013), the new interactive tools and platforms make the public not only consume content initially produced for television in a unique way but also produce new content from it. The television spectator currently speaks about audiovisual content in different social networks, participates in discussion groups, and produces content derived from characters and narratives. This audience may influence the original work itself. Nevertheless, the understanding of an active audience may be erroneously associated only with the fan, with the notion of a spectator who ostensibly interacts with the work, producing content, for example.

In this research, all audiences that maintain an affectionate relationship with the work are considered fans, even though a portion of these fans devote more time circulating their opinions on social networks and producing content for participatory platforms. The production of content by fans, the amplification of the old word of mouth, with circulation on social networks and interactive platforms, is also a contemporary Brazilian phenomenon.

A spontaneous campaign on the internet can cause difficulties for broadcasters in Brazil, mainly due to the speed with which it propagates and the difficulty that executives have in assessing the real size and penetration of the crisis. Often this crisis may be amplified by the broadcaster. On June 28, 2015, for example, journalist Zeca Camargo from the cable news channel GloboNews, surprised by the commotion from the death of country singer Cristiano Araújo, questioned the media attention given to the musician. The outrage that his statements caused among fans of the artist immediately resonated on social networks. Zeca Camargo apologized live the next day on Globo Television, on *Video Show*. This program had a much larger audience than the one that carried the original comment. Thousands of people watched

GloboNews, but millions of people watched *Video Show*. Unfortunately, Zeca Camargo got the singer's name wrong during the apology, generating another wave of negative messages and protests on social networks, including a lawsuit for moral damages moved by the singer's family. The amplification of a crisis often arises from the inability of the broadcaster to deal with the situation.

TELENOVELAS TAPPING INTO NEW MEDIA

During the last 20 years, the author of this chapter has worked intermittently for Globo Television as a director, series and telenovela head writer, and transmedia producer. Therefore, this research integrates practical experience and market sources with theoretical sources. Monaco (2010) ponders that some academics examine their multiple positions as series fans and researchers of television series and their fan groups. They see themselves as vulnerable in these multiple roles and hide them from other scholars. She considers the advantages of being explicit about the process and how localized identity and emotional recall inform research choices. Hills's (2002) research on fans also considers that academia may reject the idea of hybrid identities that unite not only within the academy but also outside it. In the case of the author of this chapter, the hybrid identities would be of scriptwriter, audiovisual director, and researcher.

The author of this chapter was invited to implement a transmedia narrative project for a 9:00 p.m. telenovela written by Silvio de Abreu called *Passione* (initially aired 2011). This was the first transmedia experience of a primetime telenovela. In addition to the traditional website with a summary of the telenovela episodes, character profiles and backstage material, we produced content for several platforms and social networks. This included a game, branded content, and an initiative that extended some of the telenovela's scenes on the internet. Characters would look directly into the camera and say what they were feeling after a scene, usually a cliffhanger scene. This content was available online on the telenovela's website right after the broadcast of each episode. Through this experience, we learned that having the characters in social media was a bad idea for many reasons. For example, fans had more time to create and produce material for "fake" profiles of the characters. The nonofficial profiles were humorous since fans had no ethical ties to the original narrative. There was no way we could control this fan production since fans take action online independently. Interestingly the nonofficial profiles had more followers than the corporate created ones. We also learned that we should invest in transmedia content that only the station could provide, involving actors, for example, or studio scenery. These were avidly consumed online.

Fans produce content because of the affection they have for the narrative, and it is this affection that makes them search for more content produced by their peers and also by the broadcaster.

Fechine (2015) observes, "The universe triggered by the project is not limited to the strategies proposed by producers and, for this reason, is not entirely under their control" (p. 325). This control involves the response from consumers to calls for action from producers that may deviate from the producer's goals. In the 2018 telenovela *Deus Salve o Rei (God Save the King)*, written by Daniel Adjafre, fans were invited to participate in the production. Fans visited the studios where the scenes were recorded, met the actors, took part in workshops, and even participated as extras in the production. There was an implicit understanding by the broadcaster with these fans that they would produce content from the experience that would help promote the telenovela. Many of these fans also had the purpose of producing content for their followers. Even though there is no way to control what is shared, these fans knew that the broadcaster could deny the opportunity in the future.

Malhação Sonhos (Young Hearts or *Young Dreams)* was another telenovela the author of this chapter cowrote with Paulo Halm. The story has a young cast and universe and aired on the 5:30 p.m. time slot in 2016. Through a crowdsourcing experience, with around 8,000 total entries, the narrative incorporated two fanfiction scenes and was a Digital Emmy Nominee that same year. The authors of the fanfiction scenes were invited to visit the set and watch their scenes being produced. Jenkins, Ito, and Boyd (2016) observe that there is currently a tendency of no clear separation between content producers and fans. In the case of a telenovela, there is a clear separation. The authors of the fanfiction scenes do not necessarily want to write 150 episodes of a telenovela or have the technical knowledge to do so. There is an ethical dimension when a large broadcaster uses content produced by amateur writers. While the first has commercial interests, the latter is produced out of affection for the narrative. In this case, both parts gained what they expected from the exchange and this produced a kind of balance. More and more producers of corporate media incorporate public participation as a means of increasing program engagement in a competitive market, especially in journalism and variety programs.

It is necessary to consider the real power of this new spectator who can be called the content-producer-fan. Audience numbers guide the longevity and integrity of a program on broadcast television. Social media tools and new technologies increase content circulation of content created by producer-fans. In the case of Brazil, the fans have not yet exhibited their full power to influence mass audiences of national telenovelas. Nevertheless, fan contributions may enrich the narrative of a telenovela. For Nogueira, the reverberation on social networks does not replace audience ratings and focus groups. Nogueira shares, "Whoever is talking on the social network is the one who loves or hates [the program]. But the group that does not manifest itself so clearly is the group that participates in the research. I think it is important to listen to these people because they are the vast majority."

A telenovela author has the liberty to change their story based on what they read in social media. However, using social media as a thermometer is a risk since, in Brazil, the repercussions on social networks is not an accurate reference for the broader audience for broadcast television. According to the annual study of the Media São Paulo Group (2019), the penetration of open television is higher than that of the internet in Brazil. Geographically, Globo TV's signal covers 97.2% of all households with a television in Brazil. Between 6:00 p.m. and 10:00 p.m., when telenovelas are being aired, approximately 70% of these televisions are on. According to the media measurement and analytics company Comscore 46,170,641 Brazilian accessed social media networks. While Facebook had a 55.7% penetration within these users, Instagram and Twitter had only 16.3% and 10.4% each. Also from Comscore, television metrics that orient the price of publicity only consider the 15 leading markets for their surveys. It is necessary to take into account the business model of broadcast television, supported by advertising, where only 15 cities are essential for rates, whereas social media activates all cities in Brazil.

The pact between the consumers and the telenovela includes a tacit understanding that the television business model contains the exhibition of commercials in (merchandising) and outside the plot. This model does not drive the spectator away from the main product consumed and desired while watching a telenovela, a good story. This story provokes the imagination, dreams, and desires of the active television audience. This audience, interspersing fiction with their own experiences, texts and expectations, consumes primetime telenovelas, plots and characters daily. The characters' clothes, accessories, attitudes, and lifestyles are also objects of desire. The consumers will decide how and when to watch the stories that touch them and provoke wishes and desires. The question is how television, and its most popular content, the telenovela, will join other screens and possibilities in order to make commercial audiovisual content viable.

Johnson (2019) draws a parallel between companies that are natives to television and audiovisual content companies that are digital natives. The former are content providers through broadcast transmission, cable, satellite, and digital television. These companies, such as Globo Television, extend their services on online digital platforms, have a history of production, acquisition and delivery of content and have access to large catalogues of collections. Those that are digital natives, in turn, offer online services and have a television service for the entire internet ecosystem. These companies, like Netflix, Amazon, and Hulu, started to produce content and invest a large number of resources in it. Netflix invested $15 billion on content during 2019. For Johnson, the great advantage that native television companies have over digital natives is the collection, and the public has already established a relationship with it regarding telenovelas. Digital native companies have an essential data advantage over their competitors. The data that these companies collect from their users plays a central role in the entire business model. Consumer data provides a means to expand audiences and create new forms of engagement, as well as new business models.

Netflix, for example, attributes features to its content to drive the recommendation algorithm based on user data. The production of an original series may also depend on this system. The US series *House of Cards* (2013–2018), the first original series on the platform, was based on the data and streaming metrics of 33 million users, according to Carr (2013). Netflix does not need to focus on content with mass appeal. It can bet on content with attractiveness to specific audiences already identified by the service. This segmented and diverse audience makes up the mass audience for an uneven catalogue. No user has access or interest in its entirety.

What surveys and research institutes do for traditional television, with a sophisticated algorithm, the digital platform itself can offer. These organizations extract value from the data in the form of forecasts, analyze data sets that serve their objectives, and thus create competitive advantages. However, if these procedures were enough, all production of these platforms would be a success. What is observed is series cancellations and discontinuity, an adjustment of content similar to what occurs on corporate television and broadcast companies.

TELENOVELAS SLIDING FROM TELEVISION TO DIGITAL PLATFORMS

Currently, the majority of open channels in Brazil, as in other parts of the world, seek technological solutions for online consumption of their content. Solutions could take the form of live transmission of streamed programming, the exhibition, differentiated hybrid business models of programs belonging to their collection, and original productions on digital platforms. Telecom groups also explore mergers and acquisitions to scale and integrate technologies and talents needed to develop digital content and service offers. The transmission itself of audiovisual content for television has also transformed. Cable or satellite transmission was the primary form of distribution of what was seen on television until recently.

Globoplay is a Brazilian subscription video on-demand service owned by Globo Group. It was launched in Brazil on October 26, 2015, and offers video streaming and on-demand content of programs from Globo Television's archived library as well as original programs and international shows. Globoplay also offers live streaming of the Globo Television free-to-air channel. In January 2020, 81 telenovelas were available for viewers.

Telenovelas figure between the ten most popular content in the Globoplay digital platform. Telenovelas that are on the air make it to the list of the five most viewed content, along with international series and films as a whole. Nevertheless, the platform does not invest in this narrative, preferring to produce original series, following the experience of international VOD groups in Brazil. New audience metrics, which include the different media of the same product, could keep the business model supported by advertising for a while. However, soon telenovelas may become unviable without a hybrid business model involving publicity, syndication, and VOD investment. Even though massive audiences are not the core of a VOD platform model, telenovelas may be the key for Globoplay to attract a Brazilian audience. Brazil has a unique multi-platform audience. The history of television in Brazil is not the same as the history of other countries. Perhaps, the construction of a VOD catalogue should also have in mind this uniqueness.

CONCLUDING REMARKS

As long as the telenovela continues to be part of Brazilian culture, it will continue to be a mass product, even if we start considering the sum of the audience across many screens and platforms. As a mass product, it may be consumed on any platform, medium, or screen and will continue to be a telenovela of Brazilian television. The universe of a telenovela has an intersubjective dimension with its characters, territories, and plots forming parts of the reality of millions of Brazilians who consume, interact and relate in different ways with the production. How the telenovela will slide to other platforms, maintaining the characteristics that guarantee its success, will be the biggest challenge for Brazilian television. The narrative has survived approximately 70 years maintaining its public through a dialogue with the audience, transforming in format and approaching new themes. However, the continuity of this process, involving other media, does not depend only on authors, directors, and production teams.

The Brazilian telenovela is the equivalent of US blockbuster films, of the world's bestselling books, and of the live performances that fill stadiums. However, where culture and the market go together, the telenovela depends on the management of corporate companies and the people behind these corporations. They need to observe and preserve relationships with the Brazilian public, whether through traditional surveys, data, sensibility, and creativity of authors, and presenting themes that society needs to discuss and debate.

REFERENCES

Adorno, T. & Horkheimer, M. (1944; 1986). *The cultural industry*. Jorge Zahar.
Almeida, H. B. (2001). *Muito mais coisas: Telenovela, consumo e gênero*. Instituto de Filosofia e Ciências Humanas, Universidade Estadual de Campinas.
Almeida, H. B. (2002). *Melodrama comercial: Reflexões sobre a feminilização da telenovela*. Cadernos Pagu.
Baccega, M. A. (2015). Fãs de telenovelas: Construindo memórias, das mídias tradicionais às digitais. In M. I. V. de Lopes (Ed.), *Por uma teoria de fãs da ficção televisiva brasileira* (pp. 65–106). Sulina.
Bourdieu, P. (1997). *On television*. Jorge Zahar.
Brazilian Institute of Geography and Statistics (2010). https://censo2010.ibge.gov.br.
Carr, D. (2013). Giving viewers what they want. *The New York Times*. https://www.nytimes.com/2013/02/25/business/media/for-house-of-cards-using-big-data-to-guarantee-its-popularity.html.
Comscore. (2019). Perspectivas do cenario digital Brasil. https://www.comscore.com/Insights/Presentations-and-Whitepapers/2017/Perspectivas-do-Cenario-Digital-Brasil-2017.
Fechine, Y. (2014). Trasmediação e cultura participativa: Pensando as práticas textuais de agenciamento dos fãs de telenovelas brasileiras. *Revista Contra-campo* (33), 5–22.
Fechine, Y., Gouveia, D., Teixeira, C., Almeida, C., Costa, M. & Cavalcanti, G. (2015). Governo da participação: Uma discussão sobre processos internacionais em ações transmídia. In M.I.V. Lopes (Ed.), *Por uma teoria de fãs da ficção televisiva brasileira* (pp. 321–357). Editora Meridional.
Figueiredo, V. L. F. de. (2011). O teatro das sombras: A crítica das imagens técnicas e nostalgia do mundo verdadeiro. *Revista Significação* (35), 183–199.
Fiske, J. (1987). *Television culture*. Methuen.
Fiuza, S. (2008). *Autores: História da teledramaturgia* (vol. 2). Editora Globo.
Granada, E. (2020). Rosane Svartman Paulo Halm talk new hit ´A life worth living´. *Variety*. https://variety.com/2020/tv/global/rosane-svartman-paulo-halm-new-globo-hit-a-life-worth-living-1203475441/.
Grupo de Mídia São Paulo. (2019). Midia Dados. https://www.gm.org.br/midia-dados-2019.
Hills, M. (2002). *Fan cultures*. Routledge.
Jenkins, H. (2006). *Convergence culture: Where old and new media collide*. University Press.
Jenkins, H., Ford S., & Green, J. (2013). *Spreadable media: Creating value and meaning in a networked culture*. University Press.
Jenkins, H., Ito, M., & Boyd, D. (2016). *Participatory culture in a networked era*. Polity Press.
Johnson, C. (2019). *Online TV*. Routledge.
Livingstone, S. (2010). Media consumption and public connection. In Couldry, N., Livingstone, S. & Markham, T. (Eds.) *Media consumption and public engagement* (pp. 23–41). Palgrave Macmillan.

Lopes, M. I. V. de et al. (2015) Autoconstrução do fã: Performances e estratégias de fãs de telenovela na internet. In M. I. V. Lopes (Ed.), *Por uma teoria de fãs da ficção televisiva brasileira* (pp. 17–64). Sulina.

Lopes, M.I.V. de & Lemos, L. P. (2019). Brazil: Streaming, all together and mixed. In M.I.V. Lopes and G.O. de & Gómez (Eds.), *Television distribution models by the internet: Actors, technologies, strategies* (pp. 69–96). Sulina.

Mittel, J. (2015). *Complex TV: The poetics of contemporary television storytelling.* New York University Press.

Monaco, J. (2010). Memory work, autoethnography and the construction of a fan-ethnography. *Participations, Journal of Audience & Reception Studies*, University of West England, UK, v. 7, n. 1.

Muanis, F. (2018). *A imagem televisiva: Autorreferência, temporalidade, imersão.* Appris.

Oguri, L., Chauvel, M., & Suarez, M. (2009). O processo de criação das telenovelas. *Revista de Administração de Empresas, 49*, 38–48.

Section III

HISTORICAL AND PERIOD DRAMA

Chapter 10

Korean Historical Television Dramas

Cultural Meanings, Confucian Values, and Transcultural Identities

Suji Park and Carolyn A. Lin

The Korean Wave or Hallyu (or Hanliu) refers to the widespread dissemination of Korean serial television dramas overseas that began in the late 1990s (Chuang & Lee, 2013), which overtook the popularity of Chinese language serial dramas in the pan-Asia region. Today Korean television dramas have garnered unwavering viewer loyalty, as these have gained widespread popularity in Eastern Europe and Latin America (Korea Creative Content Agency, 2013). These dramas, with English subtitles, delivered through satellite networks, are being watched by millions of Asian and Asian American viewers in the United States (Chuang & Lee, 2013). This soap opera power from the East has been said to rival that of telenovelas on the global stage (Park, Yun, & Lee, 2011).

Existing research on the Korean Wave phenomenon has examined Asian viewers' interest in and reception of Korean culture as well as improved cultural ties between Korea and other Asian countries (e.g., Kim, 2009; Tse, 2012). Due to the relative newness of the Korean Wave phenomenon in the United States, little is known in terms of social implications and cultural impact of Korean dramas on Asian American audiences. This chapter will utilize a set of interdisciplinary theories to analyze Asian Americans' Korean drama viewing motives and transcultural identity as well as their relations to Asian Americans' cultural-ethnic values and community social capital. Specifically, this chapter is organized to present the following discussion: (1) cultural images of Korean historical dramas; (2) the historic roots and contemporary implications of these cultural images; (3) audience gratifications obtained from viewing Korean historical dramas; (4) Asian American's transcultural identity and social capital. In addition, the current chapter will propose a conceptual framework to integrate the different theoretical components and a set of research propositions to help guide future research.

VISUAL IMAGES OF KOREAN DRAMAS

Kotler (cited in Han, Chang, & Hwang, 2008) considered the concept of "image" associated with an object or event as an individual's unique set of subjective beliefs, ideas, and impressions concerning that entity. Based on an individual's perception or knowledge about the entity, which could have been developed through prior personal experience, the individual may rationalize the way that they interpret the meanings of a given image associated with an object or entity (Barry, 1997). Research has shown that the cultural images projected by Korean dramas have captivated a large following in the pan-Asian region, as the storylines of these dramas infuse Eastern tradition with a sense of Western modernity (Jung, 2009).

In particular, the images presented by Korean historical dramas (called Sa Guek) typically highlight unique visual elements that appear "foreign" and are fascinating to Korean drama fans overseas (Haut, 2010). Period visual presentation of these epic dramas consists of Korean ethnic clothing of the era, architecture, artwork, furniture, scenery, and locales. Appealing visual presentations have enabled these historical dramas to establish iconic Korean cultural images, which provide an interesting contrast between Korean culture and native cultures of overseas audiences (Haut, 2010).

Other visual elements that drive popularity of Korean historical dramas are their visual presentations of Confucian-style themes that are strongly appreciated by Asian viewers (Ryoo, 2009). Previous research suggests that core images of Korean television dramas are reflected by a set of Confucian-tradition-oriented values, which are visually presented as nonsexual, pure, and eternal love in a twist-and-turn romantic tragedy plot (Chan & Xueli, 2011; Lin & Tong, 2007). These plot devices of pure and eternal love, such as family bonds and filial duties, are a strong draw for Asian viewers who appreciate and identify with the roots of their cultural values (Hogarth, 2013; Ryoo, 2009).

A good example of this kind of visual storytelling is the program, *Jewel in the Palace* (Korean title *Dae Jang Geum*). As one of the most popular Korean historical dramas in history, it showcases very elaborate visuals that are based on family-centered and pure love storylines. The historical text of the show also encodes the sociopolitical relationships between Korea, China, and Japan (Lin & Tong, 2009). *Jewel in the Palace* at one time was aired in 91 countries around the world, including China, Iran, Nigeria, Dubai, Mexico, Venezuela, the United Kingdom, and the United States (Jo, 2013). Though the show was produced in 2003 in Korea, it marked the third most favored Korean drama by overseas fans from 17 countries in 2019, following *Hotel Del Luna* and *Descendants of the Sun* (Korean Foundation for International Cultural Exchange, KFICE, 2020). Within the United States, this show was aired by AZN television, which is known as the satellite network for Asian America (Korea Tourism Organization, 2005). Forbes (MacDonald, 2019) reported that the streaming providers, including Rakuten Viki, Netflix, Amazon Prime, and Hulu, have aired a large number of Korean dramas over the last two decades available to US audiences.

Similar to historical dramas, other Korean nonhistorical television dramas embody the cultural images of Eastern (Confucian) values to make them appealing to worldwide viewers. For instance, a contemporary Korean drama, entitled *Cheon-guk eui Gyedan/Stairway to Heaven* (*Escalera al Cielo* in Spanish), was the most popular afternoon television program aired in 2013 in Colombia. Over 40% of Colombian viewers surveyed in a study reported watching at least six episodes of this drama, each week (Madrid-Morales & Lovric, 2015). Another Korean drama, entitled *Hotel Del Runa* was the most favored Korean drama in 2019 across the United States, the United Kingdom, UAE, Turkey, and South Africa. *Descendants of the Sun* was the most preferred Korean drama in China and Vietnam in 2019 (KFICE, 2020). Hence, as cultural differences satisfy international viewers' curiosity about Korean culture, they help attract loyal fans as well.

Korean television dramas, with their luscious visual images, good-looking actors, emotionally absorbing plots, and exotic Eastern cultural setting, are a visual entertainment product that communicates a set of cultural images through storytelling. For instance, Faiola (2006) reported that exceptionally good-looking and masculine leading men in Korean dramas should receive strong credit for the popularity of Korean dramas. It could be argued that the appeal of Korean television dramas is rooted in the cultural images that they convey in an aesthetically pleasing fashion as an expression of Confucian-based cultural values.

CULTURAL VALUE APPEAL

Cultural values are comprehensive concepts that play a significant role as standards of conduct for people who live in a given society (Singelis & Brown, 1995). For example, the East Asian cultures—China, Japan, and Korea—share and emphasize the values of "Interpersonal harmony, relational hierarchy, and traditional conservatism" (Zhang, Lin, Nonaka, & Beom, 2005, p. 2). As a cultural philosophy, Confucianism emphasizes the importance of respecting and complying with tradition and social authorities established by hierarchical rules and status to achieve harmonious relationships with other people. To present cultural images with historic realism (Chuang & Lee, 2013; Lin & Tong, 2007), Korean historical television dramas often project Confucian values in their storylines. These storylines typically feature such traditional values as family-centrism, patriarchal relations, filial piety, obedience, respect for one's elders, and harmonious interpersonal relationships (Cho, 2011; Hogarth, 2013; Tse, 2012).

In contrast to their US soap opera counterparts, male protagonists in Korean dramas are monogamous and often devote themselves to the object of their affection and sacrifice their lives for love. Couples in Korean dramas typically must overcome tragic obstacles to preserve their love, which usually results in much suffering and tears, before they can achieve their romantic union at the end (Chan & Xueli, 2011). By focusing on the cultural images of pure love or fairytale-like romance, Korean historical dramas successfully distinguish themselves from the US soap operas, which regularly show relational infidelity and overt scenes of sexual intercourse (Hanaki et al., 2007; Lin & Kwan, 2005).

Themes of devotion, loyalty, and traditional conservative attitudes toward sexuality have drawn the worldwide audience to appreciate the unique cultural values conveyed in Korean serial dramas. For instance, Chan and Xueli (2011) found that Singaporean female viewers enjoyed Korean dramas due to nonsexual pure love for which an ideal male character tends to sacrifice everything. Neighboring Asian countries or regions—including China, Japan, Taiwan, Hong Kong, and most Southeast Asian countries—are familiar with and respect these Confucian values. Therefore, Korean dramas have been accepted and favored by these viewers via subtitles without the common resistance associated with a language barrier (Chuang & Lee, 2013).

In essence, the traditional cultural values portrayed in the storylines of Korean historical television dramas are what set them apart from other television programs. Beloved Korean historical dramas have Asian ethos and cultural values with which Asians and Asian Americans are likely to empathize and identify (Hogarth, 2013). Espiritus's study (2011) showed that young Filipino females preferred Korean dramas to US and Mexican television dramas that present overly liberal values. Hogarth (2013) argued that Korean dramas become popular as they elicited a sense of nostalgia when Confucian values were still prevalent and followed by the Chinese and many other Asians who adopted those values. A study by Lee (2006) uncovered similar findings showing that one of the reasons why Japanese females became avid viewers of Korean dramas was because the young characters behave very differently from those depicted in Japanese television dramas. In Japanese television dramas, teenagers often do not show respect for their parents and seniors, whereas teenagers in Korean dramas use Korean honorifics when interacting with their parents and elders to show obedience and respect.

At the other end of the spectrum, hierarchical family structures are often depicted in Korean historical dramas. This view of an ordered world—even though it reflects varying degrees of cultural reality in Asian societies—is not wholeheartedly embraced by all Asian fans. Viewers who share ethnic and cultural identity with Koreans are said to be more likely to feel a sense of "Asian levels of identification" (Haut, 2010, p. 20). Therefore, the Confucian-styled cultural narrative could prompt Asian viewers to reflect on their own suffering from a male-dominant family structure and to experience strong empathy toward characters in these dramas (Haut, 2010).

TRANSCULTURAL FANDOM

Not unlike the popular television programs exported by Hollywood, Korean television dramas have become a welcome cultural product for their overseas fans. For example, these dramas have inspired not only Asian viewers (Cho, 2011) but Western viewers—in countries such as Spain and Latin America (Madrid-Morales, & Lovric, 2015)—to create fan clubs and form fandom culture. This transcultural fandom phenomenon has further boosted the popularity of Korean pop culture in general. For instance, the Korean drama *Winter Sonata* that ignited the Korean Wave in Japan in 2002 instantly made the male protagonist, Yong-Joon Bae, a transcultural star in Japan (Hanaki et al., 2007; Lee, 2006).

Transcultural fandom, as conceptualized here, is different from transnational fandom. While the former reflects fan obsession with popular cultural icons that share certain historical, cultural and/or linguistic commonalities, the latter describes international celebrities who do not share such a common cultural background. For example, transnational fandom could be exemplified by the popularity of US actor, Tom Cruise, who is admired by his fans from around the world, even though his sociocultural background and identity are different from that of his non-US fans. By comparison, transcultural fandom could be described by fan relations with Korean television drama stars who share pan-Asian culture with their Asian and Asian American fans. Transcultural fans embrace and identify their fandom objects as part of their own popular culture scene. Jung (2011, p. 35) describes how male Korean Wave stars accentuate the image of Pan-East Asian "soft masculinity" that originated from Japanese "beautiful boy" illustrations.

This transcultural fandom has played a role in transforming Korean drama fans into fans of other Korean popular cultural products. For instance, Japanese viewers who follow Korean dramas enjoy Korean pop music, fashion, food, and tourism (Lee, 2006). Likewise, Korean dramas and music have exerted a strong influence on bilateral cultural ties between Korea and China, by providing sociocultural information that helped construct new and modern images of Korea (Han, Chang, & Hwang, 2008; Jang, 2012). As transcultural fandom stems from shared appreciation of Korean television dramas, it communicates a unique cultural identity too. It is important to understand how the relations between this transcultural fandom and transcultural identity—as well as what a transcultural identity could mean for Asian American viewers—who are in search of, attempt to establish or intend to maintain their hybridized cultural background and values.

TRANSCULTURAL IDENTITY

Cultural identity is a composite of a hybrid set of nationality, religious affiliation, and ethnicity (Anagondahalli & Turner, 2012). Oyserman and Sakamoto's (1997) typology on Asian American ethic identity highlights Asian Americans' family relatedness, pride in heritage-connectedness to traditions, awareness of discrimination-barriers, and achievement as being integral to their group membership. These authors contend that Asian American ethnic identity is best illustrated by the interdependence and group connectedness of its ethnic community. When an individual embodies a specific ethnic background encounters and is exposed to foreign cultures or their own ethnic culture in various forms, the individual could experience a crisis in his or her cultural identity (Morris, Mok, & Mor, 2011). This cultural identity crisis may help facilitate the individual's interest in exploring and affirming his or her true cultural identity.

Asian Americans have vastly different racial, ethnic, and cultural origins. Combining Asian Americans with Pacific Islanders, there are 56 ethnics groups who speak over 100 languages in the United States (Centers for Disease Control and Prevention, 2013). Hence, a more inclusive way to examine the Asian American cultural identity would be to consider the implications of a fusion of cultures. Asian Americans who "melt" at least one ethnic culture with the mainstream US culture could be described as Americans with a transcultural identity. Operationally speaking, this transcultural identity is represented by the mixture of more than one ethnic culture, whereas an individual does not necessarily identify with a bicultural or multicultural identity but an integrated transcultural identity.

The scholar Oh (2011) proposed a model to analyze the journey that second-generation Korean Americans may experience in seeking their cultural identity. Specifically, he noted that Korean Americans in the "ambivalence stage"—or the earliest stage where they are not quite sure whether they wish to emotionally invest in the Korean culture—are not critical of Korean films, even if they are not highly interested in the Korean ethnic culture. His model further suggested that second-generation Korean Americans in the "exploration stage" are curious about and interested in understanding their ethnic identity. Upon entering the "immersion stage" next, they would seek exposure to the Korean culture, associate themselves with friends of a similar cultural background, and reject the dominant (white) culture. Following that, if they decide to enter the "integration stage," they would then embrace their ethnic identity and develop an understanding of the meaning of "being culturally American and of the limitations of Korean cultural practices" (Oh, 2011, p. 189).

If the multistage model proposed by Oh (2011) is applied, it is not difficult to see that exposure to Korean historical dramas may awaken Asian Americans' underlying desire to explore their transcultural identity. Especially among second-generation Americans, some could experience a cultural identity crisis. Past research indicates that Asian entertainment content has played a significant role in maintaining and strengthening the ethnic identity of Asian Americans across generations. For instance, Korean immigrants try to maintain their ethnic identity by watching Korean programs such as Korean dramas and Korean music videos (commonly known as K-pop) via satellite television networks (Lee, 2004).

Korean television shows provide feelings of closeness to Korean culture for first-generation Korean immigrants and second-generation Korean Americans born and raised in the United States (Park, 1990). Through observing and enjoying traditional philosophy and values illustrated in Korean dramas, Asian American viewers, including Korean Americans, can rediscover the roots of their cultural values (Hogarth, 2013). Ju and Lee (2015) showed that young Asian Americans could reminisce about their ethnic culture and transcultural identity via Korean pop culture. They enjoyed Korean romance dramas as well, due to the positive portrayals of Asians in these programs, which elicited vicarious satisfaction and comfort.

Park (2008) highlighted three major reasons why Asian American audiences are drawn to cultural images embodied in Korean dramas. First, Asian American characters in television programs and films are uncommon in the United States. Second, for those few Asian American performers that do appear in the US media, they are often cast in roles that reflect a certain degree of racial or ethnic stereotyping. Third, Korean pop culture contents provide a venue for Asian American youths to help define and reinforce their transcultural identity. According to both Jung (2009) and Oh (2011), Asian American youths are attracted to Korean pop culture content because they enjoy and can identify with the hybridized cultural images at varying degrees.

VIEWING GRATIFICATIONS

The concept of uses and gratifications (also described as viewing needs or motives) asserts that television viewers are cognitively active audiences who select their viewing choices from a wide variety of media channels/content categories to satisfy a set of cognitive and affective needs (Lee & Laramie, 2010). According to Rubin (2002), audience choices of specific viewing content may vary, due to the differences in their social and psychological make-up, which may generate differential viewing gratification expectations. McQuail, Blumler, and Brown (1972) propose the following functional dimensions of media consumption: diversion, personal relationship, personal identity, and surveillance. As the diversion function offers audiences a temporary escape from reality, the "personal relationship" function allows them to develop parasocial, mediated, or real life (e.g., fan clubs) social relations with media characters. The personal identity function can provide audiences a "personal reference, reality exploration, and value reinforcement" as members of a social group (Katz, Blumler, & Gurevitch, 1973, p. 513). Through the surveillance function, media present news, events, and information that are valuable for viewers to learn about the world around them.

Advances in communication and information technologies, in conjunction with the growth of market globalization, have enabled the diffusion of foreign media content through internet, satellite television, and cable television. The influx of television shows from different countries has created a different set of potential attractions and gratification opportunities from what local television content could not typically provide (Jiang & Leung, 2012). For example, a study on Korean drama viewing gratification revealed that highly educated and well-informed Chinese citizens tended to watch more foreign television programs to meet their entertainment and information learning needs (Jiang & Leung, 2012).

It is logical to assume that Asian American viewers may be motivated to watch Korean historical dramas to meet their diversion, personal relationship, personal identity, and surveillance needs (McQuail et al., 1972). Watching Korean historical dramas may offer these viewers opportunities to immerse themselves in images of social harmony, develop a pseudo-social relationship with Korean drama characters, confer their personal identity as Asian Americans, and learn about a distant world with close cultural proximity.

Hence, the gratifications sought and obtained from watching Korean dramas can be utilized as a source for affirming an individual's transcultural identity. A by-product that could result from the process of searching an individual's Asian cultural roots and transcultural identity would be the establishment or enhancement of social ties with the Asian American community. To derive social benefits from this transcultural identity-driven social ties,

Asian Americans could tap the technology affordances—offered by online social networks—to cultivate and maintain the transcultural social capital that they desire.

SOCIAL CAPITAL

According to Bourdieu (1986), cultural capital refers to a disposition that is loosely defined as an individual's "institutionalized" cultural class (e.g., social values, political beliefs, music taste, viewing preferences) and social capital reflects the social resources that an individual acquires due to his/her membership in a social network. An individual's cultural capital could supply resources that enable him or her to be inducted into a social network and to have access to the social capital of that social network. This type of social capital could provide bilateral, multilateral, and/or collective material and social backing for an individual to enhance their socioeconomic capital.

Social capital availability could be determined based on social relationships between individuals, the nature of those relationships, the strength, and collectivity of those associations (Adler & Kwon, 2002). Three main benefits that an individual could draw from his or her "social capital" could include (1) useful information, (2) social influence, control, and power affiliated with the authority, and (3) social solidity and support (Adler & Kwon, 2000). In practice, social capital generally falls into two categories: (1) intracommunity capital (via strong social ties), stemming from individuals such as families and friends, that shares some common group identity and social purposes; and (2) intercommunity capital (via weak social ties), deriving from attributes such as religious, ethnic, gender, and socioeconomic status, that typically operates across social boundaries (Astone, Nathanson, Schoen, & Kim, 1999). Access to these two types of social capital is similar to connecting to the commonly referenced strong-tie and weak-tie network in the communication literature.

Social capital can be differentially sought and utilized, according to the collective resources available through a social network (Robison, Schmid, & Siles, 2002). Putnam (2000) conceptualizes social capital with two dimensions. Bonding social capital evolves around close friends or family members in an intra-community strong-tie network. Bridging social capital extends from individuals who network with each other under special circumstances (e.g., professional work) (Ellison, Steinfield, & Lampe, 2007). The advent of communication and information technologies, especially social network services such as Facebook, has greatly enhanced people's ability to cultivate, expand, and maintain the social capital associated with their social networks.

Williams's (2007) study found that people access "bonding social capital" from their strong-tie network more often in an offline setting and utilize their "bridging social capital" from their weak-tie network more often in an online setting. Choi, Kim, Sung, and Sohn (2010) contend that cultural content could make a difference in terms of how and what type of social capital is built, expanded, or solidified. Donath and Boyd (2004) suggest that as technology affordances provided by online social network sites (SNS) could strengthen bonding social capital by enabling efficient reinforcement of strong ties, cultural contexts could influence which type of social capital could be strengthened.

As SNS are an important channel for building social capital, research has found that both US and Korean users who share common interests to engage in collaborative action facilitate communication via SNS (Choi et al., 2010). For example, SNS-based interaction between college students was found to encourage ethnic minorities to develop social capital by building trust and establish "norms of reciprocity" (Valenzuela, Park, & Kee, 2008, p. 4); an interaction effect between race and Facebook users of nonwhite students also influenced their collaborative action on political participation. Another study suggests that compared to their non-Asian American counterparts, Asian American college students tend to have fewer friends on SNSs, are more connected to their strong-tie networks and engage those in their weak ties networks less often (Hargittai & Hsieh, 2010). In a similar vein, other research reported that minority Facebook users that have friendship networks on SNS with more racial or ethnic homogeneity tend to have higher SNS use frequency as well (Lewis, Kaufman, & Christakis, 2008). These findings seem consistent with the thesis of another study, which found that those who identify themselves with individualistic instead of collectivistic culture tend to have more friends online (Rosen, Stefanone & Lackaff, 2010).

In sum, these empirical findings imply that racial or ethnic minorities have smaller friendship networks on SNS, compared to white users. Both ethnic minority and white users primarily have friends on SNS that share homogeneous ethnic cultures. Racial or ethnic minority SNS users utilize these social media venues to bond with friends who share their ethnic culture and to build social capital. It can be argued that Asian Americans who are interested in and enjoyed the cultural images communicated by Korean historical dramas may find such images to be resonating with their own aspirations for a transcultural identity. One venue for Asian Americans who intend to seek or express their transcultural identity could involve sharing their viewing experiences of Korean dramas with friends on SNS. Hence, by exchanging and discussing the meanings and values of the cultural images embodied in Korean dramas, Asian Americans may in turn strengthen their social bond and social capital with each other.

PROPOSED CONCEPTUAL FRAMEWORK

Based on the literature review, a conceptual framework is proposed to help integrate the different theoretical elements. This proposed conceptual framework could be utilized for future critical analysis explaining the cultural image appeal of Korean historical television dramas and their implications on viewing enjoyment, cultural identity and/or social capital. The same framework could be applied to empirical research examining the interrelationships between the different variables. Asian Americans who enjoy Confucian-themed cultural images and are seeking culturally related viewing gratifications will be interested in watching Korean historical dramas. While exposure to these television dramas will generate viewing gratifications, such exposure and viewing gratifications will also facilitate/enhance viewers' transcultural identity. Both viewing gratifications and transcultural identity, in turn, will strengthen these viewers' transcultural social capital.

RESEARCH PROPOSITIONS

To aid future research that aims at elucidating the theoretical links between the described concepts, a set of preliminary research propositions are proposed below:

> Proposition 1: Cultural image appeals will motivate Korean historical drama exposure.
>
> Proposition 2: Viewing gratifications sought, including diversion, personal relationships, social identity, and surveillance, will motivate Korean historical drama exposure.
>
> Proposition 3: Exposure to Korean historical dramas will contribute to the cultivation of Asian Americans' transcultural identity and viewing gratifications obtained.
>
> Proposition 4: Viewing gratifications obtained will contribute to the cultivation of Asian American's transcultural identity.
>
> Proposition 5: Asian Americans' transcultural identity and viewing gratifications will contribute to transcultural social capital.

CONCLUSION

The current chapter reviewed a set of interdisciplinary theories from the fields of cultural studies, sociology, and communication to provide a synthesis between cultural values, social capital as well as visual media uses and gratifications from a transcultural perspective. It proposes that cultural images of media content, which communicate a set of specific cultural values, will help cultivate, enhance, and maintain audiences' transcultural identity. The concept of transcultural identity is operationalized as a cultural identity that is represented by the fusion of more than one ethnic culture. More research is needed to fully explicate the cultural meanings of the images conveyed by Korean historical dramas on their international viewers from a transcultural perspective.

The popularity of Korean historical dramas outside of the East Asian region, such as Europe and Latin America, suggests that cultural images conveying Eastern Asian cultural values could draw strong audience interest. Hence, future research addressing the transcultural perspective proposed here should consider audiences who either share, or do not share Confucian cultural heritage, but find resonance with the cultural images embodied in Korean historical television dramas. In the age of global media markets, additional work that deciphers the attractions of pure and eternal love, family bonds and social harmony—as television drama themes through visual presentations—will have practical implications for domestic and overseas culture industries.

REFERENCES

Adler, P. S., & Kwon, S. W. (2000). Social capital: The good, the bad, and the ugly. In E. L. Lesser (Eds.), *Knowledge and social capital* (pp. 89–115). Butterworth-Heinemann.

Adler, P. S., & Kwon, S. W. (2002). Social capital: Prospects for a new concept. *Academy of Management Review, 27(1)*, 17–40. doi: 10.5465/amr.2002.5922314.

Anagondahalli, D. & Turner, M. M. (2012). Predicting psychological ripple effects: The role of cultural identity, in-group/out-group identification, and attributions of blame in crisis communication. *Risk Analysis, 32*, 695–712. doi: 10.1111/j.1539-6924.2011.01727.x.

Astone, N.M., Nathanson, C.A., Schoen, R., & Kim, Y.J. (1999). Family demography, social theory,and investment in social capital. *Population and Development Review, 25(1)*, 1–31.

Barry, A. M. (1997). *Visual intelligence: Perception, image, and manipulation in visual communication.* SUNY Press.

Bourdieu, P. (1986) The forms of capital. In J. Richardson (Ed.), *Handbook of theory and research for the sociology of education* (pp. 241–258). Greenwood.

Centers for Disease Control and Prevention (2013, May 6). CDC celebrates Asian American & Pacific Islander heritage. Retrieved from: SJ Revised_4-1_The Korean Wave.docx.

Chan, B. & Xueli, W. (2011). Of prince charming and male chauvinist pigs: Singaporean female viewers and the dream-world of Korean television dramas. *International Journal of Cultural Studies, 14*, 291–305.

Cho, Y. (2011). Desperately seeking East Asia amidst the popularity of South Korean pop culture in Asia. *Cultural Studies, 25*, 383–404.

Choi, S. M., Kim, Y., Sung, Y., & Sohn, D. (2010). Bridging or bonding? A cross-cultural study of social relationships in social networking sites. *Information, Communication & Society, 14*, 107–129.

Chuang, L. M. & Lee, H. E. (2013). Korean wave: Enjoyment factors of Korean dramas in the US. *International Journal of Intercultural Relations, 37*, 594–604.

Donath, J. & Boyd, D. (2004). Public displays of connection. *BT Technology Journal, 22*, 71–82.

Ellison, N. B., Steinfield, C., & Lampe, C. (2007). The benefits of Facebook friends: Social capital and college students' use of online social network sites. *Journal of Computer-Mediated Communication, 12*, 1143–1168.

Espiritu, B.F. (2011). Transnational audience reception as a theater of struggle. *Asian Journal of Communication, 21*, 355–372.

Faiola, A. (2006 August 31). Japanese women catch the 'Korean Wave.' *The Washington Post*. http://www.washingtonpost.com/wp-dyn/content/article/2006/08/30/ AR2006083002985.html.

Hargittai, E., & Hsieh, Y. P. (2010). Predictors and consequences of differentiated practices on social network sites. *Communication and Society, 13*(4), 515–536.

Han, E., Chang, W., & Hwang, G. (2008). The mediating effects of the national image on the relationship between the Korea Wave and a company's brand equity. *International Marketing Review, 16*, 18–41.

Hanaki, T., Singhal, A., Han, M. W., Kim, D. K., & Chitnis, K. (2007). Hanryu sweeps East Asia. *The International Communication Gazette, 69*, 281–294.

Hogarth, H. K. (2013). The Korean Wave: An Asian reaction to Western-dominated globalization. *Perspectives on Global Development and Technology, 12*, 135–151.

Huat, C. B. (2010). Korean pop culture. *Malaysian Journal of Media Studies, 12*, 15–24. http://umepublication.um.edu.my/public/index.php.

Jang, S. H. (2012). The Korean Wave and Its implications for the Korea-China relationship. *Journal of International and Area Studies, 19*, 97–113. http://iia.snu.ac.kr/iia_publication/iia_publication_jias.htm.

Jiang, Q. & Leung, L. (2012). Lifestyles, gratifications sought, and narrative appeal: American and Korean TV drama viewing among Internet users in urban China. *International Communication Gazette, 74*, 159–180.

Jo, H. (2013, October 13). Analysis of popularity of Dae Jang Geum in different countries. *Kukmin Daily News*. http://news.kukinews.com/article/view.asp?page=&gCode=kmi&arcid=0007648170&cp=nv.

Ju, H., & Lee, S. (2015). The Korean Wave and Asian Americans: The ethnic meanings of transnational Korean pop culture in the USA. *Continuum, 29*(3), 323–338.

Jung, E-Y (2009). Transnational Korea: A critical assessment of the Korean wave in Asia and the United States. *Southeast Review of Asian Studies, 31*, 69–80.

Jung, S. (2011). *Korean masculinities and transcultural consumption: Yonsama, Rain, Oldboy, K-Pop idols*. Hong Kong University Press.

Katz, E., Blumler, J. G., & Gurevitch, M. (1973). Uses and gratifications research. *Public Opinion Quarterly, 37*, 509–524.

Kim, S. (2009). Interpreting transnational cultural practices: Social discourses on a Korean drama in Japan, Hong Kong, and China. *Cultural Studies, 23*, 736–755.

Korea Creative Content Agency (2013). Retrieved March 20, 2014 from http://www.kocca.kr.

Korean Foundation for International Cultural Exchange (2020). *Global Hallyu Trends*. http://kofice.or.kr/b20industry/b20_industry_01_view.asp?seq=1049&page=1&find=&search=.

Korea Tourism Organization (2005, September 5). *'Korean Wave' lands on U.S.* http://english.visitkorea.or.kr/enu/FU/FU_EN_15.jsp?cid=289174.

Lee, C. (2004). Korean immigrants' viewing patterns of Korean satellite television and its role in their lives. *Asian Journal of Communication, 14*, 68–80.

Lee, S. (2006). *The Korean Wave in Japan: Winter Sonata and its implications through audience perception*. ICA. http://web.a.ebscohost.com.ezproxy.lib.uconn.edu/ehost/detail?vid=2&sid=c5ed1173-95fb-4245-8837-.

Lee, T. & Laramie, T. (2010). *The motives and consequences of viewing television dramas*. ICA, Singapore. http://web.ebscohost.com.ezproxy.lib.uconn.edu/.

Lewis, K., Kaufman, J., & Christakis, N. (2008). The taste for privacy: An analysis of college student privacy settings in an online social network. *Journal of Computer-Mediated Communication, 14*(1), 79–100.

Lin, A. & Kwan, B. (2005). The dilemmas of modern working women in Hong Kong: Women's use of Korean TV dramas. *Asian Communication Research, 2*, 23–42.

Lin, A., & Tong, A. (2009). Constructing cultural self and other in the Internet discussion of a Korean historical TV drama: A discourse analysis of weblog messages of Hong Kong viewers of Dae Jang Geum. *Journal of Asian Pacific Communication, 19*, 289–312.

Lin, A. M. & Tong, A. (2007). Crossing boundaries: Male consumption of Korean TV dramas and negotiation of gender relations in modern day Hong Kong. *Journal of Gender Studies, 16*, 217–232.

Madrid-Morales, D., & Lovric, B. (2015). Transatlantic connection: K-pop and K-drama fandom in Spain and Latin America. *The Journal of Fandom Studies, 3*, 23–41.

MacDonald, J. (2019). Deciding which Korean dramas will appeal to US viewers. *Forbes*. https://www.forbes.com/sites/joanmacdonald/2019/05/17/deciding-which-korean-dramas-will-appeal-to-u-s-viewers/#325309f451e6.

McQuail, D., Blumler, J.G., & Brown, J.R. (1972). The television audience. In D. McQuail (Ed.), *Sociology of mass communications* (pp. 135–165). Penguin.

Morris, M. W., Mok, A. & Mor, S. (2011). Cultural identity treat: The role of cultural identifications in moderating closure responses to foreign cultural inflow. *Journal of Social Issues, 4*, 760–773.

Oh, D. C. (2011). Viewing identity: Second-generation Korean American ethnic identification and the reception of Korean transnational films. *Communication, Culture & Critique, 4*, 184–204.

Oyserman, D. & Sakamoto, I. (1997). Being Asian American: Identity, cultural constructs, and stereotype perception. *The Journal of Applied Behavioral Science, 33*, 435–453.

Park, D. (1990). *The meanings of television viewing: An interpretive analysis of four Korean groups in the U.S.* PhD dissertation. University of Texas.

Park, J-S (2008, June 20). The high tide of the Korean Wave (36): The Korean Wave and Korean-Americans. HANCINEMA. http://www.hancinema.net/the-high-tide-of-the-korean-wave-36-the-korean-wave-and-korean-americans-14214.html.

Park, S., Yun, G.W., & Lee, S. Y. (2011). Emergence of Asian dramas as a global melodramatic genre: The case of Korean television dramas. In D. Rios & M. Castaneda (Eds.), *Soap operas and telenovelas in the digital age: Global industries and new audiences* (pp. 37–54). Peter Lang.

Putnam, R. D. (2000). *Bowling alone: The collapse and revival of American community.* Simon & Schuster.

Robison, L. J., Schmid, A. A., & Siles, M. E. (2002). Is social capital really capital? *Review of Social Economy, 60*, 1–21.

Rosen, D., Stefanone, M., & Lackaff, D. (2010). *Online and offline social networks: Investigating culturally-specific behavior and satisfaction.* Hawaii International Conf. on System Sciences. http://www.computer.org/csdl/proceedings/hicss/2010/3869/00/07-08-08.pdf.

Rubin, A. M. (2002). The uses-and-gratifications perspective of media effects. In J. Bryant & D. Zillmann (Eds.), *Media effects: Advances in theory and research* (pp. 525–548). Erlbaum.

Ryoo, W. (2009). Globalization, or the logic of cultural hybridization: The case of the Korean wave. *Asian Journal of Communication, 19*, 137–151.

Singelis, T. M., & Brown, W. J. (1995). Culture, self, and collectivist communication: Linking culture to individual behavior. *Human Communication Research, 21*, 354–389.

Tse, L. (1999). Finding a place to be: Ethnic identity exploration of Asian Americans. *ADOLESCENCE, 34*, 121–138. http://web.ebscohost.com.ezproxy.lib.uconn.edu/ehost/.

Valenzuela, S., Park, N., & Kee, K. F. (April, 2008). *Lessons from Facebook: The effect of social network sites on college students' social capital.* International Symposium, Austin, TX. http://citeseerx.ist.psu.edu/viewdoc/download?doi=10.1.1.168.3640&rep=rep1&type=pdf.

Williams, D. (2007). The impact of time online: Social capital and cyberbalkanization. *Cyber Psychology & Behavior, 10*, 398–406.

Yang, F. C. I. (2008). Rap(p)ing Korean wave: National identity in question. *East Asian Pop Culture: Analysing the Korean Wave, 1*, 191–216.

Zhang, Y. B., Lin, M-C., Nonaka, A., & Beom, K. (2005). Harmony, hierarchy and conservatism: A cross-cultural comparison of Confucian values in China, Korea, Japan, and Taiwan. *Communication Research Reports, 22*, 107–115.

Chapter 11

Thoroughly (Un)Modern *Downton Abbey*

Interrogating Gender/Sexual Dynamics and Whiteness Boundaries

Gordon Alley-Young

Julian Fellowes's television series *Downton Abbey* (*DA*) (2010–2015) chronicles the life of the fictional Earl of Grantham's family and servants in rural Yorkshire from 1912 to 1926. *DA* garnered high ratings and record awards nominations for US public television (PBS) by blending soap opera with a successful period drama formula of paralleling aristocratic and servant life (Byrne, 2014; Cuccinello, 2016). Television audiences learn history through shows like *DA* that might privilege drama over accuracy (Bedwell, 2019; Brown, 2015; Byrne, 2014; Delsandro, 2017). Audiences embracing *DA* and its lifestyle aesthetic may overlook problematic social ideologies and cultural politics (e.g., nostalgizing a culturally unified past, conservative social traditions) (Baena & Byker, 2015; Braga, 2016). *DA* set social media records for PBS during season five with over 190,000 total tweets and 24 million total impressions (Cuccinello, 2016).

This chapter analyses gender, sexuality, and whiteness in *DA* using cultural studies, history, critical identity perspectives, and postcolonial writings. I argue that while the series creator/actors, its fans, and/or critics may interpret Lady Edith and Sprat, and Barrow as progressive in their gender/sexuality role performance, these characters represent progressive and problematic representation/identity discourses. While this television series presents the Edwardian-Georgian periods as lacking in racial diversity, this chapter argues that *DA* is a useful text for exploring evolving definitions of whiteness based on religion, nationality, and social class via characters Lady Cora, Atticus Aldridge, and Thomas.

METHODOLOGY

This chapter uses Fiske's (2011) protocol for studying television via primary, secondary, and tertiary texts. The primary texts are all 52 episodes of the *DA* television series from six seasons (2010–2016) watched in their entirety, what Krippendorf (2004) calls a census sample. Representations were recorded of Lady Edith, Spratt, and Barrow's sexuality and/or gender role and representations of Lady Cora, Atticus, and Branson's whiteness via references to religion, social class, and nationality. Analysis notes both latent (i.e., symbolic/obscured) and manifest (i.e., literal/visible) content (Krippendorf, 2004). Primary text content was read through the relevant content of secondary texts (i.e., television publicity and criticism) (Fiske, 2011). Primary and secondary text content are then read through tertiary texts (e.g., viewer-created blogs, fan sites, and fan fiction/artwork) (Fiske, 2011).

Fiske (2011) argues for vertical (i.e., similar themes/meanings/motifs across these three levels) and horizontal (i.e., themes/meanings/motifs in the primary text genre reflected in other textual genres like history, scholarship, documentary, film, pornography, advertising) intertextuality. This vertical and horizontal textual juxtaposition provides a textual basis for criticism of identity construction in *DA*. The chapter examines how Lady Edith and Spratt fall short as gender progressive characters, how the depiction of Barrow is representative of the power/privilege differentials in media representations of LGBTQ+ lives, and how the seeming absence of race in *DA* makes it a valuable text for studying the evolution of racial discourses around whiteness.

Thoroughly Modern Edith

This section discusses whether Lady Edith and Septimus Sprat should be characterized as modern or progressive for appearing to step outside of gender roles expected of Edwardian-Georgian men and women. Despite being the second eldest daughter to Earl and Lady Grantham (Robert and Cora Crawley), Lady Edith Crawley's life is filled with disappointment. Notably, Anthony Strallan, her fiancé, leaves her at the altar (season three). Edith conceives a secret love child with subsequently murdered Michael Gregson in season four, a secret that later threatens Edith's engagement to Bertie Pelham, Marquess of Hexham (season six). Expected to marry but lacking options, Edith first writes a column on societal change, later becoming owner/editor of *The Sketch* (inherited from Gregson). Edith's career in male-dominated publishing parallels Septimus Spratt, butler for the Dowager Countess, who, anxious for his position, secretly writes a women's advice column as "agony aunt" Cassandra Jones.

Viewers, critics, Fellowes, and actress Laura Carmichael construct Edith as bucking 1920s gender roles. Ivie (2016) likens Edith to television's *Mad Men's* (2007–2015) character Peggy Olsen, an aspiring 1960s advertising executive, Sulcas (2016) foregrounds Edith's "evolution," and Miller's (2016) interview with Carmichael labels Edith "modern" five times. In a PBS publicity video, creator Fellowes calls Edith an "everyman" who "challenges her own destiny" while Carmichael calls her "a modern woman" and a "rebel" who is "awakened" (Masterpiece, 2014). Mahon (2016) blogs that Edith is the "strongest" Crawley sister who at series end is "a thoroughly modern woman of the 20th century" and a "Feminist Fan Favorite." Mahon (2016) declares, "Edith Crawley, you CAN have it all!"

Hollywood embraced independent women during this period (i.e., 1920s–1930s) but stereotyped women's careers as substitutes for marriage/motherhood (i.e., 1930s–1970s, later decades) (Boozer, 2010; Malone, 2017). Victorian literature also promoted familiar (i.e., companionate) marriage because marriage allowed women greater social agency (Schaffer, 2016). Lawler (2014) argues of Edwardians, "Everyone—aristocrat or servant—knows his place, his relational responsibilities [. . .] [unburdened] by the modern individualistic freedom of figuring out one's place in the world" (p. 28). Edith's working-class counterparts had to stifle their personal lives to get domestic service positions (Horn, 2013).

Edith's career developments are prompted with the experiences of loss, loneliness, and lacking a social role. She seeks columnist work after Strallan departs. Edith becomes editor and owner of *The Sketch* upon Gregson's disappearance and death. Later Edith relocates to London immediately after breaking with Bertie because her work is in London. When Edith's father asks about her happiness in London, she circumvents emotion by highlighting her new role, "I'll have Marigold. Anyway, I'm a spinster, aren't I? And spinsters live alone." Similarly, when Henry Talbot discloses that his fears about the dangers of racing prompted him to leave the profession even as he fears losing his identity and his wife's love, Edith responds, "Well, then, you must find something to do!" Henry, unassuaged, concedes, "Yes, I must, mustn't I?" Edith's response lacks empathy and emotional support similar to researchers' descriptions of men's communication (ten Brummelhuis & Greenhaus, 2018). Edith's patriarchal advice prescribes self-reliance, avoids emotion, and endorses social convention (i.e., work makes the man).

Edith's advice mirrors Spratt's turn as agony aunt Cassandra Jones, cited among *DA*'s most memorable storylines (Masterpiece, 2019). US café society columnist Maury Henry Biddle Paul (aka, Polly Stuyvesant, Dolly Madison) (Young, 2015) might be the inspiration for Sprat. Nevertrustaduck394 (2015) declares Spratt an "agony aunt supreme!" Spratt progressively seeks class mobility but is regressive for depriving a woman writer of a voice, when so many struggled to be heard, and for upholding patriarchal norms. EditorBee (2015) argues, "It's not surprising [. . .] that terrible and sexist advice was being doled out by a man." Spratt/Cassandra writes, "Your husband is losing interest? Well, here's step one. Take a look in the mirror." Spratt/Cassandra, like Edith to Henry, lacks empathy and prescribes self-reliance and encourages women to live according to the male gaze. Butler Spratt upholds this male gaze when he tells the Dowager that he observed Lady Mary with Anthony Foyle, Lord Gillingham at a hotel (season five).

Bertie perpetuates the male gaze when advising Edith, as editor, whom to include in a society feature, saying, "Best clothes and prettiest faces. Nobody cares about anything else" (season six). Similarly, footman Andy tells assistant cook Daisy, "I don't think that you need to change your hair," and Daisy replies, "What? Are you a fashion expert now?" (season six). Spratt, Bertie, and Andy's examples reflect the findings of a study that argues the most well-known fashion brands are designed for and led predominantly by men (Brown, Haas, Marchessou, & Villepelet, 2018). Similarly, men originated (i.e., Englishman John Dutton in 1691) and helped popularize (i.e., Benjamin Franklin, the 4th Earl of Chesterfield) advice columns in the 1700s (Carey, 2009; Weisburg, 2018). Similarly, men also created the communication form labeled mansplaining in 2008 (Rothman, 2012). Female post–World War I agony aunts were similarly unsympathetic and patriarchal, advising women to return to being wives/mothers after wartime work and to choose husbands with earning potential (Carey, 2009; Cawthorne, 2016). US columnist Dorothy Dix urged women to accept powerlessness/despair as their lot in life and not wallow emotionally (Weisberg, 2018).

Alternately, *DA* viewers learn of British scientist Dr. Marie Stopes, who espoused modern sexuality and gender. Mary offers Anna Stopes's book *Married Love or Love in Marriage* (Stopes, 1918) so that Anna can purchase a diaphragm for Mary's affair with Anthony Foyle in season five. Stopes encouraged women's sexual desire and encouraged couples to plan their families to maximize their love bonds. Stopes became a sympathetic agony aunt to thousands of men and women who sought her advice on their sexual dilemmas (Lambert, 2018).

Calling Edith modern evokes a 1920s definition of modern that fails to meet 2020s standard. Edith is strong through her adversities but sacrifices her emotional health. Edith is a full-time wife and mother and a Marchioness by the time of the *DA* feature film directed by Fellowes and Engler in 2019. Upon learning that Bertie will be away from home serving the Prince of Wales when her baby is due, Edith expresses resentment about losing a career she loved, her boring dinner guests, and dictated social obligations. Edith tells Bertie that a regular woman in the lodge would have her husband present during childbirth. Edith's expectation that Bertie be involved in family and childbirth reflects modern, emotionally intelligent thinking but her lodge comment overlooks how her working/middle-class contemporaries were disenfranchised. Edith demonstrates that choice and self-determination are ideals and that all levels of society must evolve and change in order for all women to advance. Likewise, Spratt's class mobility is progressive, but he reaches his goals by reinforcing the marginalization of women.

The Gay for Pay Problem and Carte Blanche Histories

Thomas Barrow's roles in *DA* include serving as first footman, head valet, under-butler, and finally butler. Barrow, as he is called by the family, has been critiqued as an anti-hero for bullying fellow staff, stealing wine from the cellar, getting a military discharge by deliberately sustaining war injuries, trading on the postwar black market, and for trying to blackmail a former lover, a closeted Duke (Byrne, 2014). Critics argue that Barrow, while complicated, illuminates previously hidden LGBTQ+ lives and history (Brown, 2015). For example, in season three, Barrow is almost arrested for mistakenly assuming footman Jimmy was gay and kissing him. Barrow subsequently suffers through quack medicine to change his sexuality (i.e., pills, electroconvulsive therapy, injections) during season five. Carson tells Barrow in season three, "You have been twisted by nature into something foul." Barrow in defense, argues, "I am not foul, Mr. Carson. I am not the same as you, but I am not foul." After a failed suicide attempt in season six, Barrow leaves briefly at series end to take over as butler when Mr. Carson's health falters. The privilege and protection Barrow enjoys is atypical of 1920s LGBTQ+ lives, which is problematic since Barrow is the only in-depth LGBTQ+ character in *DA*. Relatedly, having Rob James-Collier, a heterosexual/cisgender actor, portray Barrow is indicative of a problematic trend of LGBTQ+ representation within the larger media.

Heterosexual and/or cisgendered actors receive frequent recognition for LGBTQ+ roles, taking both top acting Oscars in 2019, while no actor has won the best actor Oscar while being openly LGBTQ+ (Advocate, 2018; Ellenzweig, 2006; Martin, 2018). Casting directors argue that they choose the best actors for LGBTQ+ roles, but critics argue that casting the majority of LGBTQ+ roles with heterosexual/cisgender actors constitutes attempts to normalize gayness as heterosexual masculinity (Kirst, 2017; Martin, 2018). LGBTQ+ actors cite how "gay for pay," or straight actors paid to perform sexually for homosexual audiences in pornography due to internalized homophobia and/or fetishizing of heterosexual hypermasculinity has influenced mainstream media portrayals of LGBTQ+ sexuality (Kirst, 2017; Reynolds, 2016). Similarly, Wirthlin (2009) argues that fad lesbian advertising imagery, likely featuring heterosexual models for straight male pleasure, lacks agency and power to not threaten heterosexual identity. Kirst (2017) has dubbed this, the gay for pay problem (GFPP) in Hollywood because it denies LGBTQ+ performers opportunities to self-represent (Kirst, 2017).

In an interview actor Rob James-Collier said he requested that Barrow kiss the closeted Duke of Crowborough in season one, while also noting his heterosexuality by saying that he fears appearing too authentic when acting in opposite sex love scenes and inauthentic in same-sex love scenes (Love, 2010). Bloggers write gay relationship fan fiction featuring Barrow and chauffeur-turned son-in-law Thomas Branson, played by Alan Leech (Archive of Our Own, 2012–2019). James-Collier and Leech encourage this fiction by flirting and holding hands during interviews (Mavity, 2015). James-Collier and Leech's displays of affection can be read as opposing homophobia by normalizing male same-sex intimacy and/or they can be read as perpetuating the GFPP as two perceived heterosexual actors role playing homosexual intimacy to publicize James-Collier's television performance of homosexuality with perceived heterosexual costars like Cox. Sánchez et al. (2009, pp. 78–79) found that "straight," "straight-acting" and "able to be pass as a straight man in public" is how many gay men were defining masculinity and such labels can determine one's access to romantic/sexual partners and ultimately one's self-worth.

Barrow's depiction also perpetuates myths of gay affluence and privilege. While marginalized in society, LGBTQ+ people are stereotyped in the media as affluent urbanites in order to subvert LGBTQ+ advocacy for civil rights (Hettinger & Vandello, 2014). Likewise, Barrow is protected from prosecution for homosexuality, a crime until 1969 in the United Kingdom, by aristocratic privilege both in the series, when Lord Grantham-Robert Crawley blocks a police investigation of Barrow kissing sleeping footman Jimmy (season three).

In the *DA* film spin-off, Barrow meets Chris in a pub and they go to Turton's, a gay nightclub, where they are arrested in a raid. The king's valet Richard Ellis uses carte blanche, his royal household credential card, to have Barrow released uncharged. Ellis and Barrow kiss and dream of the future without another thought to working-class Chris who could have lost his job, home, reputation, and/or family. Byrne (2014) argues that period dramas treat feminism and sexuality with "uncensored modernity . . . to appeal 'to a contemporary audience'" (p. 316). This impacts audiences whose perception of LGBTQ+ history is influenced by period dramas (Brown, 2015). LGBTQ+ subjects in *DA* are largely privileged. For example, consider real-life writers Lytton Strachey, Virginia Woolf, Oscar Wilde, and fictional characters the Duke of Crowborough, Peter Pelham, 6th Marquis of Hexham, and Robert's private school peers. Brown (2015) labels Barrow's homosexuality a glass closet or open secret that heightens the sense of Barrow's privilege.

GLAAD (2016) argues that while LGBTQ+ characters today appear more frequently and positively, though media representations focus "largely on those who are white, male, and affluent." Some argue that even imperfect LGBTQ+ media representations have the potential for positive impact. Others point to former US-Republican Representative Aaron Schock, whose love of *DA* led him to redesign his congressional office like the Abbey's famous red room using government funds, subsequently repaid, while also pursuing an anti-LGBTQ+ political legacy as a then-closeted member of Congress (Bedwell, 2019; Cuccinello, 2016). Schock arguably received *DA*'s messages about privilege and its aesthetic trappings, but missed its points about the importance of making hidden LGBTQ+ lives visible.

The Absence and Presence of Race in *DA*

Fellowes argues that *DA* reflects the lack of racial diversity in rural Georgian-British towns (Cox, 2013). One exception is African American jazz singer Jack Ross in season four. Jack's cultural difference is marked by rising-pitched Middle Eastern sounding oboe instrument-family music, both when he arrives to perform for Robert's birthday (season four) and when he is unseen, on the other end of the phone with Rose (season four). Similarly, in *The Maltese Falcon* of 1941, Asian-styled woodwind music denoted the arrival of queer character Joel Cairo (Epstein & Friedman, 1995). Jack and Rose's romance culminates in a brief flirtation with marriage. Mary dissuades Jack by arguing, "Do you think you can survive what they'll do to you? Because I don't believe Rose could" (season four). Jack, fearing for Rose, ends their relationship.

DA's characters more often engage with racial/cultural difference through problematic popular cultural representations in film (e.g., *The Sheik*), musical theatre (e.g., *Chu Chin Chow*), music (e.g., Al Jolson's song *April Showers*), radio (e.g., the king opening the 1924 British Empire Exhibition, critiqued for its colonialist perspective), and cuisine (e.g., kedgeree, an Anglicized Indian dish). *DA*'s "Spanish" flu outbreak in season two fits a culturally problematic pattern of assigning foreign/non-Western names to public health pandemics (Aronson, 2010; McCauley, Minsky, & Viswanath, 2013).

DA explores how the religion, nationality, and/or social class of Lady Cora Crawley, Atticus Aldridge, and Thomas Branson challenge inherited Victorian/colonial whiteness definitions that hinged upon both race and social position (Bonnett, 1998). India's colonial elite (1859–1930) deemed domiciled whites too poor, uncivilized, locally educated, and culturally integrated to hold top positions (Mizutani, 2006). Twentieth-century US and working-class British definitions of whiteness emphasized white, Anglo-Saxon, Protestantism (Alley-Young 2008; Bonnett, 1998).

Edward I's 1290 edict expelling Jews from Britain created racial discourses labeling the Jews as having a dark/melancholy complexion and this characterization persisted into the early modern period (Kaplan, 2013). Green (2016) argues that challenges to Jewish whiteness persist into the twenty-first century. British laws changed to allow Catholic (1828) and Jewish (1858) parliamentarians and yet the first Jewish parliamentarian, London-born Baron Lionel de Rothschild, was called a "foreign nobleman" by his opponents (Grube, 2007, p. 28). Late Victorian Britishness started to be defined more by shared morality due to perceived crises of sexuality and violence in the name of Irish nationalism (Grube, 2007).

Ajtony (2013) cites Englishness versus otherness as a defining theme of *DA*. Lady Cora's otherness is acknowledged before her Jewish roots. When daughter Mary objects to marrying middle-class Mathew in season one, and to selling the Abbey in season three, Mary cites her British aristocratic identity to distinguish herself from her American-born mother Cora, who deems these nonissues. Robert acts similarly when his wife Cora supports Lady Sybil's marriage to Thomas, their chauffeur (season two). Cora's support for Sybil's education in season one leads Cora's mother-in-law, Violet, to posit that Americans "live in wigwams." Violet characterizes Cora's taste in flowers as Southern Italian Catholic. Mary attributes Cora's tears at Sybil leaving for nursing school to her "American blood."

The Cartesian dualism characterizing Imperial Britain positioned white British subjects as intellectual, objective, and civilized in contrast to physical, emotional, and savage colonial others (Descartes, 1968; Mohanram, 1999; Pfeifer, 2009). Such thinking perhaps led the British Indian Army to kill 400–1,000 unarmed Sikh festival attendees in Amritsar, Punjab (season five). Cora is a privileged aristocrat who would likely never face such brutal treatment, but referencing her "blood" (symbolic of physicality/emotion) and class ignorance/"wigwam" (symbolic of savagery from a mindset claiming civility) positions her, as other. Edith similarly deems emotion as not-British, saying, "I envy it. All those Latins screaming and shouting and hurling themselves into graves" (season four). Lawler (2014) deems Cora's identity as geographically unbound versus her aristocratic family, whose identities derive from ancestral British homelands.

Atticus Aldridge's whiteness is challenged due to his Jewish ancestry and nationality. Atticus is Baron and Lady Sinderby's son, from the prominent Aldridge banking family. Ultimately Rose and Atticus marry (season five) and move to New York where Atticus works in banking. While courting, Atticus visits Rose while she works with exiled Russian Empire aristocrats. Rose tells Count Rostov how Atticus's family thrived in Britain despite being exiled from Odessa in the anti-Jewish pogroms. Count Rostov angrily replies that Atticus's family were not and are not Russian. This challenges Atticus's white identity by denying his European ancestry. Rose recognizes that identity is co-cultural by saying, "I mean, you're English now, but you're still Jewish. What's the difference?"

At Rose and Atticus's engagement dinner (season five), Rose's mother, Lady Flinshire, remarks on the Aldridges's recent Yorkshire roots compared to other noble families who have more established ancestries and thus a greater claim to Britishness. She states, "I always think of you [Jewish] as nomads, drifting around the world." Lord Sinderby cites his wife's fifteenth-century English ancestry. Both sides' claims to historical British identity are questionable as the concept of Britain originated in the seventeenth century (James, 2011).

Son-in-law Thomas Branson's nationality, class, and religion challenges British aristocratic whiteness definitions. Thomas began as the Crawley's chauffeur, during which time he courted and fell in love with their youngest daughter Sybil over their shared socialist politics. Sybil joins the Voluntary Aid Detachment as a nurse (season two) during World War I and at the end of this season they elope to marry and relocate in Dublin, where Thomas works as a reporter. The couple return after Thomas becomes embroiled in Irish nationalist politics in Dublin. Sybil has her baby at the Abbey but dies in childbirth (season three). Thomas stays on as the estate agent but later he and daughter Sybbie relocate to America, only to return at Mr. Carson and Mrs. Hughes wedding reception.

When first back at the Abbey as a newlywed, Thomas refuses to wear tails to dinner stating, "I don't own a set of tails. Or a dinner jacket, either. I wouldn't get any use out of them" (season three). Violet reconciles Thomas's dress with aristocratic standards explaining, "You don't change on the first night of a voyage." Thomas's figurative voyage is to find a place in this new aristocratic world. The white tie he wears to the ball in the post-series film signals that he has arrived but dancing with Lady Bagshaw's maid, and secret lovechild, Lucy, reflects his working-class sensibilities. Thomas and Lucy straddle both worlds.

Having Matthew enlist Thomas to play cricket for the house team (season three) is another means of reforming Thomas's social class. Levett (2017) describes how cricket was used to delineate white British identity in early twentieth-century colonial relationships. Shome (1999) argues how colonial dress, culture, and uniforms function as forms of colonial control. Thomas asserts, "You won't make a gentleman of me, you know. You can teach me to fish, to ride and to shoot, but I'll still be an Irish Mick in my heart." At the game, Thomas, in full cricket whites, pauses on the field midway between the working-class village players and the Crawley family's tent. Upon seeing his baby, a biological connection to his new world under the tent, he voyages forward to the Crawleys.

The scholar de Nie (2004) argues the British press used references to Irish identity as culturally coded shorthand for poverty, racial/religious inferiority, and a lack of Britishness between 1798 and 1882. While the Premier Duke (of Norfolk) also the Premier Earl (of Arundel) of Britain, Edward Fitzalan-Howard, is Catholic, he is emphasized to be an English Catholic (Heaven, 2015). Violet references the Duchess of Norfolk as a friend who is "more Catholic than the Pope" (season three). Thomas's plans to christen his daughter in the Catholic church becomes the subject of a racialized conflict between the family and their minister, Mr. Travis. Mr. Travis calls the "Roman Church" "un-English" and Catholicism "pagan falderal" that, in his opinion, does not please God like Anglicanism does. Robert questions baptizing the baby into a "different tribe" and Thomas replies, "She will be baptized into my tribe." Nomad and tribe are racially coded words. Carson at one point questions how loyal Catholics are to the Crown (season three). The film answers Carson's charge by having Thomas save King George V from an assassin, thus completing the process of making Thomas into a British gentleman.

This discussion of whiteness definitions underscores Hall's (1997) argument that race is a floating signifier that relies on social context for its meaning. This discussion of evolving whiteness definitions through the characters Cora, Atticus, and Thomas is only part of a much larger discussion that explores how this system of white racial privilege oppressed, often violently, the black and brown citizens of the British Empire, and the world. *DA* briefly acknowledges this substantial history of oppression by references to slaughter in Amritsar (season five) and Jack and Rose's curtailed romance (season four).

CONCLUSION

There are as many different types of audiences for *DA* as there are possible interpretations of the series. Some viewers are those drawn to *DA* for the fairytale of aristocratic life in Edwardian/Georgian Britain and the relatedly intricate lives such environs produced. Others seek to connect with history through period drama in a way they cannot with history texts. Neither audience is mutually exclusive nor exhaustive of *DA* audiences.

Whether questions of gender/sexuality, or race, are being considered this study highlights how both are socially constructed, context bound, and continually changing. Critics and audiences quickly identify with favorite characters but spend less time critically dissecting the social issues, discourses, and identity politics such characters embody. Audiences and critics cite characters' singular words and actions as evidence that the identity of a marginalized social group of people has been positively reimagined. The reality is that identity is brought into being through its recurrent performance, what Butler (1990) called a gender performative, in which popular culture participates by reifying progressive identities demarcating social changes.

Future extensions of this study could consider how parodies of *DA* on stage (e.g., comedy, pantomime), in books such as Kelly's *Downton Tabby* (2013), on television such as the costume drama called *Downton Draggy* (2019), speak to or extend the criticisms stated in this examination. Such research might consider how such texts function as both fan culture and social resistance/critique. Additional studies could also consider how uses of and references to popular culture texts (i.e., music, television, theatre, literature, fashion, film) are used in period television dramas with predominantly white casts to engage with issues of cultural difference in superficial and problematic ways. *DA* fans' engagement with the series and people during the Edwardian-Georgian eras is similar to Coontz's (1992) observation that homogeneous white 1950s television families provide the schema through which US television audiences problematically and nostalgically imagine the 1950s as devoid of cultural conflict and social problems. Will *DA* audiences think of Edwardian-Georgian Britain as a period of benevolent aristocrats, contented servants, modern women, and gay freedom? This popular reimagining of history can make it more difficult for audiences to realize the histories of real Edwardian-Georgian people, the work of whom likely made *DA*'s privileged version of history possible.

REFERENCES

Alley-Young, G. (2008). Articulating identity: Refining postcolonial and whiteness perspectives on race within communication studies. *The Review of Communication, 8*(3), 307–321.

Ajtony, Z. (2013). Various facets of the English stereotype in *Downton Abbey*, A pragmatic approach. *Topics in Linguistics*, (12), 5–14.

Archive of Our Own. (2012–2019). Thomas Barrow/Tom Branson. Archive of our own. https://archiveofourown.org/tags/Thomas%20Barrow*s*Tom%20Branson/works.

Aronson, S. M. (2010). Racism and the threat of influenza. *Rhode Island Medical Society, 93*(1), 3. http://www.rimed.org/medhealthri/2010-01/2010-01-3.pdf.

Baena, R., & Byker, C. (2015). Dialects of nostalgia: Downton Abbey and English identity. *National Identities, 17*(3), 259–269.

Bedwell, M. (2019, September 20). The 'Downton Abbey' movie erases Thomas's gay history, And ours. *LGBTQ Nation*. https://www.lgbtqnation.com/2019/09/downton-abbey-movie-erases-thomass-gay-history/.

Bonnett, A. (1998). How the British working class became white: The symbolic (re)formation of racialized capitalism. *Journal of Historical Sociology, 11*(3), 316–340.

Boozer, J. (2002). *Career movies: American business and the success mystique.* University of Texas Press.

Braga, P. (2016). How to apply the multi-strand narrative of American TV shows in a British series: The Downton Abbey's case. *Communication & Society, 29*(2), 1–16.

Brown, L. (2015). Homosexual lives: Representation and reinterpretation in *Upstairs, Downstairs* and *Downton Abbey*. In J. Leggott & J. Taddeo (Eds.), *Upstairs and downstairs: British costume drama television from The Forsyte Saga to Downton Abbey* (pp. 263–274). Rowman & Littlefield.

Brown, P., Haas, S., Marchessou, S., & Villepelet C. (2018, October). Shattering the glass runway. McKinsey & Company. https://www.mckinsey.com/industries/retail/our-insights/shattering-the-glass-runway#.

Butler, J. (1990). *Gender trouble: Feminism and the subversion of identity.* Routledge.

Byrne, K. (2014). Adapting heritage: Class and conservatism in Downton Abbey. *Rethinking History, 18*(3), 311–327.

Carey, T. (2009). *Never kiss a man in a canoe: Words of wisdom from the golden age of agony aunts.* Boxtree.

Cawthorne, E. (2016). How to be a man: Tips from 1930s agony aunts. *BBC History Magazine.* https://www.historyextra.com/period/modern/how-to-be-a-man-tips-from-1930s-agony-aunts/.

Coontz, S. (1992). *The way we never were: American families and the nostalgia trap.* Basic.

Cox, J. (2013, March 22). *Downton Abbey*, the period piece & the question of race. Atlanta Black Star. https://atlantablackstar.com/2013/03/22/downton-abbey-the-period-piece-the-question-of-race/.

Cuccinello, H. C. (2016, March 6). Downton Abbey by the numbers: Farewell to a Multimillion-dollar dynasty. *Forbes.* https://www.forbes.com/sites/hayleycuccinello/2016/03/06/downton-abbey-by-the-numbers-farewell-to-a-multimillion-dollar-dynasty/#4b4dcb43bad8.

Delsandro, E. G. (2017). What would Lady Mary do? Teaching the twentieth-century novel in the era of Downton Abbey. *Pedagogy: Critical Approaches to Teaching Literature, Language, Composition, and Culture, 17*(3), 513–523.

de Nie, M. (2004). *The eternal Paddy: Irish identity and the British Press, 1798–1882.* University of Wisconsin Press.

Descartes, R. (1968). *Discourse on method and the meditations.* Penguin Books.

EditorBee. (2015, November 10). Downton Abbey: Truth and consequences. *The armchair Anglophile.* http://www.armchairanglophile.com/downton-abbey-truth-and-consequences/.

Ellenzweig, A. (2006). Beyond the mountain. *Gay & Lesbian Review Worldwide, 13*(3), 14–15.

Epstein, R. & Friedman, J. (Producers/Directors). (1995). *The celluloid closet* [Documentary film]. US: Sony Pictures Classics.

Fiske, J. (2011). *Television culture* (2nd ed.). Routledge.

GLAAD. (2016). *GLAAD media reference guide* (10th ed.). *GLAAD*. https://www.glaad.org/sites/default/files/GLAAD-Media-Reference-Guide-Tenth-Edition.pdf.

Green, E. (2016, December 5). "Are Jews white?" *The Atlantic*. https://www.theatlantic.com/politics/archive/2016/12/are-jews-white/509453/.

Grube, D. (2007). Religion, Power and Parliament: Rothschild and Bradlaugh Revisited. *History, 92*(1), 21–38.

Hall, S. (1997). *Race: The floating signifier* [transcript]. Media Education Foundation. https://www.mediaed.org/transcripts/Stuart-Hall-Race-the-Floating-Signifier-Tranjscript.pdf.

Heaven, W. (2015, July 2). Have posh Catholics had their day? *Catholic Herald*. https://catholicherald.co.uk/issues/july-3rd-2015/have-posh-catholics-had-their-day/.

Hettinger, V., & Vandello, J. (2014). Balance without equality: Just world beliefs, the gay affluence myth, and support for gay rights. *Social Justice Research, 27*(4), 444–463.

Horn, P. (2013). *Life below stairs: The real lives of servants, the Edwardian Era to 1939*. Amberley Publishing.

Ivie, D. (2016, January 31). *Downton Abbey's* Laura Carmichael on why Lady Edith is a lot like Peggy Olson and which scenes are the most boring to shoot. *New York Magazine*. http://nymag.com/#_ga=2.3590518.750622042.1578079662-1627039614.1577121520.

James, S. (2011, February 28). Peoples of Britain. *BBC History*. http://www.bbc.co.uk/history/ancient/british_prehistory/peoples_01.shtml.

Kaplan, M. L. (2013). The Jewish body in black and white in medieval and early modern England. *Philological Quarterly, 92*(1), 41–65.

Kelly, C. (2013). *Downton Tabby: A parody*. Simon & Schuster.

Kirst, S. (2017, December 17). Call Me By Your Name is the latest gay-for-pay Oscar bait. https://www.them.us/story/call-me-by-your-name-gay-for-pay-oscar-bait.

Krippendorff, K. (2004). *Content analysis: An introduction to its methodology* (2nd ed.). Sage.

Lambert, V. (2018, August 23). The world's first agony aunt […]. *Daily Mail*. https://www.dailymail.co.uk/femail/article-6092399/Letters-written-worlds-agony-aunt-written-100-years-ago-revealed.html.

Lawler, P. A. (2014, Spring). *Downton Abbey's* astute nostalgia. *Intercollegiate Review*, 28–29.

Levett, G. (2017). The 'white man's game'? West Indian cricket tours of the 1900s. *International Journal of the History of Sport, 34*(7/8), 599–618.

Love, R. (2010, August 9). Rob James-Collier: Gay kiss is my idea. *Digital Spy*. https://www.digitalspy.com/tv/a274582/rob-james-collier-gay-kiss-is-my-idea/.

Mahon, E.K. (2016, March 11). *Downton Abbey*, Why Lady Edith is the true heroine of the series [blog post]. *Scandalous Women*. http://scandalouswoman.blogspot.com/2016/03/downton-abbey-why-lady-edith-is-true.html.

Mahmud, T. (1999). Colonialism and modern constructions of race: A preliminary inquiry. *University of Miami Law Review, 53*(4), 1219–1246.

Malone, A. (2017). *Backwards & in heels: The past, present and future of women working in film*. Mango Publishing Group.

Martin Jr., A. L. (2018). The queer business of casting gay characters on U.S. Television. *Communication, Culture & Critique, 11*(2), 282–297.

Masterpiece. (2014, January 12). Cast & creator on Lady Edith. *PBS*. https://www.pbs.org/video/masterpiece-downton-abbey-season-4-cast-creator-lady-edith/.

Masterpiece. (2019). Six *Downton Abbey* moments to remember before the movie. *PBS*. https://www.pbs.org/wgbh/masterpiece/specialfeatures/six-downton-abbey-moments-to-remember-before-the-movie/.

Mavity, A. (2015). Rob James Collier and Allen Leech: Downton Abbey interview. https://www.youtube.com/watch?v=YuREQZ7Cgbk.

McCauley, M., Minsky, S., & Viswanath, K. (2013). The H1N1 pandemic: Media frames, stigmatization and coping. *BMC Public Health, 13*(1). https://www.ncbi.nlm.nih.gov/pmc/articles/PMC3907032/.

Miller, J. (2016, March 10). *Downton Abbey's* Laura Carmichael discusses Lady Edith's happy ending. *Vanity Fair*. https://www.vanityfair.com/hollywood/2016/03/downton-abbey-finale-lady-edith.

Mizutani, S. (2006). Historicizing whiteness: From the case of late colonial India. *ACRAWSA e-journal, 2*(1). https://acrawsa.org.au/wp-content/uploads/2017/12/CRAWS-Vol-2-No-1-2006.pdf.

Nevertrustaduck394. (2015, November 8). Per ardua ad astra. *Tumblr*. https://nevertrustaduck394.tumblr.com/post/132828255882/septimus-spratt-agony-aunt-supreme.

Pfeifer, T. (2009). Deconstructing Cartesian dualisms of western racialized systems: A study in the colors black and white. *Journal of Black Studies, 39*(4), 528–547.

Reynolds, E. (2016). Why straight men are going 'gay for pay' on camera. *News Corp Australia*. https://www.news.com.au/lifestyle/relationships/sex/why-straight-men-are-going-gay-for-pay-on-camera/news-story/14b2f3f268197a92f3c590cf75920d6e.

Rothman, L. (2012, November 1). A cultural history of mansplaining. *The Atlantic*. https://www.theatlantic.com/sexes/archive/2012/11/a-cultural-history-of-mansplaining/264380/.

Sánchez, F. J., Greenberg, S. T., Liu, W. M., & Vilain, E. (2009). Reported effects of masculine ideals on gay men. *Psychology of Men & Masculinity, 10*(1), 73–87.

Schaffer, T. (2016). *Romance's rival: Familiar marriage in Victorian fiction.* Oxford.

Shome, R. (1999). Whiteness and the politics of location: Postcolonial reflections. In T.K. Nakayama & J.N. Martin (Eds.), *Whiteness: The communication of social identity* (pp. 107–128). Sage.

Stopes, M. (1919). *Married love or love in marriage.* The Critic and Guide Company. http://digital.library.upenn.edu/women/stopes/married/1918.html.

Sulcas, R. (2016, February 1). Laura Carmichael discusses Edith's evolution on *Downton Abbey*. *New York Times*. https://www.nytimes.com/2016/02/01/arts/television/laura-carmichael-discusses-ediths-evolution-on-downton-abbey.html.

ten Brummelhuis, L. L., & Greenhaus, J. H. (2018). How role jugglers maintain relationships at home and at work. *Journal of Applied Psychology, 103*(12), 1265–1282.

Weisberg, J. (2018). *Asking for a friend: Three centuries of advice on life, love, money, and other burning questions from a nation obsessed.* Nation Books.

Wirthlin, K. (2009). Fad lesbianism: Exposing media's posing. *Journal of Lesbian Studies, 13*(1), 107–114.

Young, A. (2015). *New York café society: The elite meet to see and be seen, 1920s–1940s.* McFarland and Company.

Chapter 12

From *The Crown* to *Madmen*

Historical Television as Commentary on Twenty-first-Century Ideologies

Nettie Brock

History frequently acts as a costume that other genres of television use to masquerade their messages. Dramas, comedies, procedurals, all take on different hues, when disguised as historical fiction. In some cases, the historical nature of a show is more important than the other generic attributes, due to the ideological commentary that the series is able to impart. In particular, there are several shows that are available online for streaming. These shows were produced in the last 10 to 15 years and portray life of the 1950s and 1960s as well as comment upon life in the 2010s, through churning eras of change.

Hunt (2006) says, "History needs to be humanized and made accessible to a broad audience through the experiences of 'iconic' historical personages" (p. 848). For audiences to fully understand history, it needs to be made relatable in ways that the narrative possibility of television allows. However, he points out that most historical narratives center on those "iconic historical personages" and the "marginalised people, ideas, social structures or processes mak[e] only fleeting appearances" (p. 848). Despite this claim, the 2010s featured a handful of television shows that presented history, primarily through historical characters who are neither famous nor "iconic." In this way, these television series fulfill White's (2010) assertion that

> historical narratives are not only models of past events and processes, but also metaphorical statements which suggest a relation to similitude between such events and process and the story types that we conventionally use to endow the events of our lives with culturally sanctioned meanings (p. 1542).

This chapter examines programs that use their historical settings as models for referencing current ideological issues and "endow the events" of these eras "with culturally sanctioned meanings." Ideological exploration is not contained within a single genre, neither is historical television. Thus, we can look at *The Crown* (2016–present), *Endeavour* (2012–present), *Grantchester* (2014–present), *Call the Midwife* (2012–present), *Father Brown* (2013–present), *The Marvelous Mrs. Maisel* (2017–present), *Masters of Sex* (2013–2016), and *Mad Men* (2007–2015) all in a meaningful way. These shows explore issues of gender equality, racism, sexuality, in various degrees with nuance and a clear sense of twenty-first-century sensibilities. As the characters struggle with mid-twentieth-century morality, they are relatable to audiences, who continue with similar ethical quandaries. This chapter will analyze the ways in which these shows make commentary on modern times using the historical context of the series as a template.

The 1950s and 1960s character representations and story narratives are significant. Three major events were in progress during this time period: the Civil Rights Movement, the Women's Liberation Movement, and the sexual revolution. These major events depict issues that parallel those that occurred in the 2010s and resonate with contemporary audiences. Recent social movements have foundations from the 1950s and 1960s, signaling a need for viewership to be reminded of previous contexts. This chapter reviews each movement in turn, the modern necessity of those reminders, and moments on the television programs when they manifest. The power of these representations as ideological teaching devices for modern audiences will then be discussed. First, however, it is useful to briefly review each of the television programs, in order of release.

TELEVISION SERIES

Mad Men (2007–2015) is the story of the Sterling Cooper Advertising Agency in New York City in the 1960s and 1970s. The employees of Sterling Cooper include Don Draper, Peggy Olsen, and Joan Holloway. They navigate their lives and the cultural mores of the era. Don Draper sleeps with countless women over the course of the series. Peggy Olsen and Joan Holloway all bristle against the restraints of being a woman in this particular time period, while coming into their own as feminists.

Call the Midwife (2012–present) is based on the memoirs of Jennifer Worth (2009), which focus on her adventures in London's East End during the post–World War II period, when National Health first began. The television series focuses on the nuns and midwives who live in the Nonnatus House during the period. The characters frequently deal with the prevailing postwar issues of the day, the discursive movements in its storyline in particular.

Endeavour (2012–present) is the prequel to *Inspector Morse* (1987–2000) and the early story of Oxford detective Endeavour Morse, as he begins his career in the 1960s. He is presented with a series of cases, which intersects with the tumultuous problems of the era. Additionally, Morse has several friends and occasional girlfriends who are a part of these movements.

Masters of Sex (2013–2016) tells the story of William Masters and Virginia Johnson, who pioneered human sexuality research in the 1950s and 1960s. These two real-life characters are central to the sexual revolution, and their manifestations on television frequently grapple with sex and sexuality in parallel to their research.

Father Brown (2013–present) and *Grantchester* (2014–present) are crime procedurals that take place in the years shortly after World War II. Father Brown is a priest in rural England and Sidney Chambers is the vicar in the Cambridge suburb of Grantchester. These men are also amateur sleuths. They butt heads with the local constabulary, but are always triumphant in their pursuit of truth. Additionally, these lead characters are forward thinking and open-minded. They open their hearts and apply their skills to assist prosecuted minorities to prove their innocence.

The Crown (2016–present) traces the story of Queen Elizabeth II. The story begins just before Elizabeth ascends to the throne and follows her life almost to the modern era. This analysis will look primarily at the first and second seasons, which covers the 1950s and a portion of the 1960s. Elizabeth herself is frequently portrayed as grappling with a changing world and the role that she, and those around her, play within that world.

Finally, *The Marvelous Mrs. Maisel* (2017–present) centers on Miriam Maisel from New York City, in the wake of the dissolution of her marriage. Midge, as she is called by her friends, does not know what to do after her husband Joel leaves her. She eventually becomes a stand-up comedian, who primarily targets the social mores of the era and their absurdity.

These eight television shows have particular styles and tell dramatically different stories. However, because of the era in which they are set, the shows represent similar ideologies and agendas. The sections below will examine three of these ideologies and the places on these programs that such ideologies manifest.

THE CIVIL RIGHTS MOVEMENT

Brown v. the Board of Education, the US Supreme Court ruling that racial segregation was unconstitutional, was handed down in 1954 and Martin Luther King Jr. was assassinated in 1968 (King, 2015). What unfolded between those two events—including the lynching of Emmett Till, the Montgomery bus boycott, and the Selma to Montgomery march—changed the world, making a lasting impact on race relations in the country. In response to the 2013 acquittal of George Zimmerman who murdered Trayvon Martin, a group of black organizers created a movement centered around the Twitter hashtag #BlackLivesMatter (*Herstory*, n.d.). In the years that followed, numerous African Americans were killed in moments of senseless violence. A myriad of protests emerged to oppose this treatment, just as occurred in the 1950s and 1960s; most prominently by NFL player Colin Kaepernick, who made a decision to kneel during the national anthem at his games. He defended his actions, saying:

> I am not going to stand up to show pride in a flag for a country that oppresses black people and people of color . . . it would be selfish on my part to look the other way. There are bodies in the street and people . . . getting away with murder (Wyche, 2016, para. 3).

By 2020, there continues to be violence against African Americans, and public protests against maltreatment of people of color. The programs in this study do not feature African heritage characters in major roles. However, *Call the Midwife*, set in London, introduced a black nurse from Jamaica in season seven. She is frequently confronted by the racial tensions of the era and her presence is unique in these series. Also, almost all the shows include moments where civil rights become an important part of the narrative conversation.

Grantchester and *Father Brown* feature episodes centered around the local cricket club, which is a very common trope of British crime procedurals. In these episodes, the main point of conflict is with South Asian men who have joined the team. Early in season three of *Grantchester* features a murdered batsman from Pakistan, Zafar Ali. Zafar is in a relationship with a local white girl named Annie. She is pregnant with his child, but her mother believes that he "doesn't belong" in their society. The mother also defends the murder of Zafar, by saying that "Annie is supposed to be with Neil" who is a white veterinarian. Annie's father is the root of this hostility, as he is openly racist. He even rejects Annie and her unborn child at the end of the episode.

Father Brown's cricket episode in season three, "The Last Man," takes the opposite tack and puts the Indian man, Dr. Chandraty, who is the team captain, in the position of a potential murderer. Everyone suspects him of murdering a local blackmailer. Much suspicion is spurred by the cricket team's openly racist secretary, suggesting Chandraty is "unsuitable" to be on the team and "surely there's someone more officer material." Father Brown spearheads the investigation specifically to disprove Chandraty as a suspect. In the end, Chandraty was found to have nothing to do with the murder and everyone's fears were unfounded.

While these episodes are singular opportunities for exploration of racism during the era, other episodes more prominently discuss the Civil Rights Movement, as well as similar prominent issues in Britain and the United States since 2010. On *Endeavour*, in season five, "Colours," the action occurs against a backdrop of racially triggered riots occurring across Oxford. A debate club argues over whether "immigrants" should be sent back to their "ancestral" lands. A salon with a "No Coloureds" sign draws protesters shouting, "integration for the nation." Also, a young woman is murdered. She is the stepdaughter of the speaker on the pro-side of the debate, a well-known Nazi sympathizer. A young black man is suspected in her murder. Morse has to wade through this milieu to find the true murderer. Similarly, in *Grantchester* season four, an African American religious leader gives a talk in Grantchester about "religion's role in the Civil Rights Movement," only to be interrupted by protesters carrying signs that say things such as "Keep Britain white." When the reverend's son is murdered, Sidney has to uncover whether his death was the result of the protests or some other nefarious reason.

In the two US series, no stories prominently feature characters of color nor have much interaction with the Civil Rights Movement. *Mad Men* and *The Marvelous Mrs. Maisel* received criticism for their representations of a majority white version of the 1950s and 1960s (cf. Colby, 2012; Smail, 2019). Both shows featured stories with African American characters later in their run. On *Mad Men*, in early season seven, two African American secretaries become prominent. They have a conversation in which one, Dawn, tells the other, Shirley, that she needs to keep her head down and not be noticed by the bosses. When they are noticed, Joan, the white, female director of personnel, begins moving the secretaries around to satisfy the white men in charge and the secretaries' preferences. As part of this process, Bert, a white, male account executive, tells Joan that neither Dawn nor Shirley can be the face of the company by sitting at reception. Several times in this story, the white men express their reluctance at having black women in the office but are stymied in their attempts to fire the women because they do not want to look bad. In the end, Dawn gets promoted to director of personnel, as Joan is also promoted.

On *The Marvelous Mrs. Maisel*, Midge goes on tour with Shy Baldwin, a famous African American singer and his predominantly African American band. Shy's blackness and Midge's whiteness is barely addressed in the show until later in season three with "Kind of Bleau." Midge suggests Shy accompany her to her hotel room. Shy must explain that in Florida, where they are performing, he is not allowed to stay in the same hotel as white people. Midge's nonplussed expression indicates her profound ignorance about anti-black exclusion laws and customs. Such anti-black exclusion is rarely mentioned again.

These few examples are not the only story arcs that parallel recent racial incidents and the incidents of the Civil Rights Movement, but they are the most prominent. Such story arcs paint a picture of the 1950s and 1960s that resonate today. The main characters are accepting of people of color and typically advocate for the character of color to stand on equal footing. Besides the white savior complex present in these episodes, these shows seem to be advocating for an end to racial inequality, a message that was prevalent in 1960, but one that is imbued with the nostalgia, hopefulness, and inspiration that today's era—full of many of the same issues at the heart of the Civil Rights Movement—wishes upon both the past and the present.

THE WOMEN'S LIBERATION MOVEMENT

Betty Friedan's (1963) *The Feminine Mystique* is considered by many as catalytic in the Women's Liberation Movement. Levine (2015) describes how the book arrived at a "moment when the country was poised on the verge of profound social transformation" and that it inspired the "second-wave feminism" that came in the years that followed (p. 41). By 1968, the movement had grown considerably, and a group of activists demonstrated at the Miss America pageant—which was memorialized into legend as "bra-burners"—although no bras were actually burned (Inskeep, 2008). In the 2010s, women, and the role they play in society, once again rose to the fore. The 2016 presidential election saw the first female candidate advance beyond the primary stage. Hillary Clinton won the popular vote, although eventually lost the electoral college vote. Other discursive events in past years have also engaged with women's liberation and equal rights.

On October 5, 2017, the *New York Times* published an article exposing stories of sexual harassment and assault by Hollywood executive Harvey Weinstein. The #MeToo movement took off and was embraced by celebrities and audience members alike. The movement began with Tarana Burke, an activist and organizer, who was confronted by her own assumptions about sexual harassment in the early 2000s. When she rejected the disclosure of a young girl's sexual harassment, Burke's guilt over the situation led her to realize what she should have said was "me too" (Ohleheiser, 2017). She has been working with the #MeToo movement since 2006 to help young girls find the right language to describe and understand their experiences (Jefferson, 2018). However, the #MeToo movement did not truly reach nationwide attention until October 2017, in the wake of the *New York Times* article and a tweet by actress Alyssa Milano. In fact, in the week following Milano's tweet, 1.7 million tweets included the hashtag and 45% of Facebook users in the United States had at least one friend who posted #MeToo (Lewis, 2018).

The #MeToo movement is the twenty-first-century version of the bra-burning legend, creating a dialogue in which women are able to talk about their struggles against the patriarchy.

Many of the shows in this study feature major characters who are female and are struggling with legitimacy in their lives and careers. Queen Elizabeth in *The Crown*, Virginia Johnson in *Masters of Sex*, and Midge in *The Marvelous Mrs. Maisel* are all women in a man's world, who are working to take their rightful place in that world. Queen Elizabeth constantly has to prove that she is just as smart and capable as the powerful men who surround her. In the first season, with the episode "Scientia Potentia Est," Elizabeth is struggling with her lack of education. When she discovers that 79-year-old Winston Churchill survived a stroke and hid his illness from her, she realizes that her strength is not in formal educational preparation, but in her ability to "ensure proper governance." Elizabeth then scolds Churchill in a private meeting, effectively shaming him for his behavior and convincing him to step down in the next few years. She defies the expectations of her gender to prove that she is not just a woman, she is the queen.

Virginia Johnson begins *Masters of Sex* as a nightclub singer-turned-secretary who is going through a divorce. She ends the series as Dr. William Masters's wife and well-respected research partner. However, the journey to this end is difficult and convoluted. She engages in a sexual relationship with Masters almost from the beginning of the series, even though he is married at the time. Her credibility is often called into question by the other doctors who surround Masters. Additionally, she does not have the necessary credentials to qualify her for the work that she is doing. She frequently has to deal with the consequences of being a divorced woman pursuing the typically masculine field of medical research, as well as simply being a woman in the 1950s and 1960s. Johnson also fights against these constraints to become an equal partner with Masters. She briefly abandons Masters's research to work with a female doctor at the university. In doing so, she is able to demonstrate that she is just as capable a researcher as Masters, thereby proving herself worthy of standing beside him as both a researcher and his wife.

Finally, Miriam Maisel is thrown out of the comfort of being a wealthy housewife, when her unfaithful husband leaves her. She does not know what to do with herself, but eventually realizes that she is adept at comedy and wants to become a stand-up comic. Her family rejects Midge's aspirations, regularly dismissing her assertions that she needs a job and loves what she does. Her mother repeatedly tries to find her a new husband, rather than listening to what Midge truly desires. However, Midge is determined to succeed and does not care what others think of her. She understands that she has the ability to make a living and should not have to depend upon her well-situated parents or her husband. One major roadblock for Midge, besides her family, is a general sense that women do not belong in comedy, if they do not have a "schtick." This becomes clear, when Midge meets Sophie Lennon, a very successful female comedian. Sophie presents herself as a low-class housewife from Queens, while in reality she is a ritzy socialite. She affects an accent and relies heavily on crude humor as her "schtick." Midge is furious, when she discovers the truth about Sophie. Her fury is exacerbated when Sophie suggests that there is no way for Midge to succeed without taking similar steps. In contrast to Sophie, Midge's comedy routines frequently critique the role of women in society. Much of this comes from Midge's previous tenure as a well-to-do, traditional housewife.

There are also shows in this study with female main characters, but in traditionally feminine positions. These characters redefine, and emphasize the importance of those roles. Two such characters exist in *Mad Men*, Peggy Olsen and Joan Holloway. Peggy eventually manages to break free from the secretarial pool and become a copywriter in the agency. She moves to McCann Erickson to become copy supervisor, after realizing that she does not need to "make men feel at ease" at her new job. Peggy became an iconic representation of modern feminism, when she carried a box of her belongings and a painting of an "octopus pleasuring a lady," while smoking a cigarette. Joan Holloway, like Peggy Olsen, rises through the ranks at the advertising agency, to eventually become a full partner at the agency. However, when she moves to McCann Erickson, she does not hold the same power that she did at Sterling Cooper and Partners. Instead, she is confronted with significant sexism. She threatens to reveal this sexism at the agency to the *New York Times*, a seemingly prescient fiction piece, two years before the nonfiction Harvey Weinstein story broke. Joan eventually decides to accept a deal and leave the firm.

Similarly, the women on *Call the Midwife* are constantly pushing beyond their traditional roles to become something more. The main characters of the show are all in the traditionally female jobs as midwives. That does not mean that they lead traditional lives; this plot point is most prominently manifested through Beatrix Franklin (known as Trixie in the show). Trixie is the longest-serving midwife at the Nonnatus House. She is also the most modern member of the staff. She wears pants, bleaches her pixie-cut hair blonde, and openly flirts with any single man. She is also an alcoholic who enters Alcoholics Anonymous at the end of the fourth season. Trixie bristles against the restrictions of living in the 1950s. She wants to be free and to be her own person, but cannot do so because of the era in which she lives.

Within the other shows in this study, there are multiple episodes and plot lines that focus on sexism and the role of women in society. All these shows grapple with women's equality and how that equality becomes palpable. They talk about autonomy and oppression, and present options for women outside the standards of heteronormativity. On these shows, women are allowed to be breadwinners and independent. They are encouraged to take control of their lives and they do so with aplomb.

THE SEXUAL REVOLUTION

The sexual revolution has less of a beginning point as the previous two. There are several noteworthy events that occurred in the 1950s and 1960s that evolved into sexual revolution. First, there are studies done by Kinsey (1948; 1953) on sexual behavior and those done by Masters and Johnson (1966; 1970). Other factors, including the discussion presented earlier about the Women's Liberation Movement, contributed to the sexual revolution. First, oral contraception was approved for use by the public in 1960 (Junod, 2002). In 1953, Hugh Hefner published the first edition of *Playboy,* which promoted "libertine [life]styles" and paved the way for a normalcy of sex (Batura, 2017). The 1964 decision in *Jacobellis v. Ohio* was one of several that occurred in this period of time regarding obscene content in the media. This one resulted in the famous statement by Justice Potter Stewart that he will not try to "define the kinds of material I understand to be embraced within [hardcore pornography], and perhaps I could never succeed in intelligibly doing so. But I know it when I see it" (Jacobellis v. Ohio, 1964). These are defining events that occurred in the 1950s and 1960s surrounding the sexual revolution, and they point to a sexual freedom not previously witnessed.

The twenty-first century has seen a general normalcy of sexual freedom. However, issues of autonomy and agency in sex lives have continued to persist. In 2016, the Department of Health and Human Services grew concerned with the number of states that were attempting to defund Planned Parenthood, because they perform abortions. President Obama passed a law protecting Planned Parenthood at the federal level (Calmes, 2016). Discourse surrounding abortion and autonomy have proliferated recently. The #MeToo movement is part of this discourse. The issue of bodily agency has also been raised, just as in the 1960s, with the rise of pornography. One moment when this became particularly prevalent was in the publication and popularity of *Fifty Shades of Grey* (James, 2012). This book became the bestselling book of all time by Amazon UK, when it sold more than 4 million copies in six months (Meredith, 2012). The book spurred several sequels and film adaptations, as well as a plethora of other sex-positive, kink-centered book and film series.

Three shows in this study that directly discuss sexual freedom are *The Crown, Mad Men,* and, of course, *Masters of Sex.* In *The Crown,* Princess Margaret frequently struggles as the younger sister of the queen and to overcome her inability to live a free life. Her labors come to a head in episode

2.4, "Beryl," when she meets Antony Armstrong-Jones. Margaret has not recovered from being denied a marriage to Peter Townsend in the previous series. She is depressed and barely functioning. Armstrong-Jones is an aristocratic photographer who demonstrates to Margaret an alternative lifestyle. He is openly "queer" and does not treat Margaret as a revered princess. Margaret has Armstrong-Jones photograph her for her birthday picture. She is half-naked in this picture, which is not considered obscene by today's standards but fairly racy for a public image at that time. It is published in the newspaper. Elizabeth is outraged, but Margaret has learned to love herself and allow herself the freedom to be sexy and desirable. She ends up marrying Armstrong-Jones.

On the other end of the spectrum, *Mad Men* features characters with no problem with sex and will sleep with anyone. Don Draper sleeps with numerous women over the course of the series. Don has no qualms with his promiscuity because he was raised in a whorehouse and was surrounded by sex throughout his life. The female characters also have sex frequently on the series. Peggy becomes pregnant and gives her child up for adoption in an early season. She does not realize that she is pregnant until she gives birth, and then she refuses to even touch the child. She does not tell the father, until much later. She has one other major relationship on the series, but does not sleep around more than that. Joan sees men and marriage as a means to get out of her job and give her the life she has always wanted. At the same time, however, she worries about becoming a housewife and being bored by such a lifestyle. Consequently, she has relationships and sleeps with several high-powered men. At the end of season 2, Joan is raped by her fiancé. She marries him and attempts to become the housewife he wants her to be. Even marriage does not stop Joan's desire for sex; she conceives a child with Roger Sterling and contemplates aborting it. However, she decides instead to raise it as her husband's child. She and her husband eventually divorce, and Joan returns to sleeping with a variety of professional men. In the end, Joan owns a production company and is without any male companionship.

Masters of Sex is about the sexual revolution and one of the studies of sex and sexuality that heavily contributed to the sexual revolution. Masters and Johnson's studies examine the human sexual response (1966) and sexual inadequacy (1970). The television show covers these same issues. They represent characters being impotent and sterile. One of the first questions that Dr. Masters asks Virginia Johnson when he is interviewing her for the position is "why would a woman fake an orgasm?" Issues surrounding sex from a clinical perspective are front and center throughout the series. Additionally, the characters are all having sex with one another. Again, by the end of the series, Masters and Johnson are getting married, as they did in real life. However, the road that leads to that end is a long one, as the show is heavily focused on adultery and without standard sexual mores.

The other shows in this study are also extremely liberal with their discussion of sex. There are episodes of all the shows discussed in this study, in which characters are having affairs, or the sexual revolution becomes an important part of the plot. On *Call the Midwife*, female characters are constantly getting pregnant out of wedlock with disastrous consequences. Sidney Chambers, on *Grantchester*, eventually enters into a sexual relationship with his childhood friend Amanda, much to the dismay of his housekeeper. This relationship ends in disaster, because Sidney chooses God over Amanda. He is a vicar, after all. Clearly, there are numerous elements of the sexual revolution present in these series and the abundance of sex points to a normalcy of this ideology.

CONCLUSION

According to Nichols (1996), "Our present, aligned to the film's representation of past events, may construct a dialectical 'will to transform' as our specific intentionalization toward the future" (p. 57). He borrows this idea from both Sigmund Freud and Hayden White. Freud calls this idea *Nactraglichkeit*, which translates vaguely to afterwardness. By this, Freud suggests a way "in which new knowledge transforms the meaning of memory and all but recreates the past" (Goldin, 2016, p. 408). White's concept is "willing backward" which is, in its essence, the idea that "every generation writes its own history" (Helo, 2016, para. 14). By looking to the past, we are both changing our perception of that past, to make it something that fits into our modern understanding of the world, and also looking to ourselves to transform our futures.

Nichols (1996) goes on to say, "As we view a film retrospectively, in the mode of 'willing backward,' we model a future on the basis of our present situation as it is mediated by how we now understand our past situation" (p. 57). Representations of the past can create a base for viewers to model their futures upon. These television shows do precisely this. This is not to suggest that there are particular ideological leanings or messages that these shows are sending to their audiences. These shows are representing a past that parallels many of the ideological problems that are currently plaguing society. The shows then let the audience draw connections between the past, the present, and the future however they see fit.

This chapter has focused on the ways in which these shows have represented the ideologies surrounding racism, sexism, and gender norms. It studies eight historical shows aired in Western, English-speaking countries in the last 10 years, each presenting discursive storylines that parallel the eras in which they are set with modern times. The current analysis has demonstrated the ways in which these shows allow viewers to ruminate on the future by talking about the past. In the finale of the seventh season of *Call the Midwife*, the midwives and nuns are reeling from the death of one of their colleagues and the assassination of President Kennedy. Sister Monica Joan admonishes them, saying,

> We are not what we have lost. We are not what has been taken from us. You are all too willing to embrace the void. If you do not cherish what remains, you will all become as nothing. You will be nothing. We are not broken. We are each as whole as we will ever be again. And in the end, when we cease to be, we will all become memories.

Consider her words as an admonition to the audience: do not forget what came before and do not forget the everyday moments of the past. The tribulations of those who came before will become immaterial, if we cannot learn from the past.

REFERENCES

Batura, A. (2017, September 29). How Hefner invented the modern man. *New York Times*, 1. ProQuest Recent Newspapers: *The New York Times*.

Jacobellis v. Ohio (US Supreme Court June 22, 1964). https://www.law.cornell.edu/supremecourt/text/378/184.

Calmes, J. (2016, December 15). Obama shields federal funds for Planned Parenthood. *The New York Times*, A19.

Colby, T. (2012, March 14). Mad Men's handling of race has been brave—and painfully accurate. *Slate Magazine*. https://slate.com/culture/2012/03/mad-men-and-race-the-series-handling-of-race-has-been-painfully-accurate.html.

Goldin, D. (2016). Nachtraglichkeit revisited. *Psychoanalytic Inquiry, 36*(5), 408–419. https://doi.org/10.1080/07351690.2016.1180913.

Helo, A. (2016). Letting go of narrative history: The linearity of time and the art of recounting the past. *European Journal of American studies, 11*(11–2). https://doi.org/10.4000/ejas.11648.

Herstory. (n.d.). Black Lives Matter. https://blacklivesmatter.com/herstory/.

Hunt, T. (2006). Reality, identity and empathy: The changing face of social history television. *Journal of Social History, 39*(3), 843–858. https://doi.org/10.1353/jsh.2006.0005.

Inskeep, S. (2008, September 5). Pageant protest sparked bra-burning myth. In *Morning Edition (NPR)*. NPR; nfh. https://msu.idm.oclc.org/login?url=http://search.ebscohost.com/login.aspx?direct=true&db=nfh&AN=6XN200809051110&site=ehost-live.

James, E. L. (2012). *Fifty shades of Grey* (1st Vintage Books ed.). Vintage Books.

Jefferson, J. (2018, April 3). #MeToo Founder Tarana Burke talks sexual assault, stigmas and society. *Vibe*. https://www.vibe.com/featured/tarana-burke-me-too-feature.

Junod, S. W. (2002). Women's trials: The approval of the first oral contraceptive pill in the United States and Great Britain. *Journal of the History of Medicine and Allied Sciences, 57*(2), 117–160. https://doi.org/10.1093/jhmas/57.2.117.

King, R. H. (2015). Introduction: The Civil Rights Movement, a retrospective. *Patterns of Prejudice, 49*(5), 435–439. https://doi.org/10.1080/0031322X.2015.11 03438.

Kinsey, A. C., Pomeroy, W. B., & Martin, C. E. (1975). *Sexual behavior in the human male*. Indiana University Press; JSTOR. www.jstor.org/stable/j.ctt173zmh5.

Kinsey, A. C., Pomeroy, W. B., Martin, C. E., Gebhard, P. H., Brown, J. M., Christenson, C., Collins, D., Davis, R. G., Dellenback, W., Field, A. W., Leser, H. G., Remak, H. H., Roehr, E. L., & Bancroft, J. (1981). *Sexual behavior in the human female*. Indiana University Press; JSTOR. www.jstor.org/stable/j.ctt173zmgn.

Levine, S. (2015). The Feminine Mystique at fifty. *Frontiers, 36*, 2, 41–46.

Lewis, H. (2018). The year women said: Me Too: Six writers on the strengths and weaknesses of the feminist rallying call. *New Statesman, 5440*, 30. edsglr.

Masters, W. H., & Johnson, V. E. (1966). *Human sexual response*. Bantam Books.

Masters, W. H., & Masters, V. J. (1970). *Human sexual inadequacy*. Bantam Books.

Meredith, C. (2012, August 1). Fifty Shades of Grey becomes the bestselling book of all time. *Express.Co.Uk*. https://www.express.co.uk/news/uk/336759/Fifty-Shades-of-Grey-becomes-the-bestselling-book-of-all-time.

Nichols, B. (1996). Historical consciousness and the viewer: Who killed Vincent Chin? In V. Sobchack (Ed.), *The persistence of history: Cinema, television, and the modern event* (pp. 55–68). Routledge.

Ohleheiser, A. (2017, October 19). The woman behind 'Me Too' knew the power of the phrase when she created it 10 years ago. *Washington Post*. https://www.washingtonpost.com/news/the-intersect/wp/2017/10/19/the-woman-behind-me-too-knew-the-power-of-the-phrase-when-she-created-it-10-years-ago/.

Smail, G. (2019, December 9). Mrs. Maisel finally recognizes midge's white privilege, but still fails to see its own. *Bustle*. https://www.bustle.com/p/mrs-maisel-recognizes-midges-white-privilege-but-fails-to-see-its-own-19435569.

White, H. (2010). The historical text as literary artifact. In V. B. Leitch (Ed.), *The Norton anthology of theory and criticism* (2nd ed., pp. 1536–1553). W. W. Norton & Co.

Worth, J. (2009). *Midwife: A memoir of birth, joy, and hard times*. Macmillan Reference USA.

Wyche, S. (2016, August 27). Colin Kaepernick explains why he sat during national anthem. http://www.nfl.com.

Chapter 13

The Story of Zheng Yang Gate
Chinese Television Representation of Female Entrepreneurs

Mei Zhang

Chinese economic reform and opening to the West since 1978 ushered fundamental changes in Chinese culture and society. Women have access to an unprecedented means of educational opportunities, employment prospects, and leisure pursuits. This chapter studies Chinese television representation of female entrepreneurs, which constructs nonconformist enterprising capabilities and traditional feminine qualities. In particular, *The Story of Zheng Yang Gate* (2018), a television serial drama which was originally released in 2018 (40 years after the implementation of economic reform), is the focus of the current chapter. The chapter examines female protagonist's strategies for survival and success as well as discusses the role of television in contemporary Chinese media discourse.

In traditional patriarchal Chinese society, women had little to no political power, social status, or domestic authority, with some not even having names of their own. They lived to manage household chores and serve their families at home. After the Communist victory in 1949, the official slogan, "women hold up half the sky," attempted to liberate women and promote gender equality, which led to their new double responsibilities of sustaining a career and shouldering domestic duties.

The eras following 1978 saw transformations in many realms of society. However, stereotypes persist. Cheng (1997) finds more stereotyping of women in Chinese television advertising than that in the United States; Chinese women are often portrayed in domestic roles of "cooking and cleaning" (p. 312). At the same time, numerous venues promote renewed interest in beauty and femininity with advice columns, cosmetic advertisements, and television commercials. As a result, college women appreciate different paths to beauty, from body image enhancement to cosmetic surgery for personal and professional success (Zhang, 2012). With streaming services and video platforms in and outside China, Chinese television continues to play an important role in disseminating information and promoting new cultural values in the twenty-first century.

The Story of Zheng Yang Gate (2018) [Zhengyangmen xia xiao nvren; 《正阳门下小女人》; hereafter *The Story* in the following analysis] is a 48-episode television serial drama which was first aired in October 2018, 40 years after the implementation of Chinese economic reform. The show chronicles the life of Xu Huizhen, the female protagonist, in half a century from the 1950s following the founding of the People's Republic of China through the 2000s. Xu managed to cope with many challenges in her personal life and family business through volatile periods of Chinese politics, thereby redefining television images of Chinese women and female entrepreneurs. *China Daily* refers to Xu as "a rags-to-riches female entrepreneur" (Xu, 2018).

This chapter classifies the show as a historical drama in the sense that it spanned about fifty years of modern Chinese history. This fifty-year period witnessed important political movements in China—including the government takeover of private businesses, national mobilization for iron and steel production, the subsequent three years of natural disasters—resulting in severe food shortages and a campaign targeting bourgeois social elements. *The Story* depicts Chinese culture and history through the experiences of the main female character at home, in her business, and in the neighborhood. Employing Kenneth Burke's (1969) dramatistic pentad, this chapter studies Chinese television representation of female entrepreneurs, which constructs nonconformist enterprising capabilities and traditional feminine qualities. It examines the female agent's identity negotiation and strategies for survival, success, and happiness in response to changing scenes in Chinese society and her family situation, as well as discusses the role of television in contemporary Chinese media discourse.

CHINESE TELEVISION IN THE REFORM ERA: CULTURAL HEGEMONY VIA EDUTAINMENT

The founding of the People's Republic of China in 1949 changed Chinese culture and communication in fundamental ways. The government centralized state media control and the press served as the party government's "mouthpiece." Mobilizing mass media to support political campaigns, the government attempted to instill new Communist principles such as loyalty to the party, class struggle, self-reliance as a nation, and isolation from the West. These principles were designed to replace traditional Confucian core values of family and harmony. The Chinese economic reform, which initially started in rural areas in 1978, affected many Chinese institutions and impacted Chinese thought patterns (White, 1993).

Using the metaphor of the collapsing Great Wall, a defining cultural heritage of the Chinese civilization, Chu and Ju's (1993) study found radical changes in Chinese society and values about a decade after the reform. Their research indicates that Chinese became more assertive, no longer subscribed to Communist ideals or traditional Confucian values, and had a tendency to appreciate Western ideas. According to Tang (2005), the power of the Chinese political system to control Chinese public opinion and behavior has decreased tremendously in the race for marketization and consumer society. As long as the citizens do not challenge the party government's political supremacy, there is room for liberal ideas and press freedom. Tang (2016) calls the current Chinese system "populist authoritarianism," characterized by a combination of authoritarianism, nationalism, popular support of the central government, and political activism at the local level.

Driven by the rhetoric of the socialist market economy (Lu & Simons, 2006), Chinese economic reform has led to decreasing control of media content and diverse entertainment programming. Even the Xinhua News Agency, China's official wire service, has developed "a combination of a neo-authoritarian media model and a developmental media model with Chinese characteristics," which means that the organization must perpetuate the political status quo while "making profit as a commercial corporation" (Hong, 2012, p. 131). The Chinese television industry is no exception to the impact of decentralization in China and globalization internationally. As Chinese television goes international, Western programs have become available in China. Viewers in China have access to imported television shows from countries such as South Korea and the United States. Domestic television programs must be able to sustain themselves and adapt to audiences who have access to a wide variety of alternative entertainment.

Guided by what Xie (2014) calls the ideology of neoliberalism, Chinese television needs to support the party and look for new market strategies to make a profit. As a result, the government controls what major news events are covered, while stations have leeway for entertainment programs. Therefore, the television industry has the dual function of propagating government policies and providing entertainment to increase revenues. Chinese television is "non-liberal, anti-liberal and neoliberal, all in one" (Yu, 2011, p. 33). The industry "has been increasingly commercialized, liberalized, and even privatized to some extent to both increase its capacity and audience appeal" (L. Li, 2019, p. 4722). At the same time, it is important to remember that television remains an essential form of mass media where the Chinese government exercises its control in Chinese political culture (L. Li, 2019).

Much has been studied about Chinese television. Yuan and Ksiazek (2011) state that Chinese television viewers are highly interested in entertainment programming "with high entertainment value such as drama" (p. 194), which calls for television adaptation to viewer interests and responses. According to Keane (2005), Chinese television drama has gone through three stages since its beginning in 1958: the "industrial" period of 1958–1989, the "market" period of 1990 to 2002, and the "interpersonal" period since 2003. Keane (2005) notes that "mainstream melody" replaced "socialist realism." This shift afforded a continuation of the educational functions of Chinese drama television, promoting economic reform and material prosperity via hegemonic ideological control in the 1980s reform era. In other words, popular television drama aiming at "ideological persuasion" has replaced pre-reform Chinese socialist drama via "direct propaganda" (Ma, 2014, p. 523).

Keane (2005) classifies Chinese television drama into three broad categories: (1) historical and political themes, (2) social and reform themes, and (3) contemporary popular cultural themes focusing on modern life and romantic love. Media provide people with preferred collective memory of the past (Yang, 2016). Television drama's nostalgia diverted viewer attention from serious political issues of the past to love affairs in ordinary people's daily lives (Cai, 2016), thereby focusing on entertainment instead of critical reflection of history. Haili Li's (2019) study of a family reality show reveals collectivist Chinese family values and individualistic tendencies, including parental sacrifice, hope for children, and children's freedom of choice. Brown et al. (2013) find that in the reform era, romantic scenes are prevalent in China from sex talk to sexual portrayals, a radical change from the pre-reform era when such scenes were rare or forbidden. Such media entertainment is one indication of the lessening official control of citizens' personal lives while maintaining the ideological supremacy of the party government.

Besides entertainment programming, Chinese television commercials have developed rapidly in the reform era and help to transmit cultural values. Zhang, Song, and Carver (2008) find that Chinese television commercials featuring older adults promote health, family, and product quality. This corresponds to traditional and universal values in Sun's (2013) study. Sun (2013) asserts that Chinese television commercials promote traditional Eastern values (tradition, economy, health, knowledge, etc.), modern Western values (sexuality, success, beauty, leisure, etc.) and universal utilitarian values characterized by product quality and effectiveness. Lin (2001) argues that Western values are common in Chinese television commercials and points out the continuity and changes in Chinese values as depicted in Chinese television. Lin proposes a "continuum" rather than a "dichotomy" to understand cultural differences because "the core values remain stable, but a more contemporary interpretation of those core values may emerge" (p. 92).

The new changes in Chinese television in the reform era suggest a model of government-led cultural hegemony via edutainment. Gramsci's (1971) concept of hegemony is relevant here as China continues to develop a capitalist-style market economy under the control of the Communist Party. Instead of constant class struggle and waves of political movements in the pre-reform era, the government employed persuasive strategies to promote policies of economic reform and opening to the West, in order to identify with the public and seek citizen support. Through this economic reform process, Chinese television helps to promote new cultural values and educate the public via entertainment shows such as serial dramas. Television and other forms of mass media constitute important channels for the Chinese government to exercise its cultural hegemony (B. Casey, N. Casey, Calvert, French, & Lewis, 2002; Gitlin, 1980). Indeed, Zhang (2008) argues that Chinese rhetorical practice under economic reform has changed from coercion, blame, and negative labels to persuasion, praise of role-model actions, and tributes to outstanding citizens. Despite an abundance of available research on Chinese television in the reform era, little scholarly work has focused on rhetorical studies of Chinese media edutainment under the framework of cultural hegemony.

RHETORICAL STUDY OF MEDIA TEXTS

The study of rhetoric focuses on language, culture, and the persuasive thrust of all types of communication. Dating from the classical period of ancient Greece, the scope of rhetoric has expanded to include not only speeches, but also written texts, visual images, media messages, and online discourses. According to Foss, Foss, and Trapp (2014), "symbolic choices" and rhetorical discourse construct reality for us (p. 2). Indeed, Hinds and Windt (1991) argue that even the cold war reality was rhetorically created and shaped perceptions of the political actuality following World War II. In their "Rhetorical Studies in a Media Age," an introduction to the pioneering anthology of *Rhetorical Dimensions in Media*, Medhurst and Benson (1984) call for rhetorical examination of different forms of media in response to the lack of research in that area. Gronbeck (1984), Barton and Gregg (1984), and Schrag, Hudson, and Bernabo (1984) have studied television programs from rhetorical perspectives and demonstrated that the rhetoric of television is an important domain of scholarly inquiry into media, persuasion, contemporary culture, and society.

When discussing the rhetoric of mediated texts in popular culture and its impact on our beliefs and actions, Sellnow (2018) states, "Mediated popular culture texts communicate to and for us regarding what we think we ought to and ought not to believe and do during every waking moment" (p. 4). Likewise, Brummett (2018) emphasizes the importance of studying rhetorical dimensions of popular culture and suggests that we can incorporate critical perspectives in rhetorical studies of media and popular culture texts. In Chinese communication studies, research on Chinese rhetoric remains a relatively new field. Since Oliver's (1971) study of Chinese rhetoric, scholars have contributed to comparative rhetoric (Garrett, 1991; Lu, 1998; Xiao, 2004), Chinese political rhetoric (Huang, 1996; Lu, 2004), and the rhetoric of Chinese economic reform (Kluver, 1996; Lu & Simons, 2006). Studying Chinese television from a rhetorical perspective can contribute to an increase in rhetorical understanding of Chinese media.

A BURKEIAN SCENE/AGENT ANALYSIS

Burke's (1969) dramatistic pentad includes scene (setting), agent (person/persons performing the act), act (action by the agent), agency (means for the act), and purpose (goal) to understand human motives. To conduct a Burkeian analysis, rhetorical critics examine the five terms featured in the discourse, particularly the ratio or relationship between two of the five. Beyond the content, critics may study the larger context and pentadic elements which produce the discourse (Foss, Foss, & Trapp, 2014). While recognizing scholarship on the cognitive motive that drives the act of the agent, Benoit (1996) argues for additional understanding of the motive which the discourse reveals in the rhetorical act. According to Birdsell (1989), "Different pentadic formulations may be possible within a single text, each contributing to the ultimate interpretation of the text in a different, but equally valuable way" (p. 209). In the following discussion, it is argued that *The Story of Zheng Yang Gate* features the scene/agent ratio in portraying the images of the protagonist, Xu Huizhen.

The Story centers on a series of scenes in relation to Xu's personal circumstances, business situations, and neighborhood settings, which are featured alternately as the stories unfold in the Chinese historical and political contexts. *The Story* started with one of the sad scenes that featured Xu, a pregnant woman and a deserted wife, who was going into labor. She was desperately seeking help in a street on a freezing windy day. Many people ignored her until a stranger by the name of Cai Quanwu took her to the hospital, where she gave birth to a baby girl. This scene featured a miserable woman dying for help and a kind-hearted man coming to her rescue, setting a scene/agent portrayal of the main characters in many stories to follow.

China's national scene involved several episodes of political and economic campaigns, from state takeover of private businesses to state encouragement of private companies in the fifty years of Chinese history. Under such a large sociopolitical context, Xu, as an active agent in the television narrative, successfully adapted to the changing scenes, met the challenges, acted decisively, and ultimately triumphed at home, in her business, and in the community. *The Story* ended with a happy scene on a sunny day, when Xu's corporation merged with another. Xu transferred the leadership position to her oldest daughter, and all the main characters gathered to celebrate as one big family and business entity, including Xu's ex-husband. The opening scene denotes sadness and division, which resulted in Xu's unfortunate circumstances. As a result of Xu's resilience, and abilities to adapt and defy dreadful conditions, her life is on a good course. The concluding scene signifies happiness and harmony.

At Home: A Wife and Mother

At the home front, Xu Huizhen, whose name means "wisdom" and "sincerity," was thrown into numerous difficult situations. She became a single mother who had to take care of a newborn baby, managed a family bar, and found ways to survive financially. She also navigated social biases against divorced women and fended off several men's interests in her beauty. Ironically, the tragedy of her ex-husband abandoning her ultimately paved the way for her personal and professional successes. She had to be strong and resourceful under such formidable situations. First, Xu acted decisively and chose to marry Cai Quanwu, whose name means "complete nothing." Cai was the man who had saved her life by taking her to the hospital in the opening scene. He was an orphan, appeared to be dumb, had no money or good looks, hardly ever talked, and did odd jobs to make a living using his physical strength. The neighborhood paid little attention to him and looked down on him.

Cai was pleasantly shocked and overjoyed that Xu, a beautiful bar owner whom he worked for, would want to marry him. Just as their names indicated, they were on the opposite ends of life in many ways. Second, Xu managed her family matters as head of the household following her marriage. She told Cai what to do, raised successful children with Cai's help, and eventually became a grandmother, handing over the business to her oldest daughter. Third, Xu took care of the children from her ex-husband's new marriage with her cousin, again with the help of Cai.

Though it took quite much time and emotional struggle, Xu forgave her ex-husband who left her in a helpless situation. She decided to bear no malice to He Yongqiang, whose name means "forever stubborn." She was literally her nieces' aunt-mother, who made it possible for them to succeed in the hotel and travel businesses that she later developed. Xu came a long way from refusing to allow her oldest daughter to communicate with her ex-husband. Fourth, Xu exhibited talent and artistic taste in feminine beauty, art appreciation, and leisure pursuits. After overcoming initial difficulties in her personal life and bar business, Xu found time to pursue leisure activities and resumed her interests in fashion, painting, calligraphy, and antiques. These all worked to expand her life beyond family and work.

In Business: A Businesswoman and Entrepreneur

Xu's business scene was not a set environment; it changed in response to shifts in Chinese political culture. In the 1950s, the government policies moved from co-ownership of private businesses to gradual removal from private ownership. In the 1980s, the government began to encourage private ownership and the establishment of joint ventures with international investment. Xu adapted to the various circumstances. In the early business years, her status altered from a bar owner to a bar co-owner to an employee at the bar. Later, by following Chinese economic reform policies, she eventually became a bar owner again. Such changes responded to the government regulations toward private businesses in the national movements to support dominant ideologies at different historical periods. As a result, Xu transformed herself from a small neighborhood businesswoman to a leading entrepreneur in the city. Her business ventures included a bar, a restaurant, a hotel, and a tourism company. She not only survived political movements but also thrived in the new reform era, becoming a force to be reckoned with in the business field.

First, Xu conducted her business with honesty and integrity, which earned her credibility and customer trust. For example, starting at the very beginning when she was struggling to survive with her bar business, she never added water to the alcohol in order to gain illegitimate money. Her honesty was an unusual practice among bar owners. She would rather go out of business than lose her business ethics. Second, Xu cooperated with government representatives when she had to collaborate with the government managing the bar. Later she had to turn over the ownership, and eventually work as an employee. Even during such difficult times, she willingly helped with business ideas despite being unfairly treated at times.

Third, after her bar was returned to her, Xu constantly looked to expand her business and beat her competitor business friend. She often came up with new ideas and took risks in several business ventures. Her ambition, competitiveness, and resourcefulness led to continuous real estate expansion. Her venture grew from a small neighbor bar to many urban company buildings. Fourth, Xu demonstrated compassion and cared about her workers' well-being. An employee was a former government worker who had mistreated Xu, when Xu lost bar ownership. Having to feed many children at home, that employee struggled with daily necessities and never imagined that Xu would offer her financial assistance. Xu's generosity moved the employee deeply and boosted the loyalty and morale of all employees.

In the Neighborhood: A Leader and Member

Xu's neighborhood and the community in which she lived went through different phases of Chinese political movements. At each historical period, Xu took the lead in supporting government policies and demonstrating optimism, regardless of how the movement would affect her family life or personal future. First, Xu supported the Great Leap Forward (1958–1960), which was the government campaign to collect and melt down metal equipment, tools, and household goods to develop homespun steel production, among other endeavors. The government goal was to develop a heavy steel industry and catch up with Western nations, partly via backyard furnaces in urban and rural China. She collected all her relevant household items and donated them to the collection center. To stay on top of the donor list against her competitors in the neighborhood competition, she even donated all the cooking equipment, which meant she might not be able to cook at home.

Second, Xu served her community with sincerity and resilience. She was named neighborhood committee head to oversee daily community activities and to make sure every household was in compliance with government policy. Then the government launched the Cultural Revolution (1966–1976), after the failure of the Great Leap Forward and the subsequent famine. The movement was designed to purify China from Western influences and bourgeois ideas. Those who previously studied in the West or owned private businesses became suspects. For a period of time, Xu was relieved of her position and put under neighborhood house arrest because her private business background was considered dubious. Xu waited for better days to come and never exhibited pessimism or loss of hope. When she was released, she still treated those who had mistreated her well and served the community without holding grudges. Third, Xu found ways to help others in the community as a compassionate community member and friend. When her friend and business competitor was deserted by her ex-husband and became emotionally unstable, Xu went to her house, provided emotional support, and helped her cope with the predicament.

A Nontraditional and Traditional Female Entrepreneur

In the three scenes of home, business, and neighborhood, Xu adapted adroitly to her surroundings and defied old traditional Chinese female expectations. Despite all that happened to her personally, professionally, and politically, she never exhibited hatred or the desire to retaliate. She never disliked government employees who gave her a hard time or other individuals who mistreated her and deprived her of personal freedom. She did not complain about her ex-husband leaving her; she blamed arranged marriage beyond his or her control. Rather, she strove for the best at home and beyond, and tried to help others in need. She agreed to Cai's use of their family money and food to help her ex-husband's family, during the era of national food shortages. She was thrown into impossible circumstances and rose above these. She took initiative, adjusted, and succeeded rather than scapegoating and blaming others. She beat the odds with her hard work, self-sacrifice, insight, and vision for the future. In other words, she focused on what she could do to change her circumstances, overcome adversity, and embrace the future.

As an all-powerful agent in the television show, Xu exhibited new nonconformist capabilities and traditional feminine qualities. Xu defied rough circumstances and exhibited traditional masculine qualities in order to survive and thrive. She was in charge of everything at home and made all the important family decisions. Challenging traditional expectations of a woman, she made the marriage decision for both herself and Cai by asking Cai to marry her. Even their children took her last name, instead of Cai's. She was a beautiful woman and a business owner, someone that Cai could never dare to imagine marrying. Cai was pleasantly surprised, agreed to the marriage, and was grateful that his boss would choose him as a lifetime partner.

All that Cai needed to do was support Xu's decisions. He followed her instructions, took care of household chores such as cleaning and getting the children ready for school in the morning. She gave him self-confidence and transformed him from someone virtually invisible in the community to a happy father and respected businessman. His marriage to Xu was a defining moment in his life. Their roles reversed the traditional expectations of a family, where the wife tended to be in supportive or subordinate roles. Likewise, in Xu's business adventures, Cai was her employee and later her partner, always listening to her and following her orders. One scene toward the end of the television show portrayed Cai holding an umbrella for Xu, while she was outside briefing her management personnel at an important meeting. It was customary for the Chinese to use umbrellas for protection against the sunlight. Xu was obviously in a dominant position with Cai supporting her in a subordinate place. Furthermore, Xu strived for success and competition in her business career, a traditionally male-dominated field.

On the other hand, Xu shared traditional feminine qualities. During her moments of weakness, she needed her husband in her life to encourage her, support her, bring her happiness, and enable her business success during difficult times. When her venture into international business failed and she suffered huge financial losses, she felt desperate and drank heavily. With the support of her husband, her children, and her nieces, she recovered from her losses, regained self-confidence, and became successful again. When one of her daughters ran away with a boyfriend whom Xu did not want as a son-in-law, Cai comforted Xu and searched high and low to find her. When another daughter wanted to move to the United States with a Chinese American boyfriend, Cai was again by her side comforting and relieving her of worries.

Therefore, Cai was her behind-the-scenes "rock," listening to her, following her decisions, doing all household chores traditionally expected of a wife, helping her raise successful children, as well as protecting her safety and well-being in the community. Xu could not have done it all by herself; she needed a husband as a partner in life and career. In addition, she demonstrated the feminine side by being compassionate and caring toward employees and community friends.

CONCLUSION

Using Burkeian analysis, this chapter discusses Chinese television representation of female entrepreneurs via the 50-year narrative of protagonist, Xu Huizhen. The show constructs images of a successful female entrepreneur who beat all odds. Her multiple identities as a businesswoman, wife, mother, aunt, friend, and neighbor all worked together to portray a panoramic image of a superwoman. In her constant adaptation to drastic changes, she was politically attuned. She demonstrated leadership during political movements while strategically managing family, business, and community relationships. She adapted to changing scenes, survived challenges, and transcended traditional expectations of Chinese women. In that process, she transformed herself, family, and business, while impacting her community in a positive way. Instead of being a victim of her circumstances, she changed her situations through active agency. She adroitly adjusted to, and redefined, her situations in different historical periods and different phases of her family life.

This chapter affirms Chinese television's dual political-economic function of promoting government policy and providing entertainment. Produced 40 years after Chinese economic reform, *The Story* reflects a tribute to the government's years of economic reform efforts via a unique Chinese female entrepreneur. She embodies both nontraditional and traditional virtues and attributes. While core Chinese values are retained, Xu's interpretations of such values are given new meaning. The female protagonist's happy ending suggests government hegemony to maintain the status quo via popular entertainment.

The protagonist in *The Story* was played by an award-winning star actress, Jiang Wenli. It would be interesting to examine whether a television star's screen credibility might have an effect similar to what McCracken (1989) has discussed, regarding celebrity endorsement and product meaning transfer. Furthermore, Chinese television has all heterosexual romantic scenes without diversity or attention to nonheterosexual behavior in Chinese society (Brown et al., 2013). Future research may study gender and sexuality diversity, or the lack thereof, in television representation and its impact on Chinese viewers in a globalized world.

REFERENCES

Barton, R. L., & Gregg, R. B. (1984). Middle East conflict as a TV news scenario: A formal analysis. In M. J. Medhurst & T. W. Benson (Eds.), *Rhetorical dimensions in media: A critical casebook* (pp. 33–46). Kendall/Hunt.

Benoit, W. (1996). A note on Burke on "Motive." *Rhetoric Society Quarterly, 26*(2), 67–79.

Birdsell, D. S. (1989). Ronald Reagan on Lebanon and Grenada: Flexibility and interpretation in the application of Kenneth Burke's pentad. In B. L. Brock, R. L. Scott, & J. W. Chesebro (Eds), *Methods of rhetorical criticism: A twentieth-century perspective* (pp. 196–209). Wayne State University Press.

Brown, J. D., Zhao, X., Wang, M. N., Liu, Q., Lu, A. S., Li, L. J., . . . Zhang, G. (2013). Love is all you need: A content analysis of romantic scenes in Chinese entertainment television. *Asian Journal of Communication, 23*(3), 229–247.

Brummett, B. (2018). *Rhetoric in popular culture* (5th ed.). Sage.

Burke, K. (1969). *A grammar of motives*. University of California Press.

Cai, S. (2016). Contemporary Chinese TV serials: Configuring collective memory of socialist nostalgia via the Cultural Revolution. *Visual Anthropology, 29*, 22–35.

Casey, B., Casey, N., Calvert, B., French, L., & Lewis, J. (2002). *Television studies: The key concepts*. Routledge.

Cheng, H. (1997). 'Holding up half of the sky'? A sociocultural comparison of gender-role portrayals in Chinese and US advertising. *International Journal of Advertising, 16*(4), 295–319.

Chu, G. C., & Ju, Y. (1993). *The Great Wall in ruins: Communication and cultural change in China*. State University of New York Press.

Foss, S. K., Foss, K. A., & Trapp, R. (2014). *Contemporary perspectives on rhetoric* (30th anniversary ed.). Waveland Press.

Garrett, M. (1991). Asian challenges. In S. K. Foss, K. A. Foss, & R. Trapp (Eds.), *Contemporary perspectives on rhetoric* (2nd ed., pp. 295–314). Waveland Press.

Gitlin, T. (1980). *The whole world is watching: Mass media in the making & unmaking of the new left*. University of California Press.

Gramsci, A. (1971). *Selections from the prison notebooks*. International Publishers.

Gronbeck, B. E. (1984). Audience engagement in "family." In M. J. Medhurst & T. W. Benson, (Eds.), *Rhetorical dimensions in media: A critical casebook* (pp. 4–32). Kendall/Hunt.

Hinds, L. B., & Windt, T. O., Jr. (1991). *The Cold War as rhetoric: The beginnings, 1945–1950*. Praeger.

Hong, J. (2012). From the world's largest propaganda machine to a multipurposed global news agency: Factors in and implications of Xinhua's transformation since 1978. In W. Tang & S. Iyengar (Eds.), *Political communication in China: Convergence or divergence between the media and political system?* (pp. 117–133). Routledge.

Huang, S. (1996). *To rebel is justified: A rhetorical study of China's Cultural Revolution Movement 1966–969*. University Press of America.

Keane, M. (2005). Television drama in China: Remaking the market. *Media International Australia incorporating Culture and Policy, 115*, 82–93.

Kluver, A. R. (1996). *Legitimating the Chinese economic reform: A rhetoric of myth and orthodoxy*. State University of New York.

Li, H. (2019). Representations and public discourse of Chinese family cultures across media platforms. *International Journal of Media & Cultural Politics, 15(2)*, 239–247.

Li, L. (2019). I'd rather be the ferryman in the Gold Rush: The television drama production industry in post-2008 China. *International Journal of Communication, 13*, 4722–4737.

Lin, C. A. (2001). Cultural values reflected in Chinese and American television advertising. *Journal of Advertising, 30(4)*, 83–94.

Lu, X. (1998). *Rhetoric in ancient China fifth to third century B.C.E.* University of South Carolina Press.

Lu, X. (2004). *Rhetoric of the Chinese Cultural Revolution: The impact on Chinese thought, culture, and communication*. University of South Carolina Press.

Lu, X., & Simons, H. W. (2006). Transitional rhetoric of Chinese Communist Party leaders in the post-Mao reform period: Dilemmas and strategies. *Quarterly Journal of Speech, 92*, 262–286.

Ma, W. (2014). Chinese main melody TV drama: Hollywoodization and ideological persuasion. *Television & New Media, 15(6)*, 523–537.

McCracken, G. (1989). Who is the celebrity endorser? *Journal of Consumer Research, 16*, 310–321.

Medhurst, M. J., & Benson, T. W. (1984). Rhetorical studies in a media age. In M. J. Medhurst & T. W. Benson (Eds.), *Rhetorical dimensions in media: A critical casebook* (pp. ix–xxiii). Kendall/Hunt.

Oliver, R. (1971). *Communication and culture in ancient India and China*. Syracuse University.

Schrag, R. L., Hudson, R. A., & Bernabo, L. M. (1984). Television's new humane collectivity. In M. J. Medhurst & T. W. Benson (Eds.), *Rhetorical dimensions in media: A critical casebook* (pp. 47–58). Kendall/Hunt.

Sellnow, D. D. (2018). *The rhetorical power of popular culture: Considering mediated Texts* (3rd ed.). Sage.

Sun, Z. (2013). Cultural values conveyed through celebrity endorsers: A content analysis of Chinese television commercials. *International Journal of Communication, 7*, 2631–2652.

Tang, W. (2005). *Political opinion and political change in China*. Stanford University Press.

Tang, W. (2016). *Populist authoritarianism: Chinese political culture and regime sustainability*. Oxford University Press.

White, G. (1993). *Riding the tiger: The politics of economic reform in post-Mao China*. Stanford University Press.

Xiao, X. (2004). The 1923 scientific campaign and Dao-Discourse: A cross-cultural study of the rhetoric of science. *Quarterly Journal of Speech, 90*, 469–494.

Xie, S. (2014). Similarities and differences or similarities in differences? China's TV programming in global trend of neo-liberal imperialism. *China Media Research, 10*(1), 91–101.

Xu, F. (2018). Acclaimed actress returns to the small screen with new drama. China Daily. http://www.chinadaily.com.cn/a/201810/16/WS5bc58830a310eff303282a98_1.html.

Yang, M. (2016). Rhetorically re-configuring China's past and present through nostalgia: Chinese media coverage of the 50th anniversary of *The Red Detachment of Women*. China *Media Research, 12*(2), 4–14.

Yu, H. (2011). *Dwelling Narrowness*: Chinese media and their disingenuous neoliberal logic. *Continuum: Journal of Media & Cultural Studies, 25*(1), 33–46.

Yuan, E. J., Ksiazek, T. B. (2011). The duality of structure in China's national television market: A network analysis of audience behavior. *Journal of Broadcasting & Electronic Media, 55*(2), 180–197.

Zhang, Y. B., Song, Y., & Carver, L. J. (2008). Cultural values and aging in Chinese television commercials. *Journal of Asian Pacific Communication, 18*(2), 209–224.

Zhang, M. (2008). Rhetoric in the service of reform: A study of Chinese discourse in transition. *Intercultural Communication Studies, 17*(2), 304–318.

Zhang, M. (2012). A Chinese beauty story: how college women in China negotiate beauty, body images, and mass media. *Chinese Journal of Communication, 5*(4), 437–454.

Chapter 14

Exploring Gendering in Iranian Television Drama Serials

Ali Zohoori

Television as a cultural arm of society plays an undeniable role in (re)constructing cultural values, behavioral norms, and certain ideological worldviews (Gerbner, Gross, Signorielli, & Morgan, 1980). Television, by taking advantage of its programming genres, promotes certain models of lifestyles among its viewing audiences. Serials are the most popular television genre across different demographics by virtue of their close similarity to its audiences' everyday life. The popularity of television serials genre transcends cultural differences, as does its power of reconstructing certain cultural norms such as gender.

The purpose of this exploratory study is to examine Iranian television drama serials' portrayals of gender and the extent to which the serials represent men and women's characters as equal or unequal. As Hall (2003) points out, representation is about power and "has to be understood here, not only in terms of economic exploitation and physical coercion, but also in broader cultural or symbolic terms" (p. 259). Given Iranian women's historical struggles in trying to gain equal social and political power, this study will investigate the representations of women in Iranian television drama serials to find out about the construction of gender as a reflection of the Iranian society's attitudes toward women.

This study would be the first about which we are aware to explore gendering, which excludes sex and sexualization dimension, in Iranian television drama serials. This exclusion is a result of the restrictive programming policy of the *Islamic Republic of Iran Broadcasting* (IRIB). The IRIB's programming policy is based on the rigid application of Islamic provisions—as well as the masculine nature of Iranian culture—as delineated by Hofstede (2001).

THE 1979 ISLAMIC REVOLUTION AND IRANIAN TELEVISION SERIALS

Following the 1979 Islamic revolution, the new religious government changed the name of the Iranian radio and television network to the *IRIB*, and placed it under the control of the Iran Supreme Leader. The IRIB set a new policy banning Western-made television programs and focused on domestic productions, including drama serials dominated by religious content. During the past four decades, over 900 television serials have been broadcast by the IRIB.

In retrospect, the tumultuous history of television in Iran has been affected by the tension between tradition and modernity and dominated by the patriarchal dimension of Iranian culture. In general, Iranian women have historically been marginalized and isolated from participating in social and public discourses, both in real life and on the stage.

On television, as in real life, Iranian women have been assigned the role of the good wife and nurturing mother and rarely presented as independent human beings. Iranian television has reinforced the unequal social status of women and portrayed them as being bewildered by their emotional issues and dependent on wise and capable men.

THE IRIB POLICY ON THE PORTRAYS OF WOMEN IN TELEVISION SERIALS

Basing its rationale on the Islamic view on Muslim women in the family and in Islamic society, the IRIB has set a strict programming policy with respect to the portrayals of women in its television serials. The intricate policy includes the following:

1. Depictions of women, including their make-up, acting, and customs, shall be void of any sexual suggestions or references.
2. Scenery and sets pertaining to women's rooms include a bookcase, study desk, praying set, religious books, and items which do not connote negative personalities of modest women.
3. The frequency of camera shots depicting women's characters shall not exceed those of male characters. Further, framing of women shall not focus on women's sexual attributes and place them in men's gaze.
4. Regarding character roles, women shall not be portrayed in careers such as police officers or firefighters. Women's characters shall demonstrate their compassion and modesty.
5. Characterization of women shall show them in a positive light and as pious and educated.

6. The dialogs of female protagonists shall not be void of religious connotation and shall avoid sinful language.
7. Female protagonists shall not give the impression that they are not interested in having children and raising them. They shall be kind to their spouse and children, avoid arguments with their spouse, preserve their sexual appeal for their spouse, and in interaction with male strangers, practice chastity and inhibition (Mirkhandan & Gharehbaghi, 2017).

To summarize, the above policy for the most part reinforces gender disparities and influences male audiences' evaluation of women, which will be explicated by the modern feminist theory, social drama theory, cognitive theory (SCT), and cultivation theory as follows.

THEORETICAL BACKGROUND

Many feminist theories have explained the media's role in perpetuating gender roles and gendering of women. Frederickson and Roberts (1997) suggest that modern feminism has led to two arguments about feminism today. On the one side, contenders of modern feminism point out the idea of owning and celebrating one's sexuality by being in control of the context of a situation to indicate women's power. On the other side, modern feminist rhetoricians believe "maintaining more values from the previous wave of feminism, argues that power will never be reached until women are equally depicted on film in age standards, in positions of leadership, and by distinction of extra-familial aspirations, among other inequalities" (p. 176).

These modern feminist theories merit their advantages as well as challenges in reading the text about gender relationships and gendering in media. Given the current unequal position of women in masculine and patriarchal Iranian society, the modern feminism theory which suggests women's power will only be attained when they are equally presented in the media—with respect to age standards, leadership, and family position and aspirations—is more relevant to the purpose of this study.

Nonetheless, modern feminist theories have a Western-biased nature. For example, post-feminist theories emphasize women's empowerment through their individuality and choice regarding sex, marriage and family life, work, and lifestyles. Obviously in emerging collectivistic countries, like Iran, these theories are hardly applicable to women who are subjugated and marginalized by their patriarchal societies. However, new development in feminist media research has become increasingly global by stressing the importance of international and multidisciplinary research (Steiner, 2014).

Kincaid (2002) introduced drama theory by describing how characters and plot can induce emotional involvement in audience members and lead them to identify with characters. According to Kincaid (2002), character identification is a complex construct that includes wanting to be like (and feeling similar to) a character. The more emotionally induced the audience members are with the characters in a drama, the more they identify with the characters. As such, the drama genre works through character identification and emotional involvement in the story to impact its audiences.

Within the drama, characters set goals (as determined by the storyline and plot devices). As the drama gains momentum, characters face complications to reach these goals and the drama evokes strong emotional responses in the audience accordingly. In this study, the implication of drama theory is that the more Iranian television drama serials represent female characters as inferior to and dominated by male characters, the more audience members perceive and accept female characters' roles by becoming emotionally involved with them. In other words, Iranian television drama serials do not only tell stories about gender relationships, but they also tell stories about how the Iranian society structures gender relationships and how their audiences remember the serials' characters, and internalize represented gender relationships into their lives.

The internalization of gender relationship can be further explained by the SCT which explains how "the principles of attention, retention, production, and motivation, with media exposure most likely to affect audience behavior when members are attending to attractive and/or similar models realistically performing uncomplicated, personally relevant, and rewarded behavior" (Sink & Mastro, 2017, p. 6). Studies based on SCT have demonstrated that under certain conditions media representations of reality can and do affect audiences' cognitions and behaviors (Nabi & Oliver, 2009). According to Dill and Thill (2007), people's repeated exposures to media's representations of gender roles socialize them to these roles, they internalize what they learn about the scripts or schema about these gender roles, and later apply them to their interaction with people who resemble these roles (Hall, West, & McIntyre, 2012).

A study by Johnson and Holmes (2009) revealed that people "look to relationships presented in film to learn what to expect from real-life relationships" (p. 353). The study also found that genre-specific exposure is more likely to change audiences' beliefs and expectations about real-life interactions and relationships. Additionally, Bussey and Bandura (1999) demonstrated that media's representations of gender relationships are more unrealistic and maintain stereotyped personality attributes, potential, and aspirations of depicted characters.

Cultivation theory is also useful in explaining the effects of repeated exposures to gender representations in media on audiences' cultural perceptions of reality, though more passively (Gerbner, Gross, Morgan, Signorielli, & Shanahan, 2002). Cultivation theory contends that heavy viewers of television dramas form perceptions of reality that are consistent with those observed on television. According to Eyal, Raz, and Levi (2014), continuous exposure to specific cultural messages, like the presentation of gender, will affect how the audience identifies with those messages over time.

Cultivation theory can explain the influence of the depictions of gender on television serials on their audiences, where audiences' perceptions and endorsements of gender role norms are based on their attitudes and values toward gender relationships. A meta-analysis by Morgan and Shanahan (1997) supported the above assertion and provided a small but significant role for television to cultivate stereotypical perceptions of gender roles among its viewers. In sum, both SCT and cultivation theory have received support from empirical research.

In light of the reviewed theoretical background and the issues of gendering and gender relationships in Iranian television drama serials, this study poses the following research questions:

RQ1: What are the qualities of gender relationships and gendering on Iranian television drama serials?

RQ2: Will male characters significantly surpass female characters in number and screen time?

RQ3: Will male characters significantly outnumber female characters in the following portrayals: dominance, sexualization, competence, morality, mental state, other-orientations, age, and occupational roles?

METHODS

This author used a mixed method of explorative and descriptive designs to analyze gendering in the content of the sampled Iranian television drama serials and coded the units of analysis himself. Whereas the explorative design formulates new categories out of the sampled content, descriptive design works through the content with a deductively formulated category system and counting the occurrences of those categories in a nominal way or in category frequencies (Mayring, 2014). Although the scientific value of traditional quantitative content analysis cannot be dismissed, the lack of access to Farsi-speaking (Farsi, also known as Persian, is Iran's official language) coders prevented the use of quantitative content analysis of the serials.

Population and Sample

The IRIB television networks have broadcast over 900 television serials since 1979. Less than 1% of 900 serials was produced between 1979 and 2000 due to the post-revolution's tumultuous period and the 1980s Iraq-Iran war. Therefore, this study focused on the drama serials produced and broadcast between 2000 and 2018. The author selected the 10 drama serials with the highest audience ratings as the study population.

The threading subgenre among the 10 serials was family and, to a lesser extent, spirituality. The number of episodes varied across the 10 serials, ranging from 10 to 34. Using a purposive sampling, the author chose the first, the middle, and the last episodes in each of the 10 serials to analyze gendering in their contents. The rationale for the selection of these episodes was based on Gledhill's (2003) reflection on television serial by outlining, "The serial refers to a fiction, which is divided into a sequence of parts, so that a strong sense of linear progression is maintained across episodes as the plot unfolds from beginning, through a middle, to the end" (p. 367). Further, Gledhill stresses her point by referring to how television serials follow the beginning, middle, end formula used in the majority of popular fictions, with "an abstract three-part movement: equilibrium, disruption, equilibrium restored" (p. 368).

Two key terms in this study are genre and serial. The term "genre" refers to the grouping together of individual stories with respect to similar plots, stereotypes, settings, themes, styles, emotional effects and so on. In other words, genre uses the convention of intertwining format and medium, subject matter, setting and locations, narrative pattern, character types, and plots (Gedhill, 2003). In television discourse, popular genres reinforce certain normative values, myths, or stereotypes such as gendering in public cultural knowledge.

Genre uses the format of serials in television as part of its convention. Serials are best defined by contrasting them to series. Whereas series are made of separate and different stories and don't follow certain scheduling patterns, serials consist of related subplots running simultaneously, intertwining different characters' lives, and broadcast once or more per week usually in 30 to 60-minute slots (Gledhill, 2003).

Units of Analysis

The author established the units of analysis by using categories already developed in previous studies as well those unique to the nature of the selected serials, while keeping in mind the mutual exclusivity of categories. The first category was *character gender*. The author measured the distribution of male and female characters and their respective average screen time for the sampled three episodes in each of the selected 10 drama serials. The author included the characters, who were assigned as *main characters* (recurring, regular characters who were central to the storyline), *minor characters* (infrequent, semi-regular, or one-time characters in supporting roles), or *background characters* (noncentral characters with at least two lines). The tri-level coding of characters was based on Strinati's (2004) classification.

The *age category* was determined based on the physical appearance of the character, that is, overall look, body posture, hair color, thinning of hair, wrinkles, and divided into three categories of *young age* (18 to 34 years old), *middle age* (35 to 49 years old), and *old age* (50+ years old) following Ferrante et al.'s (1988) and Milner and Collins's (2000) age classifications, as cited in Prieler (2016).

To measure the four constructs of *dominance, sexualization, competence*, and *orientation*, the author adopted the following categories from Sink and Mastro's (2017) study. *Dominance* was defined as a character having power over others and was measured by the character's *verbal aggressiveness, physical aggressiveness*, or *a combination of the two*. Due to the IRIB restrictive programming policy, any sexualization of characters in Iranian television is forbidden. Therefore, the only subcategory under the sexualization category used in this study was the *attractiveness of the character's face*. *Competence* was conceptualized in terms of three subcategories: *articulate, motivated*, and *intelligent*. *Articulate* was measured based on a character's ability to express him- or herself clearly and effectively. *Motivation* was ascertained based on the extent to which a character was presented as driven or inspired to action. *Intelligence* was assessed based on a character's demonstrated intellect and brainpower.

The *others-orientation* category was a derivation of Sink and Mastro's (2017) traditionally feminine (i.e., warm) characteristics of liked, family-oriented, and kind. The author assessed the others-orientation in terms of *being involved with* and *supportive of family, friendship*, and *expression of subtle love toward the opposite sex*. While *family orientation* and *friendship* are self-explanatory, *expression of subtle love toward opposite sex* was measured by implied and restrained verbal expressions of love. No other forms of expressing love are allowed in Iranian television serials by the IRIB; these include direct verbal expression and nonverbal expressions, such as holding hands, hugging, and kissing. Finally, the author created an *occupational roles* category by combining Mastro and Behm-Morawitz's (2005) list of occupations with those specific to the serials' plots.

The author constructed the remaining two categories, character's *morality* and *mental state*, according to the explorative nature of the study and the contents of the serials. The *morality category* was conceptualized in terms of *honesty, dishonesty/conniving*, and *piousness*, given the emphasis of the IRIB programming policy on including religious messages in television serials.

The *honesty* and *dishonesty* constructs were measured in both the character's *verbal expressions* (being truthful or lying) and *nonverbal behaviors* (following the righteous path or cheating and conniving). *Piousness* was measured by the extent to which the character *followed the Islamic dress code, performed prayers, recited from the Koran,* and *observed religious rituals.* The *mental state* category was based on the character's psychological reactions to events and people in the storylines. This category was measured by how the character demonstrated *happiness, melancholy, anger, seriousness,* or *nervousness* verbally and/or nonverbally.

ANALYSIS OF FEMALE AND MALE CHARACTERS

Based on the study's mixed method of explorative and descriptive designs, the author analyzed gendering in the content of the three sampled episodes for each of the 10 selected Iranian television drama serials. The first part of this analysis answered the first research question:

> RQ1: What are the qualities of gender relationships and gendering on Iranian television drama serials?

In total, there are 20 female lead characters in the sample. The analysis of the data showed that more than one-half of lead female characters were young, attractive, intelligent; some were dedicated to the family or society causes, and very few involved in socially disapproved activities of crime, spying, or cheating. Also, among the lead female characters were a few middle-aged and older women who played the roles of the mother, grandmother, or servant. They tended to be pious as well as an anchor of the family, advice-giver, and/or kind and caring. Out of 89 female characters across the analyzed 30 episodes, only two female characters (2.2%) appeared in non-Islamic dress. One female character, a French-educated woman, did not wear chador or scarf. She covered her hair with a European hat and had little make-up. The other female character portrayed a French Jewish girl, played by a French actor. The stories in which these two female characters appeared took place in the early twentieth century, which justified their non-Islamic dress code in the historical context of the storylines. Female characters who played negative roles in the serials mostly appeared with colorful head scarfs, instead of a traditional chador or a black scarf.

Among the 20 lead female characters, only four appeared to be independent-minded (20%). They set goals in their lives and were determined to achieve them. The other female characters followed a male-defined destiny.

The lead female characters were all from middle-class or affluent families. The young female characters generally appeared with little make-up and without lipstick. The younger women could drive. Family feuds were more common between men and women, with men having the upper hand. An interesting observation among the female characters was a devil who appeared as an innocent and attractive young woman. She subtly attempted to seduce a family man and destroy his family life. The creation of the devil character seemed somewhat brazen for the IRIB religious programming doctrine, where a devil was a powerful woman. Yet this portrayal also served the patriarchal nature of Iranian society, where women are demeaned and discriminated against in the public (Human Rights Watch, 2015).

> RQ2: Will male characters significantly surpass female characters in number and screen time?

To respond to the above research question, the analysis of the date revealed that male characters (N = 267) outnumbered female characters (N = 89) significantly in their roles. Also, male characters' average screen times (45 minutes) exceeded that of female characters (24 minutes). As such, one can argue that these drama serials reinforced the perception of men dominating women on the television screen in Iranian society. This message is also echoed to a greater extent in the analysis data, when answering the third research question:

> RQ3: Will male characters significantly outnumber female characters in the following areas: dominance, sexualization, competence, morality, mental state, other-orientations, age, and occupational roles?

Compared with male characters (44%), female characters (56%) were more likely to be attractive, motivated, intelligent, honest, nervous, family-oriented, and portrayed as office workers and nurses. Also, all characters portrayed as housekeepers were women. This data communicates at least two messages. On the one hand, female characters (55%) were more likely to possess high personal qualities such as motivation, intellect, and honesty than male characters (45%). On the other hand, compared with male characters (26%), female characters (74%) were more likely to be stereotyped regarding their mental state and occupational roles. Both female and male characters seemed to be equal in their expressions of happiness and subtle love toward the opposite sex.

Compared with female characters (29.5%), male characters (70.5%) were more likely to be dominant and aggressive (both verbally and physically), articulate, dishonest, pious, angry, serious, and friendly. Male characters (83%) outnumbered female characters (17%) significantly as older adults.

Male characters also held those occupational roles generally assigned to men in a masculine society. Excluding occupational roles of housekeeping, front-office work, and nursing, which are typically assigned to women in a masculine society like Iran, male characters (83%) outnumbered female characters (17%) in all other occupational roles depicted in the serials. The roles of clergymen, soldiers, and government employees were all occupied by male characters, which is a testimony to the Iranian government's discriminatory attitudes toward women.

Further, the number of male characters (85%) involved in antisocial activities were significantly higher than female characters (15%). Male characters (90%) also occupied significantly higher police/security agent roles than did female characters (10%). While the female characters (54%) in the serials seemed to be treated more positively regarding their personal attributes—such as motivation, intellect, honesty, and family orientation—the male characters (78.5%) seemed to possess more of the socially assigned masculine attributes, including dominance, age advantage, and occupational roles.

DISCUSSION AND IMPLICATIONS

Iranian women have historically faced a challenging dilemma. Before the Islamic revolution of 1979, Iranian women enjoyed a limited freedom as long as they didn't engage in anti-monarchy activities. Then, the prevalence of Western values in Iranian society allowed media producers to exploit women by sexualizing them in their stories. The backlash of the objectification of women in the media came after the Islamic revolution. The new religious government forbade any form of women's sexualization in the media and imposed many restrictions on Iranian media to combat Western values and their influence on Iranian society.

While Iranian women were liberated from being sexually exploited in media as before, they lost their rights to express their individuality and their freedom to fully participate in society, under a new inequality imposed by religion and patriarchy. Throughout the years, the Islamic government has set policies in order to circumvent Iranian women's participation in social and political life, unless sanctioned by the government. Today, fewer women work in public sectors. They are forbidden from attending certain sporting events; they are segregated in public spaces such as classrooms, movie theatres, concerts, and religious ceremonies. Additionally, they must cover their hair and avoid attention-drawing make-up. They also cannot be seen with non-family-related men in public.

As explained previously, the *IRIB* is following government policies regarding the appearance of women in television shows. The IRIB programs, including its television serials, have maintained and reinforced the government's policy of discriminating Iranian women under the pretext of protecting them against sexualization and other "evil" Western values. Nonetheless, Iranian women have strived to be present in television programs as actors, directors, producers, and production crew, despite the imposed restrictions and discrimination. This chapter, by exploring gendering and gender relationships in Iranian television drama serials, attempted to illustrate the disparity between male and female characters in the serials. It should be noted that the exploratory nature of this study and an absence of theory-driven hypotheses (i.e., SCT and cultivation theory) do not allow for generalizations about gendering in the serials. Research questions lead the research. Subsequent data indicated what could become reinforcement effects of patriarchal attitudes toward women.

Both exploratory and descriptive analyses of television serial content provided a better understanding of differences between the male and female characters in serials. Male characters outnumbered female characters in several categories, such as dominance and aggressiveness, piety, antisocial behavior, age advantage, and several occupational roles. Female characters were more visible in stereotyped roles of devoted wives, caring mothers and grandmothers, nurses, office secretaries, and most importantly, housekeepers. The silver lining in the representations of female characters was in the depictions of such personal qualities as motivation, intellect, and honesty. Nevertheless, male characters dominated the screen in frequency and time.

This study showed that despite the complex picture of female characters offered in serials—featuring mixed clichés and stereotypes while trying to capture reality—programming decisions are made by men and in accordance with culturally masculine subjectivity. Such television representations are worrisome, given the proven influence of television serials on individuals' appreciation of gender differences, emotional involvement and identification with serial characters. Further, it explains the potential internalization of characters' lives and relationships into one's own life, as supported by the social cognition, cultivation, and drama theories.

The results of the data analysis point to the status quo function of these serials in maintaining women's inequality and men's domination on the screen and beyond. If women are underrepresented in Iranian television serials, the implicit message is that they are less significant in society. It is desirable to direct future research toward examining the effects of Iranian television drama serials among Iranians, particularly young Iranian women.

As an exploratory study and as the first one to disseminate the selected topic in Western scholarly publications, this chapter has endeavored to promote a better understanding of gendering in Iranian television drama serials. It also helps encourage readers and scholars to become more interested in learning about other Middle Eastern or Islamic cultures such as Iran, which have been overlooked in the past by communication discipline. In sum, television in general, and television serials in particular, have the potential to make significant contributions to elevating gender equality in society and influencing gender politics. However, in Islamic countries such as Iran, the television industry has yet to fully develop its potential as a cultural force to influence the beliefs and attitudes toward gender equality among people and society alike.

REFERENCES

Bussey, K., & Bandura, A. (1999). Social cognitive theory of gender development and differentiation. *Psychological Review, 206*(1), 676–713. https://www.ncbi.nlm.nih.gov/pubmed/10560326.

Dill, K. E., & Thill, K. P. (2007). Video game characters and the socialization of gender roles: Young people's perceptions mirror sexist media depictions. *Sex Roles, 57*, 851–864. doi:10.1007/s11199- 007-9278-1.

Eyal, K., Raz, Y., & Levi, M. (2014). Messages about sex on Israeli television: Comparing local and foreign programming. *Journal of Broadcasting & Electronic Media, 58*(1), 42–58. doi.org/10.1080/08838151.2013.875021.

Frederickson, B., & Roberts, T. (1997). Objectification theory: Toward understanding women's lived experiences and mental health risks. *Psychology of Women Quarterly, 21*(1), 173–206. doi.org/10.1111/j.1471-6402.1997.tb00108.x.

Gerbner, G., Gross, L., Signorielli, N., & Morgan, M. (1980). Aging with television: Images on television drama and conceptions of social reality. *Journal of Communication, 30*, 37–47. doi:10.1111/j.1460-2466.1980.tb01766.x.

Gerbner, G., Gross, L., Morgan, M., Signorielli, N., & Shanahan, J. (2002). Growing up with television: Cultivation processes. In J. Bryant, & D. Zillmann (Eds.), *Media effects: Advances in theory and research* (pp. 43–67). Routledge.

Gledhill, C. (2003). Genre and gender: The case of soap opera. In S. Hall (Ed.), *Representation* (pp. 337–384). Sage.

Hall, S. (2003). The spectacle of the 'other'. In S. Hall (Ed.), *Representation* (pp. 225–279). Sage.

Hall, P., West, J., & McIntyre, E. (2012). Female self-sexualization in MySpace.com personal profile photographs. *Sexuality & Culture, 16*(1), 1–16. https://link.springer.com/article/10.1007%2Fs12119-011-9095-0.

Hofstede, G. (2001). *Culture's consequences: Comparing values, behaviors, institutions, and organizations across nations* (2nd ed.). Sage.

Human Rights Watch. (2015, October 28). Women's rights in Iran. https://www.hrw.org/news/2015/10/28/womens-rights-iran#.

Johnson, K., & Holmes, B. (2009). Contradictory messages: A content analysis of Hollywood produced romantic comedy feature films. *Communication Quarterly, 57*(3), 352–373. doi.org/10.1080/01463370903113632.

Kincaid, D. L. (2002). Drama, emotion, and cultural convergence. *Communication Theory, 12,* 136–152. doi.org/10.1111/j.1468-2885.2002.tb00263.x.

Mastro, D. E., & Behm-Morawitz, E. (2005). Latino representation on primetime television. *Journalism & Mass Communication Quarterly, 82,* 110–130. doi.org/10.1177/107769900508200108.

Mayring, P. (2014). *Qualitative content analysis: Theoretical foundation, basic procedures and software solutions.* Klagenfurt, Austria: Leibniz Institut. http://nbn-resolving.de/urn:nbn:de:0168-ssoar-395173.

Mirkhandan, S. H., & Gharehbaghi, M. H. (2017). Bayesteh haye Islami baznamai shakhsiat zan dar film va serial (Islamic requisites of portraying women in film and serial). *Journal of Religion and Cultural Policy,* 57–79(in Farsi). http://political.ihss.ac.ir/.

Morgan, M., & Shanahan, J. (1997). Two decades of cultivation research: An appraisal and meta- analysis. In B. Burleson (Ed.), *Communication yearbook 20* (pp. 1–45). Sage.

Nabi, R. L., & Oliver, M. B. (Eds.). (2009). *The SAGE handbook of media processes and effects.* Sage.

Prieler, M. (2016). Gender stereotypes in Spanish- and English-language television advertisements in the United States. *Mass Communication and Society, 19,* 275–300. doi: 10.1080/15205436.2015.1111386.

Sink, A., & Mastro, D. (2017). Depictions of gender on primetime television: A quantitative content analysis. *Mass Communication and Society, 20,* 3–22. doi:10.1080/15205436.2016.1212243.

Steiner, L. (2014). Feminist media theory. In R. S. Fortner & P. M. Fackler (Eds.), *The handbook of media and mass communication theory,* (1st ed., pp. 359–379). John Wiley & Sons, Inc.

Strinati, D. (2004). *An introduction to theories of popular culture* (2nd ed.). Routledge.

Section IV

COMEDY DRAMA

Chapter 15

Being a Black Man on *Being Mary Jane*
Considering Complexities of Black Masculinity in a Female-centric Drama

George L. Daniels

When Black Entertainment Television (BET) premiered *Being Mary Jane* in 2013, the television program made history as the network's first original scripted series (Harris & Coleman, 2018). Four million viewers tuned in to watch the first episode of a show featuring Mary Jane Paul, a successful black woman played by Gabrielle Union, who was making it in the television news business. The creator of *Being Mary Jane*, Mara Brock Akil conceived of a program depicting the complexities of a single black woman's life. The complexities can be placed in four quadrants: her love life, her work life, her family life, and her alone moments. Even as *Being Mary Jane*, the show about a perfectly imperfect single black woman, was being hailed in popular press as "revolutionary" (Carter, 2015); media researchers have begun to publish scholarly articles and book chapters on the program (Cheers, 2018; Harris & Coleman, 2018; Moody-Ramirez, 2019; White, 2019). To date, research has given little attention to men like Andre who played key roles in the show. This chapter fills the black male gap in the scholarship on *Being Mary Jane*. The series' popularity was its "relentless drive to show humanity" (Romano, 2015). As Connell and Messerschmidt (2005) note, masculinity is not a fixed entity embedded in the body or personality traits of individuals. Rather, "Masculinities are configurations of practice that are accomplished in social action and, therefore, can differ according to the gender relations in a particular social setting" (p. 836).

Specifically, this chapter examines the gender relations between Mary Jane Paul's character and five black men who played roles as her significant other—Andre, David, Sheldon, Lee, and Justin. Analysis goes further in reviewing the roles of her father, Paul Patterson (Richard Roundtree), her two brothers—Paul Junior and Patrick, and her coworker, Mark Bradley. In the show's first two seasons, Mark was a closeted gay news anchor and next-door neighbor. The nine black male characters are examined using the Black Masculine Identity Model, which suggests five factors that determine black masculine positionality (Jackson & Dangerfield, 2002).

BLACK MALE CHARACTERS ON TELEVISION

Historically, commercial television has been criticized for its failure to reflect African American culture adequately and its tendency to distort the few aspects of black culture it did include (Dates, 1993). For about 40 years (1949–1993), US commercial television has depicted symbolic images of issues and citizenry. The overwhelming number of depictions of African Americans in primetime, network, weekly programming has been nondramatic (p. 268). Bogle's (2001) *Primetime Blues* devotes separate chapters from the 1950s through the 1990s examining African American images, performers, and messages of primetime weekly series.

Four television situation comedies in the 1980s emphasized black male characters (including children) as leads or major contributing actors. The programs *Benson, Webster, Different Strokes* and *The Jeffersons* reinforced the importance of success, professionalism, competence, and individualism.

A decade later, the cultural representation of African Americans on network television resulted in what Gray (1995) identifies in three major categories. He describes older shows such as *Julia*, and *Room 222* as assimilationist programs in which individual black characters are integrated into a white world. Titles such as *Family Matters, Amen, Fresh Prince of Bel Air, What's Happenin'*, and *Sanford and Son* are classified as pluralist or separate-but-equal discourses. In these programs, predominantly black casts demonstrate that African American families have the same basic problems as whites. While critical of its failure to address issues of economic inequality, Gray perceives *The Cosby Show* as a transitional program to themes of diversity with "the show's use of Blackness and African American culture as a kind of emblematic code of difference" (p. 89). Elsewhere, the black middle-class response to the show was mixed, with a reluctance among the black middle class to be negative about one of the few positive portrayals of blacks on television while also wanting a more realistic portrayals.

BLACK MASCULINE IDENTITY MODEL

In the field of intercultural communication, Jackson and Dangerfield (2002) developed the Black Masculine Identity Model featuring five factors affecting black masculine positionality. These factors are struggle, community, achievement, independence, and recognition. Masculinity can be conceptualized along the twin registers of self-efficacy and historical symbiosis. Self-efficacy refers to the degree to which an individual feels he or she has control over his or her life. Historical symbiosis is the attachment one has to certain life space and or relational history defined by cultural experiences. The other element of the model is the mandala (a circle within a square), a symbol of self that is naturally motivated to move toward growth, perfection, and completion. This process occurs at conscious, subconscious, and unconscious levels. According to Jackson and Dangerfield, black masculine identities are deployed and negotiated with "struggle" at the center of the exchanges between the other factors of community, achievement, independence, and recognition. These four factors are all important aspects of repositioning Black Masculinities to counter pathological depictions.

MEET MARY JANE PAUL

BET's *Being Mary Jane* would fit Gray's (1995) definition of a transitional program. Cheers (2018) argued that black women were having a phenomenal rise in prominence on television and behind the scenes in 2017. Even as it premiered for its second season in 2015, *Being Mary Jane* with its cast of predominantly African American characters was listed as part of the Black History Month programming for BET. It was touted for its "second-screen strength," or the use of another device to enhance viewing (Romano, 2015). That second screen has been researched in a string of recently published studies on *Being Mary Jane* (Moody-Ramirez, 2019; Smalls, 2019; White, 2019).

As scholars have recounted, the opening scenes of the program featured Andre, Mary Jane Paul's love interest coming to her front door for a so-called booty call (Harris & Coleman, 2018). In addition to a lovemaking session that journeys through the television anchor's lavish home, viewers see her dilemma hours later when she discovers Andre's previously hidden wedding band under her foot (p. 43).

Moody-Ramirez (2019) focused on the fourth season of the program in her comprehensive analysis of online communicative patterns between *Being Mary Jane* executives who posted Facebook content and audience members who experienced it. At least nine Facebook groups existed with the title "Being Mary Jane." Smalls (2019) textually analyzed tweets posted during the first episode of *Being Mary Jane*. Her analysis showed that at least among Twitter users watching the pilot episode, Mary Jane was constructed as a modern-day Jezebel (loose woman), which extended to a larger conversation on whether current television shows continue to perpetuate negative narratives about black women (p. 163).

White (2019) acknowledged that when this first episode aired in 2013, she was turned off by the fact that an African American, single woman was involved in an affair with a married man. In the same research, White (2019) called attention to the intimate, complex, yet beautiful relationships Mary Jane had with other female friends and acquaintances. The closeness of the women led to White's research on the representation of sisterhood in the BET show. In her analysis of the most common words in Facebook posts, Moody-Ramirez (2019) found six of the words were either "man," "men" or the names of two of the men in Mary Jane Paul's life. The name "Justin" ranked number one with 56 occurrences, and "Lee" was the third highest ranking name. These findings help set the stage for the focus of this study.

RESEARCH METHOD

YouTube the video sharing service changed everything about television. It developed a culture of its own and became a threat to the conventional business model of television (Moylan, 2015). This study used the conversations surrounding clips from *Being Mary Jane* posted on YouTube as a way to convey the social viewing aspect of the images of black masculinity contained in the television drama. Over its five seasons, *Being Mary Jane* broke new ground in introducing the black male's struggle personally and professionally in innovative ways. The series reflects the nuances and complexities of black masculinity in the second decade of the twenty-first century. Yet much of this nuance and complexity is not often reflected in the online comments, suggesting limitations of the social viewing aspect of the program.

Rather than an in-depth plot analysis of the multiple seasons of the show, this study offers nine brief character profiles, noting whether they challenge or support long-held stereotypes of black men. To capture the essence of the characters, drama episodes where the characters first appeared, or were most prominent, were viewed multiple times by the author using the Amazon Prime Video Streaming Service. In cases where the male character remained a constant player in the program over multiple seasons, three to four "key events" or "turning points" were identified for analysis. Because of the number of characters, only a brief biological sketch is provided followed by a short summary of the role he played in the personal and/or professional life of Mary Jane Paul.

Then, the profiles are positioned within Jackson and Dangerfield's five factors that determine black masculine positionality (struggle, recognition, independence, achievement, and community). Some excerpts from dialogue are used to illustrate application of the framework.

Finally, the third phase of the analysis takes an account of social viewing of these images of black men through snippets, excerpts, and scenes. While much has been said/written on Twitter and Facebook about *Being Mary Jane*, this chapter used comments on YouTube to gauge the range of reactions from those who viewed *Being Mary Jane* in segments rather than full episodes. Instead of an exhaustive, systematic analysis of commentary where some segments garnered hundreds of comments from YouTube audiences, this study includes one or two examples to illustrate specific points, discussions, or debates on issues of black masculinity, which is the focus of this chapter.

RESULTS

Examining YouTube, Burgess and Green (2018) discuss how the now Google-owned platform has transformed significantly since debuting in 2005. That transformation is reflected in YouTube's business model, interface, and cultural role. What was once a disruptive "Web 2.0" start-up in the first decade of the twenty-first century has steadily become one of the most powerful platforms in a digital media environment. The Pew Research Center in 2018 reported YouTube had eclipsed Facebook as the most popular social media platform (Hills, 2018). More recent data on actual usage updated in early 2020 showed YouTube's 1.9 billion monthly active users placed it just ahead of the 1 billion Instagram users but in second place to the 2.2 billion monthly active Facebook users (Kallas, 2020). For mainstream television producers like those at BET and its parent company Viacom, YouTube was integral to the success of a TV show as a place where the company could post clips, highlights, trailers, previews, reviews and other "goodies" (Moylan, 2015). As of this writing in early 2020, BET Network's YouTube channel had 2.19 million subscribers. In this research, analysis is restricted to the clips posted by the network.

THE MEN OF *BEING MARY JANE*

Andre. As noted earlier, the opening scenes of the pilot episode depict Mary Jane Paul's encounters with her love interests. The first of whom was a marketing firm executive Andre Daniels. While some might interpret his character's appearances in eight episodes of the drama as reflective of the brute stereotype of black men, Andre Daniels reflects the struggle explained by the Jackson and Dangerfield (2004) Black Identity model. The following dialogue from season one shows this internal struggle primarily from the unknowing involvement of the Mary Jane Paul character:

Andre: "Let me just explain what I was trying to do."
MJ: "What are you going to say? You bumped your head and forgot you were married? You forgot a wife and kids? Are you crazy? Every time we kissed, every time we made love, every promise you made me."
Andre: "Was real."
MJ: "No it's not."

The dialogue was contained in a four-minute compilation BET Networks posted on YouTube in February 2014, months after the show's premiere in July 2013. Designed to give the audience a quick recap of the "craziness that is Mary Jane and Andre's relationship," it depicts the trouble Andre's character has in choosing between his affair with Mary Jane and his wife and two children. Andre (Played by Omari Hardwick) says to his wife, "No matter what goes down between me and you, there'll never be a day when you can threaten to take my kids." Elsewhere in this same four-minute clip, BET shows Andre Daniels encountering David Paulk, Mary Jane's supposedly ex-boyfriend. David is outside Mary Jane's home when Andre punches a keycode to enter the driveway and the code fails. Mary Jane's on-again, off-again relationship with David extends multiple episodes during the first season of the program.

David. A mixed-race executive, who is the son of an African American father and a Caucasian mother, David Paulk has not only developed a relationship with Mary Jane but with her family as well. In one episode, Mary Jane's mother invites David to sit with the family at a very public fundraiser, insinuating that the two's nuptials were imminent. David's character is further developed as the producers shine light on the challenges of single women desperate to become mothers. After one of their numerous sexual encounters, Mary Jane retrieves David's sperm from a used condom and places it in a vial in her refrigerator.

For David the dilemma of whether or not to propose to Mary Jane is confounded with his own romantic relationship with a white female. BET released a one-minute compilation entitled "David still loves Mary Jane" that includes interviews with David about the relationship. The clip includes him admitting his feelings for Mary Jane, but also declaring, "Some things aren't meant to be." David's indecision about his own marital situation reveals the process of struggle in Jackson and Dangerfield's (2004) framework. Even while her relationship with David is off-again, Mary Jane meets a powerful attorney, Sheldon DeWitt, who holds an invitation-only event that Mary Jane attends with David. Following the event, Mary Jane is able to obtain an exclusive interview with Sheldon and a relationship between the two of them begins.

Sheldon. When he comes to town, Sheldon DeWitt is introduced on the show as a civil trial lawyer who's spent more than 20 years taking on corrupt multibillion-dollar corporations. In retirement, he is holding events to encourage people to give back. Mary Jane engages his attention by rattling off some cases Sheldon has been involved with in an effort to get an interview. He initially declines, but then agrees to be interviewed, on tape, at his office. That is how their relationship begins.

DeWitt's ability to articulate the black man's struggle is amplified by his very thoughtful conversations with Mary Jane. This is after the suicide of a prominent Yale Law School educated, black, male attorney named Brian Ellis. The attorney took his own life only a few months after Mary Jane's friend and journalist, Terrence McGhee, also committed suicide.

Hours after the incident, Sheldon invites Mary Jane over to his apartment where he greets her with a taste of étouffée, a Cajun dish from the US south. He uses this moment as a launch point for an exchange with Mary Jane about the plight of black men. Below, is part of their conversation:

Sheldon: Did you know that étouffée literally translates to suffocate, to smother?
MJ: What's your point, I'm guessing you're trying to make one?
Sheldon: My point is that black men today like Brian Ellis have been smothered literally their whole lives, smothered as they claw their way up the ranks, smothered by corporate greed, smothered by racism by oppression, smothered by hatred smothered by fear, smothered by a system that never wanted to see them succeed.
MJ: And, why do you think that is?
Sheldon: Jealousy, Obama's wall was inspired by Michael Jordan's dunk inspired by John Coltrane's solos, inspired by Malcolm X's thoughts.
MJ: Can you drive the car straight because I have low blood sugar.
Sheldon: Black men represent freedom and that's what they're trying to squash. So many black men, myself included, have been surveilled, have been bullied.

As the above dialogue demonstrates, Sheldon's character is the most illustrative of the historical symbiosis where masculinity is conceptualized through a relational history attached to an asymmetrical cultural experience. Describing the systemic process of "smothering," Sheldon verbalizes struggle presented in the Jackson and Dangerfield's (2004) Black Masculine Identity Model.

Sheldon DeWitt's sophisticated conversations connect with Mary Jane's level as a journalist. His traditional courtship strategies for Mary Jane (i.e., making dinner for her, refusing intimacy initially) are impressive. When

Mary Jane discovers he does not desire to be married or have children, she promptly ends the relationship.

The irony is the retired attorney's seasoned experience and wisdom are not enough to satisfy Mary Jane. After her relationship with Sheldon fails and a solid relationship does not materialize with David, Mary Jane relocates to New York City for a new job as a morning reporter for "Good Day USA." She meets Lee Truitt in the "Big Apple."

Lee. Initially introduced in season four, Lee Truitt's character is complicated by the fact that he has children in his home country of England and they come to visit him in New York. Lee is a comedian who makes Mary Jane laugh and treats her well. Zoe, the mother of his two children, asks Lee to be the sperm donor for a third child that she would carry with her newfound lesbian lover. Lee turns her down because he says he loved Mary Jane and needed to focus on a future with her. Despite the fact that Mary Jane's family embraces Lee and he scores points with Mary Jane's father, the boyfriend from the United Kingdom, is not enough for Mary Jane. Part of their unraveling is depicted in the following dialogue:

MJ: I slept with Justin.
Lee: What did you just say?
Lee: You're obviously still that broken girl I met on that first night. It's my fault for trying to put the pieces back together.

The role of the black man, even fathering two children by another woman, but willing to have a new life and marriage with another woman is depicted in Lee's character. In the Jackson and Dangerfield's (2004) framework, Lee's character represents the independence reflected in one's self-authorization, autonomy, and freedom of self-expression. He had a larger profile at work and was willing to be in a relationship with a very high profile, on-air, broadcaster. For Mary Jane, the relationship did not compare with the one she was developing with a senior producer at her network, Justin, with whom Mary Jane had worked previously.

Justin. Unlike Mary Jane's previous love interests, Justin Talbot has a dual role as a boyfriend in her personal life and manager at her network in her professional life. He is driven and extremely ambitious. This is similar to Mary Jane Paul's character. He understands what it takes to be successful and has made it his goal to help Mary Jane succeed. In Jackson and Dangerfield's (2004) framework, Talbot demonstrates self-efficacy and achievement in negotiating his masculinity. *Being Mary Jane*'s producers developed his character to show what happens when a man acquires some wealth, which Mary Jane discovers by snooping around. Initially, Mary Jane is caught off guard by Justin's romantic interest in her, which initially Justin discounts as something that "can't happen again."

In one scene of the episode in season four, BET released a seven-minute clip entitled "Can MJ and Justin's New Found Love Stand the Test of Garrett" (Garrett Keswick is the executive producer of Mary Jane's news program). During the clip, Garrett explains how problematic it is having the senior producer, the person who rules on story assignments and production details, having a romantic relationship with on-air talent. He announces that he is sending Justin to cover stories out-of-state to avoid him having influence on Mary Jane's work assignments. Even though the BET clip obtained more than 45,000 views, there were only 13 comments. Commenters posted remarks either expressing support for Mary Jane or Justin. There was little or no discussion about Justin's masculinity as expressed in the clip.

In many ways, Justin's professional success mirrors the professional success of Mary Jane's father, Paul Patterson, who is retired.

Paul. Men in Mary Jane's life come and go throughout the five seasons of the series. However, her father, Paul is a parental mainstay. Viewers are given a clear view of his profile as the first African American chief operating officer for Advantage Airlines. His success allows his family to achieve a level of social status in their community in Atlanta, Georgia. Numerous scenes depict Paul Patterson giving fatherly advice to Mary Jane, her younger brother Paul Jr., and her older brother, Patrick. He is an ideal positive portrayal among black male characterizations. In season two, Mary Jane speaks with her father, who calls her by her birth name, Pauletta. The conversation happens after a failed cryopreservation fertility procedure she underwent as part of a "Modern Day Motherhood" segment on her show:

MJ: It's frightening because it's finally donning on me what if I can't have babies at all.
Paul: Baby, maybe that's not such a bad thing.
MJ: Why would you say something like that?
Paul: Because I'm not convinced that you really want children.
MJ: Do you think I would suffer public embarrassment because I don't want to have kids?
Paul: Call it a father's intuition. Call it 38 years of watching and raising a child who from college, to grad school, to newsroom, always went after what she wanted and got it. Call it doing the analysis and finding it strange that the only goal that has eluded you is a husband and a baby.
MJ: You're trying to make it seem like it's all within my control, like I can just cast a spell, and poof husband and baby. Getting what you and mom have, it doesn't happen like that.

Paul: What we have started in a tradition that I don't think is even relevant today. You got to throw out of your mind what we have and start focusing in on what makes you happy. Pauletta Patterson, what your mother and I have is not something you should aspire to.

This conversation in season two would turn out to be a foreshadowing of dramatic events in season four. Mary Jane's mother, Helen Patterson, rekindles a relationship with a man she knew 44 years previously. When Helen and Paul separate, Helen informs her oldest son that her old boyfriend is actually his biological father.

Paul decides to file for divorce as a result of his wife's infidelity. In the end, he changes his mind. However, the chain of events involving Mary Jane's parents shined the spotlight on a black male figure who in one era of his life married a woman, and assumed the role of father to a child fathered by another man. In another era of his life, Paul Patterson was challenged with dealing with a cheating spouse, Helen. The struggle of coping with failure and setting a good and fair example for his children reveals the achievement element of the Jackson and Dangerfield (2004) framework.

Paul, Jr. (P. J.). Introduced in the pilot episode as Mary Jane's irresponsible little brother, Paul Patterson Jr. is still in college, having sex with girls in his parents' home and selling marijuana. PJ is first presented to viewers twirling mattress signs on the street corners of Atlanta and complaining about how he has to get up out of his parents' home.

In later episodes, PJ reflects the concept of independence in Jackson and Dangerfield (2004) Black Masculine Identity Model as the family celebrates his graduation from college and his being offered major career opportunities. By season two, PJ holds a meeting with a real estate investor who commends him for his decision to switch his major to architecture. He is offered a job as a project manager in California. In that role, PJ puts together a team of like-minded real estate agents and developers from Inglewood's black community, and oversees foreclosed properties. In an episode, an Asian American female investor asks, "Who better than the son of the first black COO of Advantage Airlines to lead the charge?" She compliments PJ on being a "risk taker" who "has the balls to go after what he wants." This characterization underscores the black male independence attribute in PJ's character.

Patrick. Patrick's degree from Morehouse College was not enough to keep him from hitting bumps in the road. Those bumps included a bout with substance abuse, a failed business and failed romantic relationships, and a daughter who has two children by two different fathers. His struggles are woven into various episodes, particularly in the first two seasons. In the first episode, he asks Mary Jane for a $500 loan. In season two, when the mother of his elementary school-aged daughter is incarcerated, Patrick is forced into the role of a single father. In season two, Patrick and his father are playing golf and his father offers to help him find a higher profile job more fitting for a "Morehouse Man," but Patrick turns him down. This decision reflects Jackson and Dangerfield's (2004) independence factor because he is determined to deal with life's challenges his own way. At the same time, Patrick's character evolves more into a reflection of the community factor in the latter seasons of the show. By season four, Patrick Patterson invites Civil Rights Activist DeRay McKesson (who makes a cameo appearance) to speak at Black Lives Matter rallies in Atlanta. His community organizing opens new doors for him as a leader and change agent. Patrick's community engagement includes him mentoring a young man, who is struggling with own identity as a closeted gay male. The brief subplot near the end of season four was the second time the show addressed the issue of black male homosexuality.

Mark. In the very first or pilot episode of Being Mary Jane, viewers are introduced to her next-door neighbor Mark who also works as a news anchor at Mary Jane's Atlanta network. Mark is the consoler, with a shoulder on which for Mary Jane to cry. Even as he's comforting her, his partner, a white man, comes into the room and gives him a kiss. This quickly dispels any confusion about Mark's role in Mary Jane's life. While most of the attention is on Mark's role as a serious news anchor, some attention is given to his dilemma of whether to "come out" to his viewers.

Perhaps the most poignant scene, and a turning point for Mark Bradley's journey, is when his parents come to town in season two. Choosing to hide his homosexuality from his apparently conservative parents, he convinces Mary Jane to be his fake girlfriend and asks his partner, Eric, to temporarily be away from the house, which they shared. The chain of events sparks an argument between Mark and his partner Eric. Mark tried to justify his choice to remain closeted as an effort to avoid being a double minority, that is to say black and gay. Eric, a white male, accuses him of playing the "race card" rather than admitting his own discomfort in being open with his parents about this sexual orientation:

Eric: You're a 43-year-old never married confirmed bachelor whose girlfriend is nearly always unavailable. Or somewhere else or with other people. Do you think you're fooling anyone?
Mark: Just the people that matter.
Eric: You're an ass.
Mark: Are you speaking literally or figuratively? Because now is not the time for this. My parents are going to be outside that door in a few seconds and I don't have time nor do I feel it necessary to explain my personal decisions when it comes to my life.
Eric: Your life? I thought we were in a relationship.

Mark: Yes, my life. And it's hard enough being black. And we want me to add a side dish of gay to my plate?
Eric: Yes.
Mark: For what? We can be in a relationship from here to infinity and you will never understand what it's like to live in my skin.
Eric: Neither will you until you fully accept who you are. Don't race card me. If you're still afraid of mommy and daddy, own it.

After he and Mary Jane pretended to be a couple in a relationship for two years, Mark's mother confronts him telling him she knows he's gay. She implores him to stop hiding parts of his life. His father, who admits to being homophobic, chimes in noting, "The son we raised would have had the courage to be whatever he is no matter what anybody thought about him. Instead you've been running around like a thief in the night lying and pulling others into your lies."

In Jackson and Dangerfield's (2004) Black Masculine Identity Model, the Mark Bradley character struggles with recognition along the register of self-efficacy. As successful as he is in his job as a news anchor, he does not reflect that he has real control over his own personal life and relationships. After being dragged out of the closet by his mother, Bradley ends his relationship with Eric and much like Mary Jane, struggles in his personal life.

CONCLUSION: THE SOPHISTICATED STRATEGY OF REPRESENTATION

The pilot episode of *Being Mary Jane* begins and ends with men at Mary Jane's front door, an indication that her relationships with men would be a central factor in the direction of the drama. At least in the first four seasons of *Being Mary Jane*, the producers of this successful series gave BET viewers one of the most sophisticated looks at what it means to be both black and male in the United States. Even though the focus of the show was on a black woman, the black men around her were as varied as the range of experiences that most black men have in the twenty-first century. A far cry from black men who were the lead characters in situation comedies of the 1980s, the black men in *Being Mary Jane* were professionals in the workplace with complicated personal lives. They were also successful in their careers, despite the overall societal barriers that confronted them. Like Mary Jane, all five men who were romantically involved with her had their own struggles. Viewers were privy to multilevel processes involved in black male identity struggles. While scholars like Rossie (2018) have unpacked Sheldon DeWitt's character and his refusal to give up his individuality for marriage and children in post-feminist examinations, little has been done to expand the scholarly landscape with focus on black masculinity.

This show exemplifies the possibilities when television producers take more sophisticated strategies in presenting the black male experience. Regarding sexuality, some of the men of *Being Mary Jane* were never depicted in bedroom scenes. Others were constantly having one-night stands and dealing with the negative aftermath. Furthermore, the challenges of black male homosexuality are rarely considered in television series narratives. *Being Mary Jane* addresses the unique worries and stresses black males have regarding coming out to their families.

All five of the factors in Jackson and Dangerfield's (2004) Black Identity Model were evident in portrayals of the nine men. As for the YouTube audience, as engaged as they may have been in social viewing, the comments on the YouTube videos reviewed in this study do not reflect an intentional or robust discussion about the lived experiences of black men. Perhaps social viewing as examined in previous studies (Moody-Ramirez, 2019; Smalls, 2019) is reflective of the emphasis that the show placed on black women rather than on black men.

REFERENCES

Burgess, J. & Green, J. (2018). *YouTube: Online video and participatory culture* (2nd ed.) Polity.

Bogle, D. (2001). *Primetime Blues: African Americans on Network Television.* Farrar, Straus & Giroux.

Carter, K. L. (2015, April 14). A TV revolution: The cast, creator and a network executive talk to BuzzFeed News about their revolutionary series about a perfectly imperfect single black woman. *BuzzFeed News.* https://www.buzzfeednews.com/article/kelleycarter/being-mary-jane-and-bet.

Cheers, I. M. (2018). *The Evolution of Black women in Television: Mammies, Matriarchs and Mistresses.* Routledge.

Connell, R.W. & Messerschmidt, J.W. (2005). Hegemonic masculinity: Rethinking the concept. *Gender & Society, 19,* 829–859.

Dates, J. L. (1993). Commercial Television. In J. L. Dates & W. Barlow (Eds.), *Split image: African Americans in the mass media* (pp. 267–327). Howard University Press.

Fierce Black Women. (2015). Healthy Love Lessons From 'Being Mary Jane' & Dr. Love. https://fierceforblackwomen.com/2015/07/27/healthy-love-lessons-from-being-mary-jane-dr-love/.

Gray, H. (1999). *Watching race: Television and the struggle for 'Blackness'.* University of Minnesota.

Gray, H. (2000). Black representation in the post network, post civil rights world of global media. In S. Cottle (Ed.), *Ethnic minorities and the media: Changing cultural boundaries* (pp. 118–129). Open University Press.

Gray, H. (1995). Television, Black Americans and the American dream. In G. Dines & J.M. Humez (Eds.), *Gender, race and class in media: A Text-Reader* (pp. 430–437). Sage.

Harris, F.L. & Coleman, L.S. (2018). Trending topics: A cultural analysis of Being Mary Jane and Black women's engagement on Twitter. *Black Scholar, 48*(1), 43–55.

Hills, M.C. (2018, March 23). Survey: YouTube is America's most popular social media platform. *Forbes.com* https://www.forbes.com/sites/meganhills1/2018/03/23/social-media-demographics/#5dd866f4783a.

Howard, N.R. (2019). Real, respectable, or both: Respectability on Being Mary Jane through the Words of Mara Brock Akil. In S.B. White & K.L. Harris (Eds.), *Representations of Black womanhood on television: Being Mara Brock Akil* (pp. 47–65). Lexington.

Jackson, R.L. & Dangerfield, C.L. (2004). Defining masculinity as cultural property: Toward an identity negotiation paradigm. In R.L. Jackson (Ed.), *African American communication and identities* (pp. 197–208). Sage.

Kallas, P. (2019, September 2). Top 15 most popular social networking sites and apps [2020] https://www.dreamgrow.com/top-15-most-popular-social-networking-sites/.

Moody-Ramirez, M. (2019). Race, gender, and participatory dynamics: Facebook representations of *Being Mary Jane*. In S.B. White and K.L. Harris (Eds.), *Representations of Black womanhood on television: Being Mara Brock Akil* (pp. 133–151). Lexington.

Moylan, B. (2015, April 23). A Decade of YouTube has changed the future of television. *TIME.com* https://time.com/3828217/youtube-decade/.

Rossie, A. (2018). Being Mary Jane and postfeminism's emergent feminisms. In J. Keller & M.E. Ryan (Eds.), *Emergent feminisms* (pp. 25–41). Routledge.

Romero, A. (2015, February 2). Every February, TV makes history. *Broadcasting & Cable*, 14.

Smalls, M.W. (2019). Social TV and stereotypes: The social construction of #BeingMaryJane on Twitter. In S.B. White & K.L. Harris (Eds.), *Representations of Black womanhood on television: Being Mara Brock Akil* (pp. 153–175). Lexington.

White, S.B. (2019). Girl, you know I got you: The ideology of sisterhood on Being Mary Jane. In S.B. White & K.L. Harris (Eds.), *Representations of Black womanhood on television: Being Mara Brock Akil* (pp. 67–85). Lexington.

Chapter 16

HBO's *Insecure* and Issa Dee

Black Women's Interpretations on Facebook

Morgan W. Smalls

Social television is the practice of watching television, while using an additional device to engage with the programming, such as a tablet, computer, smartphone, and so forth (Doughty et al., 2012). Social television encourages audience interaction in digital spaces and "constitutes a fundamental shift in how people interact and socialize around television content" (Cesar & Geerts, 2011, p. 347). Social network platforms, such as Facebook, allow users to engage with television by "sharing images, videos, links, [as well as] have groups of discussions of topics of interest [and] create and maintain personal network[s]" (Pires de Sá, 2015, p. 56). This exploration of social television centers on black women's engagement in *Insecure: The Discussion Forum* Facebook group during the third season of the HBO show, *Insecure*, created by award-winning actor Jo-Issa Rae Diop (known as Issa Rae) and Larry Wilmore. Vee M. Dee, an African American female, created the forum on November 28, 2016, as a space to provide commentary on *Insecure*. As of March 2019, the forum had 16,845 members. This study investigates Facebook users' interpretation of the black female main character, Issa Dee, played by the actor Jo-Issa Rae Diop Rae, with a research emphasis on black women stereotypes. Specifically, this research looks at ways in which the stereotypes were discussed, challenged, or ignored by Facebook users. For clarity, when referencing Jo-Issa Rae Diop, the content creator, "Rae" will be used. When referencing Issa Dee, the character, Issa will be used. This is to make the distinction between the actor/creator "Rae" and the character "Issa."

INSECURE: THE HBO COMEDY DRAMA SERIES

Insecure debuted in October 2016 and continues the recent trend of casting African American females as main characters in primetime and cable television shows. *Insecure* is rated TV-MA and "this comedy series looks at the friendship of two modern-day black women, as well as all of their uncomfortable experiences and racy tribulations. As they navigate the tricky professional and personal terrain of Los Angeles, best friends Issa (Rae) and Molly (Yvonne Orji) face challenges of being black women who defy all stereotypes" (Home Box Office, 2019, para). *Insecure* is recognized by the African American community, as evidenced by the show's NAACP award nominations, and mainstream media and arts, particularly since the viewership is 61% non-black (Nielsen, 2017b). In 2020, *Insecure* was nominated for 11 Emmy awards including, outstanding lead actress in a comedy series, outstanding supporting actress in a comedy series and outstanding comedy series (Television Academy, n.d.).

THEORETICAL FRAMEWORK

This study employed black feminist thought (Collins, 1986) and participatory culture theory (Jenkins et al., 2009). Black feminist thought centers on black women's experiences and the ways in which intersecting forms of oppression such as racism, sexism, and classism are contested. Tyree and Williams (2016) outlined four central themes that permeate Collins's original construction of the theory. Tyree and Williams (2016) outlined the first tenet as women positively define and value self while challenging controlling, negative or narrow images of black womanhood. Second, black women work to demolish interlocking forms of oppression regarding race, class, and gender (Collins, 2000). Black women value knowledge production and utilize both intellectual thought and political activism to achieve goals (Tyree & Williams, 2016). Lastly, black women recognize they are building upon a unique cultural heritage providing necessary skills to challenge the status quo, resist and transform their lives (Collins, 2000).

While participating in the discussion forum, users, in this case those who self-identified as a black woman, are a part of the participatory culture, which is "a culture with relatively low barriers to artistic expression and civic engagement, strong support for creating and sharing creations, and some type of informal mentorship whereby experienced participants pass along knowledge to novices" (Jenkins et al., 2009, xi). This theory aids in understanding user engagement with media such as discussion forums to create, contest, and negotiate shared meaning regarding topics of interest.

Participatory culture is an ideal model because it operates under the assumption that media fans can be understood as "active producers and manipulators of meaning" (Jenkins, 2012, p. 23). Fans engagement with media highlights the social experience as viewers of television become "spectators who transform the experience of watching television into a rich and complex participatory culture" (Jenkins, 2012, p. 23). Fans build communities where they have the opportunity to "construct their cultural and social identity through borrowing and inflecting mass culture images, articulating concerns which often go unvoiced within the dominant media" (Jenkins, 2012, p. 23). Participatory culture and black feminist thought can shed light on how black women engage in the social television experience. Moreover, it has the opportunity to operate as a space where the media can be critiqued and challenged.

LITERATURE REVIEW

Stereotypes of Black Women

Scholars such as Bogle (2001), Dates and Barlow (1993), Collins (2000), and West (1995) traced the origin of stereotypes of African Americans. Bogle (2001) assessed African American images in US motion pictures from *The Birth of a Nation* (1915) to films in the late 1990s. He identified the Mammy and Tragic Mulatto as two of the first female stereotypes. They were examples of "character types used for the same effect: to entertain by stressing Negro inferiority. . . . All were merely filmic reproductions of black stereotypes that had existed since the days of slavery and were already popularized in American life and arts" (Bogle, 2001, p. 4). Lemons (1977) noted how the stereotypical portrayal of "Aunt Jemima or Mandy the maid" and the "ol' mammy" were "part of the popular culture of America at the turn of the twentieth century" (p. 102).

Collins (2000), Thompson (2009), and West (1995) noted how several caricatures such as the Mammy, Jezebel, and Sapphire are long-standing representations of black women in US popular culture. The Mammy is a "faithful, obedient, domestic servant," who is physical but asexual, doting on her white family at the expense of her own (Collins, 2000, p. 80). The Jezebel is sexually aggressive and manipulative, especially when it relates to using her sexual power over men. Collins (2000) defines her as "a deviant Black female sexuality" with an insatiable sexual appetite (p. 89). The Sapphire is a "hot-tempered [woman] who berates black children and emasculates men, generate[ing the] misperception of black women as [angry] unattractive and asexual" (Thompson, 2009, p. 3).

Scholars have written about how these stereotypes successfully perpetuate themselves in the twenty-first century (West, 1995; Collins, 2000; Springer, 2008; Cheers, 2018). Several tropes have been attached to black women in the media and though not an exhaustive list, the current "media landscape is populated with Gold Diggers, Modern Jezebels, Baby Mamas, Uneducated Sisters, Rachet Women, Angry Women, Mean Black Girls, Unhealthy Black Women, and Black Barbies" (West, 2018, p. 139). These stereotypes are dynamic and possess the ability to shape shift and fit current times. For example, West (2018) noted the "Mammy, Sapphire, and Jezebel images ... have been replaced by corresponding contemporary images that serve a similar function, including the Strong Black Woman, the Angry Black Woman, and the Video Vixen" (p. 140). There are also iterations of these. For example, the Freak, Gold Digger, Whole, Hoochie, Video Vixen and Thot are all rooted in the Jezebel stereotype, woven with the thread of hypersexuality and promiscuity. These stereotypes belittle, misrepresent, and project an inaccurate and limited view of black women. This concise review of black women and stereotypes is helpful in historically situating and framing contemporary representations of black women in media.

Black Women, Social Television, and Stereotypes

According to Nielsen (2017), the television viewership, smartphone ownership, and tech/social media usage of black women outpace other races. In fact, "Facebook (72%) is the top social media networking site used by Black women" (Nielsen, 2017, para 2), providing a platform for black women to engage in conversations relevant to them. Brock (2009) identified how the internet provides an extension to conversations once reserved for black spaces such as black neighborhoods, black newspapers, and black talk radio. For example, specifically related to black Twitter's engagement in the second-screen experience, Williams and Gonlin (2017) explored the connection between the show *How to Get Away with Murder* starring African American female television characters and the second-screen discourse on black womanhood via Twitter. Analyzing season one, they found that "communal viewing of the television series ... and resulting discourse on Twitter demonstrates insider access to a shared cultural history of Black womanhood, culture specific nostalgia, and the intergenerational transfer of knowledge" (Williams & Gonlin, 2017, p. 985).

Research has shown that stereotypes of black women persist in television shows, such as *Ugly Betty* (Kretsedemas, 2010), *Being Mary Jane* (Smalls, 2019) and reality television (Tyree, 2011). Extending the conversation, Smalls (2019) investigated *Being Mary Jane* with a specific focus on the social construction of the black female character, Mary Jane Paul on Twitter.

Themes from the first episode showcased "viewers' perception of Mary Jane Paul as a modern-day Jezebel, their conflicting relatability to the character and viewers' disappointment with her choice to [knowingly] participate in an affair [with a married man]" (p. 169). Also, Moody-Ramirez (2019) examined *Being Mary Jane* and the "participatory dynamics of online audiences on Facebook" in a qualitative analysis of season four of the series Facebook page (p. 134). Using a black feminist lens, findings indicated that "historical stereotypes of African American women are still prevalent (while not as strong)" (Moody-Ramirez, 2019, p. 148). Comments compared the main character to the stereotype of a jezebel or independent black woman and users expressed a desire to move away from that portrayal. Those prior studies, and the methodological and theoretical applications, have created context to further contribute to the public discourse about representations and narratives of black women in the United States on television and in digital spaces.

Although studies have focused on representations of black women in television (Kretsedemas, 2010; Tyree, 2011), social media (Smalls, 2019; Moody-Ramirez, 2019) and popular culture (Muhammad & McArthur, 2015) using qualitative methods, none have focused on *Insecure* and the character Issa Dee. Moreover, none have specifically focused on how black women perceive or characterize Issa's representation on Facebook. Black women's access to a second screen, and familiarity with the social networking site, Facebook, underscores their ability to participate in social television. The problem is that the manner in which African American women are portrayed in television and simultaneously discussed online has not been studied enough to truly understand the relationship between black women, television and the second-screen experience using the platform of Facebook. In alignment with the unique second-screen experience, the main research question to explore this phenomenon is: Do the black women who participate in *Insecure: The Discussion Forum* on Facebook align Issa's character with any historical or contemporary stereotypes of black females?

RESEARCH METHOD

Consistent with the overarching goals of qualitative research, this research used textual analysis. Textual analysis has become a preferred approach of scholars who critically examine media content (Fürsich, 2009). Since this study focused on the written reactions and discourse created on Facebook in response to *Insecure*, textual analysis was ideal for acquiring and analyzing data.

Data Collection

The author collected data from *Insecure: The Discussion Forum* on Facebook. The focus was on season three. All threads posted in the group, during 24 hours from each episode's original airing were collected. These were copied onto a Microsoft Word document file for later analysis. A thread consists of the original post that started the conversation along with any comments, replies, pictures, gifs, memes, and other images used within the online conversation in 2018.

Sample

All "commenters" within the discussion forum needed to meet the inclusion criteria. These social media users must have the following characteristics: (1) self-identified as a black female; (2) started a thread or comment/reply under a thread devoted to discussing season three of the show; (3) discussed the show within 24 hours of the episode's airing; and (4) specifically discussed the Issa character. The researcher used Facebook profile photos, profile descriptions, comments, bio information and other markers of identity—evident in the user's profile page or engagement in the forum—to identify the user as a black female. The manner in which a person portrayed herself in the forum, as a member of the digital community, was key. If a person's identity could not be determined, the comment was not included. Then, for each episode, all posts were ranked from the highest to the lowest in terms of user engagement, based on the amount of reactions (e.g., like, love, haha, wow, sad, angry) and comments carried on the thread. The researcher then pulled the top five threads (inclusive of original post, comments and replies) that related to the research question. This totaled 5 threads and a minimum of 100 comments per episode.

Data Analysis

A qualitative thematic analysis uncovered the themes that existed in the comments posted in the social media Facebook forum. Fereday and Muir-Cochrane (2006) outlined a hybrid process of both inductive and deductive thematic analysis that guided this line of research. In reporting the study findings, pseudonyms were used for each commenter to protect identity.

FINDINGS AND DISCUSSION

Of the 40 threads and 1,256 comments in the *Insecure: The Discussion Forum*, 273 specifically described Issa in a way that did not align with the stereotypes of a black woman. Instead, the forum participants' described Issa's traits in a dynamic, nuanced, and realistic way. Issa was labeled by forum members as an insecure and imperfect woman who also exemplified personal strength and growth in season three. The three main themes used to describe Issa highlighted her character as follows: (1) her insecurity, with terms such as "indecisive, broke, desperate, dependent, and insecure"; (2) her imperfections, with terms such as "irresponsible, self-centered, crazy, impulsive, dumbass and imperfect"; and (3) her strengths, with terms such as "helpful, capable, intelligent, honest, adorable, genuine and strong."

ISSA DEE: A COMPLEX CHARACTER

Comments depicted Issa as a fully developed character who exhibited flaws and strengths. Based on comments categorized as insecure, imperfect and strengths, users described Issa's character in ways that displayed a multilayered protagonist not constrained by stereotypes. Black women's interpretation of Issa displayed an ability to focus on and highlight aspects of Issa that showed a negotiated reading of the main character. Their description of Issa and their participation in the discussion forum showed them to be analytical in their decoding of Issa. Based on Facebook forum members' comments, the three themes of Issa's insecurity, her imperfections and her strengths are outlined below.

Theme One: Issa Is Insecure

According to the American Psychological Association (2020), insecurity, by definition, is characterized as "a feeling of inadequacy, lack of self-confidence, and inability to cope, accompanied by general uncertainty and anxiety about one's goals, abilities, or relationships with others." In the discussion forum, 68 comments (24.9%) indicated that Issa was both emotionally and economically "insecure" with additional terms such as "dependent," "passive," "indecisive," "scared," and "flaky" used to describe her. The Facebook users believed that this insecurity influenced both her personal and professional decisions. Forum members' portrayal of Issa showed her as the antithesis of the Strong Black Woman or Superwoman image because she did not "have it all," personally or professionally.

During the first half of the season (episodes 1–4), users noted how Issa's interactions with Daniel highlighted her financial and emotional insecurity. For context, Daniel is a former fling and she begins the season sleeping on his couch to save money. Issa vacillates about her feelings for him both in words and actions, which users pinpoint as supporting evidence of her insecurities.

For example, in episode two, forum users identified her insecurity as Alex noted, "Issa got issues—Daniel is the flavor of the moment—like she said she don't know what she is passionate about or what her feelings are, she just wandering & taking peoples feelings along with her . . . smh #insecure at its finest" (August 20, 2018). Another user Cheryl stated, "Her and Daniel really have something different this time and she's not letting it go anywhere because she's so damn insecure" (August 26, 2018), while Brittany noted, "She was still being indecisive at times, but opening up more. It kinda sends mixed signals being in that [Daniel's] bed tho" (August 26, 2018).

While Issa was living with Daniel, forum comments also mentioned her financial instability. Again, in episode two, users learned that Issa had a 425-credit score. In response, forum members, such as Anjerrika wrote, "I cried when they showed that. Like Issa all fucked up" (August 19, 2018). Kimberly noted, "I felt bad for her . . . she can't afford to take any more L's" (August 19, 2018). Forum members' reactions to Issa's credit score underscored their stance that Issa was financially insecure. In these examples, commentators highlighted the various ways to showcase Issa's emotional and economic insecurity, including her interactions with Daniel, lack of transparency with her feelings, reliance on him for shelter, and low financial credit score.

Comments during the second half of the season (episodes 5–8), focused more on Issa's interactions with Nathan, which, according to users, further highlighted her insecurities. For context, over the season, their relationship quickly progressed and dissolved. In episode six, after a few episodes of spending time together and having sex, Nathan disappeared and halted all communication with Issa without explanation. Consequently, Issa showed up to his house unannounced, broke into his room and snooped through his belongings (episode seven). In response to the episode, Aiysha commented, "That was craziness. She was doing too much" (September 23, 2018). Deidre noted "Issa, while being clearly insecure, had never delved to the depths she did by searching Nathan's drawers and trying to access his computer. She's never exhibited that level of thirst. Wasn't characteristic of her. I was kinda disappointed" (September 24, 2018). This comment assumed it was common knowledge that Issa was insecure, but the intensity of Issa's feelings, combined with her actions was a new and surprising showcase of her emotions to users. In addition, there were several other comments about the scene showing Issa at the height of her insecurity, such as Evelyn's comment, "Crashing uninvited to his place is just a NO-NO!! You must be very desperate and insecure to do that! . . . Issa looked real crazyyy with her dried ass mohawk!" (September 24, 2018). Issa was described by commenters as emotionally, mentally, relationally, and financially unstable; these descriptions were not directly connected to a stereotype.

Theme Two: Issa Is Imperfect

In season three, commenters often highlighted Issa's flaws in 53 or 19.4% of the total comments. Using terms to describe her, such as "crazy," "has issues," "self-centered," "impulsive," and "dramatic," they repeatedly indicated that Issa was not a perfect black female character. Although her imperfections were not attributed to her race, it was clear that she was a black female character exhibiting traits not deemed desirable. Commenters painted Issa as an imperfect character who had areas of her life, qualities, or behaviors that did not meet expectations of black female commenters in the forum.

Moreover, comments indicated that Issa did not make the best decisions, particularly in her relationships with men. For example, in episode four, Issa unexpectedly ran into Nathan, played hooky from work, spent the day with him, and took him back to her home. She was critiqued for her actions as Heidi wrote, "To me the 'too fast' was that she brought him to her home. Hanging out is ok, but you don't know him for him to be in your space" (September 2, 2018). For context, this was the second time she interacted with him. She met him first as his Lyft driver. In episode five, Issa was at Coachella Valley Music and Arts Festival for a fun weekend with her friends, and users outlined her poor decision-making, attributing it to her impulsiveness. While at Coachella, Issa drank alcohol, ate weed gummy bears, took the drug "molly" from a stranger, and had sex in a Ferris wheel with Nathan. In response to her actions, comments described Issa and her behavior, such as Jeanni's post, "she was high on the ferris wheel so irresponsible raw sex" (September 10, 2018). Along the same vein, Katuri posted, "The bitch was poppin Molly and edibles all day" (September 10, 2018). Lauren concluded, "The girl was high, [having sex] on a damn ferris wheel. . . . In this moment, pill-popping Issa is NOT a role model! (September 10, 2018). In these examples, commenters were clear that Issa was irresponsible, and many assumed she had unprotected sex. Furthermore, although some commenters were surprised by Issa's actions, others noted that her irresponsibility was common knowledge. Gabrielle wrote, "Yall acting like you expect Issa to consistently make sound choices or something. Her imperfections are front and center in the storyline. She would DEFINITELY be the kind of person not to use a condom every time" (September 10, 2018). Based on the comments in the forum, Issa was viewed as someone who exhibited poor decision-making skills.

Comments mentioned that Issa was a "user" of men, as one of her imperfections. While Issa lived with Daniel, commenters noted her lack of financial contribution or personal maintenance of Daniel's home. When one commenter began a thread praising Issa for being helpful in episode two by "deep cleaning this man's funky apartment," user Leah stated,

> Welll . . . to be honest Kelly [her friend] had to point out to her that she needed to help Daniel out in some way. Because she had been at his apartment for over 2 weeks rent free and not once did it seem like she tried to clean his place or be of assistance to him (August 20, 2018).

Other Facebook forum members also made this distinction and noted how Issa's actions were prompted by her friends' suggestions. Lauren wrote, "Well she only cleaned the apartment because Kelli guilted her into sleeping on that man's couch for free. She wasn't chipping in any way the least she can do is be a great friend and resource to him" (August 20, 2018). These comments in the discussion forum pointed out the selfishness members noticed in Issa's decision to live with Daniel until she became more financially stable.

Issa Is Improving

While users' comments made it clear they were cognizant of Issa's flaws, they also expressed that Issa had admirable qualities and strengths. Users noted that as the series progressed, Issa began to exhibit better decision-making skills and displayed an effort to improve personally, relationally, and professionally. Throughout season three, the season in focus, 58 comments or 21.2% of the total comments noted how Issa was "smart," "honest," "friendly," "growing," and "trying to make better decisions." This theme provided a balance to the two previous assessments of her character and contributed to users' painting Issa as an overall flawed but growing individual. Highlighting Issa's complexity is important because black feminist thought challenges stereotypes of black women and advocates replacing them with "authentic female images" (Collins, 1986, p. S17). The forum members' classification of Issa as improving also supported Fiske's (1986) assertion that television, as a text, can have multiple meanings and provides "space for resistance and negotiation" (p. 391). The discussion forum allowed insight into how commenters perceived, wrote about, and negotiated the various traits of Issa.

There were several comments that prompted insight into the ways she had grown. Discussing episode two, users commented that Issa deep cleaned Daniel's apartment only after being prompted, so she was more of a selfish user. However, there were oppositional readings regarding the meaning of her cleaning and other behavior. A thread by Rose concluded,

> So . . . Issa deep cleaned this man's funky apartment, gave him emotional support when he was feeling low (one of the reasons married men live longer), listened to him blabber about beats, got him into the club on the strength of her own connections and PUSHED him to seize the opportunity to follow his

destiny.... She sounds like a great friend and roommate to me (August 20, 2018).

In addition to pointing out that Issa was supportive and became helpful around the house, Facebook forum commenters recognized growth in Issa for not engaging in penetrative sexual intercourse with Daniel, a person whom she had sex with in a prior season. In discussing episode three, Sametta noted, "Issa was right to not let him substitute her in the same damn bed he'd just banged 'light skin love' in" (August 26, 2018). Taylor, another commenter on episode three wrote, "Yep. Women need to stop thinking they can casually fuck someone they have legit feelings for . . . I was proud . . . she's getting better at this decision making thing lol" (August 26, 2018).

Forum members also noted that Issa showed maturity and bravery by accepting a less-than-ideal job as a part-time property manager at an apartment complex, to ensure that she could move into her own apartment. They viewed her employment decisions as an indicator of growth. After Issa made the decision to move out of Daniel's place at the end of episode three, users such as Yvonne supported her actions, writing comments such as, "Issa needs to get to a place where she is standing on her own 2 feet and functioning independently. . . . Her getting her own spot is growth. She should've never been there to begin with . . . Issa need to go" (August 26, 2018). Even though the timing of Issa's decision to quit her full-time job and acceptance of the part-time manager position was questioned, users still perceived these changes as growth. Several comments indicated optimism for her future. In a thread posted during episode four, when Issa quit her job, Bridget indicated that although Issa quit her full-time job, she had multiple sources of income. Bridget stated "She has her property manager job and drive lyft. I think she'll do just fine" (September 3, 2018).

Not only did users mention that Issa was maturing, sacrificing, and making better decisions relationally and professionally during the third season, but they also highlighted her emotional growth. In episode four, when Issa played the game, "truth or dare" with Nathan, users commended her honesty and vulnerability about her mistakes in a past relationship. For instance, one user, Eva, stated, "I applaud her for that. She didn't have to she wanted to be honest with him" (September 3, 2018). Another user, Francis, in response to Issa's display of honesty, stated, "Issa is always lying and it was like she took a step back, thought before she acted which has not really been what she's known for . . . that's growth. . . . She's finally setting realistic goals . . . legit having real expectations for herself and others" (September 3, 2018). In addition, another comment by Gabrielle noted, "I think it was brave of her to just put it out there. I think it only helped her in this situation" (September 3, 2018). These examples suggested that forum members believed Issa was showing growth, often in the same episodes in which she was also making potentially detrimental decisions, such as quitting her job and inviting Nathan, a stranger at that time, into her home. Comments revealed a complexity in the way black women described Issa's character.

The discussion forum provided a balanced and nuanced understanding of Issa Dee. Comments in the forum painted Issa in a complicated way that did not directly align her with a stereotype. She was a black woman, with traits that could be interpreted as aligning with stereotypes; however, users' comments indicated they did not see her that way. The themes that the research identified indicated how users recognized multiple truths simultaneously. Issa was described as someone financially and emotionally insecure, and held toxic traits such as selfishness and irresponsibility. These negative traits did not hinder an understanding of ways in which Issa had grown, truly showing a nuanced and complex character. Findings in the forum supported Williams and Gonlin (2017) stance that "support networks may also be facilitated online" (p. 984).

Castle Bell and Harris (2017) noted, "it is critical for audiences to be cognizant of the ways in which, race, gender, and class collide to influence their interpretations of characters on the screen (Collins, 2000) and to examine how television impacts how viewers then position traditionally marginalized group members in daily life" (p. 149). Black women's forum comments provided a holistic interpretation of Issa, highlighting tenets of black feminist thought. They challenged the controlling, negative, or narrow images of black women by providing a complex and nuanced description of Issa, posturing her personality and interpreting her actions on a continuum in a way that negative stereotypes do not. Moreover, through their collective interpretation of Issa as a flawed, yet growing character, the social media users' participation in the forum showed how participatory culture functioned as black women users operated as active producers, "reviewers," and challengers of meaning in response to this series. This collective participation and meaning-making showed how the forum members' commentary and interaction became a social activity, showcasing community and shared learning. This process also allowed for the creation of a space where forum members could use a critical lens to discuss ideas of gender, race, sexuality, class, and other standards promoted within the media industry (Jenkins, 1992; 2012). This space allowed them to demonstrate the tenets outlined in black feminist thought.

CONCLUSION

This study sought to understand the role that black women's participation in social television had on constructing the character of Issa Dee in the *Insecure:*

The Discussion Forum Facebook group, based on the HBO comedy series *Insecure*. This study used a textual method and thematic analysis to interrogate the third season of comments posted in the forum. Issa was not significantly described by black women in a way that aligned with a stereotype of a black woman. The analysis revealed the black women in the discussion forum portrayed Issa as a dynamic woman with insecurities, imperfections, and strengths. The forum participants' descriptions of Issa shed light on a variety of traits that assisted in portraying Issa in a holistically flawed, yet realistic way. Although the discussion forum participants pointed out her flaws in their comments, they also highlighted redemptive qualities of Issa and recognized her personal growth in season three. The discussion forum members painted Issa in a manner that showcased her in multiple ways, which did not limit her to a stereotype. This speaks to the ways black feminist thought and participatory culture were on display in the forum by challenging interlocking forms of oppression through the creation of a complex, interactive, multidimensional, and nuanced reading of Issa.

More scholars should seek to understand how modern representations of black women impact the lived experiences of black women both within and outside of the digital spaces. Given the political climate and the increasing tension that is laden with intersections of race, class, and gender in the United States, it is necessary to interpret how black women are interpreting content and how larger media companies, which wield financial power and influence in the media industry, impact how black women are portrayed in relation to their lived experiences. Moreover, those who engage in social television should be critical of the ways in which their curated content aligns or diverges from historical images that seek to control and disempower minorities in general, and black women specifically.

REFERENCES

American Psychological Association. (2020). Insecurity. Retrieved January 25, 2021, from https://dictionary.apa.org/insecurity.

Bogle, D. (2001). *Toms, coons, mulattoes, mammies, and bucks: An interpretive history of Blacks in American films*. The Continuum International Publishing Group, Inc.

Brock, A. (2009). "Who do you think you are?": Race, representation, and cultural rhetorics in online spaces. *Poroi An Interdisciplinary Journal of Rhetorical Analysis and Invention, 6*(1), 15–35. https://doi.org/10.13008/2151-2957.1013.

Castle Bell, G., & Harris, T. M. (2017). Exploring representations of Black masculinity and emasculation on NBC's Parenthood. *Journal of International and Intercultural Communication, 10*(2), 135–152. doi: 10.1080/17513057.2016.1142598.

Cheers, I. (2018). *The evolution of black women in television: Mammies, matriarchs and mistresses.* Routledge.

Cesar, P., & Geerts, D. (2011, January). Past, present, and future of social TV: A categorization. In *Consumer Communications and Networking Conference (CCNC), 2011 IEEE* (pp. 347–351). IEEE.

Collins, P. H. (1986). Learning from the outsider within: The sociological significance of Black feminist thought. *Social Problems, 33*(6), S14–S32. https://doi.org/10.2307/800672.

Collins, P. H. (2000). *Black feminist thought: Knowledge, consciousness, and the politics of empowerment.* Routledge Classics.

Dates, J. L., & Barlow, W. (1993). *Split image: African Americans in the mass media.* Howard University Press.

Doughty, M., Rowland, D., & Lawson, S. (2012). Who is on your sofa?: TV audience communities and second screen social networks. *Proceedings of the 10th European Conference on Interactive TV and Video,* July 04-06, 2012, Berlin, Germany [doi:10.1145/2325616.2325635].

Fereday, J., & Muir-Cochrane (2006). Demonstrating rigor using thematic analysis: A hybrid approach of inductive and deductive coding and theme development. *International Journal of Qualitative Methods, 5*(1), 1–11. https://sites.ualberta.ca/~iiqm/backissues/5_1/PDF/FEREDAY.PDF.

Fiske, J. (1986). Television: Polysemy and popularity. *Critical Studies in Media Communication, 3*(4), 391–408. http://doi.org/10.1080/15295038609366672.

Fürsich, E. (2009). In defense of textual analysis: Restoring a challenged method for journalism and media studies. *Journalism Studies, 10*(2), 238–252. https://doi.org/10.1080/14616700802374050.

Home Box Office. (2019). HBO NOW. https://play.hbonow.com/series/urn:hbo:series:GV7xdwg1cosPDWwEAAABT?icid=hbo_signin_now.

Insecure: The Discussion Forum. (n.d.). In *Facebook* [closed group]. https://www.facebook.com/groups/338796316478604/.

Jenkins, H. (1992). *Textual poachers: Television fans and participatory culture.* Routledge.

Jenkins, H. (2012). *Textual poachers: Television fans and participatory culture.* Routledge.

Jenkins, H., Purushotma, R., Weigel, M., Clinton, K., & Robison, A. (2009). *Confronting the challenges of participatory culture: Media education for the 21st century.* https://mitpress.mit.edu/books/confronting-challenges-participatory-culture.

Kretsedemas, P. (2010). "But She's Not Black!": Viewer interpretations of "Angry Black Women" on Prime Time TV. *Journal of African American Studies, 14*(2), 149–170. https://doi:10.1007/s12111-009-9116-3.

Lemons, J. (1977). Black Stereotypes as Reflected in Popular Culture, 1880–1920. *American Quarterly, 29*(1), 102–116. doi:10.2307/2712263.

Moody-Ramirez, M. (2019). Race, gender, and participatory dynamics: Facebook representations of Being Mary Jane. In S. B. White & K. H. Harris (Eds.), *Representations of Black womanhood on television: Being Mara Brock Akil* (pp. 133–152). Rowman & Littlefield.

Muhammad, G. E., & McArthur, S. A (2015). "Styled by their perceptions": Black adolescent girls interpret reinterpretation of Black females in popular culture. *Multicultural Perspectives, 17*(3), 133–140. doi:10.1080/15210960.2015.1048340.

Nielsen. (2017, November 12). Reaching Black Women Across Media Platforms. http://www.nielsen.com/us/en/insights/news/2017/reaching-black-women-across-media-platforms.html.

Nielsen (2017b). For us by us? The mainstream appeal of Black content. https://www.nielsen.com/us/en/insights/news/2017/for-us-by-us-the-mainstream-appeal-of-black-content.html.

Pires de Sá, F. (2015). The co-viewing 2.0: Detaching from history and applying in the new media age. *Kultura, 5*(11), 55–64.

Smalls, M. (2019). Social TV and stereotypes: The social construction of #BeingMaryJane on twitter. In S. B. White & K. H. Harris (Eds.), *Representations of Black womanhood on television: Being Mara Brock Akil* (pp. 153–176). Rowman & Littlefield.

Springer, K. (2008). Divas, evil Black bitches, and bitter Black women: African-American women in postfeminist and post-civil rights popular culture. In C. Brunsdon & S. Spigel (Eds.), *Feminist television criticism* (2nd ed., pp. 72–92). Open University Press.

Television Academy (n.d.). *Insecure-Emmy Awards, Nominations and Wins.* https://www.emmys.com/shows/insecure.

Thompson, L. (2009). *Beyond the Black lady.* University of Illinois Press.

Tyree, T. (2011). African American stereotypes in reality television. *Howard Journal of Communications, 22*(4), 394–413. doi:10.1080/1646175.2011.617217.

Tyree, T. C. M., & Williams, M. L. (2016). Flawless feminist or fallible freak? An analysis of feminism, empowerment and gender in Beyoncé's lyrics. In A. Trier-Bieniek (Ed.), *The* Beyoncé *effect: Essays on sexuality, race and feminism* (pp. 124–142). McFarland.

West, C. (1995). Mammy, sapphire, and jezebel. *Psychotherapy Theory Research & Practice, 32*(3), 458–466. https://doi:10.1037/0033-3204.32.3.458.

West, C. (2018). Mammy, Sapphire, Jezebel and the bad girls of reality television. In J.C. Chrisler & C. Golden (Eds.), *Lectures on the psychology of women* (5th ed., pp. 139–158). Waveland Press.

Williams, A., & Gonlin, V. (2017). I got all my sisters with me (on Black twitter): Second screening of *How to Get Away with Murder* as a discourse on Black womanhood. *Information, Communication & Society, 20*(7), 984–1004. https://doi:10.1080/1369118X.2017.1303077.

Chapter 17

Pregnancy and the Back-to-Work Narrative

How Television Comedy Dramas Navigate the Social Norms of Motherhood

Elizabeth Fish Hatfield

Audiences frequently witness their favorite characters experiencing one common, human experience: the journey to parenthood. As television writers and directors employ this narrative tool, the characters they develop must make sense of their new identities as parents, wrestle with back-to-work decision-making during maternity leave, and return to work. Watching televisual pregnancy, audience members "learn what pregnancy should be like and develop an idea of what childbirth will entail" (Hall, 2013, p. 48), as the narrative format of television makes these ideas "easy to process" (Hall, 2013, p. 50). Research has shown that depictions of pregnancy and childbirth on television are used by audience members to learn about the birth process, even if they frequently lack realistic representations of the experience (Hall, 2013; Luce et al., 2016; Morris & McInerney, 2010).

Unlike the established body of work examining pregnancy and birth representations in the media, little research has specifically addressed the narrative arc that follows delivery: maternity leave (Fisher, Valley, Toppinen-Tanner, & Mattingly, 2016). Yet, it is during maternity leave that new moms must integrate their new, culturally dominant mother identity with existing roles they have already internalized such as worker and family member. The back-to-work decision, one frequently constrained by financial and personal needs, forces individuals to actively contend with the fact that US culture idealizes staying home as best for children (Pew Research Center, 2013), even as most women go back to work after having a baby (Percheski, 2008).

This study considers the postpartum leave period and return to work for television characters in dramatic comedies, with a focus on the shows' messages regarding gender, work, and the desire to "have it all" as a mother in the United States. Utilizing existing research on motherhood and media representation, this project uses thematic analysis to analyze how new parenthood and the return to work are framed before, during, and after having a baby on television situation comedies. As researchers find that "setting realistic expectations about the parenthood transition and return to work process early on" (Fisher et al., 2016, p. 143) is important for overall better outcomes, the role of media representations as forms of anticipatory socialization takes a central role in that process.

MATERNITY LEAVE AND MEDIATED MOTHERHOOD

About 70% of women in the United States take maternity leave after having a child (Lake, June 25, 2019). For those taking time off work, the average leave of 10 weeks ends due to financial pressures related to the fact that only 13% of US workers receive paid leave (Paquette, August 19, 2015). Women are more likely to return to work (versus choose to stop working after having a child) due to future income potential, and less likely to return to work when family income or childcare costs are high (Barrow, 1999, p. 51). While 8% of women do stop work temporarily during their childbearing years, this number skews higher for women with greater earning potential (Percheski, 2008). These women may "opt-out" temporarily (Belkin, October 26, 2003) knowing their strong network ties offer a privileged position should they decide to opt back in (Kirby et al., 2017).

While being a good mother has been expanded beyond earlier limited definitions of a white, middle-class, stay-at-home mom, the pervasive and impossible demands of the intensive mothering ideology have been argued both as an ongoing lived experience (Hays, 1998; Johnston & Swanson 2006), and one replicated and promoted through the media (Douglas & Michaels, 2004). As Feasey (2012) notes, "The contemporary media environment is saturated by romanticised, idealised, and indeed conservative images of selfless and satisfied 'good' mothers who conform to the ideology of intensive mothering" (p. 3). The mediated, transformative experience of motherhood (McGannon et al., 2015) begins with a "good" or "bad" delivery experience for television moms (Feasey, 2012), framed by an element of control over the birth plan. Arguably, birth on television offers a powerful learning experience for women in the United States, who have often not experienced the birth process closely before going through it (Cummins, 2019).

Mediated motherhood still frames the experience as a path to fulfillment for women (Kinnick, 2009), though representations of motherhood have changed significantly from the 1950s satisfied, stay-at-home mother as normative

(Feasey, 2012). Sitcom mothers now present working, more emotionally complex women, even as they are still distinct from non-mother characters (Feasey, 2012). Feasey's (2013) research on modern sitcom representations of motherhood argues that television mothers "struggling to construct and maintain appropriate mothering behaviors" (p. 27) offer important social commentary on the good mother ideal and our contemporary parenting environment. As for fathers, the 1980s introduced mediated dads who represented the "new man" ideology: softer, more involved in childcare and housework, and shifting from the dominant father-as-breadwinner image (Patton, 2014). Even so, sitcom mothers continue to retain the bulk of childcare and family management while outsourcing housework for their upper-middle-class television families (Bressler, 2014; Hatfield, 2017).

SEARCHING FOR TELEVISION MOMS

This project analyzed five television shows that aired during the period of 2012–2019. While at least 11 series met the criteria for data, for a more consistent comparison, series with longer formats (60 minutes) or a focus on parenting outside the United States were excluded. The final collection for analysis included episodes from five, multiple-season, award-winning sitcoms featuring pregnancy and post-pregnancy narratives. These programs are *The Office*, *Black-ish*, *The Mindy Show*, *Life in Pieces*, and *How I Met Your Mother*. Episodes containing a pregnancy and post-pregnancy story arc were included in analysis, for a total of over 50 episodes.

While the data did not feature significant diversity in sexual orientation or class, some racial diversity is represented in the sample. The groundbreaking show *The Mindy Project* was developed by and stars a South Asian woman. The show was recognized with awards during all four of its seasons, including Most Exciting New Series at the Critics' Choice TV Awards in 2012 ("Awards," 2020). Additionally, the show *Black-ish*, another well-received, award-winning series, depicts an upper-middle-class African American family.

METHOD: THEMATIC ANALYSIS

To analyze the episodes, thematic analysis was employed. Developed by Braun and Clarke (2012), this qualitative method benefits researchers who desire to identify "what is common to the way a topic is talked or written about and of making sense of those commonalities" (p. 57). Just as this study considers mediated depictions of family and parenthood, thematic analysis has been used to study both parenting (Lynch & Morison, 2016; Rowland, 2016; Thomassin et al., 2019) and media narratives (Howard, 2019; Lynch & Morison, 2016) supporting the fit of this approach with the current project.

Following Braun and Clarke's six-part process (2012), this project required collection and familiarization with data, coding and deep description, identification of codes, and finally the organization of codes into themes and patterns within the data. The final step, the written report, offers a summary of the findings as: "Themes should connect logically and meaningfully and, if relevant, should build on previous themes to tell a coherent story about the data" (Braun & Clarke, 2012, p. 69). For this project, the story being told is about the negotiation of parenthood, identity, and roles in the earliest days of parenthood.

FINDINGS

The research process elicited a chronological organizational structure highlighting the disconnect between expectations, cultural norms, and reality during delivery/maternity leave, preparing for the return to work, and the actual return to work. As themes emerged during the analysis process, the current project shifted as identity and transformation quickly presented as topics underpinning the postpartum experience. This section discusses findings related to the time periods of early maternity leave, preparing for work, and returning to work, along with the identity construction that characterizes each for the television parents in this study.

The Motherhood Transformation: Transition, Identity, and Realignment

For our characters, the transition to parenthood was dramatic, funny, and more real than expected from previous literature. During delivery and in the early maternity period, new mothers are shown grappling with this instant identity, negotiating between their expectations and actual experiences, and dealing with external expectations for the enactment of good motherhood. While characters began to assume the mother identity even before the delivery, audiences see that expectations for decisions relating to motherhood come from both internalized personal perspectives and external voices of judgment.

Within the birth episode(s), characters frequently commented on their new, transformative identities, as noted by *The Office*'s Pam, "We're really parents now," *The Mindy Project*'s Mindy, "I'm a mom," and *How I Met Your Mother*'s Marshall, "Well guys, I'm a dad." The new identities of mom and dad, assumed at birth, reflect similar experiences during these first moments. A feeling of euphoria is shown, such as Lily and Marshall who are "gloriously happy," and Mindy, who notes her baby is the "best thing she ever cooked." Viewers also see fear related to the care of the baby:

"How is the hospital letting us leave?" Jen, *Life in Pieces*

"It's our first baby and I am just a little nervous." Danny, *The Mindy Project*

"I can't tell if he's breathing. Is he breathing?" Bow, *Black-ish*

However, while the early days of parenthood reflect parallel experiences, gendered expectations for parenting responsibilities creep in early as the pressure to be a good mother begins. As Pam from *The Office* comically feeds the wrong baby in her hospital room without the latching problem she has been experiencing, and Jen from *Life in Pieces* brings in extreme consultants to help with her milk supply, these moments demonstrate that mothers must make early choices about their babies that are highly influenced by cultural pressures. The dads, while supportive, are on the sidelines of these scenes reflecting the culturally prescribed, central position of mothers even in these first days. New dad Greg of *Life in Pieces* tells Jen, "You don't have to do this, just say the word and we will get your formula." Greg wishes to help alleviate the pressure facing Jen to manage and make this decision about feeding the baby. Other television shows reflect the internalized nature of social expectations through the mother's beliefs. Though Mindy of *The Mindy Show* is of South Asian descent, the character was raised in Boston and adheres to typical American parenting ideals. While cultural differences do impact Mindy's relationship, some challenges seem to come from husband Danny's Italian heritage culture, personal choices, and strict adherence to gender roles during early parenting decisions. We see Mindy's belief in her own maternal instinct as she rejects Danny's input on how the baby should be delivered and raised, telling him, "You have to just let me be a mom the way I know how to." Lily of *How I Met Your Mother* worries about Marshall being rough with the baby, reflecting intensive mothering philosophies of the sacred child who must be protected at all times.

The comedic nature of the shows included in this study plays upon the growing cultural awareness that mothering is not innate but learned, and pressures to be a certain type of mother begin immediately. Yet, with intensive motherhood remaining a deeply ingrained cultural belief, the shows' funny moments remind audiences of the difficulty and time needed to push past restrictive social norms. Thus, television mothers notice early on that their own expectations for parenthood (often a filtered version of intensive mothering) frequently differ from the lived experience. The characters demonstrate that enacting intensive motherhood is exhausting and often impossible, forcing them to reconsider what they thought they knew. Television characters must accept their inability to control what happens as a new parent and yet find a way to still feel like they are doing a good job. We see this when Mindy delivers without the epidural she had hoped for and Bow from *Black-ish* experiences postpartum depression. Another way this is portrayed is through behavior framed as irrational, such as Danny's removal of all technology from the house and his rule that Mindy should not take the baby out during maternity leave. These restrictive rules mirror good mother ideologies of sacrifice, but ultimately make Mindy miserable. The character struggles to accept that she cannot adhere to these goals and tries to hide her trip out of the apartment from Danny. In *Life in Pieces*, Jen and Greg attempt to avoid being "high strung parents" about dirt and germs and are shown facing an even dirtier situation than if they had just relented earlier on. As Jen tells Greg, "It's happening, isn't it? We're becoming the crazy parents." In the face of failure, these women negotiate what it means to be a good parent.

The pressure to be a good mom comes from within, but also from other characters on these series. These external critics reinforce the ideology of intensive mothering as they criticize the new mothers and their choices. Criticism came in many forms within the shows: Dwight from *The Office* says "I will when you lose the baby weight"; Joan in *Life in Pieces* chides, "Where's her hat? It's chilly in here"; and Morgan from *The Mindy Project* says, "I thought you were gonna wuss out and cut your hours like those moms who love their kids."

The last example, in particular, highlights the awareness by television writers of the impossible task of mothering today. Going back to work means you love your baby less than others, but cutting work hours means you give up a career to avoid the strains of trying to have it all. Characters reflect on and frequently reject these criticisms within the episodes, just as they feel the pressure to adhere to intensive mothering while simultaneously rejecting it as an impossible standard. As each character spends more time parenting, we see their understanding of motherhood mature with confidence. The challenges of early decision-making become easier as the mothers negotiate a new vision for acceptable motherhood.

Transitioning Back-to-Work: Ideology, Identity, and Replication

On the shows studied, fathers returned to work quite quickly following the birth. Though it varied, we see that television mothers enjoyed choices related to maternity leave and took several months off work without significant concern of financial stress. The longest leave noted was Lily's on *How I Met Your Mother*, at five months, a luxurious and unrealistic amount of time for most US mothers and families. Toward the end of the mother's leave, childcare arrangements frequently became a storyline. Here, the narratives mirrored what research has shown—mothers took charge of the nanny search as an extension of their own good mothering. However, before finding childcare and returning to work, the ideology that a parent is the best caregiver for a child is represented by the pressure the mothers feel to act selfless as part of a good mother identity during maternity leave. We see characters adhere to, yet struggle with this pressure, such as Pam and Mindy who feel excited to finally have a reason to leave the baby home. For others, the pressure for selflessness emerges through fear of letting others care for the baby even as it affects their other relationships and happiness. When Jen accidentally cuts herself, Jen and Greg face her worry about leaving the baby. After spending several hours walking around an emergency room, eating, and hanging out, Greg jokes, "It's kinda like we are on a date." Jen initially adhered to cultural notions of selflessness, but when forced, learned that taking time for oneself was worth it.

For Mindy and Danny, Danny's strong belief that having a parent care for children is best permeates several episodes as Mindy debates her desire to enact the good mother identity and also go back to work. After a failed, but hilarious attempt at becoming a "stay-at-home MILF," Mindy goes back to work while Danny tries staying home. He too finds it difficult to do all the tasks a home demands yet cannot see the double standard he imposes on her as he continues to push Mindy to stay home. It is only after Danny must leave town to take care of his father that he accepts Mindy must go back to work. During this time, Mindy realizes that she actually wants to work and enjoys it. This feeling forces her to consider whether she is in fact being selfish and if Danny is right. Mindy's refusal to adhere to intensive mothering ideologies of selflessness ultimately leads to the couple's break up.

Though mothers (and some fathers) are shown enacting selflessness to their own detriment within these shows, when the time comes to return to work each becomes focused on finding the ideal nanny. As identified by Buzzanell et al. (2005), television mothers in this sample sought nannies that made the return to work acceptable while the nanny search itself represented the couple's move toward further gendered parenting roles. For the three characters searching for a nanny, the narrative was presented as dramatic and emotional. Mothers enacted emotional labor as they sought out the perfect nanny. For Jen, a nanny needed to be an ideal substitute for her mothering, "How do I know she is gonna make the same decisions I would make?" For Mindy, a nanny needed to solve her and Danny's parenting differences: "I need to find a nanny so good with Leo that I can keep working." Each show presents challenges within the search, as nannies fail to meet the mothers' high standards or budget. These mothers are shown struggling to hand the babies over on day one to the new nannies, while the dads slowly coax them away. The mothers, just a few episodes ago concerned that they would be unable to take care of a newborn, have gone from "how can we do this" to "only I can do this" in just a few short episodes.

The Good Working Mom: Environment, Stereotypes, and Spillover

The shows in this study represented a range of perspectives on how the work of home should be divided, with some couples being more egalitarian and others more traditional. Two of the mothers, Bow and Mindy (interestingly, both medical doctors and the two nonwhite moms in the study), decide to try staying home after facing hostile work environments upon their return to work. After feeling socially left out on her first day back, Bow says, "Dre, I've been back to work so many times. Why is it so hard this time?" Having already established a 20-year medical career and financial security, Bow decides to stay home now that her older children are grown and time with her younger children feels like it will pass quickly. Mindy attempts to stay home as a "modern mominista," taking the "focus she had at her old job and putting it into the new one." After a week, Mindy becomes bitter and bored and returns to work. As a result, four of the five new mothers ultimately go back to work. The return to work is assumed for Pam, Jen, and Lily, while Bow and Mindy struggle to decide what is best for their families. Bow and Mindy quickly realize that intensive mothering is impossible for stay-at-home mothers as well as working mothers, an interesting social commentary on the cultural pressures mothers face. However, as minority characters, arguably Bow and Mindy's attempts and struggles with staying home may represent the larger issues they face navigating cultural standards for motherhood that media messages long communicated they could not attain due to their black and brown bodies.

As characters got ready to go back to work, childcare in place, they faced situations that made the transition back more or less dramatic. The narratives facing Bow and Mindy, hostile work environments that made them feel excluded, created a challenging return to work that forced them to try staying home. For the other characters, the return to work is not dramatic, but the experience brings on emotions that challenge the new mother identity they have been cultivating during maternity leave. For example, Pam loved maternity leave and misses her daughter upon the return to work, but financially does not have a choice. These characters must now blend two dominant identities as well as manage how motherhood is presented at work. As working mothers, these characters cultivate their good working mother identity as they manage time at work and home, caregiving schedules and relationships, and work-family spillover in both directions.

For Pam, her unbounded motherhood means pumping breast milk at work (to provide it for the baby later) even as her fellow employees steal the special machine. For Mindy, childcare issues result in trying to hide from coworkers that she brings the baby to work and at other times misses out on important work meetings. For Lily, her baby's milestones, reached while she is working, make being away from the baby even harder. Each of these examples portrayed the need to accept the new working mother identity even as one continues to manage it.

CONCLUSION

This chapter addressed how television situational comedy dramas portray new parenthood and, in particular, demonstrate how fictional new mothers navigate the demand on women to enact a new good mother identity. While the author of this chapter initially thought more debate and discussion would permeate these series in relationship to work and the ideal of the stay-at-home parent, what was found instead was that a variety of situations are proposed and characters react differently to new motherhood based on their personal experiences and expectations (including the fathers). Each of these women—Bow, Lily, Mindy, Jen, and Pam—must figure out how and what it means to be a mother. In doing so, each character also must face a prism of influences shaping expectations and interactions with the world as a new mother and worker. The mother identity remains the dominant identity for women with children in the United States, and these series reflect the incredible work women do to make sense of the transformational experience that occurs upon becoming a parent.

The thematic analysis identified elements that were portrayed as characteristic of three postpartum periods: early maternity leave, before the return to work, and after returning to work. What we see across all of these periods is the impossibility of meeting the high demands of society and the process one goes through to find an acceptable place on the spectrum of motherhood. Ideologies of motherhood are subtly challenged through dramatic storylines that demonstrate the difficulty and repression that comes from such belief systems.

In early maternity leave, a transformation process imbues the new identity of mother on these characters. While the transformation is euphoric in many ways, it is also scary and new. Quickly, these characters realized adherence to their own beliefs about parenting (shaped by society and personal experience) was tough, forcing a negotiation between expectations for their own performance and the reality of parenthood. Both internal and external judgment from others serve as reminders that social norms create unrealistic standards for women and accepting this allows one to also carve out an attainable "good mother" identity.

As these characters prepared for the return to work, some debated and tried staying home while others focused on searching for a perfect nanny. The episodes reflect a pressure felt by women to enact selflessness during the maternity leave period and upon returning to work. Finding the perfect nanny or choosing to stay home both represented ways mothers navigate the ideals of selflessness perpetuated by intensive mothering ideologies. Finally, the return to work varied depending on the work environment, the characters' financial positions, and the characters' desires to work. Choosing to stay home is not presented as an ideal situation but simply another point of view from which new mothers must find their way.

Overall, the storylines from *How I Met Your Mother*, *Life in Pieces*, *The Office*, *The Mindy Project*, and *Black-ish* ultimately demonstrate the need to critically consider why one has expectations for behavior and how to accept the need to redefine the norm. These shows, funny and engaging television, reflect a society in transition but willing to examine how and why we do things. While at times, Mindy feels she "definitely did not live up to her mother of the year beer koozie," and she demonstrates what each character presents: that being a good working mom is simply that, a lot of work.

REFERENCES

Andriessen, K., & Krysinska, K. (2019). The portrayal of suicidal behavior in police television series. *Archives of Suicide Research*, 1–15.

Barrow, L. (1999). Child care costs and the return-to-work decisions of new mothers. *Children*, 6(17).

Belkin, L. (October 26, 2003). The opt-out revolution. *The New York Times*. https://www.nytimes.com/2003/10/26/magazine/the-opt-out-revolution.html.

Braun, V. & Clarke, V. (2012). In H. Cooper, P. Camic, D. Long, A. Panter, D. Rindskopf, K. Sher (Eds.), *APA handbook of research methods in psychology, Vol 2: Research designs: Quantitative, qualitative, neuropsychological, and biological* (pp. 57–71). American Psychological Association.

Pew Research Center. (2013). Breadwinner moms. https://www.pewsocialtrends.org/2013/05/29/chapter-2-public-views-on-changing-gender-roles/#whats-best-for-children.

Bressler, N. (2014). Good luck raising the modern family: analyzing portrayals of sexual division of labor and socioeconomic class on family sitcoms. In E. Patton & M. Choi (Eds.), *Home sweat home: Perspectives on housework and modern relationships* (pp. 183–200). Rowman & Littlefield.

Buzzanell, P. M., Meisenbach, R., Remke, R., Liu, M., Bowers, V., & Conn, C. (2005). The good working mother: Managerial women's sensemaking and feelings about work–family issues. *Communication Studies, 56*(3), 261–285.

Cummins, M.W. (2020) Miracles and home births: the importance of media representations of birth. *Critical Studies in Media Communication, 37*(1), 85–96. DOI: 10.1080/15295036.2019.1704037.

Feasey, R. (2012). *From happy homemaker to desperate housewives: Motherhood and popular television.* Anthem Press.

Feasey, R. (2013). From soap opera to reality programming: Examining motherhood, motherwork and the maternal role on popular television. *Imaginations: Journal of Cross-Cultural Image Studies, 4*(2), 25–46.

Fisher, G. G., Valley, M. A., Toppinen-Tanner, S., & Mattingly, V. P. (2016). Parental leave and return to work. In C. Spitzmueller & Russell A. Matthews (Eds.), *Research perspectives on work and the transition to motherhood* (pp. 129–148). Springer.

Hatfield, E.F. (2017). 'There's a thousand things I do around here': Examining mothers' roles in the gendered division of labor on sitcoms. In E. Hatfield (Ed.), *Communication and the work-life balancing act: Intersections across identities, genders, and cultures.* Lexington Books.

Hall, J. G. (2013). As seen on TV: Media influences of pregnancy and birth narratives. In K. Ryan and D. Macey (Eds.), *Television and the self: Knowledge, identity, and media representation* (pp. 47–63). Lexington Books.

Hays, S. (1998). *The cultural contradictions of motherhood.* Yale University Press.

Howard, N. R. (2019). Real, respectable, or both. In S. White and K. Harris (Eds.), *Representations of Black womanhood on television: Being Mara Brock Akil* (pp. 47–66). Lexington Books.

Johnston, D. D., & Swanson, D. H. (2006). Constructing the "good mother": The experience of mothering ideologies by work status. *Sex Roles, 54*(7–8), 509–519.

Kinnick, K. N. (2009). Media morality tales and the politics of motherhood. In A. C. Hall & M. Bishop (Eds.), *Mommy angst: Motherhood in American popular culture* (pp. 1–28). Praeger/ABC-CLIO.

Kirby, E. L., Kuhn, T. R., McBride, M. C., McHendry, G. F., Meisenbach, R. J., Remke, R. V., & Wieland, S. M. B. (2017). Opting (back) in to paid work: A capitalist, gendered, classed, careerist analysis. In E. F. Hatfield (Ed.), *The balancing act: Intersections of work-life balance in communication across identities, genders, and cultures.* Lexington Books.

Lake, R. (June 25, 2019). How long is the average maternity leave? *The Balance Careers.* https://www.thebalancecareers.com/how-long-is-the-average-maternity-leave-4590252.

Luce, A., Cash, M., Hundley, V., Cheyne, H., Van Teijlingen, E., & Angell, C. (2016). Is it realistic? the portrayal of pregnancy and childbirth in the media. *BMC Pregnancy and Childbirth, 16*(1), 40.

Lynch, I., & Morison, T. (2016). Gay men as parents: Analysing resistant talk in South African mainstream media accounts of queer families. *Feminism & Psychology, 26*(2), 188–206.

McGannon, K. R., Gonsalves, C. A., Schinke, R. J., & Busanich, R. (2015). Negotiating motherhood and athletic identity: A qualitative analysis of Olympic athlete mother representations in media narratives. *Psychology of Sport and Exercise, 20*, 51–59.

Morris, T., & McInerney, K. (2010). Media representations of pregnancy and childbirth: An analysis of reality television programs in the United States. *Birth, 37*(2), 134–140.

Paquette, D. (August 19, 2015). The shocking number of US moms who return to work after two weeks. *The Washington Post.* https://www.washingtonpost.com/news/wonk/wp/2015/08/19/the-shocking-number-of-new-moms-who-return-to-work-two-weeks-after-childbirth/.

Patton, E. (2014). Spaces of masculinity and work. In E. Patton & M. Choi (Eds.), *Home sweat home* (pp. 147–166). Rowman & Littlefield.

Percheski, C. (2008). Opting out? Cohort differences in professional women's employment rates from 1960 to 2005. *American Sociological Review, 73*(3), 497–517.

Rowland, G. (2016). *How do parents within the Orthodox Jewish community experience accessing a community Child and Adolescent mental health service?* (Doctoral dissertation). Retrieved from the University of East London.

Thomassin, K., Bucsea, O., Chan, K. J., & Carter, E. (2019). A thematic analysis of parents' gendered beliefs about emotion in middle childhood boys and girls. *Journal of Family Issues, 40*(18), 2944–2973.

Section V

CRIME AND MEDICAL DRAMA

Chapter 18

Historical Drama *Peaky Blinders*

Pitching Racial Allegiances and Ethnocentric Populism

Inna Arzumanova

Since 2013, the award-winning British Broadcasting Corporation's historical drama *Peaky Blinders* has developed an impressive fandom that spans a variety of platforms, forms of engagement, and consumption. It is a fandom that is increasingly immersive, spilling over into fans' realities in ways that gesture toward both the symbolic and the material. The series, set in 1920s Birmingham, England, traces the rise of the notorious Birmingham gang between the two world wars. It offers its fans a stylized history of Birmingham that captures discourses on war, its immediate and residual effects, colonization, Fascism, class politics, and significantly, racial politics. *Peaky Blinders* activates familiar historical narratives, wrapped in the equally familiar trappings of what constitutes historical drama, to play with notions of whiteness, of racial and ethnic otherness, of ethno-racial belonging, of racial citizenship, and to suggest narrow, ethnocentric strategies of ethno-racial alliance.

As fans eagerly consume *Peaky* merchandise, attend the *Peaky* themed festivals, get their haircuts and their suits in the *Peaky* style, and as significant award recognition continues to roll in for the series and its creators, the discourses on race become both increasingly prominent and dangerously resonant with the contemporary moment. *Peaky Blinders*, as both a text and a fandom, creates a world that is a time-warp of nostalgia, fantasy, and consumption. Its discourses on ethno-racial identity dialogue closely with the contemporary wave of xenophobia and racial violence. This chapter argues that this historical drama operates as an all too useful historical tool for the legitimation and explanation of contemporary appeals to Brexit, Trumpism, and other global formations of racial nationalism, lending these contemporary iterations of racist and xenophobic politics a historical legacy that is domesticated and sterilized through its central protagonist.

From the festival to the clothing line to a living museum, these glimpses into *Peaky* fandom suggest that audiences are looking for opportunities to engage in explicitly immersive fan experiences. Fans are using *Peaky Blinders* as an opportunity to build worlds; not just to play at televisual identification, but to resurrect the world and society that the series has described and importantly, to locate themselves in it. This begs the question: what are the worlds that fans are conjuring up? Also, what is the utility of these worlds, these costumed forays into a historical moment, for fans negotiating our contemporary sociopolitical moment? In other words, what are the social and historical architectures that *Peaky Blinders* lends fans who are looking to dialogue with their present by immersing themselves in a *Peaky* past?

These questions unfold over the course of this chapter and inform much of the analysis around the series, its treatments of race and ethnicity and how these translate to knowledge in the contemporary era. There is one plot point, however, that serves as an efficient introduction to the roles of race and racial politics in *Peaky Blinders*. The fifth season begins with the series' central protagonist, crime boss turned member of parliament (MP) Tommy Shelby, being courted by Oswald Mosley, the 1930s leader of the British Union of Fascists. While the series quickly redeems Shelby, showing his antagonism toward Fascism, it overlooks the ways the crime family's ethnocentric infrastructures and allegiances are uniquely well-suited for Mosley's equally ethnocentric Fascism. It is a telling plot point, finally making explicit what the series has been hinting for the first four seasons. Tommy Shelby's populism, commitment to nationalism, and management of ethno-racial diversity are congruent with a politics of nativism and racial violence.

Considering the rising tides of racial nationalism, xenophobia, and violent racial policing of borders that have marked the contemporary moment in the United States and elsewhere in the world, this congruence is an important glimpse into what fans are immersing themselves in. It is a congruence, in fact, that offers fans who are immersing themselves in *Peaky* fandom, an opportunity to reframe their own historical pasts as well as their contemporary political realities. The world that the series invokes is one where allegiances to the nation-state trump class solidarity. Populism disguises the commitment to personal survival and personal profit, and the presence and visibility of racial "others" is tolerated but resolved through a strict maintenance of ethno-racial homogeneity within criminal organizations. What does it mean for contemporary audiences to be rooting for Tommy Shelby, helping reinscribe populist politics through racial difference?

BIRMINGHAM AS IT IS CAPTURED AND CONJURED IN *PEAKY BLINDERS*

The first season of *Peaky Blinders* begins as many gangster films and television series do. The criminal organization is run entirely by an extended family engaged in a power struggle with outside forces such as rival gangs and, of course, representatives of the state and the police. The latter are doomed to fail in their efforts to curb the crime family but not without inflicting some wounds. It is 1919 in Birmingham and the Peaky Blinders, led by Tommy Shelby, his brothers and notably, their aunt, are a family of Romani, involved in a variety of rackets and in charge of Birmingham's Small Heath area and its communities. The series begins as the gang has inadvertently come to the attention of Winston Churchill. To deal with the Shelbys, Churchill sends in the Irish Inspector Campbell, who quickly identifies the scope of the criminal organization and makes a personal enemy out of Tommy. Campbell's presence serves as a signal that the Peaky Blinders, at the time of the audiences' introduction, are on their way up the criminal ranks. The rest of the show invites audiences to follow the Peaky Blinders' expansion, from fixing horse races to developing a sophisticated bookmaking operation and ultimately, attempting to go legal, as Tommy Shelby becomes MP for Birmingham South at the end of the fourth season.

As the story unfolds, there are several key plot dimensions that become both clear and normalized. First, the Shelby brothers are veterans of World War I, having joined as young teenagers and returned traumatized, self-destructive, and wedded simultaneously to nationalism, patriotism and, paradoxically, to self-interest. In fact, the war and the myriad ways in which it has damaged the Shelbys, functions as George Larke-Walsh (2019) has argued, to both explain and excuse the show's toxic masculinity. It also shores up the recurring misogynistic discourses that revolve around "good" women being able to save "bad" men (Larke-Walsh, 2019).

Second, the Shelbys are at the helm of the Peaky Blinders. The rest of the criminal organization is made up of direct family members, related Romani families, and significantly, men who served in the war alongside the Shelby brothers. This last category of members posits the experience of war as a form of kinship, both preserving the gang as a primarily Romani enterprise and allowing selected racial and ethnic others to participate in the organization as a way of extending their war "service."

Third, according to the show, post–World War I Birmingham is industrial, crime-ridden, principally working-class, and a hotbed of political activity. Communism and Fascism are debated alongside other political and economic ideologies like populism, monarchism, and capitalism. Each of these ideologies' utility for working-class people is refracted through the individualism of Tommy Shelby as both a working-class hero and romantic lead.

Fourth, Birmingham, here, is also decidedly multicultural and multiracial. The first episode of the show, in fact, opens in Chinatown and throughout the course of the show, audiences encounter critical characters from Chinese, Jewish, and Italian gangs. Moreover, two key members of the Peakies are Jamaican Brits (a father and son duo) and the Shelby sister's fifth season love interest (and father of her yet unborn child) is a black man named Colonel Ben Younger.

This multiracialism, according to Myers and Grosvenor (2011), Green (2011), and other scholars, reflects the realities of post–World War I Birmingham, which was at the center of the industrial boom that had overtaken the West Midlands region of England. It was a thriving trading outpost, installing factories all over the region and importing laborers to help operate machinery. These laborers were, in part, racial and ethnic immigrants from all over the British Empire and beyond. Long (2017) makes note of the city's racial and ethnic make-up at that time. Birmingham, he says of the city in that historical period, "is certainly global in aspect . . . its native, human capital complemented by those drawn from Ireland, China, Italy and the Caribbean" (p. 171).

It is within this context that *Peaky Blinders* positions itself as a useful text for contemporary fans looking to negotiate a moment wherein reactionary racial nationalisms are taking root globally alongside multiracial realities and racially heterogeneous societies. Specifically, the show works to reframe and stylize historically situated racial nationalisms, gifting contemporary white audiences with a sanitized, nationalist past that can be harnessed to better navigate the contemporary era. The show's suggested politics of racial and ethnic allegiance are not only serviceable for white audiences eager to redeem their own historical legacies but also tailor-made for the contemporary sociopolitical, global moment. These proposed allegiances are founded in the series' cultivation of ethno-racial taxonomies and its location of whiteness within these taxonomies.

TAXONOMIES OF RACE AND ETHNICITY IN *PEAKY BLINDERS*

In her exploration of *Peaky Blinders* and its uses of racialization within the context of the gangster genre, Larke-Walsh dialogues with Dika's (2000) work on *The Godfather*, noting that the Shelby family's ethnic otherness is a polite cover for what is effectively an indulgent fantasy of white power and racial violence. Their Romani heritage, at once ethnically other and both British and white, provides audiences with an opportunity to enjoy these fantasies while also disavowing a more direct invocation of white supremacist discourses. Larke-Walsh's argument is founded in what she views as Tommy's fundamental "prejudices ... towards foreigners," shaped by his "generalized idea of ethnic purity through blood and marriage ties" (p. 50). Similarly, Long also argues that the Shelbys are "disparaging and suspicious of other groups" (p. 173).

While these are both useful points of entry into the discussion of the ways in which racialization operates within the series, this chapter argues that it is precisely Tommy's varying relationships to ethnic and racial "others" that reveals the series' far more complex relationship to whiteness and, importantly, its presumed supremacy. The "foreigners" Larke-Walsh refers to are not all created equal. Ethnic others (ethnic whites) exist as opportunities for alliance building while racial others exist to confirm the Shelbys' whiteness. Consequently, it is not simply white militant violence and xenophobia that are being normalized and stylized here. The series acts as an instruction on how to produce racial and ethnic homogeneity while also dialoguing with the reality of a multiracial society. Tommy is not just "prejudiced" toward racial and ethnic others. He differentiates between ethnic others and racial others, harnessing their presence to his own ends, often forging critical and in some cases, intimate relationships with members of other groups, all the while preserving his own commitment to whiteness.

The distinction between racial and ethnic others relies on work by Roediger (2005) and Jacobson (1998), as well as scholars like Brodkin (1998) and Richards (1999). They differentiate between the two categories in order to trace the histories of new immigrants to the United States, their original characterization as nonwhite, and their subsequent battles to both formally and symbolically attain whiteness. While these scholars are concerned with the US context, and the histories of whiteness and racialization certainly differ between the United States and the United Kingdom, the categorizations of what and who represents racial difference are sourced in colonial discourse, which both contexts embrace. To say that *Peaky Blinders* offers viewers a taxonomy of otherness is to argue that the series' navigation of whiteness, and its strategies of interacting with a multiracial society, act as a useful model for contemporary fans. These fans are witnessing the rise of white nationalism within their own, contemporary, multiracial societies.

THE SHELBYS' WHITENESS WITHIN A MATRIX OF ETHNO-RACIAL OTHERNESS

The Shelbys operate as white subjects who enjoy, despite the discrimination they face at the hands of persistent anti-Romani sentiment, an allocated place within both the historical and their contemporary nation-state. Their whiteness is underscored throughout the series through their interactions with racial others, specifically, black and Chinese Brits, all of whom occupy peripheral roles within the series but serve as a useful racial contrast, producing the Shelbys's whiteness. Tommy forges alliances with ethnic others (ethnic whites), going into business with Jewish, Russian, and Italian organizations, affording their members with rich, complex storylines and opportunities to articulate a kind of belonging within the landscapes of early twentieth-century Birmingham and London. Members of racially othered groups remain narratively marginal, positioned firmly as irredeemable outsiders.

In episode four of the second season, Isaiah Jesus, one of the only two Black Peakies, tries to convince Michael Gray to accompany him into a local bar by explaining, "Look, they won't serve a Black man without a Shelby by his side." Isaiah is not exaggerating and the two quickly find themselves in the middle of a bar fight triggered by racial insults until the bar patrons discover Michael's identity as Tommy's nephew. The scene is meant to invoke the Shelbys' power within the neighborhood. What this scene accomplishes is to remind us that the Shelbys are, in fact, white and while their working-class status and Romani heritage "others" them in many ways, it would not occur to Michael that a black man might need his symbolic body in order to receive service in a bar. It is Michael's entitlement and dismay at the turn of events that reveal his own experience with racial privilege and his own default to what we might read as "white innocence."

Scholars have long identified "white innocence" as a hallmark performance of white subjectivity within legal discourse in the United States (Ross, 1990; Hunt, 2006), as an agent in shaping and understanding colonial pasts and presents (Wekker, 2016), and as a more diffused dimension of white performance. Speaking of the concept's legal invocations in the United States, Ross posits that "white innocence was a rhetorically created myth . . . cast[ing] the contemporary whites as free of responsibility" for the violence of racism, "permit[ing] white magicians to pretend . . . that the horrific circumstances of the blacks were, after all, not the white person's fault" (pp. 5–6). This functionality of white innocence casts a particularly interesting light on Michael's performance of it. He is not only clueless about the pernicious work of anti-blackness but rendered doubly innocent of complicity by virtue of white innocence and simultaneously, his own status as an oppressed, ethnic outsider (a Romani).

Michael's performance of white innocence, furthermore, is underscored by Arthur Shelby and John Shelby's reactions to the events at the bar. Michael and Isaiah do not explain to the elder Shelbys why they got into the fight; and they don't need to. Arthur immediately asks Isaiah where his father is, suggesting that he knows exactly what the source of the problem was. In a determined, organized rage, Arthur and John Shelby set out to destroy the bar, also exhibiting a variation on white innocence. Racism and, specifically, anti-black racism, clearly are not new to the elder Shelbys, but their righteous indignation, coupled with the ability to retaliate suggest that they deny any complicity in those projects. Theirs is a white innocence that is, as Hunt proposes, both "innocent of race itself . . . [and] innocent of racial perspective" (p. 499).

Isaiah's scene is brief and no more than a narrative sideline, which perfectly captures the series' use of racially othered characters. The series introduces and marks racial difference so that the Shelbys might claim both their whiteness and their own ethnic otherness in contrast to that difference. Colonel Ben Younger, a black former officer in World War I and current representative of the Home Office, is put to similar use in the series. Appearing once at the end of season four and then more consistently throughout season five, audiences first meet Col. Ben Younger when he is sent in by Winston Churchill to squash the rising tides of Communist organizing in Birmingham. As Younger drafts Ada Shelby for this cause, a romance develops between the two.

By the start of season five, audiences discover that Ada is pregnant with his child. Debating what the future might hold for a biracial child in Birmingham in 1930, Polly tells Ada, "Imagine . . . The baby's black, he's a bastard, and it's Birmingham" (season five, episode one). Having established not only Younger's racial difference but also Ada's presumed absence of that difference (she will be just fine in Birmingham, after all, without a biracial child), Polly continues, "But you don't care." The last statement is one that lights and lifts Ada's otherwise burdened face as she realizes that her own constellation of privileges, among them, racial, will save her from the burden of having to worry about violence against her biracial child. The implication is clear. Both her status as a Shelby and her whiteness will ultimately embolden her to have this child.

Younger, whose storyline is brief and whose character exploration is nearly nonexistent, is killed in a car explosion by episode five of that season. Like Isaiah, he too has served his purpose in conjuring up what Hall (1997) has famously called the "spectacle of the other," existing for little else but to explain to viewers what the shape of its counterpart is, what constitutes whiteness, and who, in this case, might be confirmed as white. It is in these brief interactions with characters whose racial difference is made spectacular that we are reminded of the Shelbys' whiteness.

In the case of black characters who labor to prop up the narrative of whiteness within *Peaky Blinders*, the spectacle Hall identifies is produced discursively. When it comes to the Chinese Brits who appear in the series, that spectacle of otherness is primarily visual. The very first episode of the series opens in Birmingham's Chinatown and the visual rhetorics are neither subtle nor particularly new, when it comes to representations of Chinese immigrant communities in the West. The community is presented as dark, loud, crowded, chaotic, marked by fear, and having an unexplainable, eroticized magic. Tommy has sent for one of the young Chinese women to cast a magic spell on his horse to help it win a race. She does it, in dramatic slow motion, bows to Tommy and runs away in deference and fear. Tommy, meanwhile, is elevated above them all on a horse, juxtaposed against this backdrop of spectacularized racial otherness and made to signal whiteness in the process.

The first episode of season five relies on much the same visual vocabulary in depicting members of a rival Chinese crime organization. Three Peakies arrive in an apartment building to carry out an assassination of two Chinese gang members. This scene is also crowded, full of mystery and intrigue. The sheets hanging out to dry work to disorient the field of vision and suggest mysterious, unseen threats. Visual and sound cues are gendered explicitly female as we hear the wails of women and children and witness them cowering in corners. That the series relies on these deeply racist, well-worn and easily recognizable spectacles of otherness is not surprising considering their purpose. These characters, and the communities being depicted, exist solely for confirming for viewers that the Shelbys and the Peakies are white. The Chinese characters have no names, no storylines, no character development and in most cases, no recurring roles. They are simply spectacles.

MODELING STRATEGIC MULTICULTURALISM: FORGING ALLIANCES WITH ETHNIC OTHERS

This chapter focused on the Shelbys' relationships to and interactions with characters who are specifically marked as racial others. It is these relationships that stand in stark contrast to how Tommy and his family network with ethnic others, complicating the notion that the Peakies are simply weary of all "foreigners" and prejudiced against them. Instead, what this difference in attitude lays bare is that within the narrative world of *Peaky Blinders*, Tommy Shelby and his clan model for viewers. They demonstrate how to navigate race and ethnicity in an environment that is increasingly multicultural and multiracial and also, an environment wherein violent backlash against that racial and ethnic heterogeneity is swelling.

There is a consistent suggestion within the series. This message is racial others are peripheral players who exist as foils to an otherwise camouflaged whiteness while ethnic others are to be tolerated and groomed for strategic alliances. Consider, for example, Tommy Shelby's long-standing relationship with Alfie Solomons, the leader of the Jewish crime organization in London's Camden Town. Throughout the series, Alfie is positioned as an unreliable but formidable antagonist to Tommy. Over the course of five seasons, Alfie undermines and betrays Tommy several times, siding with the Peaky leader's enemies and deceiving him. One of these deceptions leads directly to the kidnapping of Tommy's young son and an assassination attempt on Tommy's life. Nevertheless, their friendship only deepens throughout the course of the series, becoming more meaningful, more meditative and revealing that the two men share a mutual respect and a vision of what is framed as "honor."

The Jewish gangster, then, despite being the object of repeated anti-Semitic slurs made and violently actualized by the Shelbys and other Peakys, remains a valuable ally for Tommy. His ethnic otherness is made visible, made unsavory and inferior through anti-Semitic depiction and language, and yet, redeemed by virtue of the suggestion that alliances must be forged in order to endure. Moreover, despite the fact that Alfie is often embroiled in schemes that threaten to derail Tommy, the character of Alfie Solomons is a fan favorite, as demonstrated by fan reactions across social media platforms when the character returned (from the dead) in season five.

The Italian crime organization, the Sabini family, enjoys a similar depiction in the series. Luca Changretta and Darby Sabini are repeatedly ostracized for their Italian heritage. While Tommy never develops friendships with any of the Italian crime bosses, he does view them as serious competition. Unlike the Chinese gangsters, the Italian gangsters are treated as a sophisticated enterprise, requiring analysis, strategizing and even alliance building as opposed to a simple, easy assassination. In the middle of Tommy's war with Luca Changretta, in fact, the two meet and decide the terms of their vendetta fight, "no civilians, no children . . . no police" (season four, episode two). There are similarities between the two men such as their commitments to kinship and "traditions of honor," as Changretta calls it. So, ethnic difference is not to be breached but critical resources for alliance building are to be harnessed.

Continuously, *Peaky Blinders* attributes the kind of value and narrative significance to ethnic others that characters who are racially marked never receive. Furthermore, the series itself dictates value in granting these characters significant storylines, personal histories, endowing them with complex motivations and a respected constellation of agendas. In his negotiations of war terms with Tommy, for example, Luca Changretta explains why he chose to speak with Tommy instead of killing him immediately. Changretta wanted Tommy to know why he was targeted and why the vendetta was activated in the first place, demonstrating how the series allows ethnic others to wield and express psychosocial motivations and positions them as subjects who have a right to complex interior lives. Like Alfie Solomons, both Luca Changretta and Darby Sabini are identified as ethnic others whose ethnic heritage makes them incompatible with Peaky Blinders membership. They are also identified, however, as necessary allies.

It is this stratified approach to racial and ethnic otherness that makes Tommy Shelby and the Peakys an attractive ally to Oswald Mosley, the virulently racist leader of the British Union of Fascists, in the fifth season of the series. Mosley too was not above wielding strategic alliances with ethnic others. Furthermore, Mosley is an aristocrat masquerading as a populist to stoke racial hatred and seize power using a Fascist political agenda. The agenda includes economic protectionism and nativism, an all-too-easy analog to contemporary leaders across the globe (Boris Johnson in Britain, Donald Trump in the United States, etc.). Furthermore, Tommy Shelby engages in a kind of management of otherness that makes him appealing to Mosley, and this provides contextualization of the immense popularity of the series.

HISTORY FOR LEASE: HELPING AUDIENCES EMBRACE LEGACIES OF WHITENESS

The popularity of the series and the contours of its fandom cannot be understood outside of the historical format that it embraces, and the ways in which the conjured history becomes utilitarian in the contemporary moment. The *Peaky* past is, in fact, the stuff of classic historical drama. The history of the real Peaky Blinders gang is stylized, spectacularized, and stretched beyond the moment of their actual temporal expiration. Within the series, historical events can be convenient backdrops, adding realistic ambiance and at other times events are explicit, critical plot points. In both cases, however, *Peaky Blinders* is not only dialoguing with history but rewriting it, and offering these edits for contemporary consumption; edits that are dangerous in their imagination around racial and ethnic identity.

It is the drama's historical work, and that work's function in the contemporary moment, that is at stake here. Paul Long argues that the series' "imaginative landscapes" dialogue with history, intervening in a dearth of historical, region-specific televisual representation of the British working classes. Leaning on Thompson's (1963) classic work, Long argues that this intervention offers a representationally significant "history from below" (p. 169). While significant in terms of representation, this "history from below" also sutures the work of populist history to a ruthless and transparent investment in whiteness as the working-man's only true Britishness. If *Peaky Blinders* captures early twentieth-century debates on populism, and if the very act of writing the series is politically interventionist gesturing to a kind of populism, then what audiences are enjoying is a reification of populism as an exercise in whiteness. The series' yoking of populism to whiteness is situated in history and is easily transferable to the contemporary moment. Brexit in the United Kingdom, Trumpism in the United States, the movement around

Jair Bolsonaro in Brazil, Viktor Orbán's Fidesz-driven politics in Hungary, and many others, have all made similar populist claims.

Larke-Walsh also makes note of the series' uses of its crucial historical dimension. For her, however, the Shelby family's Romani heritage is an important clue about their Englishness. Leaning on Houghton-Walker's explorations of representations of Romani communities during the romantic period (2014), she argues that this heritage "connects them to a romanticized and pure national identity pre-modernity and seemingly untainted by multicultural influences" (p. 50). In other words, not only do the Shelbys represent an allegiance to whiteness in the face of multiracial communities and multicultural ideologies, but they also reinscribe a historical teleology wherein Englishness is romantically rural, situated in the countryside, rather than in multiracial and multicultural urban environments.

Taken together, these historical meditations within the series afford contemporary racial nationalisms a historical legacy. This kind of history is not mired in necessary racist frames and colonial residue. It vindicates these contemporary politics by offering them a historical origin full of romantics, populist heroes, loyal men, and strong (suggestively, feminist) women. An examination of the series' fandom and the industry that this fandom has spawned demonstrates that it is precisely the series' historical nature that attracts fans.

FROM *PEAKY* STORIES TO CONTEMPORARY FANDOMS: EXPORTING HERITAGE AND WHITENESS

Among fans, the series' historical draw takes on different modalities, with the notion of "heritage" figuring prominently in the fandom discourse. Fans attending the inaugural "Legitimate Peaky Blinders Festival" in Digbeth, Birmingham, in September 2019 were mostly dressed in 1920s era attire, including flapper dresses, tailored three-piece suits with suspenders and the requisite peaky flat caps. The series is famous, in part, for its soundtrack, which is an anachronistic but no less haunting combination of contemporary indie-rock and punk, which the festival delivered in spades. The festival also featured ballet, screening experiences, and most pointedly, fans could experience run-ins with actors from an immersive theater group. These were hired to recreate the atmosphere of gritty, industrial 1920s Birmingham on festival streets. Reporting on the festival, Andy Welch interviewed a pair of fans, "attending in full Peaky get-up," who explained that "the local association is really important for [them]. . . . It feels like it's part of [their] heritage. [They] didn't know anything about that era before the series started" (Welch, 2019).

The retailer Kent & Curwen's collaboration with Garrison Tailors, for example, is branded as a heritage collection. Launched in 2016, Garrison Tailors, described as "the official Peaky Blinders menswear brand," rolled out a collaboration with the London-based Kent & Curwen at the 2019 Autumn/Winter Men's London Fashion. David Beckham, who is majority owner of Kent & Curwen and a fan of *Peaky Blinders*, has frequently mentioned that he, like other *Peaky* fans, prefers this style of dress. In fact, he picked up his first flat cap from his grandfather and has been wearing them ever since. Today, his famous son wears them as well. It is a personal note that Beckham, as a fan of the series, has repeated to journalists. It captures ways in which fans use the series to articulate both their own personal and collective historical legacies; to dress in those historical legacies, importing that sartorial affect and the ideologies it drags along into their contemporary realities.

The same can be said of Murdock London's 2019 *Peaky Blinders* barbershop experience. This offers fans the opportunity to get a *Peaky* haircut in an old-fashioned barbershop setting, helping fans discipline their bodies according to their imagined historical heritage. In fact, the barbershop chain offers "bespoke grooming kits and barbershop experiences for gentlemen, inspired by the iconic [*Peaky Blinders*] characters Thomas Shelby and Alfie Solomons." Quoting the series' oft-repeated declaration, the company's Instagram account proclaimed: "Murdock London is under new management. . . . By order of the Peaky Blinders."

Demonstrating how fans' desires to both connect personal histories to a shared heritage and then, to step inside that heritage are activated, encouraged, and sanitized through the series. The Black Country Living Museum in Dudley offers a *Peaky Blinders* souvenir collection through their gift shop. The museum itself is a living open-air museum, where 26 acres have been reconstructed to simulate life and work in the West Midlands of England (named the "Black Country") from the mid-1800s to the mid-1900s (roughly the period when this region was the nation's center of industrial manufacturing). Mark Sweney of *The Guardian* reports that *Peaky Blinders* is responsible for bringing record numbers of heritage tourists to Birmingham specifically and the West Midlands region more generally. The museum is "a staple filming location in all five series of *Peaky Blinders* to date," Sweney writes, "sells out themed evenings in less than 24 hours" (Sweney, 2019). Here, you can "explore over forty carefully reconstructed shops, houses and industrial areas that represent the Black Country's story. . . . Most importantly, you'll see history brought to life before your eyes" (BCLM, 2020).

In this way, the museum reminds us that the series functions as a kind of televisual pilgrimage. The series is a pilgrimage for fans seeking to capture and articulate their own regional and resolutely nationalist heritage. The heritage is one that is steeped in an allegiance to a white working-class identity that makes currency, accumulating wealth, out of the violently racist management of their diverse environment.

CONCLUSION

The historical drama *Peaky Blinders*, in teaching audiences how to navigate the realities of racial and ethnic difference, instructs them how to maintain racial homogeneity, while also enduring within a rapidly changing, diverse environment. It is a lesson that is remarkably and tragically applicable to the contemporary political era. The Peakies display a desire to hold fast to their Romani heritage, maintain their identity as an ethnic outsider while also benefiting from whiteness. They also wish to erect and maintain strict restrictions around who belongs and who does not, constituting a body of racist, retrograde politics. The fact these politics are made inextricable from the Peakies' brand of nationalism only sutures the series more closely to the contemporary moment, when nationalism is a frequent euphemism and flag for racist violence.

Then and now, to different degrees, these racist politics have to be waged within the context of societies that are more global and more racially diverse every day. For viewers looking to publicly invest in their whiteness and to build nationalistic, racially exclusive communities and modes of socialization, *Peaky Blinders* offers a stylized instructional manual, dressed in sex, guns, and noir. More than that, it offers these viewers a historical legacy that can function to sanitize and normalize these same practices of white supremacy and racial violence in the present.

REFERENCES

Bernstein, R. (2011). *Racial innocence: Performing American childhood from slavery to civil rights*. New York University Press.
Black Country Living Museum (2020). About Us: What we're all about. https://www.bclm.co.uk/about.htm#.Xm-15OhKjIU.
Brodkin, K. (1998). *How Jews became white folks and what that says about race in America*. Rutgers University Press.
Dika, V. (2000). The representation of ethnicity in *The Godfather*. In N. Browne (Ed.), *Francis Ford Coppola's The Godfather Trilogy* (pp. 76–108). Cambridge University Press.
Green, A. (2011) The anarchy of empire: Reimagining Birmingham's civic gospel. *Midland History, 36*(2), 163–179.
Hall, S. (1997). The spectacle of the 'other.' In S. Hall (Ed.), *Representation: Cultural representations and signifying Practices* (pp. 223–290). Sage.

Houghton-Walker, S. (2014). *Representations of the Gypsy in the Romantic Period.* Oxford University Press.

Hunt, C. J. (2006). The color of perspective: Affirmative action and the constitutional rhetoric of white innocence. *Michigan Journal of Race and Law, 11,* 477–555.

Jacobson, M. F. (1999). *Whiteness of a different color: European immigrants and the alchemy of race.* Harvard University Press.

Larke-Walsh, G. S. (2019). The King's shilling: How *Peaky Blinders* uses the experience of war to justify and celebrate toxic masculinity. *Journal of Popular Television, 7*(1), 39–56.

Long, P. (2017). Class, place, and history in the imaginative landscapes of *Peaky Blinders*. In D. Forrest & B. Johnson (Eds.), *Social class and television drama in contemporary Britain* (pp. 165–179). Palgrave Macmillan.

Myers, K. & Grosvenor, I. (2011). Birmingham stories: Local histories of migration and settlement and the practice of history. *Midland History, 36*(2), 149–162.

Richards, D. A. J. (1999). *Italian American: The racializing of an ethnic identity.* New York University Press.

Roediger, D. R. (2006). *Working towards whiteness: How America's immigrants became white.* Basic Books.

Ross, T. (1990). The rhetorical tapestry of race: White innocence and Black abstraction. *William and Mary Law Review, 32*(1), 1–40.

Sweney, M. (September 2, 2019). Peaky Blinders mania puts Birmingham on global 'screen tourism' map. *The Guardian.* https://www.theguardian.com/uk-news/2019/sep/02/peaky-blinders-mania-birmingham-screen-tourism-boom.

Wekker, G. (2016). *White innocence: Paradoxes of colonialism and race.* Duke University Press.

Welch, A. (September 15, 2019). Peaky Blinders fans fill Birmingham festival with flat caps. *The Guardian.* https://www.theguardian.com/tv-and-radio/2019/sep/15/peaky-blinders-fans-birmingham-legitimate-festival-with-flat-caps.

Chapter 19

Zero Tolerance

Genre and the Politics of Reconciliation in a South African Crime Show

Ian-Malcolm Rijsdijk

In the early 2000s, South African television viewers were presented with a host of crime shows. Paid subscriber and free-to-air channels, and the public broadcaster SABC (South African Broadcasting Corporation), all produced shows that appealed to different varieties of the police procedural: *Jozi Streets* (2004, e-TV), *Snitch* (2004, M-Net), *Interrogation Room* (2004, SABC) and *Zero Tolerance* (2003, SABC). *Zero Tolerance* offered production values and narrative complexity closely modeled on US television crime dramas such as NBC's *Homicide: Life on the Street* and HBO's *The Wire*. Indeed, David Simon and David Mills were creator and writer respectively on those two shows and acted as consultants on the series. The opening credits to *Zero Tolerance* echo the abstract score and grainy montage of the credits for *Homicide*.

Zero Tolerance ran for three thirteen-episode seasons on SABC2, a channel of the national broadcaster with an emphasis on representing the diversity of South Africa's eleven official languages (*Zero Tolerance* focused on English, Afrikaans, and Setswana). Set in Johannesburg, the show followed the cases of an elite investigative unit modeled on the Directorate of Special Operations (known colloquially as the Scorpions), which was established in 2001 and controversially disbanded in 2009. In the show, the Zero Tolerance unit comprises characters from a variety of criminological disciplines—law, forensics, information technology, police intelligence—and diverse races, genders, and sexualities representing the "rainbow nation" of South Africa's immediate post-1994 years.

This chapter proposes that *Zero Tolerance* advanced the SABC's project of nation-building while, at the same time, challenging several assumptions of the nation-building discourse. The show's characters and positive representation of police investigation reflected the desire for multiracial, multilingual, and South African role models on television, but the narrative arc of the first season and the narratives of several specific episodes demonstrated the fragility of this aspirational vision of a reconciled post-apartheid South Africa. The first season, which will be the focus of this chapter, captures the essential elements of *Zero Tolerance* through the establishment of the unit's identity, its characters, and the series structure, which balances season-long story arcs and single-episode investigations. In particular, the Scorpions' zealous investigation of corrupt politicians involved in South Africa's massive arms deal with European weapons' manufacturers (see Feinstein, 2007) is utilized explicitly as the basis for the first-season arc.

The analysis of *Zero Tolerance* will also consider the genre of the police procedural in relation to its South African context. How does the country's sociopolitical history affect the genre's conventions: detectives working in pairs, interpersonal and workplace tension, forensic investigation and interrogation, and the catharsis of solving cases? The chapter will show that *Zero Tolerance* foregrounds complexity over episodic open-and-shut cases, and that it positions its diverse characters as proxies to express political conflicts, grievances, and reconciliations. *Zero Tolerance* represents the increasing distance between rainbow nation affirmation through the discourse of nation-building and criticism of the government's failure to make good on its post-independence promises to improve the lives of the majority of South Africans.

SOUTH AFRICAN TELEVISION AND CRIME TELEVISION SERIES

Studies of South African television fiction shows are relatively scarce, compared to those of South African film in international scholarship, and there is limited analysis of crime shows as a television genre. Nonetheless, there is considerable research into television as a part of media policy, as well as the crucial role of news media in the period before and after the 1994 elections (Barnett, 1999; Evans, 2014).

Television was only established in South Africa in 1976, when more than 100 other countries already had television broadcast networks (Tomaselli et al., 1989, pp. 153–155). Ironically, television expanded the dissemination of news to the country in the year when the Soweto uprising galvanized the struggle against apartheid within South Africa and abroad. In the wake of the June 1976 protests, the apartheid government sought to obscure what was happening in the towns and cities around the country by presenting what news they did broadcast as "unrest" and criminality. At the same time, the adoption of the television medium sought to reassure the country's white citizens that they were not being excluded from cultural movements in the West. As such, television offered a window on the world, but also fantasy and nostalgia, as revolution raged beyond the garden walls of white suburbia.

Like the ideology of apartheid, South African television during the early 1980s emphasized the separation of cultures. Initially, the SABC hosted one channel, which alternated its programming between English and Afrikaans content. It provided news content that focused either on overseas narratives or on local stories that avoided references to the ongoing revolution in townships around the country. The "structured absence" (Krabill 2010, p. 66) of blacks from the white social and political discourse in South Africa was reflected in television that prioritized Afrikaans local dramas (*Nommer Asseblief*; *Ko-operasie Stories*), game shows (*Flinkdink*) and imported programming in English. The English-language programs were mostly US shows such as *CHiPs* (NBC), *Miami Vice* (NBC), and *Dallas* (CBS). These were sometimes dubbed by local Afrikaans voice actors. When J. R. Ewing was shot in a season finale of *Dallas*, the program made headlines in South African newspapers.

In the run-up to the 1994 general elections, the structure and functions of the SABC were subject to intense debate, particularly regarding the broadcaster's role in nation-building as part of the reconstruction and reconciliation process (Barnett, 1999, p. 287, p. 290). The move to multilingualism across both commercial and state broadcasters provided a boon for local content producers, though the SABC found itself on the horns of a dilemma. While it needed to promote local content in indigenous languages, it also needed to be financially secure enough to fund the commissioning and production of these shows (Teer-Tomaselli, 2001).

As a genre, crime shows, particularly the police procedural, posed specific problems within the post-apartheid context. While US crime dramas such as *NYPD Blue* (ABC) and *New York Undercover* (Fox) were popular on South African television, there was a noticeable lack of locally produced shows in the same genre. The first reason for this dearth of television crime drama was related to the real work of reconceiving public-order policing in the new South Africa. Decades of police violence and extra-judicial killing, sanctioned by apartheid's discriminatory laws, resulted in a country where resistance to authority was a liberation narrative. Police had to keep up to date with changes in crime patterns and new technologies associated with criminal enterprise and crime prevention, but there was also a need for fundamental change in the relationship between the police and publics. How could the new South African Police Services (SAPS) rebuild trust with communities in which they operated?

Reproducing the conventional procedural elements of tireless, professional, and self-sacrificing detectives investigating crimes irrespective of the race, class, or ethnicity of the victims and suspects was a hard sell, during a period where the horrors of the apartheid regime were being exposed by the Truth and Reconciliation Commission (TRC). As Mhlambi argues, "It is not productive to read the 'crime scene' in South Africa through the lens of a universal theoretical paradigm" (2010, p. 163).

The position of genre within the flow of television schedules was the second reason for the sensitivity toward police procedurals in the first decade after the 1994 elections. Mhlambi's statement above refers to *Yizo Yizo* (SABC1), the controversial and groundbreaking series that merged educational television with drama to represent the violent and traumatic lives of children in township schools (Modisane, 2013, pp. 159–174; Ballot, 2005). While crime played a central role in the show, its hybrid nature largely omitted the central elements of the crime procedural.

The TRC testimonies, combined with high levels of crime in the country, resulted in a continuous discourse of violence in the media. Commercial broadcasters and the SABC produced investigative journalism shows that represented the reality of South Africa's fragile new democracy. Popular soap operas such as *Isidingo* (SABC3) frequently featured crime subplots. Between the news, current affairs, and dramas, where could one schedule a crime procedural?

As rainbowism wore off, driven by increased public critique of the arms deal and the discussion of violent crime in the media, the disentangling of crime from apartheid's political oppression became reflected in fictional and nonfictional crime narratives. Crime novels, colloquially referred to as "krimi," and true crime writing exploded on the literary scene (Naidu, 2013; Guldimann, 2020). Television content producers were quick to capitalize on this trend. For example, while following a generic buddy-cop model, *Jozi Streets* exploited criminal profiler Micki Pistorius's literary history of serial killers in South Africa, *Strangers on the Street*, for many of its episodes.

ZERO TOLERANCE: FROM POLICING MANTRA TO TELEVISION DRAMA

The police drama, *Zero Tolerance*, was strongly influenced by investigative journalism. Indra De Lanerolle, one of the show's producers, had been a senior producer at the BBC on *Newsnight* and *Panorama*, and several of the show's writers were journalists. The show's title drew on ideological approaches to public policing in South Africa at the time, as well as the high-profile Scorpions unit and its anti-corruption operations.

The term "zero tolerance" as it relates to policing is widely regarded as emerging out of an approach to policing in New York in the late 1980s. It proposes that in order to fight crime, authorities should be as strict in addressing minor infractions of the law as they would major offences, for it is through the continued commission of seemingly minor infractions (jay-walking, littering, vandalism, drunken behavior) that citizens progress toward more serious crimes. Disorderly behavior and "quality of life" offences are viewed as the origin of community disorder. Confronted with a "crime wave," zero-tolerance policing, in theory, "creates a deterrent effect and dissuades those disposed to crime from committing those crimes, at least in the target areas" (Greene, 2014, p. 173).

Zero Tolerance is often viewed in association with the "broken windows" philosophy espoused by Wilson and Kelling (1982). They argued, "if a window in a building is broken and is left unrepaired, all the rest of the windows will soon be broken . . . one unrepaired broken window is a signal that no one cares." This situation could eventually bring about dilapidation, property abandonment, and criminal elements. In the larger context of a city or even nationwide policing, this requires a policy shift from crime prevention and the targeting of "major" crimes to public-order maintenance (Sridhar, 2006, p. 1842; Kelling & Bratton, 2015).

Critics of zero tolerance policing argue that it leads to the targeting of racial and ethnic minorities, mass incarceration, and, ultimately, "makes the disparity between rich and poor that much worse" (Howell, 2015, p. 1067). In the worst-case scenario, this undergirds a police force that is increasingly prone to acts of racial profiling, extra-legal harassment, manipulation of due process, and brutality (Sridhar, 2006). The result is the erosion of trust in the police force and an increasing distance between police authorities and citizens. Indeed, Wilson and Kelling (1982) argue in their original essay that "a strong and commendable desire to see that people are treated fairly makes us worry about allowing the police to rout persons who are undesirable by some vague or parochial standard" (p. 7).

Zero Tolerance: Narratives and Characters

Season one of *Zero Tolerance* attempted, with varying degrees of success, to complete a number of objectives. First, it offered a high-quality television crime drama for South African audiences that was indigenous, authentic, and topical. Many episodes dealt with contemporary issues in South African crime: child sexual abuse and murder, "muti" killings (muti refers to traditional medicine), illegal immigration (particularly from Zimbabwe), and gang violence. The show's writers were a combination of screen professionals and well-known journalistic authors, whose own backgrounds enriched particular episodes with rich detail.

The second objective of the show was to confront, in a complex narrative form, the large-scale corruption that was taking place under the auspices of successive post-democracy governments. *Zero Tolerance* appears in a transitional period between the rainbow nation era that characterized South Africa's first years after the 1994 elections, and the African Renaissance era under the leadership of Thabo Mbeki in the early 2000s. While the unit does investigate particular crimes in each episode, in the traditional police procedural form, the first-season arc deals explicitly with a proxy for the arms deal. This involved high-ranking politicians formerly in *uMkhonto we Sizwe* (the armed wing of the African National Congress during apartheid, colloquially referred to as MK). In *Zero Tolerance*, the former MK commander Gen. Righteous Molefe is found to be taking a bribe in the procurement of missiles through South African arms company Simba Eagle Corp.

The third element that marks out *Zero Tolerance* as particularly South African, and specific to that period, involves the ways in which nation-building discourses were embedded in the episodes. It is through the analysis of individual episodes that this becomes clearer.

Zero Tolerance opens with an armed heist at Johannesburg International Airport, during which a security guard is killed. The classic trope of the mismatched pair forced to work together emerges as young recruit Denzela Ledwaba (a black woman formerly with MK) is partnered with seasoned cop Sakkie Bezuidenhout (a white Afrikaans man who, during apartheid, was a member of the notorious Brixton Murder and Robbery Squad). The heist of copper statues masks a bigger issue: the smuggling of Tanzanite gems. The storyline includes US involvement, as two FBI agents (played unconvincingly by South African actors) are tracking the illicit gem trade as a funding source for Al Qaeda in the wake of the 9/11 attacks.

This narrative extends over the first three episodes and culminates in another conventional trope of the procedural genre: local cops fighting for arrests against outside interference. The Zero Tolerance cops arrest their man and charge him on South African soil before he can be extradited "on a waiting plane" by the Americans. This satisfies the embedded liberal critique of US policy of "extraordinary rendition" that saw suspects taken to countries with poor human rights oversight, where they were interrogated at so-called black sites.

On the domestic front, Denzela's marriage to Thabo, a businessman and former MK cadre, is in trouble after she hears of his infidelity and he complains about the danger of her job. The long arc of the corrupt missile deal begins but in minor scenes, and Gen. Righteous Molefe's avuncular role in the Ledwaba family is established. Crucially, a new character is introduced, the charming Vuyo Khumalo. Episodes four through seven deal with specific crimes extracted from the newspapers at the time: prison gangs, farm murders, muti killings, and child sexual abuse and murder. In the following section, the chapter will look specifically at the sociopolitical contexts of these episodes and how they relate to a broader nation-building discourse. Running in parallel to these cases is the Ledwabas's ongoing marital strife and its effect on their young son, Siso, and the growing scale of the corrupt missile deal.

Episode eight is a strange stand-alone episode that explicitly engages with reconciliation in contrast to the previous four episodes. When bones are uncovered during an archaeological dig, the case revolves around confirming to whom they belong: an MK cadre imprisoned under apartheid or a Boer soldier. The effect of the episode is to break the rhythm of the procedural that *Zero Tolerance* had attained after its three-episode pilot and four cases.

Episodes nine and ten deal completely with the missile deal as a former cadre is found murdered after an apparent carjacking, before Denzela herself becomes the target of the forces behind the deal. This leads to Denzela's temporary suspension from the unit for episode eleven, which, somewhat incongruously, reverts to the single-case, single-episode approach.

The final two episodes of season one deal exclusively with the missile deal and its effect on the Zero Tolerance unit. Vuyo goes undercover in jail to find out who murdered a witness to Righteous Molefe's crimes. Vuyo himself is stabbed. In the hospital, more attempts are made on his life, as gangsters linked to Molefe threaten Denzela and her family. Finally realizing the true nature of his former hero, Thabo quits the company involved in the missile deal. "I assure you, everything I know will die with me," he says as he walks out, foreshadowing his death in the episode finale, as the Zero Tolerance building is sprayed with gunfire.

This overview of the season reveals how *Zero Tolerance* follows certain conventions of the police procedural. This includes the tight-knit unit containing various racial and gender tensions, and the opening episodes introducing both the unit's investigative orientation and its characters. The structure of the first season is less conventional as the show switches between single episodes and the ongoing storyline that taps into the political zeitgeist and ultimately dominates the narrative arc. Three specific episodes are examined below.

Digging Up Bones

Episode eight merges the cold case model with a political narrative, based on South Africa's apartheid past and the political and psychological fallout from the TRC. It focalizes the grand scale of South Africa's colonial and apartheid history through the lens of the crime procedural and its everyday concerns. Naidu writes, "Like the Cold War thrillers, South African crime fiction constantly excavates the past. Characters, plots, even crimes have their origin in the struggle era" (2013, p. 129).

When archaeologists uncover human bones during the renovation of a building known as the Old Fort, Thabo Ledwaba is convinced that they belong to fellow MK fighter and cellmate Moss Motau, who disappeared while in custody in 1986 and was never seen again. The forensic specialist, however, uncovers evidence that the victim died long before Motau was even born. Furthermore, some old buttons are found with the body. Sakkie, who in a previous episode is pointedly seen reading *Die Boere Oorlog*, Thomas Pakenham's history of the South African War, recognizes the buttons as belonging to a Boer fighter identified as Veldsman Wolfaardt. There is an exchange between Sakkie and Hannelie:

Sakkie: Veldsman Wolfaardt and Moss Motau. Both imprisoned at the same place. Both disappeared without a trace. Why? The struggle for freedom.
Hannelie: Asseblief, Sakkie. This whole boere-darkie-come-together-over-our-shared-struggle-for-freedom makes me sick. *Wat se* freedom did we lose in 1910?
Sakkie: You see what happens when you send our young people to Wits University?

This dialogue simultaneously recognizes the role of English colonialism in modern South Africa's racist formation and challenges the notion of white Afrikaners' "liberation" from colonial rule. The post-apartheid struggle over Afrikaner identity plays out as the young, gay Afrikaner woman, educated at an English-language university, pushes back against the older, working-class man. Holtmann describes Hannelie as "a character who signifies all that is new and positive about the new discourse as a happy, young, homosexual woman, freed from a history of deep oppression of this subjectivity" (2007, p. 26). Sakkie, an Afrikaner seeking reconciliation with black struggle history against a common English foe, critiques the historical revisionism taking place in the country.

Vuyo later dismisses Sakkie as an untransformed racist, after Sakkie refuses to arrest former security-branch colleagues, now in hiding, whom he contacts to find out what really happened to Moss Motau: "You should have gone years ago with all your kind," rages Vuyo, at which point Sakkie performs the crime show convention of handing in his gun and badge. The episode ends with Motau's family, accompanied by Thabo, Denzela, and Vuyo, laying a wreath on the dam where his remains were disposed of. Sakkie keeps his distance, then joins the gathering in the final shot.

This episode makes explicit the tension between the "one nation" and "many cultures" of the rainbow nation. Sakkie represents the problematic past of the South African police. His ability to extract the information regarding Moss Motau's death raises a question for his black colleagues: how committed is he to the transformation of South African society? The details of Motau's murder refer to various pieces of evidence given during the TRC by former policemen confessing to the murder of ANC activists. The cold case device, and the literal layering of South African history through the archaeological discovery, provides a striking but unsubtle allegory for South Africa's complex colonial history.

Farm Fables and Muti Murders

Two earlier episodes provide a more complex approach to the clash of cultures, race, and class, revealing that *Zero Tolerance* was doing far more than just mirroring the intrigues of the state. In episode five, "Farm Fables" (written by Jonny Steinberg), police in the small town of Lichtenburg investigate a brutal attack on a farmer and his wife. The title "Farm Fables" tackles head-on the heated issue of farm murders and claims of a so-called genocide of white South African farmers (see *Human Rights Watch*, 2001). The subject of farm murders (which continues to activate animosity to this day) has galvanized right-wing and neo-fascist groups around Afrikaner identity, self-determination, and land rights. Meanwhile, the ANC-led government has pushed for land reform (currently, land expropriation without compensation).

In the post-apartheid period, the descendants of people who were forced off the land after the infamous 1913 Natives Land Act—which began the formalized process of land dispossession for black South Africans—had the chance to lodge a claim for the return of that land. Though this law applied to land in rural and urban areas, access to agricultural land was at the heart of this land dispossession process. Steinberg's book *Midlands* (2002) is an investigation into one such farm murder in KwaZulu-Natal. The "Farm Fables" episode follows his approach of uncovering the complex political and social history behind a single act, recognizing the fact of the murder but questioning the sensationalism surrounding farm murders. The fable of farm murders immediately contests the narrative of white farmer genocide.

When Denzela and Sakkie are put onto the case by their boss, Enoch Molope, they question his decision.

Sakkie: We don't do murder cases.
Enoch: You are doing this one.
Sakkie: Why?
Enoch: What's your problem, Sakkie? Have you never done a murder case before?

Sakkie: I've never done one that belongs to a murder and robbery squad before.
. . .

Enoch: Our turf has always been somebody else's turf. We're Zero Tolerance. We're supposed to piss people off.

Denzela: So why are we doing it?

Enoch: Because [Detective] Visser has not solved his last three murder cases. And when farm murders are not solved, the farmers' lobby goes berserk.

Sakkie's questions lead the audience through the logical query: why would a specialized task team dedicated to corruption investigate a murder in a remote area under the jurisdiction of another investigative unit? Enoch frames the murder as a symptom of a wider threat to national unity: that farm murders will increase the possibility of retaliation and violent racial conflict. His evasive answers reiterate the unit's approach to crime investigation without fear of favor, but also aim to distract the audience from the truth that the episode is another case-as-allegory for contemporary South Africa.

This is a complex case. The black suspect, who is also a community leader fighting for land restitution, is a tenant of the white farmer who was attacked. Rather than simple revenge for past oppression, the murder is contextualized by the land-claims process. Significantly, the farmer is framed in sympathetic terms: the farmer, his wife, and the alleged killer are all members of a community struggling to deal with the weight of its history. While it appears as if the case has to do with land claims, a white private security guard, Gous, complicates matters. He represents the farm commandos, small units of predominantly white men, many with military training, who patrol farms at night. In 2003, the government described the farm commandos as vigilantes and disbanded them against the wishes of commercial farmers' organizations (*Mail & Guardian*, 2003).

Gous is very much the vigilante figure referred to here, operating in a remote area while the police (white former security-branch officers) turn a blind eye. Indeed, Sakkie's own familiarity with the local detectives troubles Denzela, sustaining the minor narrative of the unit's trust in Sakkie's commitment to transformation of the criminal justice system. The episode ends inconclusively: the apparent killer is found dead himself, so while the case of the farm murder is closed, another remains open, and is unlikely to be solved.

Episode six, "Muti Murder Central," also tackles a sensitive topic. When body parts are found in a fridge in a Johannesburg tenement, the evidence points toward muti murder. Many cases in South Africa have been reported from the North West province, and this is where the case takes Denzela and Vuyo.

Sakkie offers to go in order to provide an "outside" perspective on African culture, thereby presuming that Denzela will be unable to properly investigate the case. Enoch's retort, "We tried that, and it was called apartheid," exaggerates the cultural volatility of the situation, but does continue the debate around identity and belonging in South Africa that runs through "Farm Fables." Sakkie, raised on a farm by black caregivers, claims to be more at home in the rural areas of the country than urbanite Denzela, who, for her part, makes it clear that "witchcraft is not my thing." Enoch sends Vuyo along with Denzela, while Sakkie starts his own undercover investigation in Johannesburg, where the human remains were found.

Denzela and Vuyo interrogate a man previously accused of murdering his own daughter, and this leads them into a series of exchanges with a local "sangoma," a likely suspect in the current case. In a scene that recalls the South African film *Dingaka*, the sangoma says, "up in the mountains there is a man who can tell you about witches." This separates the almost supernatural, mystic healer living timelessly in the wilderness from the daily issues of poverty, illness, and unemployment in the urban periphery of South African cities.

At this point, the episode sets up a series of expected conundrums for the audience: How can we sympathize with a man who murders his own child? How does our trust in or dismissal of traditional medicine lead us to see the sangoma's culpability? And what is the role of traditional practices in modern urban society? This last question arises when the sangoma responds to Denzela's procedural inquiries about the case: "Where are your ancestors buried?" Denzela deflects the question, but upon her return to Johannesburg, her connections to her ancestors, her African roots, become an abiding concern for the rest of the season.

When the man accused of murdering his child is himself murdered by residents of the town, suspicion turns again to the sangoma. Ultimately, the killer turns out not to be a sangoma, but a young black doctor from a local hospital. For extra income, the doctor harvests body parts from the morgue and sells them to a contact in Johannesburg (whom Sakkie uncovers in his own investigation).

This conclusion performs a number of tasks. It allows for both Sakkie and Enoch to be right about the decision not to send Sakkie on the investigation. It offers a "victimless" crime in that the body parts belong to the already deceased, and it offers an examination of muti murders that does not stigmatize traditional healers. Rather, it puts the blame at the door of capitalism: the economy is struggling, and people will do anything for a change in their fortunes. The real problem of muti murders is also addressed through the punishment of the man who murdered his daughter—though, once again, his death remains unsolved.

One of the features of the US police drama, *Homicide: Life on the Street*, is that many cases often do not close. The easy determination of guilt that characterizes more conventional procedurals is often absent in this US television series, and though audiences may know who is guilty, they are left to grapple with the moral dilemmas and agonizing injustices at the conclusion of episodes and seasonal arcs.

Zero Tolerance is aiming for something similar. "Digging up Bones" offers a dramatic act of symbolic reconciliation in a narrative. It is free of the crimes of the present but haunted by the traumas of the past. The open-endedness of "Farm Fables" and "Muti Murder Central," however, leaves audiences to consider the complexity of crime and society in South Africa, and the ways in which history and culture act on the events of the present.

CONCLUSION

Kruger (2010) argued, "While South African content quotas remain in place ... programming in the second decade of the officially 'democratic' dispensation resembles more closely the aspirational and consumerist hue of advertising directed at the upwardly mobile than the narratives of national democratic transformation" (p. 82). After its restructuring in 1996, the SABC was holding together a number of contradictory elements: (1) how to be profitable and make content easily available to the country's diverse classes and cultures; and (2) how to be independent yet respond to the government's rhetoric of national reconciliation. In short, how to "imagine 'us' as 'one' as part of the process of nation-building" (Barker, 1999, p. 5).

Zero Tolerance is at the nexus of several of these tensions. A locally made, high production-value show that represents a diversity of race, culture, language, gender, and sexuality, it appears to satisfy many of the basic aims of the SABC. As a criminal procedural show, it represents the complexity of South Africa's nationhood in a dramatic context. While the specter of apartheid stalks the narrative of *Zero Tolerance*, the crimes and the resulting investigations lay bare the uncomfortable discussions around culture, history, and political ideology in the new democratic South Africa.

REFERENCES

Ballot, J. (2005). (Re)defining television genres: Classic narrative and edutainment in *Yizo Yizo 2*. In J. van Eeden & A. du Preez (Eds.), *South African visual culture* (pp. 242–260). Van Schaik Publishers.

Barker, C. (1999). *Television, globalization and cultural identities*. Open University Press.

Barnett, C. (1999). Broadcasting the rainbow nation: Media, democracy, and nation building in South Africa. *Antipode, 31*(3), 274–303.

De Lanerolle, I., Blecher, H., & Blecher, S. (Executive producers) (2003–2006) *Zero Tolerance* [Television series]. Ochre Pictures, SABC.

Evans, M. (2014). *Broadcasting the end of apartheid: Live television and the birth of a new South Africa*. I.B. Tauris.

Feinstein, A. (2007). *After the party: A personal and political journey inside the ANC*. Jonathan Ball.

Greene, J. R. (2014). Zero tolerance and policing. In M.D. Reisig & R.J. Kane (Eds.), *Oxford handbook of police and policing* (pp. 172–196). Oxford University Press.

Guldimann, C. (2020) A New Beginning for Good People: National identity and the new South Africa in Deon Meyer's crime fiction. In J. H. Kim (Ed.), *Crime fiction and national identities in the global age* (pp. 115–137). McFarland.

Holtmann, E. (2007). *Zero Tolerance and its women: Representations of self and nation* [Unpublished master's thesis]. University of Cape Town.

Howell, K. B. (2016). The costs of broken windows policing: Twenty years and counting. *Cardozo Law Review*, *37*(3), 1059–1074.

Human Rights Watch (2001). Farm attacks: Violent crime against farm owners. Available at: https://www.hrw.org/reports/2001/safrica2/Safarms7.htm.

Kelling, G. L. & Bratton, W. (2015). Why we need broken windows policing. *City Journal* (Winter). https://www.city-journal.org/html/why-we-need-broken-windows-policing-13696.html.

Krabill, R. (2010). *Starring Mandela and Cosby: Media and the end(s) of apartheid*. University of Chicago Press.

Kruger, L. (2010). Critique by stealth: Aspiration, consumption and class in post-apartheid television drama. *Critical Arts*, *24*(1), 75–98.

Mail & Guardian (2003). Dying days of SA's farm commando units. https://mg.co.za/article/2003-04-03-dying-days-of-sas-farm commando-units/.

Mhlambi, I. J. (2010). "It is not crime in the way you see it": Crime discourses and outlaw culture in *Yizo Yizo*. *Current Writing*, *22*(2), 152–165.

Modisane, L. (2013). *South Africa's renegade reels: The making and public lives of black-centered films*. Palgrave Macmillan.

Naidu, S. (2013). Crime fiction, South Africa: A critical introduction. *Current Writing*, *25*(2), 124–135.

Pistorius, M. (2002). *Strangers on the street. Serial homicide in South Africa*. Penguin.

Sridhar, C. R. (2006). Broken windows and zero tolerance: Policing urban crimes. *Economic and Political Weekly*, *41*(19), 1841–1843.

Steinberg, J. (2002). *Midlands*. Jonathan Ball.

Teer-Tomaselli, R. (2001). Nation building, social identity and television in a changing media landscape. In R. Kriger & A. Zegeye (Eds.), *Culture in the new South Africa* (pp. 117–138). Kwela Books.

Tomaselli, K., Hayman, G., Jack, A., Nxumalo, N., Tomaselli, R. & Ngcobo, N. (1989). Square vision in colour: How TV2/3 negotiates consent. In R. Tomaselli, K. Tomaselli, & J. Muller (Eds.), *Currents of power: State broadcasting in South Africa* (pp. 153–176). Anthropos Publishers.

Wilson, J. Q., & Kelling, G. L. (1982, March). Broken windows: the police and neighborhood safety. *The Atlantic*. https://www.theatlantic.com/magazine/archive/1982/03/broken-windows/304465/.

Chapter 20

Doctor(ed) Representations

Physician Portrayals on Medical Television Shows

David Lynn Painter, Sarah Parsloe, and Hannah Jureller

As television diffused through US society in the mid-twentieth century, programming genres adapted from literature, film, and the radio became familiar formats to viewers. For instance, *City Hospital* (1951–1953), the first television medical show, originated on the radio, and *Dr. Kildare* (1961–1966) were based on books, movies, and radio shows about the same title character. The popularity of these shows, along with *Ben Casey* (1961–1966), established medical dramas as a television programming staple (Turow, 1996). Indeed, dozens of medical dramas have captivated audiences over the past seven decades, earning critical acclaim and some of the highest ratings in television history (CTVA, 2012).

While Anne Burr starred as Dr. Kate Morrow in *City Hospital*, women and other minority groups have historically been underrepresented not only as doctors but also as leading characters in positions of power on television (Sink & Mastro, 2016; Mastro & Robinson, 2000). In particular, research indicates that televised medical dramas throughout the 1970s portrayed doctors almost exclusively as highly principled white men who were compassionate, appealing, and effective interpersonal communicators (Gerbner, Gross, Morgan, & Signorielli, 1981; Gerbner, Morgan, & Signorielli, 1982; Kalsich & Kalsich, 1984). In line with these portrayals, television viewers perceived that doctors were highly intelligent, ethical, benevolent, and personable white men (Pfau, Mullen, & Garrow, 1995). As medical television programming evolved, however, physician portrayals became less homogenous and positive (Chory-Assad & Tamborini, 2003).

Concerns over physician portrayals have animated much of the research on medical television program content (Mastro & Greenberg, 2000; Pfau, Mullen, & Garrow, 1995). Applying cultivation theory, which explains that watching television "cultivates" viewers' perceptions of reality, Bandura (1986) argued that television doctor portrayals influence viewers' perceptions, attitudes, and behaviors related to the medical world. Further, cultivation research suggests that different television programming genres may exert distinct effects on viewers (Bilandzic & Busselle, 2008; Cohen & Weimann, 2000; Morgan & Shanahan, 2010).

Using cultivation theory as our guiding framework, we conducted a quantitative content analysis of television doctors' portrayals on the most-watched contemporary medical television comedies and dramas. First, we analyzed the television doctors' portrayals on medical comedies and dramas to determine how accurately they represent the distribution of practicing US doctors' genders, ethnicities, and nationalities. Next, we examined the doctors' professional behaviors because these shows are used as training materials in medical programs; they may influence both doctors' and patients' perceptions and expectations (Bandura, 2009; Hirt, Wong, Erichsen, & White, 2013; Hoffman et al., 2018). Finally, we analyzed the television doctors' patient-centered communication practices, recognizing that these practices are critical determinants of high-quality medical care (Duggan & Thompson, 2011; Roter & Hall, 2011).

THEORETICAL FRAMEWORK

Most medical television content analyses have used cultivation theory to guide their investigations because these programs may influence viewers' knowledge about, attitudes toward, and behaviors related to health and medicine, even when they are designed to entertain (Brodie et al., 2001; Morgan, Movius, & Cody, 2009; Ye & Ward, 2010). Indeed, the elegance of cultivation theory's central proposition, that heavy television viewers are more likely to perceive that the television world accurately reflects the real world compared to otherwise similar but lighter television viewers, has generated thousands of studies in dozens of countries (Shanahan, Shanahan, James, & Morgan, 1999). Moreover, cultivation theory's focus on the effects of television viewing makes it a valuable guide for selecting the aspects of medical television programming to analyze, such as the portrayals of the television doctors' demographic characteristics, professional behaviors, and patient-centered communication practices. However, cultivation theory is not a particularly compelling theoretical framework for analyzing programming content or comparing television portrayals across genres. Thus, in addition to using cultivation theory as the basis for our analysis of television physician portrayals, we also used genre theory to explain why we expected to find differences across medical comedies and dramas.

Television Genre Theory

Adapted from literature and film studies, television genre theory explains that different programming types use different production, format, and content elements to elicit different expectations, uses, and gratifications from viewers (Lichter, Lichter, & Rothman, 1991). For example, the plots, pacing, and dialogue in television comedies are much different from those in dramas, which may make one type of programming more appealing than another to specific groups of viewers. This uses and gratifications adaptation of cultivation theory suggests that television viewers actively decide what to watch based on their expectations from specific types of shows and their needs or inclinations at that time (Abercrombie, 1996). Thus, some viewers may decide to watch medical dramas while others may prefer medical comedies, depending upon their particular needs, moods, and preferences. While some genre classifications focus on the show's subject, such as legal and medical programming, others focus on the type of entertainment format, such as comedy and drama, to define their categories. For the purposes of this study, we selected medical television shows as the content genre and then compared physician portrayals across the comedy and drama subgenres.

Medical Comedies. We conceptualize medical comedies as a subgenre of medical television programming in which the programs use 30-minute, episodic television narratives featuring recurring characters sharing humorous dialogue and dramatic situations in a medical facility. The development and popularity of medical comedies began with *MASH* (1972–1983), which depicted the doctors' flaws and idiosyncrasies in ways never before seen on television (Tapper, 2010). *MASH* also merged the comedy and drama genres into its storylines about medical professionals and support personnel stationed at the 4077 Mobile Army Surgical Hospital during the Korean War. Over its 11-year run, *MASH* was one of the top 10 highest-rated shows for 9 years, and it was nominated for more than 100 Emmy Awards, winning 14 in the television comedy category (Andrews, 2018; ATAS, n.d.-a). More recently, medical comedies such as *Scrubs* (2001–2010) and *Nurse Jackie* (2009–2015) have also received critical and popular acclaim.

Scrubs (2001–2010) was a madcap, slapstick medical comedy set in an urban hospital that has been described as the most realistic television depiction of interns and residents (Weiss, 2009). *Scrubs* was also the most-watched medical comedy since *MASH* and was nominated for 17 Emmy awards, winning two over its 10-year-run (ATAS, n.d.-b; Brooks & Marsh, 2007). Similarly,

Nurse Jackie centered on the medical personnel at a fictional urban hospital and was one of the most-watched *Showtime* television productions in history, receiving 16 Emmy nominations and winning 5 over its 6-year run (ATAS, n.d.-c; Maul, 2009). We selected *Nurse Jackie* and *Scrubs* as the most appropriate programs to sample in the medical comedy subgenre following (1) the Academy of Television Arts & Sciences' classification and (2) because they are produced in the 30-minute, episodic, situation-comedy format. Moreover, *Scrubs* and *Nurse Jackie* are the highest-rated, most critically acclaimed contemporary medical comedies, and are both used in medical training programs (Hirt, Wong, Erichsen, & White, 2013; Hoffman et al., 2018).

Medical Dramas. We conceptualize medical dramas as a subgenre of medical television programming in which the 60-minute narratives are set in a medical facility and the plotlines are driven by the emotionally charged situations and interactions in the lives of medical professionals. Although *MASH* was classified as a medical comedy, its use of dark humor in poignant situations—as well as its depictions of irreverent, substance-abusing, and authority-flaunting doctors—was also adopted in subsequently successful medical dramas. For instance, *House* (2004–2012), which focused on a fundamentally flawed but genius doctor at a fictional New Jersey hospital, was nominated for 25 Emmy Awards, won five, and is one of the most-watched fictional television shows in history (AFP, 2009; ATAS, n.d.c.).

While medical dramas have historically been populated by white male doctors, producer Shonda Rhimes wanted *Grey's Anatomy* (2005–present) to focus on "smart women competing against one another" (Rhodes, 2005, para. 9), and she used color-blind casting to depict doctors across a wide range of ethnicities (Warner, 2015). Since its inception, *Grey's Anatomy* has become the longest-running and most-watched medical drama in television history, nominated for 39 Emmy Awards and winning five over its historic run. Research indicates that *Grey's Anatomy* has been influential in shaping viewers' perceptions of doctors and popular culture at large (Quick, 2009). Therefore, *House* and *Grey's Anatomy* were sampled as representative of medical television dramas due to their (1) critical and popular acclaim and (2) because they are used as training materials for medical professionals (Hirt, Wong, Erichsen, & White, 2013; Hoffman et al., 2018).

RESEARCH QUESTIONS

Based on this discussion of the medical television comedy and drama subgenres, differences in production techniques, plots, characters, dialogue, and behaviors might lead researchers to expect differences in physician portrayals. Few researchers have compared content across subgenres (but see Jain &

Slater, 2013), and we were unable to locate any quantitative analyses of medical comedies. Thus, the purpose of this study is to analyze the most-watched, contemporary medical television comedies and dramas set in urban hospitals to describe the physicians' portrayals, professional behaviors, and patient-centered communication practices both across subgenres and in the aggregate.

Prior research on the content of medical television shows has included concerns over the doctor's gendered and racialized portrayals (Mastro & Greenberg, 2000; Pfau, Mullen, & Garrow, 1995). For example, Jain and Slater (2013) found that medical dramas and reality shows portrayed physicians' demographic characteristics differently, but that in the aggregate, they accurately represented the distribution of men, women, white, and Hispanic US doctors. However, their results also suggested that black doctors were overrepresented, while Asian and international doctors were underrepresented (Jain & Slater, 2013). Nevertheless, this study, and others like it, analyzed medical television shows by episode. In this investigation, on the other hand, we sought to account for the frequency of the television doctors' appearances in each scene of each sampled episode. Further, prior research has not explored physician portrayals in medical comedies. Thus, our first research question asks:

> RQ1: How are television doctors' demographic characteristics portrayed in medical comedies and dramas?

We also wanted to explore how accurately the television doctor's genders and ethnicities represented the distribution of practicing US physicians' identities. These comparisons may be informative, because both over- and underrepresentations of demographic groups have cultivation effect implications. Specifically, overrepresentation could lead viewers to believe that there are no disparities in television physician portrayals and reality, which could negatively influence their attitudes toward efforts to address equity and diversity in the medical world (Gates, 1992; Lewis & Jhally, 1992). Alternatively, underrepresentation could lead viewers to believe that individuals with particular gender, racial, or ethnic identities do not typically become doctors, or that they do not belong in medical professions (Gerbner, Gross, Morgan, & Signorielli, 1981; Gerbner, Morgan, & Signorielli, 1982). Thus, we asked:

> RQ2: How do the doctors' demographic characteristics portrayed in medical comedies and dramas compare to the actual demographic characteristics of US physicians?

Prior research has also analyzed television doctors' professional behaviors, recognizing that these portrayals may influence viewers' expectations regarding real-world provider interactions (Bandura, 1986; 2009). Additionally, since the medical television shows sampled in this study are used as educational tools in medical training programs, they could also influence the practitioners' perceptions about acceptable behaviors (Hirt, Wong, Erichsen, & White, 2013; Hoffman et al., 2018). Further, scholars have expressed concerns over the misleading, stereotypical, and degrading portrayals of women and minorities on television (Collins, 2011; Mastro & Greenburg, 2000)—racism and sexism that might persist in today's medical television programming. Thus, we aimed to explore how television physicians' behaviors might vary in relation to their gender and ethnic identities. Therefore, we asked:

RQ3: How are physicians' professional behaviors portrayed, based on their gender and ethnicity?

In addition to exploring television physician portrayals and professional behaviors, we also wanted to analyze how medical shows depicted patient-centered communication. These practices are defined as communication that is respectful; responsive to patient needs and preferences; acknowledges patient personhood; allows the patient to act in partnership with doctors to make medical decisions; embraces emotion and conveys empathy, reassurance, and positive rapport; and enables patients to express their doubts and concerns (Duggan & Thompson, 2011; Roter & Hall, 2011). This line of research also indicates that patient-centered communication is a powerful predictor of compliance with medical advice and other positive health outcomes.

When examining the depiction of physician patient-centered communications, we specifically wanted to compare the use of these practices across the television doctors' ethnic and gender identities because of the previously noted criticisms of minority character portrayals on television. Although research indicates women doctors practice more patient-centered communication than do men doctors in the United States (Bertakis, 2009), Jain and Slater's (2013) analysis indicated there were no gender differences in medical drama and reality show doctors' use of patient-centered communications. When comparing the use of patient-centered communication practices among white and minority doctors, however, they found that minority doctors were more courteous and made more eye contact than did white doctors (Jain & Slater, 2013). Since this study failed to include comedies in the analysis, we asked:

RQ4: How do television doctors of different genders and ethnicities use patient-centered communication practices?

METHOD

Sample

To sample episodes from shows that aired as close to the same time as possible, we specified seasons 1, 2, and 3 of *Nurse Jackie* (2009–2011); seasons 5, 6, and 7 of *House* (2009–2011); seasons 6, 7, and 8 of *Grey's Anatomy* (2009–2011); and seasons 6, 7, and 8 of *Scrubs* (2006–2009). Then, to ensure the equivalency of show time coded (24 hours of programming per show), we randomly selected 48 episodes of *Nurse Jackie* (67% of total shows during sampling period), 48 episodes of *Scrubs* (46% of total shows during sampling period), and 24 episodes of *Grey's Anatomy* and *House* (34% of total shows each during sampling period).

Unit of Analysis and Categories

We coded each scene in each sampled episode for physician portrayals, professional behaviors, and doctor-patient communication. While most prior research used each episode as a unit of analysis (e.g., Jain & Slater, 2013), this investigation accounted for the frequency of each television doctor's demographic characteristics in each scene because an appearance in an episode may not accurately account for the number of scenes within that episode the characters appeared (MacDonald, 1983). In each scene, we coded the physician portrayals by recording the number of doctors, their genders, ethnicities, and nationalities. Finally, we coded physicians as international if they were explicitly portrayed as such and/or if they had a non-North American accent; or as a US doctor if they had a US accent and did not identify as international.

Next, we coded each scene for the presence or absence of four physician professional behaviors adapted from Stanek et al. (2015): unprofessionalism, work-life balance, patient dehumanization, and communication with a patient. If the scene depicted doctor-patient communication, we coded the doctors' demographic characteristics and the presence or absence of 12 specific elements in the interaction (see Jain & Slater, 2013) that are listed in table 20.2.

Inter-coder Reliability

Two trained and independent coders double-coded 20% of the total sample. Inter-coder reliability was determined using Krippendorf's alpha and Cronbach's alpha. The reliabilities ranged from 0.88 to 1.0, with an average alpha score of 0.93, suggesting the results were reliable.

Table 20.1 Doctors' Demographics in the United States, by Subgenre and Total (in Percentages)

Demographics	U Census (N=?????) %	Comedies (n = 1731) % (M) 95% CI	Dramas (n = 1846) % (M) 95% CI	Comedies & Dramas (n = 3577) % (M) 95% CI	F	p
Men	63	63 61, 64	61 59, 63	62 60, 63	2.96	.09
Women	37	37 36, 39	39 37, 40	38 37, 39	2.71	.10
White	70*	85 83, 86	74 73, 76	79 78, 80[e]	113.77	<.001
Black	4*	14 13, 15	15 14, 16	14 13, 15[e]	2.93	.09
Hispanic	5*	0 0, 0	3 3, 4	2 1, 3	128.33	<.001
Asian[a]	21*	1 1, 3	7 6, 8	4 3, 5	153.20	<.001
US	74*	87 86, 89	97 97, 98	92[d] 91, 93[e]	174.01	<.001
International	26*	13 11, 14	2 2, 3	8[d] 7, 9[e]	174.01	<.001

*US Census statistic significantly different than medical comedies, dramas, and total statistics

RESULTS

The first two research questions inquired about portrayals of television doctors' ethnicities and genders on medical comedies and dramas as well as about how those portrayals compared to US doctor demographics. Since preliminary analysis indicated there were significant differences in the number of doctors appearing in the shows, $F(3, 3664) = 167.71, p < 0.01$, we divided the number of doctors in each demographic trait by the total number of doctors in each scene. Next, the differences in mean scores in each demographic category by medical television show subgenre (comedy and drama) were analyzed using a multivariate analysis of variance test.

Specifically, RQ1 inquired about the portrayals of the television doctors' ethnicities and genders in medical comedies and dramas. To answer this question, we referenced the results of the MANOVA [$F(1, 3592) = 59.95, p < 0.01$, Wilk's $\Lambda = 0.92, \eta^2 = 0.11$], which indicated there were significant differences in five of the eight television doctors' demographic traits across subgenres. As shown in table 20.1, the results indicated the comedies portrayed more white and international doctors, but the dramas showed more Hispanic, Asian, and

Table 20.2 Behaviors and Patient-centered Communications by Demographics (in Percentages)

	White	Minority	X^2	P	Men	Women	X^2	p
Unprofessionalism	27	44	20.50	.00	37	30	4.17	.04
Work/Life Balance	13	17	10.27	.00	5	9	4.76	.04
Dehumanization	8	12	16.31	.00	10	14	3.96	.04
Patient Communication	27	26	0.38	.53	17	31	123.62	<.001
Dr. Questions Pt.	36	39	1.78	.38	33	38	2.89	.09
Pt. Questions Dr.	42	47	1.58	.21	45	40	1.46	.23
Additional Information	29	46	19.03	.00	38	23	20.75	<.001
Navigation	6	6	.03	.88	6	8	1.40	.24
Verbal Empathy	28	21	21.83	.00	22	32	9.99	<.001
Nonverbal Empathy	12	6	19.34	.00	9	10	.59	.44
Eye Contact	83	84	.04	.85	82	83	.34	.56
Active Listening	78	82	1.59	.21	80	75	2.87	.09
Courtesy	25	16	5.21	.01	25	18	6.63	.01
Casual Conversation	30	13	21.58	.00	21	35	20.42	<.001
Humor	15	13	.57	.45	14	17	2.00	.16
Self-Disclosure	14	10	1.90	.17	13	13	.06	.80

US doctors ($p < 0.01$). However, the differences in percentages of men, women, and black television doctors between subgenres was not significant ($p > 0.05$).

To answer RQ2, which asked how the television doctors' demographic characteristics compared to US physicians' demographic characteristics, we used the data from the US Census Bureau (2014) and then calculated Bayesian 95% confidence intervals using R for all of the television doctors' demographic variables in each subgenre (Sundar, 2014). Then, we determined whether the US Census statistic for each demographic variable fell inside or outside of the confidence intervals. If the real-world statistic fell outside the confidence intervals, the difference was considered significant at $p < 0.05$; but if it fell inside the confidence intervals, the difference was considered not significant. As also shown in table 20.1, the percentages of men and women doctors portrayed in comedies, dramas, and in the aggregate were not significantly different from that reported in the US Census statistics. However, there were significant differences in all ethnicity categories, compared to the real-world statistics, both by total and each subgenre's physician portrayals. In particular, the medical television shows depicted more white, black, and US (versus international) physicians than are actually practicing in the United States but fewer Hispanic, Asian, and international doctors.

The third research question asked how the physicians' professional behaviors were portrayed, based on their gender and ethnicity. To answer this question, we combined the minority categories because there were too few occurrences of Hispanic and Asian doctors to allow for meaningful cross-tabulations with the chi-square statistic. When we analyzed the doctors' behaviors by ethnicity, we found that minority physicians exhibited a higher level of unprofessionalism as well as more struggles with work/life balance issues and dehumanization behaviors than white physicians, who engaged in more patient communication than minority doctors ($p < 0.05$) (see top four rows of table 20.2). Alternately, when analyzing the physicians' behaviors by gender, we found that men were portrayed as more unprofessional, while women had more work/life balance issues and exhibited more dehumanization, but communicated with their patients more frequently than men ($p < 0.05$).

Finally, the fourth research question asked how television doctors of different genders and ethnicities use patient-centered communication practices. The results of the cross-tabulations with the chi-square statistic displayed in table 20.2 indicate that minority doctors provided their patients with significantly more additional medical information, but that white doctors exhibited more verbal and nonverbal empathy, courtesy, and engaged in more casual conversations with their patients, $p < 0.05$. Alternately, we found that more men doctors communicated with their patients, provided them with additional medical information and were more courteous, whereas women doctors exhibited more verbal empathy and engaged in more casual conversations with their patients, $p < 0.05$.

DISCUSSION

Overall, the purpose of this investigation was to analyze television doctors' portrayals, behaviors, and patient-centered communication practices in the most-watched medical television comedies and dramas. The first result of this analysis indicated that these shows accurately represented the distribution of US physicians' genders. While this finding suggests that women have made significant progress in television portrayals over the past 50 years, it is nonetheless disheartening to realize that less than 40% all US doctors are women. Further disheartening was our finding that there were significant differences in television doctors' ethnicities both by medical television subgenre and in comparison to the demographics of US doctors. Moreover, when parsed by the television doctors' demographic characteristics, we found significant differences in all four professional behaviors as well as nine of the 12 patient-centered communication practices.

When analyzing the television doctors' professional behaviors by ethnicity, we found that medical television shows underrepresented Hispanic, Asian, and international doctors while white, black doctors were overrepresented in comparison to the distribution of ethnicities among practicing US doctors. Specifically, white and black doctors were overrepresented by 9% and 10%, respectively. On the other hand, Hispanic and Asian doctors were underrepresented by 3% and 17%, respectively. While the finding that white doctors are overrepresented is in line with prior analyses over the past several decades, it remains troubling that they continue to dominate television physician portrayals, particularly on medical comedies.

Our concerns about the misrepresentation of television doctors' ethnicities are based on research suggesting they may influence viewers' perceptions and attitudes toward practicing physicians in the real world. For instance, cultivation researchers have found that heavy television viewers' perceptions of Latinos (Mastro, Behm-Morawitz, & Ortiz, 2007) and Asians (Ramasubramanian, 2011) were significantly more negative than light television viewers' perceptions. Additionally, research also indicates that *The Cosby Show*'s viewers believed that there were more successful black doctors than non-viewers because Bill Cosby played a doctor (Inniss & Feagin, 1995).

Based on the existing literature, this line of research suggests that racism and sexism continue to influence patients' perceptions and expectations. For instance, Greene, Hibbard, and Sacks (2017) found that white male patients most frequently selected physicians with names they perceived as belonging to a white man. Additionally, Paul-Emile, Smith, Lo, and Fernandez (2016) found that patients have refused a physician's treatment because of the physician's ethnicity. Thus, the extent to which physician portrayals may reinforce or discourage lingering racism remains an important topic of study. Moreover, genre theory suggests that viewers may develop different expectations depending on the type of medical show they watch. In the current study, our results suggest that medical comedy viewers may perceive that doctors are generally white or black, since Hispanics and Asians were essentially absent from that subgenre. Likewise, medical drama viewers who seldom see international doctors may feel uncertain about what to expect from their interactions with physicians of international origin, or they may even perceive that such doctors do not belong in their exam rooms.

In addition to being under- or overrepresented in medical television programming, minority television doctors were also portrayed as engaging in more negative behaviors—such as unprofessionalism and the dehumanization of patients—than white doctors. Further, larger proportions of white doctors engaged in more patient-centered communication practices than minority doctors. These portrayals are especially problematic because viewers may have few examples of professional, patient-centered doctors of color. Viewed through the lens of cultivation theory, such findings suggest that contemporary medical programming may contribute to viewers' perceptions that minority and international doctors are not as competent, professional, and personable as white US doctors.

With respect to gender, we found that larger proportions of female doctors communicated with their patients, expressed more verbal empathy and engaged in more casual conversations than their male counterparts, even as they struggled with more work/life balances issues. Alternatively, male doctors provided their patients with more additional information and were more courteous, even as they were depicted as more unprofessional than women doctors. These findings appear to model traditional gender roles for viewers, where feminine communicators engage in rapport talk aimed at building relationships, while masculine communicators engage in report talk designed to accomplish specific tasks (Weinberg, Treviño, & Cleveland, 2019).

Further, work/life balance issues and unprofessionalism also have gendered associations. Women, often associated with domesticity, struggle to separate themselves from the domestic sphere while men, often associated with aggression and assertiveness, rebelliously violate workplace policies and codes of conduct. Thus, while viewers are encouraged to wonder whether Meredith Grey can "hack it" as a surgeon in the midst of her personal drama, they are expected to admire House's flagrant disregard for protocol. These findings have important theoretical and practical implications for the ways in which viewers are primed to approach real-life interactions with male and female physicians.

Clearly, these findings offer important practical implications for television writers and producers. In addition to concerns over the perpetuation of racism and sexism, our findings suggest that medical programs generally fail to model realistic and effective doctor-patient communication. In particular, fewer than 25% of the scenes in the medical television shows depicted doctor-patient communication; of the scenes that did include it, fewer than 50% showed them asking each other questions. Further, fewer than half of the doctor-patient communication scenes depicted the physicians engaging in patient-centered communication practices. Such findings highlight lost opportunities for television writers and producers to educate both doctors and patients about the importance of effective and appropriate communication practices in a medical setting. Indeed, organizations such as Hollywood, Health, & Society (n.d.) have made progress transforming popular television shows into opportunities for research-based edutainment. However, the differences in the physicians' professional behaviors and patient-centered communication patterns between medical comedies and dramas found in the current study suggest that writers may feel constrained by genre-specific conventions. As boundaries between subgenres blur, however, new possibilities may emerge.

LIMITATIONS AND DIRECTIONS FOR FUTURE RESEARCH

While we have utilized television genre theory as one theoretical lens to explore differences in doctors' portrayals, we found it difficult to neatly categorize shows as pure comedies or dramas. For instance, while *House* is officially classified as a drama, much of dialogue involves comedic quips. Similarly, while *Nurse Jackie* is officially classified as a comedy, Edie Falco, the title character actress, resisted this characterization of her dramatic performance (McNamara, 2014). In fact, an emergent subgenre, the dramedy, might better categorize both of these shows. Future research may explore how such shows blur traditional genre conventions in ways that offer greater flexibility in depicting doctor-patient interactions. Similarly, while we compared physician portrayals across subgenres, future research may analyze the ways in which plots driven by a woman protagonist (i.e., *Nurse Jackie* and *Grey's Anatomy*) portray medical personnel differently from shows that feature a man protagonist (i.e., *Scrubs* and *House*). Indeed, such analyses could center concerns about the ways in which gender norms are reinforced or challenged in medical show plotlines.

REFERENCES

Abercrombie, N. (1996). *Television and society*. Polity Press.
Abghari, M. S., Takemoto, R., Sadiq, A., Karia, R., Phillips, D., & Egol, K. A. (2014). Patient perceptions and preferences when choosing an orthopaedic surgeon. *The Iowa Orthopaedic Journal, 34*, 204–208.
Academy of Television Arts & Sciences. (n.d.-a). MASH awards and nominations. https://www.emmys.com/shows/mash.
Academy of Television Arts & Sciences. (n.d.-b). Scrubs awards and nominations. https://www.emmys.com/shows/scrubs.
Agence France-Presse (2009, June 12). 'House' is world's most popular TV show. https://web.archive.org/web/20120401043907/https://www.google.com/hostednews/afp/article/ALeqM5gGRhjVWTeAVMws-iEDRJOY3IDH7g.
Andrews, T.M. (2018, February 28). 106 million people watched MASH finale 35 years ago. No scripted show has come close. https://www.washingtonpost.com/

news/morning-mix/wp/2018/02/28/106-million-people-watched-mash-finale-35-y ears-ago-no-scripted-show-has-come-close-since/.

Bandura, A. (1986). *Social foundation of thought and action: A social cognitive theory.* Prentice-Hall.

Bandura, A. (2009). Social cognitive theory of mass communication. In J. Bryant & M. B. Oliver (Eds.), *Media effects: Advances in theory and research* (2nd ed., pp. 94–124). Erlbaum.

Bertakis, K. D. (2009). The influence of gender on the doctor-patient interaction. *Patient education and counseling, 76*(3), 356–360.

Bilandzic, H., & Busselle, R. W. (2008). Transportation and transportability in the cultivation of genre-consistent attitudes and estimates. *Journal of Communication, 58*(3), 508–529.

Brodie, M., Foehr, U., Rideout, V., Baer, N., Miller, C., Flournout, R., & Altman, D. (2001). Communicating health information through the entertainment media. *Health Affairs, 20*(1), 192–199.

Brooks, T. & Marsh, E. (2007). *The complete directory to prime time network and cable TV shows, 1946–present.* Ballantine Books.

Chory-Assad, R. M. & Tamborini, R. (2003). Television exposure and the public's perceptions of physicians. *Journal of Broadcasting & Electronic Media, 47*(2), 197–215.

The Classic TV Archive (CTVA Forum). (2012). US medical drama series guide. http://ctva.biz/US/Medical/_USmedical.htm.

Cohen, J. & Weimann, G. (2000). Cultivation revisited: Some genres have some effects on some viewers. *Communication Reports, 13*(2), 99–114.

Collins, R. L. (2011). Content analysis of gender roles in media: Where are we now and where should we go? *Sex roles, 64*(3–4), 290–298.

Duggan, A. P., & Thompson, T. L (2011). Patient-provider interaction and related outcomes. In T. L. Thompson, R. Parrott, and J. F. Nussbaum (Eds.), *The Routledge handbook of health communication* (2nd ed., pp. 414–427). Routledge.

Gates, H. L., Jr. (1992). TV's Black world turns-but stays unreal. In M. L. Anderson & P. H. Collins (Eds.), *Race, class, and gender: An anthology* (pp. 310–317). Wadsworth.

Gerbner, G., Gross, L., Morgan, M., & Signorielli, N. (1981). Special report: Health and medicine on television. *The New England Journal of Medicine, 305*, 901–904.

Gerbner, G., Morgan, M., & Signorielli, N. (1982). Programming health portrayals. In D. Pearls, L. Bouthilet, & J. Lazar (Eds.), *Television and behavior: Ten years of progress and implications for the eighties* (vol. 1, pp. 291–307). National Institute of Mental Health.

Greene, J. Hibbard, J. H., & Sacks, R. (2017). Does the race/ethnicity or gender of a physician's name impact selection of the physician? *Journal of the National Medical Association.* Retrieved online. doi: 10.1016/j.jnma.2017 .05.010.

Hollywood, Health, & Society. (n.d.). Retrieved from https://hollywoodhealthands ociety.org/.

Hirt, C., Wong, K., Erichsen, S., & White, J.S. (2013). Medical dramas on television: A brief guide for educators. *Medical Teacher, 35*(3), 237–242. https://doi:10.3109/0142159X.2012.737960.

Hoffman, B.L., Hoffman, R., Wessel, C.B., Shensa, A., Woods, M.S., & Primack, B.A. (2018). Use of fictional medical television in health sciences education: A systematic review. *Advances in Health Science Education, 23*, 201–216. https://doi.org/10.1007/s10459-017-9754-5.

Inniss, L.B., & Feagin, J.R. (1995). The Cosby Show: The view from the Black middle class. *Journal of Black Studies, 25*(6), 692–711.

Jain, P., & Slater, M.D. (2013). Provider portrayals and patient-provider communication in drama and reality medical entertainment television shows. *Journal of Health Communication, 18*(6), 703–722.

Kalsich, P.A., & Kalsich, B.J. (1984). Sex-role stereotyping of nurses and physicians on prime-time television: A dichotomy of occupational portrayals. *Sex Roles, 10*(7–8), 533–553.

Lewis, J., & Jhally, S. (1992). *Enlightened racism.* Westview.

Lichter, S.R., Lichter, L.S., & Rothman, R. (1991). *Watching America: What television tells us about our lives.* Prentice Hall.

MacDonald, J. F. (1983). *Blacks on white TV: Afro-Americans in television since 1948.* Nelson-Hall.

Mastro, D., Behm-Morawitz, E., & Ortiz, M. (2007). The cultivation of social perceptions of Latinos: A mental models approach. *Media Psychology, 9*(2), 347–365.

Mastro, D.E., & Greenberg, B.S. (2000). The portrayal of racial minorities on prime time television. *Journal of Broadcasting & Electronic Media, 44*(4), 690–703.

Mastro, D.E. & Robinson, A.L. (2000). Cops and crooks: Images of minorities on primetime television. *Journal of Criminal Justice, 28*(5), 385–396. https://doi.org/10.1016/S0047-2352(00)00053-2.

Maul, K. (2009, July 2). Showtime's Nurse Jackie campaign brings in record ratings. https://www.prweek.com/article/1271096/showtimes-nurse-jackie-campaign-brings-record-ratings.

McNamara, M. (2014, June 6). Edie Falco loves playing the lying, seriously flawed Nurse Jackie. https://www.latimes.com/entertainment/tv/la-et-st-edie-falco-nurse-jackie-20140608-column.html.

Morgan, M., & Shanahan, J. (2010). The state of cultivation. *Journal of Broadcasting & Electronic Media, 54*(2), 337–355.

Morgan, S. E., Movius, L., & Cody, M. J. (2009). The power of narratives: The effect of entertainment television organ donation storylines on the attitudes, knowledge, and behaviors of donors and nondonors. *Journal of Communication, 59*(1), 135–151.

Paul-Emile, K., Smith, A. K., Lo, B., & Fernández, A. (2016). Dealing with racist patients. *New England Journal of Medicine, 374*, 708–711. doi:10.1056/nejmp1514939.

Pfau, M., Mullen, L. J., & Garrow, K. (1995). The influence of television viewing on public perceptions of physicians. *Journal of Broadcasting & Electronic Media, 39*, 441–458.

Quick, B.L. (2009). The effects of viewing Grey's Anatomy on perceptions of doctors and patient satisfaction. *Journal of Broadcasting & Electronic Media, 53*(1), 38–55.

Ramasubramanian, S. (2011). Television exposure, model minority portrayals, and Asian-American stereotypes: An exploratory study. *Journal of Intercultural Communication, 26*(1), 1–17.

Rhodes, J. (2005, April 14). Thriving ratings for a new patient on ABC. https://www.nytimes.com/2005/04/14/arts/television/thriving-ratings-for-a-new-patient-on-abc.html.

Roter, D. L., & Hall, J. A. (2011). How medical interaction shapes and reflects the physician patient relationship. In T. L. Thompson, R. Parrott, & J. F. Nussbaum (Eds.), *The Routledge handbook of health communication* (2nd ed., pp. 55–68). Routledge.

Shanahan, J., Shanahan, J., James, S., & Morgan, M. (1999). *Television and its viewers: Cultivation theory and research.* Cambridge University Press.

Sink, A. & Mastro, D. (2017). Depictions of gender on primetime television: A quantitative content analysis. *Mass Communication and Society, 20*(1), 3–22. doi: 10.1080/15205436.2016.1212243.

Stanek, A., Clarkin, C., Bould, M. D., Writer, H., & Doja, A. (2015). Life imitating art: Depictions of the hidden curriculum in medical television programs. *BMC Medical Education, 15*, 1–8.

Sundar, D.-R. (2014). Binom: Binomial confidence intervals for several parameterizations. R package version 1.1-1. Retrieved from http://CRAN.R-project.org/package=binom.

Tapper, E. B. (2010). Doctors on display: The evolution of television's doctors. *Proceedings, Baylor University. Medical Center, 23*(4), 393–399.

Turow, J. (1996). Television entertainment and the US health-care debate. *The Lancet, 347*(9010), 1240–1243. Retrieved from https://doi.org/ 10.1016/S0140-6736(96)90747-3.

US Census Bureau. (2014). *American Community Survey.* https://census.gov/programs-surveys/acs/technical-documentation/pums.html.

Warner, K. J. (2015). The racial logic of Grey's Anatomy: Shonda Rhimes and her 'post-civil rights, post-feminist' series. *Television and New Media, 16*(7), 631–647. doi:10.1177/1527476414550529.

Weinberg, F. J., Treviño, L. J., & Cleveland, A. O. (2019). Gendered communication and career outcomes: A construct validation and prediction of hierarchical advancement and non-hierarchical rewards. *Communication Research, 46*, 456–502. doi:10.1177/0093650215590605.

Weiss, J. (2009). Goofy, cartoonish, and the most accurate portrayal of the medical Profession on TV. Slate. http://www.slate.com/articles/arts/culturebox/2009/05/Scrubs.html.

Ye, Y., & Ward, K. E. (2010). The depiction of illness and related matters in two top-ranked primetime network medical dramas in the United States: A content analysis. *Journal of Health Communication, 15*, 555–570.

Index

Aahat, 87–88
ABC, 39, 65–66, 69–71, 74–76
Abreu, Silvio de, 134
Abu-Lughod, L., 98
abuse and trauma survivors, 59–61
Adjafre, Daniel, 135
African Americans: family structures, 14; racial profiling of, 16; respectability politics, 11–12; stereotypes, 12–13. *See also* black male/masculinity; black women
Afrofuturism, 27
age category, 209
Ahmad, Nazeer, 90
Ajtony, Z., 166
Akil, Mara Brock, 219
Almeida, H. B., 130
Amazon Prime, 1, 136–37, 145, 222
ambivalence stage, 148–49
Amor à Vida (*Trail of Lies*), 98, 101–2, 104
Ang, I., 99
Anglo-Saxon formats, 111, 114. *See also* French dramas
anti-Semitism, 120
apartheid, 283–84
Araújo, Cristiano, 133–34
Asian Americans, 148–51
Asim, J., 17

audience, 112–13; gratifications, 150–51; intergenerational, 113; as typological markers, 117. *See also* fans/fandom
Avatar, 27

The Bachelor, 66
background characters, 209
back-to-work narrative, 249–58; findings, 252–57; thematic analysis, 251–52. *See also* motherhood
Bajia, Fatima S., 84, 88–89
Bandura, A., 206, 292
Barlow, W., 235
Barton, R. L., 193
Beckham, David, 274
Behm-Morawitz, E., 209
Being Mary Jane, 219–31
Bellucci, Monica, 41, 48, 49
Ben Casey, 291
Benioff, David, 52
Benoit, W., 194
Benson, T. W., 193
Berg, C. R., 26
Bernabo, L. M., 193
Bhutto, Benazir, 87
Bhutto, Zulfiqar Ali, 84
Birdsell, D. S., 194
The Birth of a Nation, 235

307

Black Country Living Museum, 274
Black Entertainment Television (BET), 219, 221–24, 227, 230
Black-ish, 251, 254
Black Lives Matter (BLM), 4, 10, 12; hoodie as a symbol of, 16
black male/masculinity, 3, 12–19; factors affecting positionality of, 220–21; fatherhood, 14; in a female-centric drama, 219–31; language, 17–19; police brutality, 15–16; stereotypes, 14–15; in television, 220
Black Masculine Identity Model, 220–21
black women: Facebook and, 233, 236, 237–39, 242, 243; participatory culture, 234–35; social television, 233, 236–37; stereotypes, 235–37; on television, 221
Blumler, J.G., 150
Bogle, D., 220, 235
Bom Sucesso (*A Life Worth Living*), 128, 130
Boudon, H., 116, 121, 123
Bourdieu, P., 151
Boyd, D., 133, 135, 152
Brazil: audiovisual ecosystem, 128; broadcasters, 127–28; media transformations in, 127
Brazilian Institute of Geography and Statistics, 128
Brazilian telenovelas, 128; audience and narrative, 131–34; digital platform, 136–38; gender violence on, 95–107; narrative format, 128–31; social media, 135–36
British Broadcasting Corporation, 27, 111, 263, 280. See also *Peaky Blinders*
Brock, André, 236
broken windows philosophy, 281
Brown, J. D., 192
Brown, J. R., 150
Brown, Michael, 10, 16
Brown v. the Board of Education, 177
Brummett, B., 194

Bryman, A., 68
Bryon-Portet, C., 118, 120
Burgess, J., 223
Burke, Kenneth, 190, 194
Burke, Tarana, 180
Burr, Anne, 291
Bush, George W., 75
Bussey, K., 206
Buzzanell, P. M., 255

Call the Midwife, 176, 178, 182, 185, 186
Camargo, Zeca, 133–34
Capaldi, Peter, 27
Carmichael, Laura, 161
Carr, D., 137
Carver, L. J., 192
Castle Bell, G., 244
Certeau, M. de, 116
Chan, B., 146
Chan, K., 76
character gender, 208
Chauvel, M., 133
Cheers, I., 221
Cheng, H., 189
Cheon-guk eui Gyedan/Stairway to Heaven, 145
China/Chinese society: political movements, 190; radical changes in, 191; socialist market economy, 191; women in, 189
China Daily, 190
Chinese economic reform, 189–91
Chinese television: classification of drama, 192; commercials, 189–90, 192; Communist principles, 190–91; cultural hegemony, 193; entertainment programming, 192; female entrepreneurs in, 194–99; neoliberalism and, 191; reform era, 190–93
Choi, S. M., 152
citizen-viewers, 122
City Hospital, 291
Civil Rights Movement, 177–80
Coker, Cheo Hodari, 10

Collins, P. H., 14, 235
Colombiana, 53
Colter, Mike, 10, 13, 15, 17–19
Coman, M., 98
comedy dramas, 3; back-to-work narrative, 249–58; *Being Mary Jane*, 219–31; *Insecure*, 233–45. *See also* medical comedies and dramas
Communism, 265–66
competence, 209
Comscore, 136
Confucianism/Confucian values, 144–46
Connell, R. W., 219
Constant, F., 71, 73
content series, 70
Cornillon, C., 75
Corroy, L., 122
corruption, 280, 282, 286
The Cosby Show, 220, 301
COVID-19, 1, 4
creative license, 3
cricket, 167
crime dramas, 3; *Peaky Blinders*, 263–75; *Zero Tolerance*, 277–88
crime novels, 280
criminal organization, 265
critical cosmopolitanism, 76
critical race theory, 11
The Crown, 176, 177, 181, 183–84
Cruise, Tom, 147
cultivation theory, 207, 292–93, 302
cultural capital, 151
cultural hegemony, 193
cultural identity, 148–49
cultural image/value appeal, 145–47, 153; Confucianism, 145–46; East Asian cultures, 145; Korean dramas, 146–47
cultural industries, 114
cultural stereotypes, 68–70
cultural stigmatization, 3

Dangerfield, C.L., 220–31
Dates, J. L., 235
De Lanerolle, Indra, 280

de Nie, M., 168
Department of Health and Human Services, 183
Descendants of the Sun, 145
detectives, 278, 280
Deus Salve o Rei (*God Save the King*), 135
Diane: The Twin Peaks Tapes of Agent Dale Cooper (Frost), 39
Die Boere Oorlog (Pakenham), 284
digital platform, Brazilian telenovelas on, 136–38
Dika, V., 266
Dill, K. E., 206
Disneyland, 67
Disneyworld, 67
diversity, 118–21
Doctor Who's 13th Doctor, 25–36; bearing witness, 32–33; case study, 27–28; family and, 31–32; fan responses, 33–35; feminism and, 30–31; gender roles, 29–30; thematic analysis, 28–29
dominance, 209
Donath, J., 152
Dorfman, A., 68
Downton Abbey (*DA*), 159–69; gender role, 160–63; LGBTQ+ representation, 163–65; whiteness, 165–68
Downton Draggy, 169
Downton Tabby, 169
dream/dreams within dreams, 48–49
Dr. Kildare, 291

Ellis, M., 43, 44
emotional realism, 123
Endeavour, 176, 177, 179
Englishness *vs.* otherness, 166
enlightened moderation, 89
Ernotte, Delphine, 119
exploration stage, 149
Eyal, K., 207

Facebook, 233, 236–39, 242, 243
Faiola, A., 145

family, 31–32; African Americans and, 14; Korean, 147
fans/fandom, 263; Korean television dramas, 147–48; *Peaky Blinders*, 273–75; response to reimagined *Doctor Who* (DW), 33–35
fantasy drama, 2; *The Game of Thrones*, 51–61; *Lost*, 65–76; *Luke Cage*, 9–20. *See also* science fiction
fascination, 43
Fascism, 264–66
Father Brown, 176–78
Feasey, R., 250, 251
Fechine, Y., 135
Fellowes, Julian, 159
female entrepreneurs in Chinese television, 193–99; business, 196–97; home, 195–96; neighborhood and community, 197; nontraditional and traditional, 197–99
The Feminine Mystique, 180
feminism, 30–31
feminist theories, 205
Fernández, A., 301
Fifty Shades of Grey, 183
Fina Estampa (*Looks & Essence*), 98, 100, 103–4
Fire Walk with Me, 39, 42, 43
Fiske, J., 131, 160, 242
flexible identities, 71–72
Ford S., 133
Foss, K. A., 193
Foss, S. K., 193
The Frame, 15
France Télévisions, 111–13, 119–21
Frederickson, B., 205
French dramas, 111–23; audience engagement, 121–23; diversity and, 118–21; mass-produced series, 114–16; regional level work, 116–17; social portrait, 117–18
Freud, Sigmund, 185
Friedan, Betty, 180
Friends, 66
Frost, Scott, 39
Frosts, Mark, 39–41, 49

Galow, T. W., 44
The Game of Thrones, 51–61; abuse and trauma, 59–61; agency, 53–59; gender representation, 52–53; viewing trends, 52
gangsters, 265, 266, 271. *See also Peaky Blinders*
Garner, Eric, 10
Garrison Tailors, 274
gendered gaze, 43, 53
gender/gender roles: in *Doctor Who*, 29–30; in *Downton Abbey* (*DA*), 160–63; as heroines/tough/violent females, 52–53; in science fiction, 25–26
gendering: in Iranian drama serials, 203–14; in Urdu television drama, 84–87
gender violence in Brazilian telenovelas, 95–107; mystification of the feminine, 106; narratives/storylines, 99–103; villains, 103–5
genre theory, 293–94, 301, 303
Gledhill, C., 208
Glevarec, H., 120
globalization, 150
global village, 72–74
GloboNews, 133–34
Globoplay, 137–38
Globo Television, 127, 128, 131, 133, 134, 136–38
Gothic texts, 40–42, 44–46. *See also Twin Peaks* (*TP*); *Twin Peaks: The Return* (*TP:R*)
Gramsci, A., 193
Grantchester, 176–79, 185
gratifications, 150–51
Gray, H., 12, 220, 221
Green, A., 266
Green, J., 133, 223
Greene, J., 301
Gregg, R. B., 193
Grey's Anatomy, 74, 75, 294, 297
Gronbeck, B. E., 193
Grosvenor, I., 266
The Guardian, 274

Hall, S., 168, 203
Halm, Paulo, 128, 135
Harris, T. M., 244
Hatchuel, S., 74–75
HBO (Home Box Office), 51; *The Game of Thrones*, 51–61; *Insecure*, 233–45; *The Wire*, 10
health disparities, 4
Hefner, Hugh, 183
Heidegger, Martin, 41, 45
heritage, 273–75
Hibbard, J. H., 301
Higginbotham, Evelyn Brooks, 11
hijab, 86
Hills, M., 134
Hinds, L. B., 193
historical and period dramas, 3; Chinese television, 189–200; *The Game of Thrones*, 51–61; Iranian drama serials, 203–14; Korean dramas, 143–54; *Peaky Blinders*, 263–75; twenty-first-century ideologies, 175–86
Hofstede, G., 203
Hogarth, H. K., 146
Holmes, B., 206
Holtmann, E., 284
Homicide: Life on the Street, 287
honor killings, 86
honor of a family, 85–86
hoodies, 15–16
horizontal textual analysis, 160
Hotel Del Runa, 145
House, 294, 297, 303
House of Cards, 137
How I Met Your Mother, 251–53, 255
How to Get Away with Murder, 12, 236
Hudson, R. A., 193
Hulu, 1, 136–37, 145
Hunt, T., 175
hybrid identities, 134

identity: Black Masculine Identity Model, 220–21; cultural, 148–49; social, 117
immersion stage, 149

immoral behavior, 86
Inland Empire, 40, 42–47
Inness, S. A., 52–53
Insecure, 233–45. *See also* black women
Inspector Morse, 177
institutionalized cultural class, 151
integration stage, 149
inter-coder reliability, 297
intercommunity capital, 151
Internet, 1, 72–74, 133, 134, 136, 236
intracommunity capital, 151
intrigue, 98
Invitation to Love, 39–40, 42
Iranian television drama serials, 203–14; female and male characters, 210–12; Islamic revolution and, 204; women in, 204–5, 210–14
Iraq-Iran war, 208
Isidingo, 280
Islamic Republic of Iran Broadcasting (IRIB), 203–5
Islamic revolution, 204
Islamization, 82, 84–87
Ito, M., 133, 135
Iwamura, J. N., 69, 70

Jackson, R.L., 220–31
Jacobellis v. Ohio, 183
Jain, P., 295, 296
Jangal, 86
Japanese television dramas, 146–47
Jenkins, H., 133, 135
Jewel in the Palace, 144–45
Johnson, K., 206
Ju, H., 149
Jung, E-Y, 149
Jung, S., 147

Kaepernick, Colin, 178
Keane, M., 192
Kelling, G. L., 281
Kennedy, R. L., 18
Kent & Curwen, 274
Khan, Sir Syed Ahmad, 90
Kim, Y., 152
Kincaid, D. L., 206

King, Martin Luther, Jr., 177
Korean Americans, 148–49
Korean historical dramas, 143–54; conceptual framework, 153; cultural identity, 148–49; cultural image/value appeal, 145–47, 153; fandom, 147–48; gratifications from, 150–51; hierarchical family structures, 147; overview, 143–45; research propositions, 153; social capital, 151–52; visual images, 144–45
Korean pop culture, 149
Korean Wave, 143, 147
Krippendorff, K., 160
Kruger, L., 288
Ksiazek, T. B., 192
Kung-Fu, 69–70

Lafky, S., 42, 43
Larke-Walsh, George, 265–67, 273
Lawler, P. A., 161, 166
Lee, S., 146, 149
"Legitimate Peaky Blinders Festival," 273
Lemons, J., 235
Lemos, L. P., 128, 130
Levett, G., 167
Levi, M., 207
Levine, S., 180
Lewdon, L., 40, 41
Li, Haili, 192
Life in Pieces, 251, 253, 254
Lin, C. A., 192
Lindelof, Damon, 67, 71
Livingstone, S., 99
Lo, B., 301
Long, Paul, 272
Lopes, M., 96
Lopes, M.I.V. de, 128, 130
Lost, 65–76; as a content series, 70; discourse of reconciliation, 74–76; flexible identities, 71–72; global village and, 72–74; imaginary kingdom, 67–68; stereotypes, 68–70
Luke Cage, 9–20; debut season of, 10; language, 17–19; police brutality, 15–16; sociopolitical commentary of, 12–19
Lynch, David, 39–43, 45–47
Lynch, Jennifer, 39

Macé, É., 112, 120
Mad Men, 161, 176, 179, 182–84
Mahon, E.K., 161
Maigret, E., 112
main characters, 209
male gaze, 43, 162
Malhação Sonhos (*Young Hearts* or *Young Dreams*), 135
Malonga, M. F., 118
Mandi, 88
Marie, V., 68
Married Love or Love in Marriage (Stopes), 162
Martin, George R. R., 52
Martin, Trayvon, 10, 15, 16, 178
Marvel Cinematic Universe, 9–20. *See also* Luke Cage
The Marvelous Mrs. Maisel, 176, 177, 179, 181
masculinity, 221. *See also* black male/masculinity
mass-produced series, 114–16
Masters of Sex, 176, 177, 181, 183, 184
Mastro, D., 209
maternity leave, 250–51
The Matrix, 27
Mattelart, A., 68
Mattelart, T., 74
Mbeki, Thabo, 282
McLuhan, Marshall, 73
McQuail, D., 150
Medhurst, M. J., 193
mediacultures, 112
Media São Paulo Group, 136
media technologies, 1
medical comedies and dramas, 3, 291–303; content analyses, 292–94; future research, 303; research questions/method/result, 294–300

melodrama: defined, 99; gender violence and, 99–106; structural elements, 99
Messerschmidt, J. W., 219
#MeToo movement, 51–52, 59–60, 180–81
Mhlambi, I. J., 280
Midlands (Steinberg), 285
Milano, Alyssa, 180
Millennium, 53
Mills, David, 277
The Mindy Project, 251–57
minor characters, 209
misogyny, 43
Mittel, J., 129
mixophilia, 120
Moin, Hasina, 84, 87, 90
Monaco, J., 134
Montpellier Méditerranée Métropole (Montpellier 3M), 114
Moody-Ramirez, M., 221–22, 237
Moore, H., 103
Moss, C., 14
motherhood, 249–58; back-to-work, 254–57; maternity leave and, 250–51; transformation, 252–54
motivation, 209
Muanis, F., 131–32
Mulheres Apaixonadas (*Women in Love*), 95, 99–100
multiracialism, 266
multistage model, 148–49
Mulvey, L., 43, 44
Murdock London, 274
Musharraf, Pervez, 89
Myers, K., 266
mystery drama. *See Twin Peaks* (*TP*); *Twin Peaks: The Return* (*TP:R*)

Nactraglichkeit, 185
narrative, of Brazilian telenovelas: audience and, 131–34; format, 128–31; love story/romance, 130
narrative arcs, 118–21
National Cinema Center, 115
nationalism, 264, 266

nation-building, 277–78
Natives Land Act of 1913 (South Africa), 285
NBC, 65
neighborhood, 116
Netflix, 1, 10, 19, 136–37, 145
new womanhood, 89–91
New York Times, 180
New York Undercover, 279
Nichols, B., 185
Nielsen, 236
Nogueira, Alcides, 128
Nogueira, Eneida, 131, 132, 135–36
Nowell, L. S., 29
Noyer, J., 116
Nurse Jackie, 293, 294, 297, 303
NYPD Blue, 69, 71, 72, 74, 279

Obama, Barack, 12, 76
O Clone (*The Clone*), 130
The Office, 251–54
Oguri, L., 133
Oh, D. C., 148, 149
On High in Blue Tomorrows, 44–46
O Outro Lado do Paraíso (*The Other Side of Paradise*), 98, 102, 105, 130
O Rei do Gado (*King of Cattle*), 130
orientalism, 69–70
others-orientation category, 209
Oyserman, D., 148

Pakenham, Thomas, 284
Pakistan Electronic Media Regulatory Authority (PEMRA), 81–82
Pakistani Urdu television drama, 81–91; gendering in, 84–87; Islamization and, 82, 84–87; new womanhood, 89–91; in post-Islamization era, 82, 87–89; progressive movement and, 83–84; women's empowerment, 87–89
Pakistan Muslim League (PML), 89
Pakistan People's Party (PPP), 83, 89
Pakistan Television (PTV), 81–84, 87, 89
Park, J-S, 149

Park, M. K., 14–15
participatory culture, 234–35
Passione, 134
Paul-Emile, K., 301
Peaky Blinders, 263–75
Perry, Tyler, 12
physician portrayals in medical television, 291–303; content analysis, 292–94; demographic characteristics, 295, 298, *298*, 299, 300; overview, 291–92; patient-centered communications, 296, *299*, 300, 302–3; professional behaviors, 295–96, 300–302; unit of analysis, 297
Pistorius, Micki, 280
Planned Parenthood, 183
Playboy, 183
Plus Belle La Vie (PBLV), 111–23; Alternate Reality Game (ARG), 122–23; audience engagement, 121–23; narrative styles, 113
post-Islamization era, Urdu television drama in, 82, 87–89
post-racial ideology, 10
The Practice, 71, 72
pregnancy and post-pregnancy, 249, 251. *See also* back-to-work narrative; motherhood
primary text, 160
Primetime Blues, 220
The Professional, 53
progressive movement and Pakistani drama, 83–84
public service media, 111, 112, 119, 123
Putnam, R. D., 151

race/ethnicity, 3; in *Downton Abbey* (*DA*), 165–68; in *Peaky Blinders*, 266–73; in science fiction, 25–27; social network sites (SNS), 152
racial and ethnic others/otherness, 267–72
racial nationalism, 263–64, 266, 273
racial profiling, 16
racial stereotypes, 68–70

racism, 4
Rae, Issa, 233
Raoul, B., 116
Raz, Y., 207
Rede Globo, 98
reflexive approach to media, 98
regional level work, 116–18
A Regra do Jogo (*Rules of The Game*), 98, 101, 105
relational television, 119
representation, 1; of Chinese women, 189–90, 194–99; gender violence, 95–107; LGBTQ+, 163–65; minority, 9; orientalism, 69–70; respectability politics, 12. *See also* gender/gender roles; race/ethnicity; women
residential segregation, 71
respectability politics, 10–12; media representation, 12
rhetorical criticism, 11. *See also* textual analysis
Rhetorical Dimensions in Media (Medhurst and Benson), 193
rhetoric of mediated texts, 193–94
Rhimes, Shonda, 12, 294
Righteous Discontent (Higginbotham), 11
Roberts, T., 205
Ronell, Avital, 41, 45–46
Rothenbuhler, E., 98
Rubin, A. M., 150

SABC (South African Broadcasting Corporation), 277–78
Sacks, R., 301
Said, E. W., 69
Sakamoto, I., 148
Scandal, 12, 74, 75
Schrag, R. L., 193
science fiction: Asians in, 26–27; gender and race in, 25–27; Hispanics in, 26; Techno-Orientalism, 27. *See also* *Doctor Who* (*DW*)
Scrubs, 293, 297
secondary text, 160

The Secret Diary of Laura Palmer (Lynch), 39
The Secret History of Twin Peaks (Frost), 41
Segato, R., 103, 106
self-agency, 57–58
self-efficacy, 221
Sellnow, D. D., 193–94
September 11 attacks, 69, 75–76
sexuality, 43; in *Downton Abbey (DA)*, 163–65
sexualization, 209
sexual revolution, 183–85
Sharif, Nawaz, 89
Shome, R., 167
showrunner, 129
Simon, David, 277
Sink, A., 209
Slater, M. D., 295, 296
Smalls, M., 236
Smith, A. K., 301
soap operas, 2–3; French, 111–23; Urdu, 81–91. See also Brazilian telenovelas
social capital, 151–52; benefits, 151; bonding, 151, 152; bridging, 151, 152; intercommunity capital, 151; intracommunity capital, 151; social network sites (SNS), 152
social cognitive theory (SCT), 206, 207
social identity, 117
social inequities, 4
social media, Brazilian telenovelas and, 135–36
social media platforms, 1–2, 111
social network sites (SNS), 152
social television, 233, 236–37
socio-anthropological approach, 97–98
Sohn, D., 152
Song, Y., 192
South Africa: crime novels, 280; crime show, 277–86; nation-building, 277–79; television, 278–79. *See also* Zero Tolerance

South African Police Services (SAPS), 279
Steinberg, Jonny, 285
Stewart, Potter, 183
Stopes, Marie, 162
The Story of Zheng Yang Gate, 189, 193–99
Suarez, M., 133
Sulcas, R., 161
Sun, Z., 192
Sung, Y., 152
superhero fiction/narratives, 9; black characters, 9–10. *See also Luke Cage*
Sweney, Mark, 274

Taguieff, Pierre-André, 120
Tang, W., 191
technology, 40–41, 45–48
Techno-Orientalism, 27
telecommunication, 45
telenovelas, 2–3
The Telephone Book: Technology, Schizophrenia, Electric Speech (Ronell), 41
television drama series, 1–5; human stories, 4–5; textual analysis, 11
Terminator, 52–53
tertiary texts, 160
textual analysis, 11, 237. *See also* rhetorical criticism
Theus, T., 43, 44
Thill, K. P., 206
Thompson, L., 235
#TimesUp movement, 51–52, 59–60
Totalmente Demais (Total Dreamer), 128
transcultural fandom, 147–48. *See also* fans/fandom
transcultural identity, 148–49
Trapp, R., 193
Trump, Donald, 4
Truth and Reconciliation Commission (TRC), 280, 283
Twin Peaks (TP), 39; as an auteur series, 40; as a Gothic show, 40–42;

as an Oedipal narrative, 42–43; technology, 40–41
Twin Peaks: The Final Dossier (Frost), 41
Twin Peaks: The Return (*TP:R*), 39; as an auteur series, 40; dream/dreams within dreams in, 48–49; *Inland Empire* and, 43–44; technology, 40–41, 45–48
Tyree, T. C. M., 234

Ugly Betty, 236
Union, Gabrielle, 219
Un Si Grand Soleil (USGS), 111–23
Urdu television drama. *See* Pakistani Urdu television drama
Uroosa, 88–89
US Census Bureau, 299

vertical textual analysis, 160
Viacom, 223
Vidas em Jogo (*Lives at Stake*), 98
Vidas Opostas (*Opposite Lives*), 98
Vietnam War, 70
viewers. *See* audience
violence against women, 52, 54, 55, 59–61. *See also* gender violence in Brazilian telenovelas
virtual orientalism, 69–70
VOD (video on demand), 128, 137–38

Walt Disney Company, 65–67
The Washington Post, 17
Weinstein, Harvey, 180
Weiss, D. B., 52
Welch, Andy, 273
West, C., 235
Westworld, 60
White, Hayden, 185
whiteness: in *Downton Abbey* (*DA*), 165–68; in *Peaky Blinders*, 267–75. *See also* race/ethnicity

White Shadow, 84
Whittaker, Jodie, 25, 28, 33–34
Williams, D., 152
Williams, M. L., 234
willing backward, 185
Wilmore, Larry, 233
Wilson, J. Q., 281
Windt, T. O., Jr., 193
Winfrey, Oprah, 18–19
Winter Sonata, 147
The Wire, 10
women, 4; in Chinese television drama, 189–90, 194–99; domestic violence against, 4; in *The Game of Thrones*, 51–61; in Iranian drama serials, 204–5, 210–14; in science fiction television, 25–36; in Urdu television drama, 81–91
Women's Liberation Movement, 180–83
Wood, Evan Rachel, 60

xenophobia, 26, 263–64, 267
The X-Files, 66–67
Xie, S., 191
Xinhua News Agency, 191
Xueli, W., 146

Yaqeen Ka Safar, 91
Younge, Adrian, 13
YouTube, 123, 222–24, 231
Yuan, E. J., 192

zannan khana, 86
Zard Dopehar, 88
Zero Tolerance, 277–88
zero tolerance policing, 281
Zhang, M., 193
Zhang, Y. B., 192
Zia-ul-Haq, 82, 84–85
Zimmerman, George, 15, 178

Contributors

Saleem Abbas is Assistant Professor in the Department of Mass Communication at Forman Christian College University, Lahore, Pakistan. His research and teaching includes gender representation in visual media, and studies of television drama.

Gordon Alley-Young is a Professor in the Department of Communications and Performing Arts at Kingsborough Community College-City University of New York, Brooklyn, New York. His research includes critical readings of teaching/learning and race/sexuality in film and television.

Inna Arzumanova is Assistant Professor of Media Studies at the University of San Francisco. Her research interests include racial and gender performances, popular culture and aesthetics, and transnational media, cultural and arts industries.

Joseph Boisvere is faculty at the Graduate Center, CUNY, Program in Comparative Literature. His research and teaching include critical theory, translational studies, and film studies/theory/criticism.

Nettie Brock is an Assistant Professor at Morehead State University in Morehead, Kentucky. Her research focuses on critical analysis of popular culture, concentrating mainly on television and transgressive storytelling devices.

Lorena Caminhas is a Research Fellow in the Interdisciplinary Research Group on Science and Technology (GEICT) at the State University of

Campinas, Campinas, Brazil. Her main fields of investigation are gender, sexuality, politics, and the media.

George L. Daniels is an Associate Professor in the Department of Journalism and Creative Media, College of Communication and Information Sciences, at the University of Alabama in Tuscaloosa, Alabama.

Jérôme David holds a doctorate and is Associate Researcher at the Interdisciplinary Center for Research and Analysis of the Media, at Paris 2 Panthéon-Assas University, in Paris, France. His research and teaching include media economics and cultural industries.

Karin A. Haberlin is a doctoral candidate in the Department of Communication at the University of Connecticut, Storrs. Her research focuses on interactions between behavioral health systems and communities.

Elizabeth Fish Hatfield is Associate Professor in the Department of Arts and Humanities at University of Houston-Downton. Her research and teaching include interpersonal, family, gender roles, culture in media, and work/life balance.

Patricia Jullia is Associate Professor in the Department of Communication at the University Paul Valéry Montpellier 3, Montpellier, France. Her research and teaching include cultural industries, digital uses, and public communication.

Hannah Jureller is an honors student studying communication and sociology at Rollins College in Winter Park, Florida. Her previous research focused on nonprofit marketing and public relations.

Carolyn A. Lin is Professor in the Department of Communication at the University of Connecticut. Her research and teaching include persuasive, strategic, and risk communication in the contexts of marketing, health, climate change, and human computer interaction. She founded the *Communication Technology Division* (AEJMC) and was editor for the *Journal of Broadcasting & Electronic Media*.

Frédéric Marty is Associate Professor in the Department of Communication at the University Paul Valéry Montpellier 3, Montpellier, France. His research and teaching include audience studies, user experience, and transmedia content.

Mary Helen Millham is a Contributing Faculty member in the School of Communication, at the University of Hartford, West Hartford, Connecticut. She teaches students via pop culture. Her research includes critical analysis of media and qualitative analysis of privacy behaviors on social media.

Gwendelyn S. Nisbett is an Associate Professor in the Mayborn School of Journalism at the University of North Texas. Dr. Nisbett's research examines the intersection of media, politics, and popular culture.

David Lynn Painter is an Assistant Professor of Communication at Rollins College in Winter Park, Florida. His teaching and research focus on electronic and interactive media content and effects.

Suji Park is Research Professor at the Institute of Body & Culture at Konkuk University, Seoul, South Korea. Her research and teaching include traditional/new media effects on emotions, attitudes, and behaviors.

Sarah Parsloe is Assistant Professor in the Department of Communication at Rollins College. Her research and teaching interests include health and disabilities, stigma, ableism, social media, and cyber-activism.

Newly Paul is Assistant Professor in the Mayborn School of Journalism at the University of North Texas in Denton. Her research and teaching interests include media diversity and political communication.

Graciela Quiñones-Rodriguez is a psychotherapist and mental health wellness expert at the University of Connecticut. She has extensive experience with community members, women, and university students in crisis. She conducts teaching and research on diversity issues. She is cofounder of La Comunidad Intelectual.

Ian-Malcolm Rijsdijk is a Senior Lecturer in the Centre for Film and Media Studies and a member of the Environmental Humanities South research program at the University of Cape Town. His research includes South African film, and film and the environment.

Diana I. Ríos is an Associate Professor with a joint appointment in the Department of Communication and El Instituto: Latino/Latin American & Caribbean Studies, at the University of Connecticut. Her research and teaching includes media, intercultural processes, ethnicity/race/gender, diverse audiences. She is founder of La Comunidad Intelectual and AAUP National Council member.

Morgan W. Smalls is an Assistant Professor in the School of Media Arts and Design at James Madison University. Her research includes social media, digital media, television, popular culture, and the intersections of communication, women, and gender.

Rosane Svartman is the Head Writer of four internationally recognized, award-nominee telenovelas. Dr. Svartman wrote and directed five series for television and has five feature films. She is the author of three theatre plays and has coordinated over 10 transmedia narrative projects.

Graeme John Wilson, born in the United Kingdom and raised in the United States, is a dual citizen of both countries. Dr. Wilson's research interests lie in the visual representation of gender and racial identities in popular media.

Mei Zhang is Professor in the Department of Communication at Missouri Western State University. Her research and teaching include rhetoric, media, and intercultural communication.

Ali Zohoori is Emeritus Professor of Communication and former department chairperson at Bradley University, Peoria, Illinois. His research and teaching included cross-cultural and international communication, and media ethics.

www.ingramcontent.com/pod-product-compliance
Lightning Source LLC
Chambersburg PA
CBHW021343300426
44114CB00012B/1063